D1527519

PHILOSOPHICAL PAPERS

PHILOSOPHICAL PAPERS

Volume 2

Peter Unger

OXFORD

UNIVERSITY PRESS

2006

OXFORD

UNIVERSITY PRESS

Oxford University Press, Inc., publishes works that further
Oxford University's objective of excellence
in research, scholarship, and education.

Oxford   New York
Auckland   Cape Town   Dar es Salaam   Hong Kong   Karachi
Kuala Lumpur   Madrid   Melbourne   Mexico City   Nairobi
New Delhi   Shanghai   Taipei   Toronto

With offices in
Argentina   Austria   Brazil   Chile   Czech Republic   France   Greece
Guatemala   Hungary   Italy   Japan   Poland   Portugal   Singapore
South Korea   Switzerland   Thailand   Turkey   Ukraine   Vietnam

Copyright © 2006 by Peter Unger

Published by Oxford University Press, Inc.
198 Madison Avenue, New York, New York 10016

www.oup.com

Oxford is a registered trademark of Oxford University Press

Library of Congress Cataloging-in-Publication Data
Unger, Peter K.
Philosophical papers / Peter Unger.
p.   cm.
Includes bibliographical references and index.
ISBN-13 978-0-19-515552-5 (vol. 1)
ISBN 0-19-515552-1 (vol. 1)
ISBN-13 978-0-19-530158-8 (vol. 2)
ISBN 0-19-530158-7 (vol. 2)
1. Philosophy.   I. Title.

B945.U543P48 2006
191—dc22   2005048843

2   4   6   8   9   7   5   3   1

Printed in the United States of America
on acid-free paper

For my wife, Susan
Our son, Andrew

And for my dear friend,
Betsy Rodman Salandria

PREFACE TO VOLUME 2

Most folks reading this Preface will already have read, I should think, the Preface to Volume 1 of this two-volume collection, *Philosophical Papers*. If you're one of those folks, you needn't read any further here, in this Second Volume's Preface. Oh, heck; you might as well read the few more words that serve to complete this one paragraph: You've been proceeding in a nicely orderly way, you have, with your first looking at what's in the collection's First Volume—at least at what's in that Volume's Preface—before looking at this Preface, for Volume 2. Good for you! Would that more of my readers were such orderly people as you are.

By contrast with those following good order, quite a few folks, I fear, won't have already read the Preface to Volume 1. In your own case, what's the reason for that? Maybe, it was sheer chance at work: This was, perhaps, the only Volume of *Philosophical Papers* anywhere near where you are, or you were, when first you hankered to have a gander at any part of this two-volume set. Well, if it's just something like that, then there's no fault on your part. Much of life is, of course, just a lot of luck, chance and happenstance.

At another extreme, you might have had both Volumes before you—each equally ready-to-hand. And, by golly, you simply chose to look *first* at the *Second* Volume. Just possibly, I guess, you might have had a decently good reason for doing that—though I haven't the faintest idea what it might be. Much more likely than that, I strongly suspect, you're an habitually disorderly person—perhaps so much so as to verge on sheer perversity. Now, if anything much like that should be so, then perhaps, and right quickly, you'd best change your ways. As I'll strongly suggest, you should try to proceed in a more orderly fashion. Now, if that seems too hard for you to do, all on your own, at this point in your life, then get some help with the issue. It needn't be professional help, I hasten to say (though, if this is just one of many ways in which you're behaving aberrantly, that might not be a bad idea). By contrast with anything as expensive, the help can be as perfectly costless, to you, as this: Find one of your most orderly friends, and place her in front of a set of volumes—whichever set it is that, at the time, you're most interested in perusing. Take note of what she does and then, after she's finished, you just proceed in the same order as she's just done. Pretty easy; don't you think?

All right, that's enough sarcasm from me—at least for the meanwhile. Quite certainly, it's enough snide chastisement. So, I'll very soon present the main part of this hopefully humorous Preface, right after saying how very little this one differs from the Preface to Volume 1: One difference between the two Prefaces is, of course, that the previous Volume's Preface gets right down to its business, without making any reference to any complementary Volume's Preface, whereas this present Preface begins with a rambling preamble, multiply mentioning the First Volume's Preface, and still rambling right along. Beyond that, the differences are, so far as I can tell, only quite automatic differences. So, in the Preface to Volume 1, there are many occurrences of the expression "Volume 1" that shouldn't be precisely the same as parallel occurrences in this present Preface, the Preface to Volume 2. Instead, for each of *those* occurrences—though not for all the occurrences of "Volume 1" in the First Volume's Preface—there should be, in this present Preface, an occurrence of "Volume 2." Context will make clear which occurrences fall into each of the two categories. And, in what directly follows this paragraph, I'll (try to) present the material in question with all the almost automatic alterations already made, without altering anything that should be precisely the same in both Prefaces. (Goodness gracious, this paragraph is boring!) Anyhow, without any interesting changes at all, what follows this paragraph's close is, or is relevantly equivalent to, the whole of the Preface to Volume 1 of *Philosophical Papers*.

Just a few months ago, I finally finished my *magnum opus*—well, my Really Big Book, anyway—a tome whose creation had been consuming me for eight very full years. With my so recently having relinquished any very vital connection with *All the Power in the World*, it's now hard, for me, to engage in substantial philosophical writing. But, that's hardly the whole story. Even years before completing that book, I decided

I wouldn't try to supply this collection, already on the drawing boards, with any intellectually ambitious Introduction—even if that might be much in vogue nowadays, as it just might possibly be. At all events, and for each of several individually sufficient reasons, in this large collection's many pages, one thing you won't find is any Introduction—none that's intellectually ambitious and, of course, none that's just so much perfectly pedestrian padding. (As James Carville might say, if he'd been advising me, "It's the papers, stupid!" Or, as I've given the Democrats a fair sum of cash, over the years, while nary a cent to the Real Protector of the Powerful's Privileges, maybe he'd leave out the "stupid." Or, maybe he wouldn't leave it out; I don't know.)

Though there's a fair lot of my shortish philosophical publication that's not contained anywhere in *Philosophical Papers*, still, this is a very sizeable collection—too big to comfortably fit between the covers of a single volume. Or, maybe in better words, there's too much to be contained in a single volume that's comfortable for a typical human being to comfortably read, while holding the whole thing in her own two hands. Accordingly, the collection is presented as a two-volume set.

In allocating papers to the set's two Volumes, I've tried to present the material thematically, by contrast with, say, a chronological presentation. Following some such principle for allocation pretty consistently, I've been able to manage, it happily turns out, a nice balance, so far as the number of selected papers goes, for the pair of Volumes: Exactly eleven selections serve to constitute the First Volume, Volume 1, and, as well, precisely that many may be found in this complementary Volume, Volume 2.

For a rough idea as to which sorts of pieces are in each Volume— where sorts are determined by thematic topic area—you may think of Volume 1 as having the alliterative subtitle "Epistemology, Ethics, Etcetera," and you may think of Volume 2 as being subtitled, almost as alliteratively, "Metaphysics and More." As each would-be subtitle indicates, in neither Volume are the selected works very neatly compartmentalized. At any rate, they're not exhaustively covered by brief terms for topic areas, with each term's proper denotation excluding that of the other topic terms. As this isn't any big deal, I'll say no more about it.

As I've already intimated, to put the point very mildly, in neither Volume will you find any intellectually ambitious Introduction, to precede that Volume's selected offerings. Nor will you find, in any of this big collection's many pages, anything else that might be taken to be some new substantial philosophical effort, not previously published. For one thing, in each of the two Volumes, I'm leaving all of the published pieces collected therein perfectly intact, just as it first appeared in published print. (Well, very nearly so: Of course, the collection's publisher, the Oxford University Press, may see fit to correct however many typographical errors some Oxford editors might find in the originally published material. And, of course, I'll allow them to format the papers so that the present presentations appear most pleasingly consistent. But, of course, none of that amounts to anything that's philosophically substantial.)

Just so, another thing you won't find in *Philosophical Papers* is this: Any remarks aimed at expressing my present views—or my later views, anyway—on questions addressed in any of the collection's published papers. (For that matter, you won't find any newly penned remarks, either, on any *other* philosophical issues.) As I'm thinking, there's little point in that. Why? Here's my thinking, about that question.

On the one hand, it may very well be, I think, that some of the presented papers grab you. In such a happy event, I'm quite sure, they'll serve to stimulate enjoyably disturbing thinking on your part. If anything much happens for you with my papers, or maybe even anything at all, it's that sort of experience that you'll enjoy. Now, in such a circumstance, you'll do far better to press on with your own responsive thoughts—prompted by my strangely challenging papers—than you'd do by gazing upon more words from me. For these further words of mine, they're likely to be more mature and mellow comments, far less happily stimulating than what's forcefully grabbed you and, accordingly, what's gotten you involved in your own enjoyable philosophic thinking. Well, that's what's on one hand.

Now, here's what's on the other hand: Unlikely though it may be, it just might happen, I fearfully allow, that my presented papers *don't* grab you—not even some very few among the twenty-two selected for the whole two-volume set. What's to be done in such a very different circumstance? Well, it's most unlikely that there's anything *I* can do to improve matters much. Do you think that, though I've entirely failed to light your fire, with all the very many presented attempts you've already seen me make toward such an end—well, somehow or other, I'll suddenly change things, very much for the better, by my heaping yet more words on you? Hardly likely, I'd say: Look, in such a sad circumstance as this, you'll be a (sort of) reader—a rather rare (sort of) reader, I hope—who's quite *dis*inclined to respond, in any very enjoyably active way, to the (sort of) sentences that a writer like *me* is so deeply disposed to produce. Let's face it; for happily active philosophical reading, I'm not your guy. Astonishing though the thought is, you'll likely do better by perusing the works of other contemporary philosophical writers. ("It's the papers, stupid!")

But, hey; let's be a little optimistic. You're a reasonably well-educated reader, I'm thinking, though you're not so very deeply steeped in recent philosophy as are most mainstream academic philosophers. So, as is then most likely, you'll be thinking that, since this collection comprises just so many papers produced by a worker in core analytic philosophy and, to boot, such a one as holds a very reputable academic post, these constituent papers are likely to be quite like those in each of just so many pretty similar collections—pretty much all of them published by academic presses (just as this present collection so obviously is). And, most likely, your related further thoughts will be a lot like these imminently upcoming ideas, even if they're not nearly so specific or detailed as what's coming right after my next colon: Except for a very few hundred other analytically-oriented metaphysicians, or epistemologists, or philosophers of language, and so on, well, there's scarcely anyone who'll find much enjoyable reading in anything even remotely like most such academical essays. Well, as you may be somewhat surprised to learn, I agree with this thinking of yours. (There's not absolute and complete agreement here, mind you. But, of course, that rarely happens among us opinionated human beings. More to the realistic point, there's agreement on the whole.) In fact, on the whole, I may have an ever dimmer view of the situation than you do. "Well, what's so optimistic about *that*?" you should now be thinking.

Nothing; nothing at all. But, as I'll remind you, the general situation isn't an all-encompassing situation. Happily for me—and for you, too, I imagine—this collection's papers were written by a very different sort of analytic metaphysician, and analytic epistemologist, and so on. Just so, the collection contains papers that, with almost every one of them, go smack against the grain of all the widely boring writing that you're so accustomed to dreading: In matters epistemological, I'm a radical skeptic, gosh-darned-it—leastways, most of the time I am. In matters metaphysical, I'm a self-styled nihilistic philosopher—very often, at least, that's my happily radical view. And so it goes. In the words of that delightfully wise cultural critic, Steve Martin, I'm a wild and crazy guy—not absolutely always, mind you, but—very much of the time, that's me.

For most browsers in any big Borders, say, or in any large Barnes and Noble store, just take a look at, say, "A Defense of Skepticism" (Paper number 1, in Volume 1) and "Skepticism and Nihilism" (Paper number 4, in that Volume). Right there, you'll find far more enjoyable stimulation, I'm sure, than in any of the dozens upon dozens of mainstream collections that, quite understandably, indeed, you won't give even so much as a two-minute lookover.

Equally, this holds true with most viewers of, say, Web-pages of Amazon.com. Or, to give such Web-surfing folks equal space here, I'll say this: In this present Volume of *Philosophical Papers*, that is, Volume 2, they'll find quite a lot to enjoy in, say, just the readily readable short selection "I Do Not Exist" (Paper number 2, in this Volume) and, directly after that, the short essay's more thoroughly exploratory companion, "Why There Are No People." Just in those two pieces, they'll find *far* more, to really enjoy, than in the whole of most any of the aforesaid analytically-oriented essay collections. I say *far* more to enjoy, and I mean just that. (Heck, if the difference was anything *much less* than that, most sensible book-buyers oughtn't give this present collection, either, so much as a two-minute lookover.)

Well, that's more than enough of such confident but self-serving comparisons. By this point, you've gotten my point, I'm sure. ("It's the papers, stupid!")

Now, even though it's just a rhetorical device, I'll again ask this question: Is there reason for you to be optimistic here, about what you'll find here, in this voluminous two-volume collection? Of course, you won't be at all surprised at the answer I provide: *Heck*, yeah! You'll become very happily embroiled, I'll bet you a quarter, in lots that's in *Philosophical Papers*.

Beyond what's in this Volume's reprinted papers, and beyond the Volume's Index, and, of course, beyond this happily humorous Preface, I'll supply you, in what's between the book's front cover and its back, little more than three lists: First, there's the (Table of) Contents for this very Volume, that is, for Volume 2 of *Philosophical Papers*. Second, there's the (Table of) Contents for this Volume's companion in the collection, that is, for Volume 1 of *Philosophical Papers*. Third, there's a lulu of a list, quickly called *Provenance of Papers*, that provides, in chronological order, quite full bibliographic information, for each of the twenty-two items reprinted in this entire two-volume collection. As with the two Contents lists, this list, too, will appear, identically the same, in both Volumes. Not obvious to sheer inspection, still, you'll soon see how very useful this list can be—especially for me!

With the next few paragraphs, you'll come to know more than enough, and more than you want, about the how serviceable are the three lists provided in this Volume. ("It's the papers, stupid!")

Even while this little prefatory production's meant to comprise mostly prose that's remarkably entertaining, it's also meant to serve certain more serious purposes. While those purposes are pretty serious, there's nothing very profound, let me tell you, in any of that: Indeed, far from concerning anything that's deeply philosophical, the points the Preface has yet to cover lie along such sensibly superficial lines as these: Beyond making some serious use of the lists lately mentioned, including what may be some legally necessary use, I'll supply you, in this Preface, with a smidgeon of authorial autobiography, and also a bit of practical advice for prospective readers. And, to top all that off—what the heck—I'll provide some blatant advertising for much other published work of mine, specifically, for all my self-standing book-length philosophical productions.

First, the smidgeon of authorial autobiography: Though I'd never have guessed it when first I wrote philosophy for publication, it's turned out that I'm more of a book-writer than a paper-writer—though, as I trust this collection makes plain, I've been a pretty considerable paper-writer, too. In retrospect, insofar as it's been papers that I've been writing, many of them turned out to be studies for books, or ancestors of books, or something of the kind. But, even so, many haven't ever been anything much like that and, most likely, they never will be. This is reflected, pretty well, I think, in what's been selected for appearance in *Philosophical Papers*: While eight of this whole collection's papers may be rightly regarded as seeds of longer and later published works, almost twice that number, fully fourteen selections, can't be regarded as being, in that way, anything like so seminal. So, for your hard-earned money— or for your institutional library's money—I've given you a nice mix here, I think. It's sort of a happy sampler, I'll suggest, with quite a nice variety of Ungerian offerings. ("It's the papers, stupid!")

From that bit of authorial storytelling, I segue to remark on the chronological list that, briefly, I call *Provenance of Papers*: My Provenance list, as I've noted, supplies bibliographic information for each of the original publications represented in *Philosophical Papers*—all those in Volume 1 of the collection and, as well, all those in Volume 2. I'm not sure how useful that may be for you. But, for me, it certainly serves a very useful purpose: In one fell swoop, I hereby thank all the relevant entities duly associated with each and every one of the twenty-two pieces listed therein, including the past and present editors of the various volumes and journals listed, their past and present publishers, and even whatever conglomerates may have, at one time or another, acquired rights regarding reprinting of the listed pieces. And, as instructed by one of these publishers, both for the one paper first appearing in *Synthese*, and for the two first appearing in *Philosophical Studies*, I'll now give my thanks by adding these very words, specifically wanted by that outfit: with kind permission of Kluwer Academic Publishers. So, that's it, guys, or corporations, or whatever "you" may be—you're all thanked now, every last one of you—especially you sticklers at Kluwer Academic

Publishers. All of you—and not just the Kluwer guys—should feel very much appreciated, by me, who does very much appreciate, in fact, your kind cooperation in the present project. Indeed, I ask that you take full notice of this fact: Not only do I thank all you folks, but—doubling everything up—I thank you all twice over: I thank you here, in this collection's Second Volume, and I also thank you in the First Volume of the set. For as happens with this most relevant part of my prefatory writing, the Provenance of Papers list also appears, in its entirety, in *both* Volumes of *Philosophical Papers*. (Surely, in the very bright light of all this clearly expressed appreciation, good fellows, all your lawyers should find useful work to do elsewhere—someplace far from me and my family.)

That said and done, I'll make some comments on two other lists I'm providing, each also appearing in both of the collection's two Volumes. These are the (Table of) Contents for Volume 1 and, com-plementing that, the (Table of) Contents for Volume 2: In each of these two (Tables of) Contents, I've grouped a Volume's eleven rep-rinted papers—including a self-styled paper wholly composed of Book Symposium material—into four numbered Parts. Just so, the First Volume has four numbered Parts, numbered from 1 through 4, and, equally, the Second Volume has four numbered Parts, also numbered from 1 through 4. For your happy perusal, I've quite delightfully la-beled each of these eight (two times four) Parts. With so many as six of the Parts, all told, in the Part's well-chosen title, there's cleverly em-bedded the title of one of my five already-existing, self-standing, solely-authored books. In each instance, there are several good reasons for doing that. But, for my money, the most operative reason is always this: All five of these self-standing works—the volumes with the cleverly embedded titles—they're all currently (2006) available for purchase. And, what's more, they're all readily available, for purchase, from this present collection's worldwide publisher, the Oxford University Press. ("It's the papers, stupid!")

Now, think about this, for a minute: If you like what's in any given one of these six Parts, or even just some of what's there, then there's a good chance, I'll bet, that you'll like the book whose title is embedded in that Part's title. Makes sense; doesn't it?

OK. So, then what?

Here's where I offer sound advice to prospective readers: In your "institutional" library—using that word for want of another that's better—you should, I'll suggest, go have a gander at the book (pretend there's just one) whose embedded title helped provide the title for the Part that contains the shorter writing, or shorter writings, that you've just so greatly enjoyed. As I just said, and as makes perfect sense, there's a good chance you'll then like what you see *there*—in the self-standing book whose embedded title is presently most salient. And, if you *do* like what you see—well, then, you should (try to) take that self-standing book home with you—along with both Volumes of *Philosophical Papers*—providing, of course, that it's perfectly legal for you to do all that. After some several days of actively living with all these legally borrowed books, it may very well happen, I'll just venture to guess, that you'll *still* like the philosophical productions that you've been perusing. Now, if you're enthralled with one of these books—or, as I hope, with many more than one—well, then you'll be happy that I've bothered to include, in this breezy Preface, some slickly effective advertisements for my writing. Anyway, at least by my lights, it's high time we encounter my Preface's main advertising section. ("It's the papers, stupid!")

Except for the very poorest among us, it's quite easy to permanently acquire, perfectly legally, a copy of any of my books, leastways any of them that's available as a paperback. For, among other convenient sources for the books I've authored, each is very readily available through the OUP's *Web-page*, whose address is, at the time of this prefatory writing, this Web-address: http://www.oup.com Now, once you're on this main OUP Web-page, you'll then have to search around there, it's true, to get onto a page where one of my books is featured, or where there's featured more than one—and this may involve rather a bit more clicking. But, for most decently well-educated Americans not yet on Medicare, that's a piece of cake. Or, as we perennial dieters prefer to say, it's a stroll in the park. ("It's the papers, stupid!")

Heck, if you're reading these words just a few years after I wrote them, you may easily be able to feast, for years and years, on a veritable banquet of my published philosophical food for thought, the whole shebang priced pretty reasonably: With a dozen or so well-placed clicks, you'll be able to acquire, for your private use and enjoyment, something that's far nicer than just some several philosophy books I've sent into the world. Very easily, but not very expensively, you'll be able to acquire a *complete **matched** set* of the books that feature nothing but Peter Unger's philosophical writing! (Well, if you acquire all the books within just a few years of my writing this sentence, your set will be as complete as then can be. Beyond that, well, who knows what more the still further future may bring?) Each of the seven volumes, I've certainly specified to the OUP—by now, maybe specified it some seven times over—each should be precisely the same trim size as all the others: the same height—I'm measuring that at some 24 centimeters, as near as I can tell;

and the same width, too—I'm measuring *that* at some 16 centimeters, with my same cheap cloth tape. (Of course, the books won't have the same thickness, even as some will be longer works while others will be shorter volumes. But, of course, that's perfectly irrelevant to any presently sensible point.) What's more, the paper cover of each book should look, most especially right where there's the book's spine, just so nicely like all the other books look. {Right now, it's true, in early 2005, my thirty-year old, my *Ignorance*, has a distinctly smaller trim size than that. But, by the time you're ready to buy a matched set of my paperback works, that should all be correctly changed. Still, you've now been forewarned, very clearly, of a (barely?) possible even long-term danger.} (Of course, even spinally presented, the books won't look precisely alike. Far from that, thank goodness! Not only will some books be thicker than others, but, often much more conspicuous, the title of any one book will look very different from the titles of (at least most of) the others. What do you want, for goodness sakes, that each book's *title* should look the same? That would be perfectly absurd!)

While the lined-up spines certainly won't look *precisely* alike, then, still and all, they'll look plenty pretty enough: Each book's spine will have, as its visually dominant feature, the same clean white background as will be gracing all its companion volumes. And, with all seven books having the very same trim size, there'll be a clean white line formed not only by the bottoms of these seven books—to be placed, I'd recommend, on a clean white shelf—but, quite as well, there'll be a clean white line formed by the *tops* of the books, as well. Think about *that*, for a minute. Very clean, very slick, very nice—almost perfectly exquisite will be that avidly awaited paperback matched set of Ungeriana. Heck, with such a nice slick look as that, I'll bet even your interior designer will give you a big thumbs up. Indeed, with a few friendly words from you—no doubt, by then a most happily satisfied customer—he (or she) might order his (or her) very own set, to grace his (or her) own den, or study or, just maybe, grand foyer. ("It's the papers, stupid!")

As I'm vividly imagining, by this point you've had quite enough of what's fast becoming a Preface both crassly and crudely commercial. So, with a more public-spirited remark, I'll now call it quits: Even if you never buy any of my works, please do return *all* your borrowed library books, *whomever* may have written them. It's the right thing to do; and, you'll feel better for it. Heck, it's about as easy as eating a hotdog, and it's nowhere near as fattening.

New York   P. K. U.
April 2005

PROVENANCE OF PAPERS
REPRINTED IN
PHILOSOPHICAL PAPERS

A CHRONOLOGICAL LIST

"An Analysis of Factual Knowledge," *The Journal of Philosophy*, LXV (1968): 157–170. Reprinted in Volume 1.

"A Defense of Skepticism," *The Philosophical Review*, LXXX (1971): 198–219. Reprinted in Volume 1.

"An Argument for Skepticism," *Philosophic Exchange*, vol. 1, no. 5 (1974): 131–155. Reprinted in Volume 1.

"Two Types of Scepticism," *Philosophical Studies*, 25 (1974): 77–96. Reprinted in Volume 1.

"The Uniqueness in Causation," *American Philosophical Quarterly*, 14 (1977): 177–188. Reprinted in Volume 2.

"Impotence and Causal Determinism," *Philosophical Studies*, 31 (1977): 289–305. Reprinted in Volume 2.

"There Are No Ordinary Things," *Synthese*, 41 (1979): 117–154. Reprinted in Volume 2.

"I Do Not Exist," pp. 235–251 in *Perception and Identity*, G. F. MacDonald ed., London: The Macmillan Press, 1979. Reprinted in Volume 2.

"Why There Are No People," *Midwest Studies in Philosophy*, IV (1979): 177–222. Reprinted in Volume 2.

"Skepticism and Nihilism," *Nous*, 14 (1980): 517–545. Reprinted in Volume 1.

"The Problem of the Many," *Midwest Studies in Philosophy*, V (1980): 411–467. Reprinted in Volume 2.

"Toward A Psychology of Common Sense," *American Philosophical Quarterly*, 19 (1982): 117–129. Reprinted in Volume 1.

"The Causal Theory of Reference," *Philosophical Studies*, 43 (1983): 1–45. Reprinted in Volume 1.

"Minimizing Arbitrariness: Toward a Metaphysics of Infinitely Many Isolated Concrete Worlds," *Midwest Studies in Philosophy*, IX (1984): 29–51. Reprinted in Volume 1.

"The Cone Model of Knowledge," *Philosophical Topics*, XIV (1986): 125–178. Reprinted in Volume 1.

"Book Symposium on *Identity, Consciousness and Value*," Precis of the Book, Reply to Sydney Shoemaker, Reply to Peter Strawson, Reply to Richard Swinburne, Reply to Stephen White, *Philosophy and Phenomenological Research*, LII (1992): 133–137 and 159–176. Reprinted in Volume 2.

"Contextual Analysis in Ethics," *Philosophy and Phenomenological Research*, LV (1995): 1–26. Reprinted in Volume 1.

"The Mystery of the Physical and the Matter of Qualities," *Midwest Studies in Philosophy*, XXII (1999), 75–99. Reprinted in Volume 2.

"Book Symposium on *Living High and Letting Die: Our Illusion of Innocence*," Precis of the Book, Reply to Fred Feldman, Reply to Brad Hooker, Reply to Thomas Pogge, Reply to Peter Singer, *Philosophy and Phenomenological Research*, LIX (1999): 173–175 and 203–216. Reprinted in Volume 1.

"The Survival of the Sentient," *Philosophical Perspectives*, 14 (2000): 325–348. Reprinted in Volume 2.

"Free Will and Scientiphicalism," *Philosophy and Phenomenological Research*, 65 (2002): 1–25. Reprinted in Volume 2.

"The Mental Problems of the Many," *Oxford Studies in Metaphysics*, Oxford: Clarendon Press, Volume I (2004): 195–222. Reprinted in Volume 2.

CONTENTS OF VOLUME 2

           STILL WITHOUT *ALL THE POWER
           IN THE WORLD*

            9.   The Uniqueness in Causation   295
           10.   Impotence and Causal Determinism   319
           11.   Free Will and Scientiphicalism   336

           Index of Names   365

CONTENTS OF VOLUME 1

PART I

Three Studies for
a Book That Wasn't

1

THERE ARE NO ORDINARY THINGS

Human experience, it may be said, naturally leads us to have a certain view of reality, which I call *the view of common sense*. This view is tempered by cultural advance, but in basic form it is similar for all cultures on this planet, even the most primitive and isolated. According to this prevalent view, there are various sorts of *ordinary things* in the world. Some of these are made by man, such as tables and chairs and spears, and in some 'advanced' cultures also swizzle sticks and sousaphones. Some are found in nature such as stones and rocks and twigs, and also tumbleweeds and fingernails. I believe that none of these things exist, and so that the view of common sense is badly in error. In this paper, I shall argue for this negative belief of mine.

It shall not be my business here to offer arguments concerning the question of whether there are any people, or conscious beings. I contrast these putative entities with mere *things*, and trust that my usage of the latter term follows one common way of allowing for such a distinction. Further, among such things, I shall discuss only those which are not living or alive; perhaps I may call them *ordinary inanimate objects*. Nothing of basic importance depends upon any such a division; it serves only to restrict my topic conveniently.

A second restriction I impose on myself is not to discuss certain more general concepts which are intended to delineate in a 'thing-like way' suitable portions or aspects of 'the external world', or of 'physical

3

reality'. Accordingly, while I shall argue that our concept of a stone, for example, is devoid of application, I shall not make any such claim for our concept of a *physical object*, or for any similarly general idea. So far as these present arguments go, then, there may well be various physical objects, indeed, even of a great variety of shapes and sizes. But whatever the shapes and sizes of any such objects, none will ever be a table, a stone, or any ordinary thing. At the same time, my arguments do not require the existence of any physical objects, but leave that question entirely open.

The arguments I will offer for my negative beliefs are variations upon the sorites argument of Eubulides, that incomparable Greek genius who also disclosed the paradox of the liar, the problems of presupposition and those of intentionality.[1] In its original form, the sorites argument appears to have concerned how many items, say beans, or grains of sand, or even some of each, will be sufficient to constitute a heap. None or one is insufficient. But, if there isn't any heap before us adding a single grain or bean, it seems, will not produce a heap. Hence, even with a million beans quite nicely arranged, there will be no heap of them. By generalization, this is a compelling argument that there are no heaps, and that our concept of a heap is relevantly incoherent. It is, we might say, a *direct argument* for this idea and, I believe, it is a sound one. Conversely, we may begin by supposing that there are heaps, and that a million beans typically arranged gives us an instance of that concept. But, then, removing a single peripheral bean gently from such a typical heap, it seems, will not leave us with no heap before us. Hence, we must conclude that even when we have but one bean left, or none at all, we still have a heap of beans. But this is absurd. Hence, we have reduced the original supposition of existence to an absurdity, and we may generalize accordingly. This, we may say, is an *indirect argument* that there are no heaps, and that our concept of them is not a coherent one. It is also, I believe, an adequate argument. Now, Eubulides' seminal contribution has long labored under the misnomer

1. See, for example, William and Martha Kneale, *The Development of Logic*, Oxford, 1962, p. 114ff. Eubulides has no writings extant, it appears, and scholarship pertaining to him is somewhat difficult, as is indicated by, e.g., Jon Moline's 'Aristotle, Eubulides and the Sorites', *Mind* 78, N.S., No. 311, 1969, pp. 393–407. Given that these four attributions are deemed highly likely, however, and that no direct writings remain, it seems likely that Eubulides discovered other things as well. But even if these four were all he discovered, they comprise a staggeringly brilliant achievement. It is a secondary intention of this paper that we come to better appreciate the brilliance of the Megarian master, as well as his great profundity.

of 'the sorites paradox'. But, in any philosophically important sense, there is no paradox here. Rather, we are given two demonstrations of the non-existence of heaps, while no important logical problems come from accepting the conclusion. It is hoped that as this paper develops, we shall better appreciate our true inheritance from Eubulides.

As a clarificatory note, let me point out that the sorites arguments just presented did not involve the notion of identity in any interesting way; we never said, or cared, *which* heap was present. Indeed, if that idea is involved at all, which I doubt, it is only in the manner in which any terribly general idea may be presupposed by, and so involved in, any argument at all, or virtually any. The arguments that I shall presently deploy similarly avoid any interesting involvement with identity. By introducing the notion, I suggest, we may obtain further arguments to the same effect; so our avoidance of it will only make things harder for our Eubulidean efforts. But even with sparse materials, it will be seen, the existence of all ordinary things may be disproved. Indeed, this may be done several times over, in each of a variety of complementary ways. In each case I shall try to keep the reasoning quite simple and straightforward: for the fundamental issues, I believe, are themselves of such a nature.

In the final section of this essay, I will discuss what I take to be the implications of these present rather restricted reasonings.

1. Ordinary Things and the Sorites of Decomposition

By *ordinary things*, as I have indicated, I mean such things as pieces of furniture, rocks and stones, planets and ordinary stars, and even lakes and mountains. This is not the only way that this expression may be used, but it surely represents no philosophic eccentricity on my part. For example, my use of the expression appears fairly close to that of W. V. Quine in his influential book, *Word and Object*.[2] Despite certain engaging departures from accepted common sense, such as his views on "the indeterminacy of translation", Quine's book does, nevertheless, operate on a foundation of common sense assumptions. The first section of the work is called, aptly enough, 'Beginning With Ordinary Things', and the book's body begins with this sentence: "This familiar desk manifests its presence by resisting my pressures and by deflecting

2. W.V. Quine, *Word and Object*, New York, 1960, p. 1ff.

light to my eyes." For Quine, then, a desk is a paradigm of an ordinary thing; his usage is much like mine. The difference between us, of course, is that while he thinks, along with almost everyone else, that there are such objects, I hold that there are no desks, nor any other ordinary things. It will not serve much of a point, I suppose, for me to list those philosophers whose usage is similar to my own. Nor shall I try to catalogue the various philosophies which rely on the supposition that there are ordinary things, however inexplicit they may be on the matter. For the nature of the issue is clear enough, and that it is of moment to various philosophers is also rather obvious.

To jolt our minds away from common sense thinking, and toward the denial of desks and stones, a bit of 'general science' may be of more help than any celebrated philosophy. Even from the early grades, we are given some simple scientific learning which in broad outline, and with fatal incoherence, is this: our ordinary things, like stones, which most certainly exist, comprise or consist of many atoms, and even many more sub-atomic particles. The point here has little to do with any niceties of such a term as 'consist', but may be put this way: in any situation where there are no atoms, or no particles, there are in fact none of our ordinary things. This should move us to deny, with proper reasoning, the existence of all alleged ordinary things.

The reasoning for this denial does not require atoms or particles. But for jolting the mind, I have found it helpful to cast it in such terms. I will do so here, choosing stones as my ordinary things and atoms as removable constituents. Accordingly, we may express these three propositions, which reasoning informs us form an inconsistent set:

(1)   There is at least one stone.
(2)   for anything there may be, if it is a stone, then it consists of many atoms but a finite number.
(3)   for anything there may be, if it is a stone (which consists of many atoms but a finite number), then the net removal of one atom, or only a few, in a way which is most innocuous and favorable, will not mean the difference as to whether there is a stone in the situation.

The reasoning here is simple. Consider a stone, consisting of a certain finite number of atoms. If we or some physical process should remove one atom, without replacement, then there is left that number minus one, presumably constituting a stone still. Whether what is left is the same stone, as it presumably is, or whether it is another one makes no difference to our cautious reasoning here: thus do we make good our resolve to foreswear reliance on considerations of identity. (Indeed, we may be more cautious still, writing our third premise so that we require only that *at least one* stone is left.) Now, after another atom is removed, there is that original number minus two; so far, so good. But after that certain number has been removed, in similar stepwise fashion, there are no atoms at all in the situation, while we must still be supposing that there is a stone there. But as we have already agreed, in (2), if there is a stone present, then there must be some atoms.

There is, then, a rather blatant inconsistency in our thought. However discomforting it may be, I suggest that any adequate response to this contradiction must include a denial of the first proposition, that is, the denial of the existence of even a single stone. Whatever one then thinks of the other two propositions is a further, much more minor matter. Whether one eventually deems them straightforwardly true, vacuously true, without truth-value, or whatever, will not be of any surpassing importance.

I call this argument, *the sorites of decomposition* or, more fully, *the sorites of decomposition by minute removals.* It is an indirect argument for the conclusion that there are no stones and, by generalization, no other ordinary things.[3] I believe this indirect argument to be not only compelling but sound. Let us consider a number of points of commentary which may help us to assess this belief of mine.

The first point we may consider is that, while this sorites of decomposition works well against the supposed existence of our ordinary things, it does *not*, in contrast, *work as compellingly* to deny the existence of physical objects. For no matter how small a thing is removed, if anything is left, which that first has been removed from, that remaining item, for all we can compellingly argue, may be a physical object. It takes some doing to argue to the contrary, and any such extra effort will only begin to approach, at best, our argument against any ordinary things. Now, none of this is to say that physical objects cannot be made to cease to exist, by cutting into them, so to say, or in any other way; nor is it to deny that. I wish only to notice the difference between how compellingly

---

3. Especially for generalizing, I have been careful not to say, in the third premise, that removing a peripheral atom *will always leave a stone.* Such a condition would be faulted, for example, by a putative stone containing a time-bomb about to explode. Innocuously removing an atom won't leave a stone there, for it has no chance to do so. But *that removal won't mean the difference* as to whether there is a stone there. So, even with threatening time-bombs, our careful premise will let us conclude that there aren't any stones and, similarly, any time-bombs either. Having this distinction before us, in what follows. I won't bother to employ it explicitly. Here, I am indebted to Terence Leichti.

our sorites works to deny an ordinary thing, a stone, for example, and how much less powerfully it works against physical objects (if, indeed, it has any power at all with regard to the latter).

Now, if one appreciates this contrast, it follows that he will be finding our sorites of decomposition quite compelling as deployed against our ordinary things: against stones and rocks, desks and tables, and planets and certain stars. While he may wish to alter the argument thus deployed, the alterations are, then, only a matter of details and niceties. While he may wish an explanation, in some depth, of why supposed ordinary things fall prey, that too presupposes agreement that our argument surely appears quite sound. The correct explanation of this appearance is, I suggest, the simplest one: the argument is as it appears to be, that is, it is a sound one. A contrast may also be drawn between ordinary things and certain particulars which are prominent in the physical sciences. A compelling argument of this sort may be given to deny stones, planets and at least certain stars, but not electrons, hydrogen atoms, and water molecules, or so it now appears.

A second point worth noting is that the central idea of this argument does not depend on atoms, or on anything else so very minute. For example, we may remove 'a speck of dust's worth' at a time to the detriment of any putative stone. For certain artifactual items, like a table, possible future cases might require decremental units which fall below the level of of unaided perception. For example, someone might conceivably construct a table 'smaller than a speck of dust'. With the proper equipment on his part, I am not sure that facts of material structure would prevent him from getting things into the intended shape, etc. And, perhaps the resulting item would be termed a table by common sense judgement. But the removal of tiny units would show this judgement also to be erroneous.

Now, in imagination we may contemplate a table, or a stone, it seems, shrinking down to the size of an atom. But that is not real. When you remove more and more small units from an alleged table or stone, you don't keep getting smaller and smaller tables or stones, or anything relevantly preservative.[4] Further, our argument implies no particular, not to say particulate, theory of matter. For all we care, the only physical reality may be a single plenum, modifications of which are perhaps poorly labeled as atoms or as particles.

As a third point, we may agree that it is somewhat arbitrary how many propositions we display in order to generate the contradiction.

4. On these points, I have profited from discussion with Raziel Abelson.

As we have it here, the third proposition is not one which entails that any stone consists of atoms, but it does entail that any stone which does consist of them may have an atom, or a few, removed without replacement. Alternatively, we might have conjoined our second proposition with our third, to pit against the assertion of existence a single more complex proposition. Alternatively yet again, we might unravel our third proposition into one which says that any stone consisting of atoms allows for such a net removal and another which says that whenever such a removal should happen to such a stone we are left with a stone.[5] It is an interesting task, then, to spell out more explicitly the specific assumptions which underlie this argument, thus increasing the number of members of the inconsistent set we may exhibit. But we may confidently say even now, I suggest, that however finely we demarcate things, the relevant propositions are accepted by almost all educated human beings. The problem, then, is to respond to the inconsistency, and the most compelling solution, I suggest, is to deny the existence of ordinary things.

As a fourth point, we should allow that our third premise, and even our second, has not been stated in a manner which is very clear or explicit. But the statement of a premise may be refined, while no substantial change in the argument will result from any relevant alteration. This is not to suggest that, in our present system of concepts, such a premise may ever be made adequately precise. It is only to notice that any attempt to move in that direction will mean no important problem for our argument. For example, one may squabble over the word 'many' or over the word 'few'. I chose these vague words because they rather faithfully express, I supposed, the unreflective beliefs on these matters which most people have, so few of us being scientists. But we may of course replace them by more definite expressions which, upon reflection, must be admitted to yield acceptable propositions. Thus, we may say, by way of illustration, that any stone consists of *at least one billion* atoms, and that removing *no more than ten thousand* leaves a stone. Again, one may complain about our use of an expression so vague as 'a way which is most innocuous and favorable'. But then we may be more explicit, always pretending, so to say, that there is real substance to the matter of whether there is a stone present or not, while always on the way toward showing how insubstantial is that very matter. In this direction, we might say, for example, that no atom is to be removed forcefully from a central position, but one may be taken gently from

---

5. I am indebted here to discussion with Michael Lockwood.

a peripheral location. We may say, again, that we are to remove in a manner most favorable *to there being a stone left there after the removal*, supposing such an actually absurd thing to have some bearing on reality. Further, we may point out that we are not supposing that in any given case one way is *the* most favorable or innocuous. At almost any choice-point, so to say, any atom or relevant group, of many millions, might be just as favorable to remove as any other. Certain *conditions*, which we may include under 'way', or which may be mentioned distinctly, may all be equally as favorable, and more so than many others; and so on. We might say, further, that there is nothing mysteriously ideal about these favorable ways, as my remarks about removing dust specks (supposing them to exist) make quite clear. For such ways and conditions, or ones near enough to them, appear to occur all the time on the face of the earth. Finally, to put a convincing cap on this whole matter, we note that all we need for our argument is this: for any putative stone, there is always *at least one* way of removing *at least one* minute item without going from (at least one or) a stone to none. With even one relevantly gradual path to follow, we can 'peel our onion' down to nothing. In fact, it seems, there are an 'enormous' number of these paths always open to us. Hence, we make our point with powerful overkill.

As a fifth point, we may reply to the Moorean gambit of clutching onto common sense at the expense of anything else, most especially any philosophical reasoning.[6] According to this way of thinking it is *always* most appropriate to reply to philosophical challenges as follows. We are *more certain* that there are tables than of *anything* in the contrary philosophic reasoning. Hence, while we may never be able to tell *what* is wrong with the reasoning, at least one thing *must* be wrong with it. But while such a generalization may prove a useful guide in addressing many philosophical challenges, is it to have *no exceptions at all*? I think that an unquestioning affirmative answer here is not only likely to be untrue, or incorrect, but is extremely dogmatic. What of the *present* case, then, *might not that* be just such an *exception*? The merits of the case must be judged in terms of the particulars. That is, of course, we consider those points, some already made, which have much more to do with the issues here at hand.

We have an inconsistency to which to respond. If we persist with our belief in ordinary things what rational responses are available? As a sixth point, we may note that any response other than our suggested

---

6. G. E. Moore, 'Four Forms of Scepticism', in his *Philosophical Papers*, London and New York, 1959, p. 226.

one involves us in the acceptance of a *miracle*, in a fair employment of that term. The miracle expected will be of one of these following two kinds, though of course someone might expect both sorts of miracle. First, tables and stones might be preserved by natural breaks in the world order, so to say, by disjoint happenings whose occurrence prevents nature from being relevantly gradual. For example, after a few atoms were successively removed, or a few minute chips, it might be physically impossible to remove another. Or, for another example, after the sixth atom or chip was removed, the removal of the seventh might occasion a drastic result: the remainder might 'go out of existence', or turn into a frog, or whatever. Such happenings as this go against our daily experience, as with sanding a piece of wood or smoothing stones. They also conflict with our scientific perspective which, taking things down to deeper levels, fits nicely with this everyday experience. To expect tables and stones to be saved by such cooperative breaks in nature is, I say, to expect a *miracle of metaphysical illusion*. Thinking nature relevantly gradual, this response has little appeal for me.

Now, given that the world is in fact relevantly gradual, and apparently quite uncooperative, the only hope for ordinary things will lie with the human mind. We must suppose, contrary to what our intuitions seem to be telling us now, and contrary to what we believe to be the rather limited power of our everyday conceptions, that we are all the time employing ideas that have precise limits. We must suppose that with, say, a trillion trillion atoms there, in a certain case, there really is a stone, whether anyone can ever tell or not. But, with one or a few, say fifty, gingerly removed from the outside, the situation suddenly changes, even if no one can ever tell. And this means that with *any* one, or *any* fifty, of the atoms gone, there is no stone there. That's the sensitivity of our word 'stone' for you! To believe in this is, I say, to believe in a *miracle of conceptual comprehension*. Thinking of our everyday thought as relevantly imprecise and unrefined, this alternative response also has little appeal for me. Accordingly, I must abandon my belief in stones.

A seventh point will now be helpful to consider. This is the point that whatever holds true of such allegedly familiar things as stones and rocks, and desks and tables, insofar as it is relevant to our topic, also holds true of swizzle sticks, sousaphones, withered tumbleweeds and hundreds of other ordinary things. The ideas of these others are less familiar and frequent for us. The ideas of stones and tables, in comparison, are like old and trusted friends. To think these familiars inapplicable may thus, for most of us, occasion greater discomfort than thinking the same about, say, 'swizzle sticks'. But the logical situation can scarcely sustain any such emotional difference. If tables will be left behind with the innocuous removal of a single atom, presumably any one of millions, then the same miracle must hold for swizzle sticks. The idea that nature may favor tables against swizzle sticks defies credibility, I hope even that of the most adamant defenders of common sense. But does anyone really think that by taking away peripheral atoms we shall ever encounter such a sensitive swizzle stick? Does anyone imagine that our concept of a swizzle stick discriminates at the required atomic level? Surely, this is quite absurd. But, then, it is just as absurd in the case of tables, and of stones.

The last matters for us in this first section come from an idea of Donald Scheid, offered by him to me in conversation. He notes that, according to common sense, if we have an ordinary thing, there is some sufficiently large 'part' of it which would *not* leave such a thing were it taken away. For example, if one ate 97 percent of an apple, in the typical fashion, one would not still have an apple there. Following Scheid, we might say that that 97 percent was an 'obliterating part' of the apple. But, then, he notes, if something is an obliterating part, then one atom less should still give us an obliterating part. In stepwise fashion, we must conclude that a single atom is an obliterating part, for any ordinary thing. But doesn't this contradict our third premise, which says that if you have a stone, then removing an atom *leaves* a stone still? I think not. Scheid's argument does not give us the negation of our conditional but, rather, a conditional with the same antecedent and the negation of our previous consequent: if something is a stone, then the net removal from it of an atom will *not* leave a stone. So far from jeopardizing our third premise, then, this gives us an additional argument from it against ordinary things. For now we may conclude that if something is a stone, then the net removal from it of an atom both will and will not leave a stone there. And so, we may conclude, nothing is a stone.

Two further points may be noticed with respect to Scheid's reasoning. First, by extending it further, we may conclude that if something is a stone, then removing nothing from it at all will leave no stone. For if one atom is an obliterating part, and so is one atom less than that, the removal of nothing will mean the obliteration of such an object. Thus we may conclude, again, that there are no stones or other ordinary things.

Though I have argued otherwise, Scheid's reasoning might be supposed to refute our third premise. The supposition that it should do so lets us make our final point. For we have just seen that *if* this reasoning should refute our third premise, it will do so in a manner which is at least as effective against our first premise, that is, against ordinary things. To preserve rational belief in such objects, however, it can never be enough to undermine some contrary propositions in such a manner as that. Rather, we must refute such contrary statements by reasoning which does *not* do as much, or worse, for our belief in ordinary things. And this, I suggest, can never be effectively accomplished.

2. Mathematical Thinking and the Sorites of Slicing and Grinding

In recent years problems of vagueness have suffered the attempts of philosophers and logicians to afford them a solution in mathematical terms. Such an employment of technical devices is, I shall argue, almost certainly out of place in this connection, and it will not provide any rational counter to our sorites arguments. This is not to place any significant limitations upon mathematics. On the contrary, it is to recommend that its proper use here is, not to rescue hopeless concepts from demonstrations of their inadequacy, but to aid in the development of better, precise ideas with which those concepts may be replaced. To evaluate my recommendation, let us look at the situation.

First, to judge by recent writings, the device more widely expected to help with vagueness, of those with a mathematical inspiration, is the assignment of new and exotic *truth-values*, most particularly of *numerical ones*. Along these lines, David Sanford, for example, has tried to develop a *logic of vagueness*. As he himself says, he is rather representative:

> ...I shall proceed from some of the basic assumptions shared by previous workers on the logic of vagueness...The first assumption I share is that an infinitely valued interpretation is appropriate in dealing with the application of sentential logic to vague sentences. The values are the real numbers between 1 and 0 inclusive.[7]

The key idea in this sort of approach, for it to be at all plausible, is that the application of a vague term appears *gradually* to become more questionable as we move further from its accepted paradigms. The gradual change in truth-values is to mirror this appearance. But in reality this device, whatever else one may think of it, leaves wholly untouched the miracles which any failure of the sorites requires. The miracle of metaphysical illusion is no more to be expected now than before, when, presumably, truth and falsity were the only values in question. But, then, what of the miracle of conceptual comprehension; is it more to be

---

7. David H. Sanford, 'Borderline Logic', *American Philosophical Quarterly* 12, No. 1, 1975, p. 29. For his treatment of sorites arguments see p. 38. For references to various other thinkers of similar persuasion see his footnotes.

expected now? There is some slight appearance to this effect. Now, with the removal of a peripheral atom, we do not go from truth to falsity, from one thing to its diametric opposite, so to say, but only from, say, unity to 0.999. So now, we go from one thing to another which is quite close by it. But as regards our required miracle, this appearance is quite deceptive, and accomplishes nothing. For *any* departure from unity, or indeed *any* change in truth-value, with the removal of a single atom, requires that our terms 'stone' and 'swizzle stick', be sensitive at least on the atomic level. That our expression 'swizzle stick' should be that sensitive quite defies credibility. For it to be that discriminating is a miracle which surpasses my capacity for belief.

The matter is not changed if we focus, not on statements, or on such things as might properly have a truth-value, but on sentences. Thus, in a relevant context, we may consider such a sentence as 'There is a swizzle stick here'. Discounting the fatal vagueness inherent in the word 'here', and perhaps also that associated with the present tense use of the verb, we may ask when this sentence first ceases to express something which is true, whatever it then does instead. At the beginning, we are assuming, there is a swizzle stick before us; so at that point the sentence doesn't fail to express a truth. As peripheral atoms come off, one by one, we are always asking whether it still does the same or whether now, for the first time, it does something else. For something else to be done, upon the removal of a peripheral atom, requires the same incredible sensitivity on the part of 'swizzle stick' as we previously noted. The distinction, then, between sentences and statements, which might prove helpful for other logical topics, does nothing to diminish the great problem here at hand. And in like manner, I suggest, further distinctions and devices of logic only get our required miracle further from our focus, and do not get its enormity to decrease by one jot. For me, then, no attempt to make it look like little is happening here can be of any use at all.

Similar considerations, I believe, will suffice to refute *any* attempt at making our miracle look small, and so look to be expected, however complex that attempt might be. So far as my acquaintance goes, the following attempt is as complex as any available. It is suggested by an idea of Hartry Field, which is in turn based on an approach of David Lewis.[8] Seeking no new logic, Lewis would assign a range of *semantic*

---

8. See the appendix to David K. Lewis, 'General Semantics' in Donald Davidson and Gilbert Harman, eds., *Semantics of Natural Language*, Dordrecht, Holland, 1972, pp. 215–216. Also, see the appendix to Hartry H. Field, 'Quine and the Correspondence Theory', *The Philosophical Review* 83, No. 2, 1974. This attempt, or something much like it, has been brought to my attention by David Lewis in conversation.

values to sentences with vague terms. For Field these are "successively higher degrees of truth", to account for the fact that relevant sentences do "not jump *suddenly* from absolute falsehood to absolute truth". But suppose two people differed as to where absolute truth is first to appear? There may be vagueness here too, Field suggests, in the term 'true', and various resolutions of it may yield various results for first appearance.[9] Thus, it is suggested, there may be a great deal of play in the whole business. Letting qualms about these 'resolutions' have no say, we might amplify upon this idea. We might say, then, that different resolutions of 'swizzle stick' and 'true' together will yield different results, and this joint yield may let the look of suddenness fade further into the background. But what is accomplished by all of this? For our sorites to be thwarted, some resolution(s) of 'true' and 'swizzle stick' must apply up to a point, atomically counted, and then, quite suddenly, after a single peripheral atom is removed, presumably *any* one of millions, the whole business no longer applies! (Otherwise, the whole business will still apply with only one atom left, which is absurd.) But that, in a new guise, is our miracle of conceptual comprehension all over again. And, it is no more to be expected now than before, despite the more complex formulation in which it appears.

For those who expect no such miracle at all, there is no response but to deny ordinary things. And this, I think, means that such a denial is the only rational response for anyone. In order to dissuade others from trying similar attempts to escape our arguments however, more may be required than to point up the reappearance of our miracle in various complex contexts. To alter the motivation behind such maneuvering, it may be best to take another, complementary tack. On this tack, we notice the 'range of phenomena' present in typical cases where philosophers have examined sorites arguments, cases where we have taller and taller 'short' men, or hotter and hotter 'cool' objects. And, we notice, also, that we have such an enticing range where we take atoms from a swizzle stick, one atom at a time, or only a few. We shall endeavor, then, to leave all such ranges well behind us. To do that, in fact, we need only return to the beginnings of all this, that is, to Eubulides and his heaps.

As fairly as I can, I will try to approach the Eubulidean problem with the notion of degrees of truth, and the range of available values that it implies. Now, according to my own idiolect, or my linguistic

9. I argue that 'true' has no such vagueness, and is instead a kind of 'absolute term', in Chapter 7 of my *Ignorance*, Oxford, 1975, pp. 272–319. But, with Field, I am supposing the opposite here; my purposes are illustrative.

intuitions, I can feel comfortable, whatever that may be worth, in saying with five beans suitably before me, 'Here's a very small heap, and so, a heap'. Perhaps, then, I should assign the value of 1, or at least 0.95, to the proposition that Oscar is a heap, where 'Oscar' is supposed to name the hopeful heap of five now before me. (When I first wrote this, I was actually playing with grains of rice, not beans in fact, to try seriously to get a feeling for the matter.) Taking away a bean from Oscar, to produce Felix (who may or may not be the same entity as Oscar), I fell less comfortable in saying a heap is before me. But it isn't all that unsettling. What am I to do; assign a value of 0.9 to the proposition that Felix is a heap? Taking away one again, now to yield Leo, I am at a loss. My sensitive intuitions seem to desert me; I know not which way to turn. Perhaps a value of 0.5 is now in order, or is that a bit too high, or too. low, and just a fake at compromise? With two beans, and only Alex before me, I feel like 0 is the value for me. But can such a sudden and great drop stand scrutiny? Perhaps we'd better go back and re-evaluate, or better yet, give up this game.

A familiarity with mathematical thinking may engender a second way of attempting to counter our attack on common sense. It may be urged that our lengthy arguments, with a step for each atom or chip, may require us to employ *mathematical induction,* and that this may be unwarranted in ordinary contexts.[10] Now, I suggest that an objection focusing on mathematical induction is, indeed, only a special case of a more general worry about our sorites of decomposition by minute re-movals. The more general worry, or objection, would be that our argument is too long: "In pure mathematics, and even in certain forms of empirical and everyday reasoning, long arguments are all right. But in certain other contexts, and you have clearly hit on one of them, restrictions of length must be imposed." This objection may be elaborated upon in a manner reminiscent of mathematical logic. It may be said that we have employed certain 'rules of inference', or that we have pre-supposed them. These rules, while perhaps good for unlimited use in some contexts, must surely be restricted in others, notably in those

---

10. There are two papers, both appearing in *Synthese* 30 (1975), which treat of sorites arguments, and of mathematical reasoning in connection with them, in a manner conformable with that recommended here: Michael Dummett's badly misnamed 'Wang's Paradox', pp. 301–24 and, though perhaps the connection with mathematical reasoning is somewhat less, Crispin Wright's 'On the Coherence of Vague Predicates', pp. 325–65. Neither of these authors, however, adopts a view as radical as that which I espouse. Further from mathematical considerations but, by my lights, the most far-reaching paper in that issue of *Synthese*, is Samuel C. Wheeler's 'Reference and Vagueness', pp. 367–79. All of these papers are to be recommended.

where we would challenge common sense. A system of logistic might even be concocted to codify formally the restrictions thought necessary and proper, and so on, and so forth. I can think of no good reasoning in support of such an objection. But more importantly perhaps, it misses the fundamental point upon which our sorites argument revolves, and which appears already to have been anticipated by Eubulides, with his heap. For we have seen that short arguments cut heaps down to size soon enough.

To bring the point home for our more 'cohesive' ordinary things, I shall provide a variant upon my original sorites of decomposition, which I call *the sorites of slicing and grinding.* I will present this sorites in two versions, the first being more suitable for most artifactual objects, like tables, as well as for the more highly structured natural items, for example, twigs and pine cones.

With regard to any table, then, no matter how large, I suggest that there will always be at least one way of partitioning by volume, say, into roughly equal fifths, or if one likes into eighths, so that the Eubulidean bafflement matches that lately encountered with the heap. Having made our partitioning imaginatively, we then envision a physical process occurring to the putative table as follows. First, one fifth of the table is sliced off and ground to a find dust, perhaps even rendered into separated atoms. The dust, if not atoms, is then scattered to the winds, or sunk speck by speck into widely dispersed regions of the sea. Then a second fifth is sliced, ground and scattered, and so on. Now, when we are down to our last fifth, there is, quite clearly, no table present.

But, then, when did we first have no table? I submit that there was none in the first place. The idea of this sorites is, then, quite simple, and very easy to comprehend. And while the argument only requires that there be at least one way of effecting a relevant partitioning, for at least one relevant fraction, say, fifths, there are in fact for any such fraction one chooses, sixths, sevenths and so on, an 'enormous' number of ways to divide bafflingly the putative table in question. Accordingly, with what might be described as powerful overkill, this sorites of slicing and grinding eliminates any objection to our challenge as requiring reasonings that are 'too lengthy for the context'. And, of course, mathematical induction plays no part here.

Let us exhibit the argument, to see that it is, indeed, not a very lengthy one: if the original item is a table, then so is what remains after an appropriate fifth has been sliced off, ground fine and scattered widely. If what remains then, about four fifths of the original, is a table, then so is what remains after another such fifth is sliced off, ground and scattered. If what remains then, about three fifths, is a table, then so is the two fifths or so that remains after the next fifth is thus treated. If that is a table, then we have one when we only have a fifth left of the original, say, a small part of the top, most of one leg and a bit of another. But, this last, we have agreed is no table. Hence, the original item is no table either, contrary to popular misconceptions. This argument is quite fully laid out. And it employs no peculiar 'rules of inference' or 'logical principles'. Moreover, it is rather shorter than many reasonings in everyday life, as well as in mathematics, science and philosophy, which are widely accepted, and scarcely ever questioned. To deny this argument, it should be clear, is to become involved in absurdity.

Some persons on whom the foregoing argument is tried might, nevertheless, attempt to resist it by thinking that an important line was crossed with the removal of a certain fifth, no matter how cleverly baffling the design of the partitioning. Such a one might, then, deny a particular intermediate premise on such putative grounds. For example, he might deny this premise: if there is a table with three fifths left, then there is still a table with two fifths left. To my mind, such a denial appears quite absurd. But even if it is granted some momentary plausibility, such a denial will be only a delaying device. For after we have removed easy fifths, we may imaginatively divide the problematic fifth itself into, say, fifths. And then we may slice and grind again. (If we have already destroyed that fifth with our original putative table, we may use a duplicate of it.) Now, if there is a table there with three fifths, i.e., with fifteen twenty-fifths, then there should be one with fourteen twenty-fifths; and so on down to ten twenty-fifths. This should decide matters well enough. If not, which I find hard to conceive, we may perform again and again the same partitioning procedure until any resister will find absurd his own putative sensitivity. But with any rationality on the part of our resisting subjects, no great length will be necessary. Fifths should often suffice; the twenty-fifths should take care of any remaining laggards.

An entirely similar argument will not work compellingly against stones, for hardly anyone, I suppose, would be convinced, without further reasonings, that a fifth of a stone was not a stone. We might get further if we asked him first to imagine something which was 'just about the smallest' item he would count as a stone, bearing in mind the realities of material structure. But even this might well fail to convince. If so, we may get a lot further by following this procedure: We cut that 'approximately smallest' stone in, say, tenths, more or less *simultaneously* grind nine and scatter their dust, or atoms. Is the remaining tenth a stone? We then repeat the procedure. After only ten steps, the remaining item, while presumably larger than the scattered particles, is only one ten-billionth of the original, which, we remember, the person originally thought of as just about as small as a stone could be. If at any place our subject thinks an important line has been crossed, we may then backtrack, if need be using a relevant duplicate. Starting with the larger item, on the 'first side of that line', we may then slice and grind in tenths, *one at a time*, in much the same manner as that lately employed with alleged tables. Thus, we may reduce to absurdity the existence of this approximately smallest stone. As it was alleged to be that small, our backtracking may well occur with the first cutting in tenths. To convince further, we may then start well on the other side of this 'small stone'; we may start, for example, with a supposed stone ten times the size of it. This latter, for our subject, would clearly be a stone if anything ever is. And, beginning with it will not add many steps to our argument. Accordingly, whether the items we treat are more like alleged tables or more like supposed stones, no suspiciously long or complex reasoning is needed to deny compellingly assertions of existence.

It may be useful to interject at this point a few remarks regarding the relation of our arguments to time. While we are casting them in a temporal form this is not crucial to our arguments. For one thing we may put our reasonings in a counter-factual form: if there is a table before us, there would still be one without a peripheral atom, and without one of the bafflingly imagined fifths. For another, we can consider differing items existing at one time, each in a different region of space. Each item might differ from the next to be considered by one peripheral atom, the last being only one atom itself. With such small differences as that, our formulation may best be, not only spatial, but also counter-factual. More realistically, we may have five objects, say, corresponding to the steps of the argument lately envisioned for tables and, if need be, some extras for our baffling twenty-fifths. For stones, as noted, a few more items might be needed.

A third mode of mathematical objection is one based on a putative distinction between fully extensional systems and those which are, in part at least, intensional. Our sorites, it might be thus objected, relies on at least one premise which is intensional, that is, which fails to be fully extensional. This occurs, perhaps, with the third premise, where we are talking about a series of decrements which may never have been effected. Which putative table, after all, has undergone decomposition atom by atom, or even in a way much like that? Our premise only speaks, it may be said, of what *would* be the case if such decompositions *were* carried out, or were to obtain in nature, or something of that sort. Further, as understood extensionally, our premise may be true and yet generate no contradiction with our other exhibited propositions. For those minute, perhaps atomic, removals which actually do occur to stones may leave them all clearly stones, as it happens. And, it might be urged, it is only an extensional sentence which makes any proper sense, and which should be used in the formulation of any worthwhile sorites argument.[11] Now, granting that there is a clear distinction of the sort intended, I can see no reason for denying importance to sentences which are intensional in the manner of our third premise. Indeed, without such sentences, we abandon any attempt to express causal relations, lawlike connections, and so on, amongst events and processes in nature. If this is the only way to escape our sorites, then we are on a path very nearly as radical as the one marked by a denial of ordinary things. It is doubtful, then, that many would wish to follow this reply.

But even if one takes the heroic stance here, no true escape from the sorites attack will be effected. For supposing that they existed in the first place, actual processes of destruction and deterioration have befallen a great many ordinary things. And, in a great *many of these* cases, it cannot truly be said that in any given *second* the situation changed from one where there was a stone, or table, or whatever, to one where there was not. If there was really a stone there at an earlier time, then so in the next second, and so on. But during seconds near the end, so to say, there clearly is no stone or table or whatever. Hence, in the actual situations in question there never were any stones, or tables, or whatever. But there is no relevant difference between *these* putative objects and *any other* ordinary things. If there ever were, are or will be any stones, or tables, or whatever, then some of these things were among them. Hence, there never were, are or will be any ordinary things at all. And, here we have reasoned only as regards actually occurring processes and, so, I suppose, in a wholly extensional manner.

Concerning the relation of our sorites to mathematical thinking, perhaps I may sum up my position in this way: the sorites, now given in two main variations, points up a contradiction in our beliefs. The introduction of mathematical complexities may draw our attention to certain *other* propositions, perhaps interestingly *related* to the ones in question, which are, in contrast, mutually consistent. But nothing can make a contradiction itself disappear, and not just disappear from our view. Our belief in ordinary things, then, may be rescued by mathematical thinking only insofar as the latter makes credible at least one of the two miracles we have already discussed several times over. This, of course, is not to be expected. Hence, in all likelihood, no mathematical

---

11. These matters were brought to my attention by David Sanford.

system can make rational for us a belief in ordinary things. None of this, of course, is to disparage mathematical thinking. On the contrary, it is to suggest that the proper service for it lies, not in the rescue of incoherent common sense, but in the formulation of more adequate descriptions of reality.

3. The Sorites of Cutting and Separating

There is another variation of our sorites which I should like to present and consider, *the sorites of cutting and separating*. My introduction of it will be a bit roundabout; I hope instructively so.

When focusing on our sorites of decomposition by minute removals, which proceeds atom by atom, or at least tiny chip by tiny chip, we may easily get the idea that *fairly sizable physical objects* are more stable, or better able to endure changes, than are ordinary things. As the atoms come off one by one, or a few at a time, we get to a situation where, even according to common sense judgements, there is no table, stone or sousaphone. It seems, however, that there is still a physical object before us, one consisting of many atoms, perhaps even many millions of them. Moreover, though I have foresworn serious inquiry here into matters of identity, we do have the thought that this remaining physical object might well be the same one as the bigger item with which we started, and which we wrongly called a table, a stone or a sousaphone. One who thinks along these lines, then, may well get the idea that 'table' names a state or phase which a given physical object may occupy, whether during a certain portion of its career or throughout its entire history. The term 'table' may thus be thought to bear much the same relation to 'physical object' as 'infant' or 'philosopher' may bear to 'man' or to 'human being'. Finally, it may be thought that terms for ordinary things, like 'table', really do apply after all, and that our conclusion to the contrary was based on a confusion as to what sort of logical role the terms have in our conceptual scheme for things, on a category mistake if you please.

Whatever we may think of the previous thoughts which may thus lead to it, however, this last idea is a *non sequitur*, and is in any case badly in error. For whatever the category or categories in which one may place a term, whether one identifies it as a term for an object, a process, a quality or whatever, if that term is incoherent, so it will remain. If 'table' is best thought of as a term for a state or a phase, it will be an *incoherent* term of *that* sort, and so it will apply to no real state or phase, just as it will apply to no real object, quality, or whatever. In any case, then, as our sorites arguments have already shown, terms for ordinary things will apply to no reality at all.

Placing this most important point to the side now, it is still a mistake to suppose that any of these terms, 'table' for example, has much to do with putative phases, or with anything of the kind. Indeed, in many cases, quite the opposite impression attends these terms from that somewhat peculiarly generated by our sorites of decomposition by minute removals. Rather than looking to denote any transitory phase, terms for many sorts of ordinary things, 'table' for example, appear to transcend particular physical objects. Thus, the term 'table' purports to preserve identity for a given table, it appears, even as sizable physical objects, in which the table may be said to consist, move hither and yon, come into being and cease to be. For example, let us consider a putative table which is, we shall suppose, initially made of a single piece of metal, say, of iron. Let us cut off a substantial piece of the metal from the rest, say, a piece somewhere between two fifths and one-half of the whole, perhaps measured by volume, and let us send it miles away. Now, we may well think that we have two rather substantial physical objects, whereas before we had but one. But the same table may be thought to exist throughout, first consisting in the one physical object, and then in the two created by the cutting, which we may call its separated 'parts'. If the parts are brought back together, and joined by solder, we may think of the result as the original table, now again consisting in one substantial material object. It is, then, not only very natural and ordinary, but in a wider respect sustained by common sense, to think of the table as existing in the interim, part here and part miles away, perhaps in California. And the same thought will occur, of course, for such putative tables as are thus cut apart but are never made whole again.

According to our common view of the matter, then, it is not very easy to get rid of tables by such a procedure of cutting and separating. Such putative ordinary things, even if they don't really exist at all, appear at least to be rather stable, and hardly like the potentially fleeting phases we extracted from our original sorites of decomposition. This newly encountered appearance of stability, however, is also an illusion. To make this plain, we may construct an additional piece of reasoning, *the sorites of cutting and separating*. This applies, first, to those ordinary things whose identity seems to transcend any particular material object, as recently indicated, like tables and sousaphones, and such rocks and stones as are 'important or well known', like Plymouth Rock and the Rosetta Stone. It applies equally, reflection will reveal, to those ordinary things whose identity appears more ephemeral, like a rock or stone of little importance or familiarity. Let us take these two cases in turn beginning with those things whose identity appears rather more stable.

We begin by assuming that if we cut a table into two roughly equal parts, and do so most innocuously and favorably, then there is still a table left in the case, no matter how widely the parts are separated. Common sense has us make this assumption. Further, even where we always choose a 'largest available part', as we always shall, no single operation of cutting and separating will be enough to take us from a situation involving a table to one involving none. By a series of such operations, however, we shall eventually have upon us a situation where there are only resultant specks of dust, or even atoms, scattered all over the solar system or even into regions far more remote. In such a situation as this last, however, we quite clearly have no table at all. To suppose that we still have one is to be committed to all sorts of absurdities, even according to the view of common sense. For one will, presumably, then suppose as well that every table that ever was still does exist and also, presumably, every mountain and every lake, every star and every planet. Hence, we have again uncovered a contradiction in our ordinary thinking. The only adequate response to it is, I suggest, to conclude that we have reduced to absurdity yet again the idea that there are, or ever were, any such things as tables.[12]

The intuitive correctness of this reasoning makes vividly clear the futility in the thought that certain ordinary things, because they are 'functionally defined', will withstand a sorites attack. But, of course, this Aristotelian approach gets ordinary thinking wrong at the start. A fake rake is not a rake (which is fake) but, supposing there to be any rakes at all, a broken rake is a rake which is broken. Further, a rake may be first

12. Underlying this sorites argument is a common sense assumption which is itself incoherent. This assumption is that we may properly distinguish between (1) removing so little from a thing that what is thus removed does not count as part of that thing but is only, say, an isolated atom or speck of dust, and (2) cutting off enough from the thing so that what is thus cut off remains as part of the thing, part of the thing now being here and part of it over there. The incoherence of such a putative distinction may be quickly shown by a sorites of accumulation: first, if what is removed is an atom, then it is not part of the ordinary thing, say the table, from which it was taken; but, second, if, instead, what is removed is only one atom greater, the additional atom on the side of that which is removed cannot mean the difference; so, what is removed is still not part of the thing. Accordingly, by stepwise reasoning, no matter how great the thing removed it will still not be part of the ordinary thing. The apparent stability of such things as tables, then, as well as our new sorites, rests on a common sense assumption which is actually quite absurd. We passed over this in order to present our new sorites. This does not, of course, reveal any defect on the part of our sorites of cutting and separating. On the contrary, it shows this reasoning to be an argument *a fortiori*.

made in a lucite cube, and in such a way that the rake will shatter if the cube does. Thus, it will *never* be much good for raking, and so on, and so forth.[13]

This sorites of cutting and separating adapts easily to application with things whose identity does not appear to transcend one sizable physical object, for example, to unfamiliar, unimportant stones and rocks. Now, I do not mean to suggest that there is a rigid distinction here between, say, such stones and typical tables. Rather, I wish only to remark a certain tendency in our thinking, and to show that it makes no difference to the matters under discussion. For the important point is that, according to our ordinary thinking, an operation of cutting and separating leaves us with *at least one* stone. No such operation performed upon any stone, including any stone which results from such an operation, is enough to mean the difference between a situation with at least one stone involved and a situation where there isn't any stone at all. Accordingly, when choosing largest resultants, we shall still have at least one stone present, we must conclude, even where all we have is specks of dust, or even atoms, widely scattered throughout the solar system and even far beyond. But, on the contrary, in such a case as that, there will truly be no stone. Thus we disclose again a contradiction in our thought, the only rational response to which is, I suggest, to abandon our supposition of existence for stones. Now it may be that this sorites will not work compellingly on every putative ordinary thing. But it will, I suggest, work on such an ample sample of things that we may say that, if none of *them* exist, then no ordinary things do. Whatever escapes direct application of this argument, I suggest, will do so for a superficial reason, which does not ensure its existence.

Historically, problems concerning ordinary things, as well as those regarding sizable material objects, have often been discussed in a context concerning perception. It is thus easy to suppose that our sorites by minute removals importantly concerns the perceptual recognition of a dwindling entity. To a certain extent, this thought is undermined by our sorites of slicing and grinding, discussed in the section just previous. Our sorites of cutting and separating, I suggest, even more powerfully shows the inadequacy of such an assessment.

We have just mentioned one valuable feature of our newest sorites variation. Another, as we remarked before, is that it undermines the

13. I am glad to find somewhat similar thoughts expressed by such an influential philospher as Roderick M. Chisholm in his 'The Loose and Popular and Strict and Philosophical Senses of Identity', in Norman S. Care and Robert H. Grimm, eds., *Perception and Personal Identity*, Cleveland, 1969, p. 97.

appearance of stability in the identity of certain sorts of ordinary things. Still another is the negative lesson it gives us about 'functional definition'. But the main value in exhibiting a variety of sorites arguments goes beyond the particular lessons each serves most clearly to teach. For as the arguments accrue, the thought that our ordinary things are real entities becomes ever more rapidly a desperate one. The devices to be imagined, to save our swizzle sticks and sousaphones, look ever more *ad hoc* and irrational. At the same time, we can more fully appreciate, from the various aspects of our present conceptions which thus prove vulnerable, the genuine difficulties one must overcome if one is to obtain ideas which truly are coherent.

Rather than continue to add to these lessons by constructing further destructive sorites, I shall now discuss a variant upon, or complementary argument to, any such decompositional piece of reasoning. This will allow us to discuss certain broad logical issues which will surely have occurred to some astute readers by now, and which we have so far ignored almost entirely.

4. Accumulation Arguments and the Place of Paradox

Near the beginning of our essay, we saw that the original sorites, concerning a heap, worked as a two-edged sword. On one edge, starting with what seemed to be a heap of things, we were forced to conclude that we still had a heap there even with nothing before us. On the other edge, starting with nothing before us, we were forced to conclude that even with a million things nicely arranged before us, there was no heap present. I think that the correct assessment of this is that the sword cuts common sense clear through both ways. And, I think that an appropriate way of putting the situation is to say 'There are no heaps'. The same duality is present in the case of any of our ordinary things. I think that the correct response is the same, and that the matter may be summed up by saying "There are no ordinary things: no tables, no stones, no planets and no sousaphones". But as there may be some objection to my thoughts, these matters merit some discussion.

As we have labeled the one edge of our Eubulidean sword *the sorites of decomposition*, so we may call the other *the sorites of accumulation*. Our original sorites of decomposition by minute removals proceeded by the stepwise removal of very small items, tiny chips or even atoms, from the putative ordinary thing in question. The sorites of accumulation which we shall here examine involves the reverse of that procedure: A series of very small items will be accumulated, in some putatively relevant manner, upon some small beginning item, or in some chosen region. It should be clear, however, that our other variations upon our sorites of decomposition also admit of reverse procedures. Accordingly, there are accumulation versions as well of our sorites of slicing and grinding, and of our sorites of cutting and separating. The points which we shall now discuss, then, while related directly only to the minute removal version of decomposition, look to be quite general in their application to these matters.

Our relevant sorites of accumulation will be a *direct* argument for the idea that ordinary things do not exist. We shall derive this result from acceptable beginnings. Each of our variations of decomposition was an *indirect* argument for that same idea; there we began by supposing existence and, then, with acceptable auxiliary premises, we reduced the supposition to absurdity. Before we proceed to the direct arguments of accumulation, I pause to note, in contrast, that there are accumulation arguments which are indirect.[14]

One such indirect argument, which proceeds by small stepwise increments, is as follows. Begin with an alleged table. Now, the addition of a single atom to what we already have, providing it occasions no substantial disruption, will never take us from a situation where a table is before us to one where there is none. But, by appropriate increments, we shall still have a table even when we have before us a spherical object many times larger than a house. Then we have no table; therefore, we didn't have any at the start. This sorites of accumulation is of interest for us in that it complements and reinforces our previous reasonings. But as it is like them in being a *reductio ad absurdum*, it presents us with no new logical form.

In turning to our direct sorites of accumulation, I shall again begin by focusing on stones as my example of putative ordinary things. And I shall again use the atom as my unit, now of increment rather than decrement. We may begin with an empty region, and say that there is *no stone in it*, or we may begin with a single atom somewhere, and say that it is *something which is not a stone*; the upshot will be the same. I will choose the latter beginning. Now, if we add a single atom to something which is not a stone, it seems that such a minute addition, however carefully and cleverly executed, will never in fact leave us with a stone. For a single

---

14. In the widest respect, I consider all of my arguments to be indirect proofs of the incoherence in common sense thinking. This is because I must conduct my arguments in an available natural language, the existence of which may be exposed as incoherent by suitable sorites reasoning. But the exposure of such faults takes us beyond the confines of this present paper.

atom, I suggest, will never mean the difference between there being no stone before us and, then, there being one there. (A process which supposedly produces a stone may be thought sometimes to involve no physical additions at all but, instead, only a rather substantial re-arrangement of that matter which is already in the relevant region or situation. But, of course, that does nothing to refute what I am advancing.)

Now, there is an asymmetry, which may be worth noting, between the proper way of formulating a premise of addition here and that of stating our third premise, of removal, with our sorites of decomposition. Before we said that if we removed an atom in a way *most favorable to there continuing to be a stone*, there would still be a stone. And this allowed us to derive our absurd result. But if we *add* an atom in a way *most favorable* to there continuing to be only something which is *not* a stone, no absurdity will ever be felt by anyone. For we shall never thus construct anything which, even according to quick common sense judgements, will be even remotely like a stone. We might well thus construct, for example, what quick common sense would call a wooden table, or a planet, or perhaps even a duck. But we will come nowhere near to producing any stone in the process, for our premise would be so formulated as to ensure such a result. Accordingly, our new premise will say, rather, that if there is, in a certain situation, only something which is not a stone, or some things which are not stones, the addition of *any* single atom, *no matter in what way*, will not mean the difference. Presumably, the ways now most relevant will be those *least* favorable to there continuing to be no stone there. But this asymmetry scarcely affects our argument, for even according to common sense, our new premise is as hard to deny as was our older one.

In any event, then, by repeated application of this new principle, we must conclude that there is no stone before us no matter how many atoms we add to our original one, and no matter how they are arranged. Even when we have before us something which 'looks for all the world like a stone', and which would prompt people to think that there is a stone there, we must conclude that there really is no stone. We have again, this time by accumulation, exposed a contradiction in our ordinary beliefs. This raises again for us the question of how to respond to such a contradiction. I submit that the proper response, as before, is to deny the supposition that stones exist.

Our accumulation argument applies most immediately to such putative stones, if any, which have, or will be formed, through such a gradual stepwise process. But it also applies to any other putative stones. For any putative stone may have a duplicate of itself constructed via the gradual sort of process here envisioned. The one object, surely, will really be a stone only if the other is; as the duplicate is not, neither is the original candidate. In other words, as I have submitted, there are no stones at all and, similarly, for any other of our ordinary things. In the parlance of logic, we may say, then, that our sorites of decomposition is an *indirect argument* for the idea that there are no ordinary things, while this correlative sorites of accumulation is a *direct argument* for that same conclusion.

Some people, however, may object to this understanding of these related sorites arguments. They would try to deny us our negative conclusion about ordinary things, perhaps claiming that the true situation allows neither a positive nor a negative proposition to prevail but, instead, presents us with a *paradox*. One form their objection may take is by way of this following argument, where a new way is suggested for combining a sorites of accumulation with a sorites of decomposition. In this way, we may make it appear that every ordinary thing, at least, is a stone. For example, we may start with a feather and, by decomposition, work down to an atom, still having to hold that a feather is before us. We may, then, by accumulation, work up to something which looks to be a stone. This time, our accumulation premise will be that adding an atom to a feather leaves a feather there still, providing only that no substantial collapse or similar result is effected in the process. Confronting what we have produced, we say that it is a stone. Reasoning by our sorites we may say it is a feather. But this may be done with any feather. Accordingly, we must now hold, not that there are no stones, but that all feathers are stones. And, similarly, so are all planets, and swizzle sticks, and sousaphones. While this reasoning is engaging, I think that it is weak. One place it goes wrong, I suggest, is where we confront what is before us. Whatever the look of things, we need not say that there is a stone before us. Indeed, we already have compelling arguments, both direct and indirect, for the conclusion that no such statement will be true. Another weakness, of course, is in insisting that a feather is still there with only one atom present. While Eubulides' contribution has often been labeled 'the sorites paradox', there is nothing here which is a paradox in any philosophically important sense. I remarked on this near the outset; I hope I have supported it by now. Accepting our negative conclusions here does not mean important logical trouble for us; we only think we have troubles while we refuse to admit their validity.

At this point, and in the second place, it may be objected that we beg the question against common sense in denying the combined argument just presented and, in particular, in denying the 'claim of observation'.

But it is very unclear what this charge can mean. For common sense does not speak with one consistent voice on any of these matters. What we have done is to disclose contradictions in our beliefs. Beliefs about atoms, to be sure, do not have an ancient claim to being part of common sense. But they now seem to be part of it, at least in advanced cultures. And, further, our arguments may be conducted wholly in terms of removing, and adding, tiny chips or specks. The premises concerning these visible items would surely be part of common sense, albeit reflective or implicit common sense. This would be true even of rather ancient times, and even rather primitive cultures. The most rational way of responding to the contradictions, I submit, is to deny application for the ordinary concepts: the concepts of stones, tables, feathers and sousaphones. These concepts do not apply. We cannot say, then, 'All feathers are stones', unless we mean it in some peculiar sense of the logicians. But a vivid way of putting our point is to say 'There are no stones'.

At this present juncture, and in the third place, it may be said that if the notion of a stone is indeed incoherent, then no genuine proposition is expressed by saying 'There are no stones'. Accordingly, it may then be urged, such a form of words is at best misleading, and in any case quite inappropriate for expressing our philosophy. As regards the part about propositions, I have little to say in reply, as I have little idea as to what a proposition may be, and only speak in such terms as a means for convenient exposition. But, in any case, I do not think that the negative form of words is inappropriate for expressing our philosophy. The following example may be helpful on this point. Suppose that some children tell stories to each other regarding certain imaginary entities, which they term 'nouls'. Now, their imaginary world, in which nouls are supposed to exist, may be so described by them that it could not possibly contain any nouls, given their own descriptions. For example, they may so use the term that on certain days nouls, if they existed, would be people, on other days mere objects, and so on. Their concept of a noul, we might say, is quite incoherent, if indeed they have so much as any genuine concept here at all. The question whether there is a genuine proposition to the effect that there are no nouls, I will not attempt to decide. But if someone, perhaps on hearing the children, asked me what nouls were, one thing I would say to him is simply this: 'There are no nouls'.

In this essay, I have been trying to offer arguments, both direct and indirect, for the denial of the existence of ordinary things, and for all that that entails. The sorts of objections to this attempt we have been recently considering have it that a negative remark is out of place. Now, I think that we have effectively countered them. But *even if* I am wrong in this thought, things will not be altered much for the philosophy I seek here to advance. For we may say 'There are no stones' at least as a sub-conclusion in a lengthier argument on these matters. And, then, we might advance as another sub-conclusion something like 'There are ever so many stones; indeed, all ordinary things are stones'. And a more final conclusion may then be put by saying that none of the previous remarks, as well as 'There is at least one stone', make any clear sense at all. Now, I should think that anyone disposed to cling to ideas of ordinary things would find little comfort indeed in these most recent radical recommendations. But even if they are not literally what I have been arguing for, they are surely in the same spirit as my own philosophy.[15]

5. Some Implications of These Reasonings

The arguments we have considered are effective, I believe, against our beliefs in ordinary things. Before we close our essay, however, it will be well to make a few remarks as to what our reasonings imply and what they do not. For it is easy to misinterpret our results so as to underestimate their importance. And, for that matter, it is also easy to misconstrue them in such a way as to exaggerate their implications. We shall try, then, to encourage a balanced and accurate appraisal.

One way to *misunderstand* our arguments is to take them as concerning *words but not things*. For while our arguments do concern words they likewise concern things (which are not words). It is true that we have shown that, in a relevant manner, terms for ordinary things are incoherent. In that that is so, those terms cannot apply to anything real. And from that it follows that there are no such ordinary things as those words might purport to designate. Accordingly, our results concern words and things alike. They thus differ from points of grammatical distinction which concern only words, and thus our points are more comprehensive. But they are also thus more comprehensive than points pertaining *only* to things and not to words, if such points there be; for our points concern things and something else besides, namely, words. The realization that our reasonings concern words, then, can hardly detract from whatever substance and importance they might have.

15. Various points discussed in this section emerged from discussions with Saul Kripke and with Ralph Silverman.

A *second misunderstanding* is to suppose that our arguments concern *kinds as opposed to things*. For in that they concern kinds of things, our reasonings concern both things and kinds. We have argued that certain kinds are never instanced; there are, then, never any things of those kinds. Things of those kinds do not exist. Accordingly, if there are arguments which concern *only* things, and not kinds, they fail, in that respect at least, to be as comprehensive as these present reasonings, which concern both. The observation that our arguments concern kinds, then, can scarcely deny them even the least bit of significance.[16]

As we have just remarked, our arguments concern words and kinds, as well as things which are neither. Concerning words and kinds, now, we might say this. First, we might say that it is in connection with *semantics* that our reasonings have what are their most obvious implications and, second, that their most obvious semantic implications concern certain *sortal nouns*, namely, those which purport to denote ordinary things. Thus, it appears quite obvious to us now that there will be no application to things for such nouns as 'stone' and 'rock', 'twig' and 'log', 'planet' and 'sun', 'mountain' and 'lake', 'sweater' and 'cardigan', 'telescope' and 'microscope', and so on, and so forth. Simple positive sentences containing these terms will never, given their current meanings, express anything true, correct, accurate, etc., or even anything which is anywhere close to being any of those things. Various other words and expressions will similarly fail to serve with distinction. Amongst these unfortunate devices are certain ones which are only marginally counted as words, namely, *certain proper names*. Accordingly, in the most relevant sense, we must count as vacuous such names as 'Venus' and 'Everest', in those uses of them which dot the philosophical literature.[17] For we may be confident that, in relevant uses, if 'Venus' names anything, it will be a planet which is in fact thus named. Similarly, it seems quite nearly certain that, in relevant contexts, if 'Everest' names anything at all it will name a mountain. But, as we have argued several times over, there are no planets or mountains. Hence, with respect to their relevant uses, these names are empty. What amounts here to the same: Venus does not exist and neither does Everest. In a similar vein, it may be noted that, in very many occurrences, *certain pronouns*, such as 'it', 'they' and 'them', either serve to make reference

---

16. This paragraph emerged from discussion with Samuel Wheeler.

17. I discount, for example, uses of 'Venus' in connection with various women. Presumably, some thoughtless parents may have attached this moniker to a baby daughter.

to some existing ordinary thing or things, or else fail in contributing to any true or realistic comment. As we have been arguing, the first of these two disjuncts never holds and, so, in all these occurrences, these pronouns do thus fail.

Now, these negative ideas, concerning names and pronouns, I take liberty in noting, can be confirmed more directly, and somewhat independently. We may do this by constructing sorites arguments directly upon the alleged named entities, and upon those which are apparently the reference of the pronouns. To be sure, these confirming arguments, in contrast to the reasonings herein advanced, do importantly involve the notion of identity. Thus, they fall outside the limits on our reasoning which we have here imposed on ourselves. I take the liberty of mentioning them despite this violation because, in the present context, their role is only an auxiliary one.

What we have said about words pertains immediately to our *thought*, for much of our thought is in terms of such words. For example, when we are under the impression that we are thinking about an object in the world, I suggest that our impression is mistaken. If we suppose that we are thinking of Venus and, thus, are thinking of some existing thing, I suggest that we are similarly in error. At best, we are thinking of something, but only in much the way we do when thinking of a fictional entity. Alternatively, it might be that we are here not really thinking of or about any (finite) entity at all. I leave these matters for future discussion, noting that, whatever their detailed outcome, our thought must make much less contact with reality than we have commonly assumed.

To turn a phrase along a familiar line, we may say that our arguments have been pertinent to *descriptive semantics*, though they concern other things besides. When done properly, we have argued, descriptive semantics shows the poverty of our language and our thought and, thus, it shows the need for the invention of new terms, that is, for good *prescriptive semantics*. It is quite unclear to me, however, how we should go about finding a suitable replacement, or replacements, for one of our ordinary terms, for 'log', to take a representative example. With respect to atomic removals, to cite one difficulty, at a given juncture in a given case, there are millions of removals which seem quite innocuous and favorable. The item resulting from one such does not seem any more 'loggy' than that resulting from any other of them. Which steps are to be ruled out; and why? I leave these matters to others for further discussion, noting that other sorites arguments must also be avoided. It may be much harder than one might first suppose, I would suggest, to achieve coherence while adequately serving anything much like our everyday concerns.

However difficult it might be, prescriptive semantics takes us in those directions which are somewhat practical. It does not touch on those issues that are philosophically most profound. For these philosophical issues concern the general features of the view, or views, which our arguments allow us to find acceptable. In this connection, it is important for us to notice that the arguments we have here exhibited, while they show common sense to be badly in error, do not force upon us a world view which is far removed from common sense. Now it may well be that extensions of, or variations upon, these present arguments will indeed require departures which are remarkably radical. But it is important to notice that the present reasonings do not themselves require so much. For one simple example, there is nothing in these arguments to deny the idea, common enough, that there are physical objects with a diameter greater than four feet and less than five. Indeed, the exhibited sorites allow us still to maintain that there are physical objects of a variety of shapes and sizes, and with various particular spatial relations and velocities with respect to each other. It is simply that no such objects will be ordinary things; none are stones or planets or pieces of furniture.

In reflection upon world views, it is easy to suppose that the challenge to ordinary things, to the existence of stones, for example, must come from some 'mentalistic' philosophy: from *idealism*, from *phenomenalism*, and so on. The present arguments show this supposition to be false, however, for they do not require us to embrace any such radical metaphysics as that. It may also be supposed, conversely, that a mentalistic philosophy must abandon ordinary things.[18] Bishop Berkeley, the chief exponent of a mentalistic view, was of an opposite opinion: he never meant to deny ordinary things but intended to reveal their true mentalistic nature. Let us now grant that Berkeley was right in thinking that his idealism did not require him to deny ordinary objects. But, especially with visible chips in mind, rationality would require even him to accept these present reasonings. Hence, while his mentalism seems not to have required it, Berkeley was wrong, nevertheless, to affirm the existence of ordinary things.

18. This is the view implicit in Dr. Johnson's futile attempt to refute Berkeley by "kicking a stone". In *Word and Object*, W. V. Quine endorses Johnson in these matters; p. 3ff. and p. 17ff.

Given the limits to which we have here confined them, our Eu-bulidean reasonings allow us to hold a world view much like that of common sense. First, in that we have foregone arguments with regard to living things, we may still believe in plants and animals, and the organs, tissues and cells presumed to pertain thereof. In that we may regard them as mere products of living things, twigs and logs and fingernails may be considered and denied by us, but perhaps that is a loss which may be accepted with equanimity. Most importantly, it may still be held that there are people, including ourselves, and, with that, also the mental or psychological items typically characteristic of per-sons, such as thoughts, feelings and experiences. At the same time, as we have already remarked, we may still hold that there are physical objects of various shapes and sizes, including many of such size and duration as to be suitable for comment, even if in fact such comment rarely has been made. We may see, then, that it is rash to suppose, as some may do, that these reasonings thrust upon us some esoteric on-tology where only events, or processes, or facts, or whatever, are al-lowed to exist, and where no physical objects or people are allowed any genuine place in the world. We can allow, of course, that some such ontological doctrine may indeed be correct; but to show it is will re-quire arguments which differ from those advanced in this essay. In-deed, so far are our present arguments from forcing us to acknowledge only events, or processes, or whatever, that they require us to deny many such items which are ordinarily acknowledged, namely, all those which involve ordinary objects. Thus, for example, the eruption of a volcano is something which can never occur. For its occurrence logi-cally requires the existence of a volcano and, as we have argued, there will never be any such thing. Likewise, the alleged fact that a certain cat is on a certain mat never can obtain. For that would require the existence of at least a mat, and we have seen that there never is any at all.

With these brief remarks, we have outlined, well enough I suggest, the situation with which our exhibited reasonings present us. Our rea-sonings, I have submitted, are as unobjectionable as they are simple. And their implied situation, it now seems clear, makes no great de-mands upon either our credibility or our imagination: on the one hand, our reasonings demand of us only a 'rather small' departure from common sense; on the other hand, as this required departure has not yet been made, our existing thought is in quite a bad way. If we are rational, we shall recognize two main options. First, we can proceed to engage in prescriptive semantics, so that a detailed view, at least largely commonsensical, may once again appear at hand. Or else we can press on with Eubulidean reasonings, in various new directions, to see whether such simple, persistent thinking might require further, much more radical departures. For my own part, that second option is compelling. But of course I am a radical skeptic, and simple, persistent thinking is all the sense I seem ever to desire.[19]

19. This present essay is meant to advance but a small part of a nihilistic viewpoint in metaphysics, ontology and the philosophy of language. For a concise sketch of more of the whole, see my paper, 'I Do Not Exist', forthcoming in Graham Macdonald, ed., *Epistemology in Perspective*, (London: The Macmillan Press), which volume is the festschrift for Professor Sir Alfred Jules Ayer. For a detailed analysis and discussion of nihilistic sorites arguments, I refer the reader to my 'Why There Are No People', forthcoming in *Midwest Studies in Philosophy*, Vol. IV: *Studies in Metaphysics*. Nihilism fits well, in a variety of ways, with skepticism in epistemology. For an extended development of skepticism, see my book, *Ignorance*, Oxford, 1975. For some relations between these two views, see my paper, 'Skepticism and Nihilism', forthcoming in *Nous*.

2

I DO NOT EXIST

It seems utterly obvious that the question 'Do I exist?' may be correctly answered only in the affirmative; of course the answer must be 'Yes.' Descartes, it may be said, made this idea the keystone of his philosophy, he found it so compelling. Hume, however, in his characteristically sceptical style, at least at times questioned the propriety of an affirmative reply. My teacher, Professor Sir Alfred Jules Ayer, to whom this essay is dedicated, customarily expressed himself in a conditional manner, which I find quite congenial:

> The sentence 'I exist', in this usage, may be allowed to express a statement which like other statements is capable of being either true or false. It differs, however, from most other statements in that if it is false it can not actually be made. Consequently, no one who uses these words intelligently and correctly can use them to make a statement which he knows to be false. If he succeeds in making the statement, it must be true.[1]

Of course Ayer is right in pointing to the absurdity of a person's trying to deny his own existence. Prepared to pay this price, in this brief essay I mean to deny my own putative existence, a position which I take to be even more radical than Hume's. This is owing not to a desire to be more perverse than any of my predecessors, but, rather, to certain arguments which have occurred to me, and which seem quite far from any of their thoughts. As may be expected of a student of Ayer's, and as I have

---

1. A. J. Ayer, *The Problem of Knowledge* (London: Macmillan, 1956) p. 50.

indicated, I appreciate the utterly paradoxical position into which these arguments lead me. But I venture to suppose that this does not reflect badly on my reasonings in any relevant regard. Rather, it may show their great scope, thus highlighting obscure defects in prevalent conceptions. With this understanding, I mean to present herein the main lines of reasoning against my own existence.

I offer my arguments as a challenge to any others that there may be, so that they may dissuade me from the path of extreme nihilism that reason appears to require. Accordingly, I shall present my ideas as forcefully as possible, not to indicate any enormous confidence on my part, but rather to provoke others to reply most promptly and effectively. For my own part, I can find nothing importantly wrong with the uncomfortable thoughts I shall thus boldly put forth. The more I reflect upon them, the more I become convinced of their essential truth or justice, for any errors I ever find are superficial mistakes, requiring at most only minor changes in formulation. As a consequence, there appears to be growing within me an inclination to expend much effort toward developing the required nihilism in great detail, no matter how painfully laborious the attempt may be. Perhaps this growth had best be stopped, but then only by an appropriate rational argument.

To compound my dilemma, I notice that, in general outline, the same view lately has been conjectured by another writer, Samuel Wheeler, or so it appears. In a pioneering paper, 'Reference and Vagueness', Wheeler conjectured that there may not be any people; I should suppose he meant to include himself.[2] While he does not offer a positive argument for the nihilistic surmise, he does disarm prevalent ideas which would point the other way. Appearing to find a similar current in another, but no adequate compelling force in the opposite direction, the situation encourages my thoughts to move, however slowly and painfully, toward their properly destructive denial. Perhaps a response to my challenge may save me from the ultimately fruitless labours I seem required to undertake.

The challenging position is this: I do not exist and neither do you. The scientific perspective, especially as developed over the last few centuries, compels this result. Now, there is nothing especially unfortunate in this as regards the human condition. For, as regards almost everything which is commonly alleged to exist, it may be argued, in like manner, that it in fact does not. There are, then, no tables or chairs, nor

---

2. Samuel C. Wheeler III, 'Reference and Vagueness', *Synthèse*, xxx (1967) no. 3–4 367–79.

rocks or stones or ordinary stars. Neither are there any plants or animals. No finite persons or conscious beings exist, including myself Peter Unger: I do not exist. So much for this challenging position. To the main arguments for it, rather briefly presented, I now turn.

1. The Sorites of Decomposition

Tables, as well as chairs, have often been believed to be paradigms of existing things or entities, but I shall argue that they do not exist at all. They are, if you will, only fictions, though nothing whatever depends on my use of such a term of convenience. My argument will be in the form of an indirect proof, wherein I reduce to absurdity the supposition of their existence.

According to our modern scientific view, if there are any tables, then each of them is constituted of, or is composed of, or comprises, or consists of, or whatever, many atoms, and still more 'elementary particles', but only a finite number of each. Now, nothing here depends on the expression 'is constituted of', or on any similar expression. Baldly put, the point is this: where and when there are no atoms present, there and then there is no table. This idea is not crucial to the argument; a 'less scientific' analogue will work as well, so far as the purer logical features go. But it is good to have nature apparently so co-operative.

Now, at the same time, according to our common-sense view of the matter, which for something like a *table* is, of course, all but definitive, one atom, or only a few, removed, or added, quite innocuously, will not make a relevant difference. If you have a table at the start, then, after an atom has been gently ticked off the edge somewhere, there will still be a table present. These simple ideas, when brought into combination, leave nothing for reason but to conclude that there really are no tables. It takes no great acumen to see this, as the reasoning is utterly simple, and most just and suitable to the subject before us.

For, if there is a table there, then it has only a finite number of atoms—say, a billion billion; it does not matter. The net removal of one, then, leaves us with a supposed table of a billion billion minus one atoms; after two are removed, the supposed table has a billion billion minus two; and so on. After a billion billion atoms have been removed, we have a table consisting of no atoms at all. In this simple fashion, I suggest, we have reduced to an absurdity the supposition that the table in question exists, or ever did exist. As this argument may be most readily generalised, we may conclude that there really are no such things as tables.

To advance discussion, it may be helpful if I give the argument just presented something like a formal shape or presentation. We begin with a supposition of existence:

(1)   There exists at least one table.

But, from our scientific perspective, we may add this second premiss:

(2)   for anything there may be, if it is a table, then it consists of many atoms, but only a finite number.

From these two premisses, we may deduce that there is at least one table which consists of many atoms, but a finite number of them. The crux and bite of my argument, however, may be supposed to come with a third and final premiss:

(3)   for anything there may be, if it is a table (which consists of many atoms, but a finite number), then the net removal of one atom, or only a few, in a way which is most innocuous and favourable, will not mean the difference as to whether there is a table in the situation.

These three premisses, I take it, are inconsistent. The assessment of this inconsistency, I submit, leads one to reject, and to deny, the first premiss, whatever one may subsequently think of the remaining two propositions.

Discounting minor matters of formulation, I doubt that many would deny our second premiss. Many more, I imagine, are liable to deny our third and final proposition. It has, I must admit, been stated in a way which leaves matters less than completely clear and evident. Accordingly, I shall try to provide some clarificatory interpretation, to the extent that this seems merited even in a very brief treatment.

I have said that an atom is to be removed in a way which is most innocuous and favourable. What do I mean by such a way? First, I mean for the removal to be *net*, of course, and in the fullest way. The process which removes an atom does not put something else in its place, or in anywhere else; nor does such a thing happen in any other way. And, what is removed is randomly cast aside, so to speak. Secondly, I mean for the net removal to take place with as little disruptive effect as possible on what remains, especially as regards the question, if it really has any substance, as to whether or not any table remains. In other words, we might say, it is most unlikely that an atom will ever be blasted out of a central position; rather, one will be gently dislodged from an outside spot. Additionally, we are to conceive of the most favourable, or least disruptive, conditions, as regards temperature, pressure, electricity, magnetism, and so on. Further, if an occasion arises where, vary conditions as we may, a single atom cannot be removed without substantial relevant disruption, then we remove as few as possible, balanced against a disruptive effect. Finally, I close this interpretation with a remark on the alleged matter of whether an entity may be *as much as possible*, or be *as well off toward being, a table*. I am supposing this matter to have substance, of course, but only on way toward exposing its absurdity. This is an indirect argument.

Thus clarified, perhaps we may profitably divide what our premiss is saying under two heads. First, it makes a 'causal' claim: there is no relevant breaking point where, no matter what is done to be gentle and to retain things, the whole business, or a substantial portion thereof, collapses, or turns into an apparent donkey, or disappears, or whatever. Rather, things are relevantly quite gradual. To deny this, I believe, is to cast aside science, and even common sense as well. And, secondly, our premiss claims that, in this rather gradual way of things, the difference made by the small removals encountered, by one atom, more or less, is never nearly so much as the difference, merely alleged as it may be, between a table's being there and not being there. To deny this premiss, then, is as much as to affirm that there comes a place where, by taking away an atom or so, presumably *any one or few of millions* still, one makes a table cease to exist. And this, I suggest, is as much as to expect a miracle.

Now, as it is stated, of course, our final premiss points to conditions, and a way, that are quite ideal. That is no fault. It may make one think, however, that the whole argument has an 'airy-fairy' character, and is quite unrealistic. But conditions close enough to those which are most favourable do occur almost all the time. And, very small bits, if not nearly so small as an atom, can be removed in stepwise fashion, for an argument to similar effect. Whatever 'airy-fairy' features are there, then, cannot be basic to the argument.

Within fine points of formulation, our third premiss thus fairly compels belief. As a move to escape our just but uncomfortable conclusion, it remains only to deny the reasoning employed. In this vein, some may object that 'the logic' I have used is what is at fault. If some 'alternative logic' is chosen, they may respond, instead of the system of rules and formulae I have employed, the integrity of our tables may be secured. But I do not believe that good reasoning can ever be captured or frozen into any such system, or that the matter is really one of choosing one or another optional pieces of logical apparatus, like so many hammers or wrenches. There is not, I suggest, here a question of this logic or that one. Without my now being less than sceptical, it is a question of whether my reasoning has been sound, and has been just and appropriate to the topic before us. Now, if I have been in error in my reasoning, or unjust to my subject matter, then such an error or injustice should be made manifest. But, excepting small points of formulation, and with a proper sceptical hesitancy, I doubt that this will be done. Of course, I am no mathematician. But, I think that a fair appraisal of the matter by those more mathematically inclined will find them to view things in much the way that I here recommend.

In a somewhat deeper vein, perhaps, it should be re-emphasised that my argument is not dependent upon the existence of atoms, at least not in any fundamental way. Perhaps there are no atoms, and in 'removing an atom' what really happens is something involving, say, an underlying plenum, which is the only existing (physical) reality. If so, then perhaps the argument presented is acceptable only provisionally; perhaps it operates only on a superficial level. But, whatever changes or profundities may be compellingly envisioned, I hardly think that the reinstatement of tables is among them.

As a related, already anticipated point, while the gradual nature of things is needed for my argument, no deep theories about material reality are important. While it is nice to have ready-made units there to remove—molecules, atoms and particles—the slightest contrivance will work about as well. Thus, from an alleged table, one may remove a tiny chip or splinter, until not a single one remains.

In the manner of G. E. Moore, some will object to my argument along the following lines. First, they will claim to be *more certain* of the existence of tables than of *anything* which I am bringing to bear against such alleged existence. And, then, they will say, with apparent caution and modesty, that, while they are *not sure which* of the things I advance is in error, there *must be at least one* weak link, or fault, in my reasoning. Now, it well may be that this Moorean reply is often, or even usually, a proper answer to a philosophical attack on common sense. But, is it *always* proper, appropriate or correct? Is common sense *always* to be believed, while philosophy, along with science, is *always* to yield? I cannot believe that this is so, and that *no exceptions* can be made to this popular Moorean doctrine. What of the *present case*, then: may not *that* be just such an exception? We have seen, I suggest, that to deny my argument amounts to supposing a miracle: the gentle, innocuous removal of a single atom, or only a few, *which is not even perceptible to the unaided senses*, takes us from a situation where a table is present to one where there is no table at all. Indeed, the removal of *any one*, or *any few*, of *millions* of removable atoms or groups, will be enough to work the trick. This is, after all, where the issue does lie. Can common sense be so powerful as to sustain such a miraculous supposition as this? I do not think so.

In contrast to its employment with tables and chairs, our argument does not seem nearly so compelling, if at all, against *physical objects.* Intuitively, we have the idea that if we consider a biggish physical object, consisting of many atoms, as we take one away and then another, and so on, what we have left is always a physical object, so long as any object at all remains. The last atom, particle or whatever, it may be supposed, is as well off toward being a physical object as is the biggish thing at the start.

Let us be a bit particular as regards the differences between our sorites against tables, or any other ordinary things, and a similar attempt against physical objects. In the first place, we cannot say, in parallel with (2), that, for anything there may be, if it is a physical object, then it consists of many atoms but only a finite number. For an atom itself is a physical object and it does not consist of atoms, let alone many of them. Nor will matters improve if we look for a finer component than atoms, for what we find may also be regarded, I suppose, as a physical object if it is any proper component at all. Nor can a parallel with (3) be accepted readily. Unlike with a table, if you have a physical object and remove an atom, you may have left no physical object at all. For that atom, now removed, may have been the only physical object there to be removed. Now, none of this is to suppose that physical objects do exist. But, as the present argument does not compellingly disprove their existence, they appear to be a somewhat extraordinary thing, whether truly existent or only alleged for all that.

All in all, it may be said, I hope, that the argument I have employed is a rather *simple* piece of reasoning. I call this sort of argument the *sorites of decomposition.* A parallel argument, going the other way, suggests itself, *the sorites of accumulation*, as well as variations upon, and combinations of, both of these forms of reasoning. In particular, counterfactual variations should be of interest to many contemporary writers.

We employed our argument against tables, which, if they exist at all, have certain more or less special features. They are in some sense functional things; they are typically man-made; and so on. But none of this, it will be easily recognised, has anything to do with the matter at hand. Our argument may be employed equally well to deny the existence of such alleged things as sticks and stones, mountains and lakes, planets, (ordinary) stars and galaxies, ships and carriages, pieces of hair and of money, bodies of horses and of generals, and so on, and so forth.

Such things as are not susceptible to decomposition withstand this form of argument: certain sub-atomic particles may provide an example. More importantly, decomposible things which are in a relevant way 'defined with precision' escape the present reasonings. Accordingly, I shall not now deny the existence of most molecules, even some 'quite large' ones, nor, perhaps, even certain crystal structures. However, something such as a blue 1968 Chevrolet four-door sedan, while according to most accounts not something vaguely described, will fall prey to our sorites. While much of physics and chemistry thus *might* remain relatively unscathed, biological entities, above the molecular level, appear to be nothing but fictions. I deny, then, not only the bodies of animals, including human beings, but also their organs, such as livers, hearts and brains, their tissues, and even individual cells, such as neurons.

Similar decomposition arguments make it clear, as well, that many alleged substances in fact do not exist at all. Unlike water and gold, which may be real, but which do not come in drops or hunks, juice and brass are only fictions. Also among the sorts of stuff that do not exist are, I should think, air and earth, meat and flesh, wood and rock, cloth and paper, and so on.

None of the things so far placed in the range of our reasonings, however, is of nearly so great an interest, I imagine, as we ourselves. Accordingly, I now turn to begin a new section, devoted to this topic, wherein I explicitly reason to deny, not without paradox, but perhaps with success, the very thing that Descartes would have me consider *certain*: my own present existence.

2. A Disproof of My Own Existence

The developing scientific perspective, especially owing to gains in biology and chemistry over the last few centuries, renders it exceedingly likely, at least, that no finite people or beings exist. In particular, and more conservatively, this perspective indicates that I myself do not exist; that I never have and never shall.

To achieve this paradoxical result, I shall again employ the sorites of decomposition. Now, the 'normal growth of the human being from conception' also provides, I believe, a sound sorites of accumulation. That sorites is naturally instanced, we might say, even though, with cellular growth not being clearly arithmetic, a unit of increment may have to be contrived: what happens during the first second; what happens during the next; and so on. But, the very artificiality of a gradual decomposition may better jar the mind. Thus, it may increase the chances for acceptance of the uncomfortable conclusion. Now, the most compelling decompositions are not yet attainable. We cannot remove, for example, one cell at a time, while keeping the remainder alive and functioning impressively. While it is not strictly relevant, I should think that this ability is not too far off for us, perhaps no more than a few centuries. In any case, if and when it can be done, I hope that it will not be. What is most relevant is that nature allow for the decompositions herein to be imagined.

As I have indicated, the unit of decrement which I shall choose is the cell. It is instructive for us now to argue at this level. As a cell consists of millions of atoms, a sorites of decomposition based on the atom can show that cells do not exist. Thus, the success of an argument against myself, or even my body, based on the cell, makes it quite clear that, in our argument against tables, the reliance on atoms was far from fundamental.

To mirror our previous argument, against tables, I now display the following three premisses:

(1) I exist.
(2) if I exist, then I consist of many cells, but a finite number.
(3) if I exist (and consist of many cells, but a finite number), then the net removal of one cell, or only a few, in a way which is most innocuous and favourable, will not mean the difference as to whether I exist.

As before, these three propositions form an inconsistent set. They have it that I am still there with no cells at all, even while my existence depends on cells. To escape this inconsistency realistically, we must suppose this. Even under conditions most favourable to me, the removal of a single cell, or only a few, *any* one or few of those in the situation, will mean the difference between my existence and no me at all. But, if I do exist, can my existence really be that tenuous? I think not. Therefore, I do not exist.

A bit more informally, the idea is this. One cell, more or less, will not mean the difference between my being there and not. So, take one away, and I am still there. Take another away; again, no problem. But after a while there are no cells at all. Indeed, as they have been replaced by nothing, in the relevant structures, it is unclear what will be there: perhaps, some salty water. Supposedly, I am still there. But given anything like the developed perspective of science, this is really quite absurd. Thus, the supposition of my existence has been reduced to an absurdity.

As before, it is important to discuss our third and final premiss. Because of the previous parallel discussion, various points may now be safely passed over. But a few new things arise in the present context which, even in a brief essay, are worthy of some consideration.

In the first place, it should be noted that, in the previous reasoning, about tables, we did not become involved in matters of identity, or persistence. There, I argued that *no* table, the same or any other, survived the decremental changes, and so *no* table existed in the first place. In contrast, the present argument does involve identity and, except for its counterfactual form, even persistence through time: I myself must survive. No new problems of importance are, I suggest, thus introduced for us. Indeed, we may abandon questions of identity entirely, and construct a general argument, upon the alleged existence of finite persons or beings, to parallel more completely our argument about tables. To play it safe with respect to such various forms as there may be of 'extraterrestrial beings', we should then make our unit the atom, or even the particle, instead of the cell. It was to honour Descartes, so to say, and to pack the punch of particularity, that I focused the argument on myself, quite directly, thus becoming involved with identity. But that involvement is not essential.

In the second place, it will be maintained, I suppose, that my argument about tables did not involve considerations of life, or of consciousness. Let us grant this point. But how might such involvements as are now upon us serve to promote my own existence, or that of any finite being? I think there is no realistic way. Let us try to interpret our third premiss quite graphically, now, to clarify its import. On its most relevant interpretation, I suggest, life and consciousness, as well as the 'capacity' for them, will be present for as long as anyone might need to appreciate our argument's point. For it is supposed, in our third premiss, that the 'way' in which a cell is removed is one which is most innocuous and favourable—that is, with respect to me, or to my own identity. How might that happen?

At the present level of reasoning, the following scenario, I suggest, is more or less appropriate. At a certain stage in the decremental process, not very far along, it seems clear, life-support systems will be brought in to keep me going as well as possible. I shall be placed *in vitro*; nourishing fluids will be pumped into me; electrical stimulation will be provided, but not in such a way that any apparatus 'does my experiencing or thinking for me'; and so on. Cell after cell is pulled away. The remaining ones are kept alive, and kept functioning 'at the highest level of achievement of which they are capable'. The added apparatus has not, in the case here described, replaced the removed cells as part of me.

In this present case, an electric wire will only be a means of support, much as a cardiac pacemaker serves even now. While *other cases* may be construed as involving the replacement of natural parts by synthetic ones, this present one is not correctly understood in such terms. Sticking to what might here most plausibly be considered myself, then, at a certain point we are down to a brain in a vat and, then, half a brain. So far, so good; but then we get down to a third of a brain, then a sixteenth. Still later, there are only fifty-three neurons in living combination. Where at the end, there is but one living nerve cell, and then it too is gone. Where will I disappear from the scene? Realistically, now, will the removal of a single cell ever, under such favourable conditions, mean my disappearance from reality? While that may be a 'logical possibility', it does not compel belief. The conclusion of our argument, in contrast, is quite compelling: I do not disappear at any time, because I was never around in the first place.

We may agree that at one time it may have been a very compelling thought that there were souls, or individual essences, one for each person. Many people even now believe in such things, and in minds, a life force, if not entelechies, ghosts, spirits, and so on. Many of these believers, I imagine, think that a person is not only real, but an immaterial, indivisible entity. Thus, I expect, they lay the ground for a hope in survival of bodily death, and perhaps even immortality. At the time of Descartes, for example, it may be that all of these suppositions fairly demanded or compelled credence. But they do not sit well, I suggest, with our developed scientific perspective. For that reason, I believe, they offer no compelling alternative now to the bleak conclusions drawn herein.

My sorites of decomposition, against my own existence, has, to be sure, required some speculative effort. But such speculation as there may be is, I submit, far from wild. Further, it does jar the mind, and lets us look anew at the process of cellular development. We may reason justly, then, about the embryo growing from a fertilised egg, and we may conclude again, less speculatively, that, just like you, I do not exist. Against this more 'natural' argument, some would object, I suppose, that I myself was once nothing but a fertilised egg. Now, while I admire attempts to be consistent, I think that, in the present case, the attempt has little to recommend it, and is in any case erroneous. If someone persists in such a thought, however, I should bid him consider whether even a sperm, or an egg, was any existing entity, much less a fertilised egg. Accumulation and decomposition arguments, it seems, may also be used to refute the supposed existence of any of them.

3. The Substance of the Argument and the
Irrelevance of Logical Inventions

The main thrust of this argument is, in light of our scientific perspective, the same in my own case and in those of a table, a stone and,
for that matter, even of a yo-yo. Let us reconsider the matter, then,
with respect to alleged yo-yos, for they give us an example which is
refreshingly light and calmly unemotional. Again the main issues seem
to turn on a suitable third premiss:

> For anything there may be, if it is a yo-yo (which consists of many
> atoms, but a finite number), then the net removal of one atom, or only
> a few, in a way which is most innocuous and favorable, will not mean
> the difference as to whether there is a yo-yo in the situation.

Now, how could such a premiss as this be false, and untrue, and inaccurate and unacceptable? Apart from minor matters of formulation, there
are, it seems clear, only two ways in which things might go wrong for it.

First, and more on 'the side of things in the world', it might be that
nature protected yo-yos, or at least one of them, by giving it a place of its
own in the world, set apart from other things, an essence if you please.
But how might anything like this actually obtain? The matter is, I think,
very important, so, even if we repeat some of our previous words, let us
try to outline the possibilities. First, yo-yos would be protected if, either
at the start or at some later point, we just could not take out any atoms
from them. Or, being realistic, and supposing that that way is not
available, they might still be saved if new atoms were to rush in whenever
crucial old ones were extracted. Or if that is out, as it surely appears to
be, it might be that at some point, even under the most favourable
conditions for relevant gradualness, a spontaneous explosion should
take place, a yo-yo's previous existence thus being preserved by such
sudden destruction. Or, failing that, which does seem more in line with
any actual experience of the world, a god on high, or a suitable natural
law, might turn an endangered dwindling yo-yo into a sousaphone,
perhaps upon the removal of the four million and twelfth atom, so that
our concepts themselves would never have to be tested on its behalf.
And so on; and so forth. There are, then, many logical possibilities for
nature to conspire, as it were, so that things would fit our term 'yo-yo'.
But we are confident that none of them actually obtain. To think otherwise, I should say, is to expect a miracle: if you will, a *miracle of
metaphysical illusion*.

With the world being so unfavourable for them, as it surely seems
to be, the only chance for yo-yos lies on 'the side of our terms and

concepts'. But what can be expected here? At the very least, we need the concept of a yo-yo to be atomically precise. Certain concepts of molecules seem to be thus precise: when you snip a hydrogen atom off the end somewhere, and do not replace it, you no longer have in the situation a molecule of that original kind. But is the concept of a yo-yo relevantly like that? I think we ask too much of ourselves if we expect ourselves to be working here in such a precise manner. Accordingly, to suppose this much for ourselves and 'yo-yo' is to expect another miracle, perhaps a *miracle of conceptual comprehension.* On either hand, then, yo-yos require a miracle; for any who do not believe in miracles, there is no rational belief in yo-yos.

Our reasonings turn up for us an implicit contradiction in our beliefs. To strive to be reasonable we must give up one at least. To deny a suitable second premiss is to have yo-yos floating around with no atoms at all, nor any matter in the situation, and that is yet more miraculous than the two apparent wonders we have just considered. The only path to consistency, then, which is even remotely reasonable or realistic is to deny existence for alleged yo-yos, for we have just covered the whole story as to what wonders a commitment to them means. If this is appreciated we may see the irrelevance of remarks about clear cases, paradigms, family resemblances, and other soothing remedies, lately influential but now happily well on the wane. Perhaps more importantly, in these more technical times, we may also thus see the emptiness in the suggestion, currently favoured by certain philosophers, that we escape the argument by assigning to relevant sentences truth values other than truth and falsity.[3] For, whatever these values may be, they do not reduce one bit the miracles that yo-yos require; at most they occasion only a mildly different description of them.

Let us suppose we have before us a yo-yo. As atoms are removed one at a time, without replacement, we keep considering singular propositions each to the effect that at the appropriate new time a yo-yo is before us. We begin, as in any *reductio,* by assigning truth. As things progress, at some particular point, atomically counted, we are for the first time no longer to assign truth! Instead, when some peripheral atom is gently removed, and there would appear to be at least virtually no significant difference in what is before us, we are for the first time to depart from our initial kind of assignment, and to assign *some other* value. Perhaps

---

3. A recent example of a philosopher who would treat of vagueness by means of exotic truth values is David H. Sanford in his 'Borderline Logic', *American Philosophical Quarterly,* XII, (1975) no. 1, 29–39. Sanford provides references to other writers of a similar persuasion.

the new value will not be falsity; it may be indefiniteness, or some numerical value just a shade less than unity, say 0.999, or some other newly
invented candidate. But whatever else it is, there will be just as much of a
miracle for us to expect. For, given that we have no miracle of metaphysical illusion to help us—that is, the world is indeed relevantly
gradual—it will take a miraculous sensitivity on the part of 'yo-yo' to
generate the difference, however we should choose to label such a wonderful discrimination. So sensitive is our concept of a yo-yo that, as a
single atom goes away at the periphery, truth or unity or whatever
is suddenly left behind! To expect that is, I submit, still to expect a
miracle of conceptual comprehension. Hence, any new values, as well as
the logical inventiveness they may occasion, are utterly irrelevant to the
issues here.

Nor will it help matters to invoke a distinction between propositions
and sentences, which may express or fail to express relevant propositions. Let us focus on the sentence 'There is a yo-yo before us now.' We
may begin as before, with a putative paradigm yo-yo, and may then
judge that our sentence expresses a proposition which is true. We then
take off peripheral atoms, one at a time, and ask whether the sentence
does something else, for the first time, with the removal of each single
one. The supposition that with a single atom something else is for the
first time done appears quite incredible, as well it should; it is but another form of our miracle of conceptual comprehension. But if this
miracle may not be expected, then, if the sentence is not to express a
truth with no atoms before us, we must conclude that our sentence never
expresses a truth.[4]

Concerning the question of our putative yo-yos, then, it appears
that only two responses are relevant: a belief in the miraculous or else
an acceptance of nihilism. And the same choice, I submit, is there with
alleged tables, and stones, and even my very own self. No matter how it
is looked at, there is not much of a choice here. Habit and emotion
appear on one side, while reason seems to be on quite the other.

4. The Scope of these Problems

The argument I have employed derives, of course, from 'the paradox of
the heap', an ancient problem devised by Eubulides, the great Megarian
thinker. In way of reconstruction, we might say that Eubulides showed

4. On these matters, I am indebted to discussion with David Sanford.

that there were and are no heaps. First, we may suppose the existence of heaps. Secondly, we note that, if any heap exists, it consists of various other entities—of grains of sand, or of beans, for example. Finally, we note that, if one bean is removed without replacement, and this is done most favourably and innocuously, what remains will be a heap. Thus, given anything like our view of reality, heaps, which many suppose to be ordinary existing things, are only fictions: there are no heaps.

I shall not here bother to detail the differences and similarities between Eubulides's original argument and my own variations upon it. So far as the compelling force goes, though, suffice it to say that our modern scientific perspective means that there is little difference between a heap and almost anything else, so to say, including myself. As far as repercussions or consequences are concerned, however, my own arguments are of course enormously more effective than the original version. While this is rather obvious, the details may be worth some presentation.

First, virtually all of our common-sense beliefs are untrue, and even as to nothing. Moreover, most of our learned studies are similarly unfortunate, at least in anything like their present formulations. Samuel Wheeler begins to put the point in a manner which is conjectural, and perhaps somewhat ironic: 'If there is no objective difference between possible persons and possible non-persons, much of what we believe about morality, psychology, etc., is in trouble.'[5] We may say, now, that the matter is not very conjectural, and that all of moral reasoning, as well as psychological understanding, looks to be in deep trouble indeed. This holds as well, of course, for the other studies concerning man. History, law and medicine are all a tissue of fictions, as are economics, linguistics and politics. Various related areas of philosophy, such as epistemology, the philosophy of language and the philosophy of mind, can contain nothing sound and true. Unless mathematics is clearly severed from connections with human beings, it too must fall prey to our sorites. Various other studies look to fare poorly. Biology, for example, is a tissue of nonentities and untruth, except as it becomes biochemistry perhaps, or something much of that sort. Astronomy too, except as it becomes astrophysics, or something similar, looks to be about anything but our universe.

Under a second head, we may notice that, while they may in some respects involve language importantly, our sorites arguments undermine all natural languages, while the argument of Eubulides hardly

5. Wheeler, in *Synthese*, xxx (1967), no. 3–4, 371.

begins to do anything here. In the first place, as there are no human beings, there is no human language or thought. Waiving that basic point, and supposing the opposite, we shall notice that our existing expressions, at least by and large, fail to make any contact with whatever is there. For example, the proper names so far given do not refer to anything real. We may confirm this by a sorites argument directly involving such famous nonentities as Cicero, Descartes, Venus, Everest, and so on. Should someone name an individual atom 'Adam', things might be different on this score. The personal pronouns, we have seen, fare little better. Except for atoms, and so on, none of our referential devices look to be of much distinction.

But then, too, the picture looks bleak for the question of whether atoms exist, and so for any other things. For we cannot, in good faith, long waive the point that there is no human language or thought, nor even any human or other finite beings. And from such a standpoint even simple arithmetic looks to be beyond comprehension, there being none of us to grasp any realities or truth which might be there. Finally, the existence of any sorites arguments themselves cannot be relevantly affirmed, there being not a one of us ever to consider any such piece of reasoning. The chain of nihilistic propositions appears to come full circle.

This undeniable absurdity is, I suggest, no blameworthy fault of our Eubulidean reasonings. On the contrary, by such means, our sorites arguments allow us to perceive the truly thoroughgoing inconsistencies in our available language and thought. Continuing to speak in the paradoxical manner they expose, we might say this. For anything like truth's sake, these arguments counsel us to begin a radical reconstruction of our means of thought and expression. No available earthly means, which is sufficiently rich for many of our purposes, fares any better than does English. I have been disclosing no peculiar subtleties of our language which may be absent in Chinese, or in ancient Greek. But what steps should we take to make things better?

With something like a heap, and sticking to Eubulides's original level of argument, moderately good steps can be taken quickly and easily. For, if there are no heaps, we can define the word 'hoap', for example, so that a hoap may consist, minimally, of two items: for example, beans or grains of sand, touching each other. But, if there are no tables, trees or cats, what are we supposed to define, and, even very roughly, what is to be the definition of it? If I do not exist, then what does exist in which, so to speak, I should have an appropriate and rather intense interest? If you do not exist, as is here argued, what does exist over there which must not be inappropriately interfered with, or harmed? I am truly in darkness on these momentous matters, with no light at all to guide me.

These problems are, I believe, of the first importance for any who value philosophy and the traditional quest after truth. But I am far from sanguine that my challenge, from which they flow, will be met with an attempt to reply which is properly serious, let alone rationally effective. For it is easiest to shun the most pervasive difficulties in philosophy, to leave it to others, in times long to come, to explain their solutions. It is easiest to presume we know in advance, without knowing the details, which way the answer *must* go, letting the social acceptance of others serve as our assurance and even foundation, rather than anything like the light of one's own reason. But I am hopeful that one or two thoughtful souls may break the common easy pattern. Perhaps they will allow me to avoid the labours, apparently painful and fruitless, involved in developing an adequate philosophy of nihilism, which it now appears is the only adequate philosophy there can be. Or perhaps, on the contrary, they will provide me with further reason for thinking that this challenge is too powerful to be met adequately, and that there is no rational hope at all for the thought that anyone might be real. That might not be cheerful, but at least it would be something. Either way, I doubt that Eubulides ever had it so good.[6]

6. I have been helped in writing this paper by discussion with various people; Ralph Silverman and Samuel Wheeler deserve special thanks.

For a discussion of related matters, I refer the reader to my paper, 'There are No Ordinary Things'. *Synthese*, xli (1979), 117–54. For a detailed analysis of sorites arguments, see my 'Why There are No People', *Midwest Studies in Philosophy*, vol. iv: *Studies in Metaphysics*. And, for a discussion of relations between the nihilistic approach of this present paper and the sceptical approach in epistemology, see my 'Skepticism and Nihilism', *Noûs*, xiv (1980), 517–45.

3

WHY THERE ARE
NO PEOPLE

Imagine, if you will, a somewhat uncommonly shaped object, one whose shape is not very irregular or bizarre, perhaps, but which is at least sufficiently so that we have no common name or expression for an object with a shape of that sort. Following this instruction, then, you have not imagined a pyramid, or cylindrical object, for those are readily spoken of in available terms. I shall call your imagined object a *nacknick*, which term you are to apply also to such various other objects as you deem suitably similar in shape to the first. In this way, we have invented a new word together: I have given you the form of the inscription, 'nacknick', and some instructions which help to delimit the meaning. But only you have enough of an idea of the word to put it to much use. That is because, according to this little story, you have not revealed your imagined shape to me, or done much else to give me a useful idea of it.

Let us change the story a bit. In this version, you do not first imagine any object. Rather, I now actually place before you an object of the sort which, we have supposed, you imagined in the first version. Pointing to this uncommonly shaped thing, I then say to you, "This object is a nacknick, as are various others that are suitably similar in shape to it." To be emphatic and explicit, in both versions I may go on to add these following words to my instructions: "Don't think that an object must be *exactly* the same as this one in shape to be a nacknick. Rather, while such exact sameness is amply sufficient, any object that differs in shape from a nacknick only minutely will also be a nacknick. There is, then, no particular limit on shapes for nacknicks. At the same time, however, many objects will differ from nacknicks, as regards their

53

shape, substantially and significantly, and these will not be nacknicks. These remarks apply, of course, not only to actual objects, which might be found in reality, but also to such merely possible objects as might be only imagined." I do not think that, in adding these explicit instructions, I would be changing the learning situation in any substantial way. Rather, I would only be making explicit what would otherwise be learned implicitly. Except for this rather minor matter, and the fact that we set out intentionally to invent a new expression, the word you have just come to understand is of a piece with much that you learned at your mother's knee. The newness and the explicit character of this experience with 'nacknick', however, let us reflect productively on what logical features are common to both the invented terms and the expressions learned in childhood.

1. The Argument from Invented Expressions

What reflection reveals, I suggest, is that a common feature of 'nacknick' and so many other terms is that they are all logically inconsistent expressions. On a par with 'perfectly square triangle', the supposition that anything satisfies 'nacknick' implies a logical contradiction. The instructions that served explicitly to introduce 'nacknick', and that now serve to govern the term, were so devised as to ensure this surprising result. Because of this, we can bring out the inconsistency in the term by reflecting on those instructions, with no need for us to enter into lengthy, complex argumentation as to what the word really means.

Our instructions endowed 'nacknick' with such a meaning that it is now governed by at least these two conditions:[1]

(1n)　If some (actual or only possible) entity satisfies 'nacknick', then any (actual or only possible) entity that differs *minutely*, in shape, from that putative satisfier *also satisfies* the expression.

(2n)　If some (actual or only possible) entity satisfies 'nacknick', then there are some (actual or only possible) entities each of which differs *substantially*, in shape, from that putative satisfier and each of which does *not* satisfy the expression.

1. In formulating these conditions, I have been helped by correspondence with John Tienson.

As stepwise reasoning shows, because it is governed by these two conditions, 'nacknick' is an inconsistent term.

We may begin by considering some shaped object, if only a possible one, that is *not* a nacknick; for, according to my instructions, and (2n), if there are nacknicks, there must be some such. Having done this, we want now to reason that, according to these same instructions, the considered object *also is* a nacknick. Well, let us now think about an alleged nacknick, perhaps even the object from which, presumably, I taught you the expression. If this is a nacknick, then, according to my instructions, and to (1n), so too is an object only minutely different in shape from it, in particular, one that is minutely more alike in shape to the object that we have agreed is not a nacknick. Now, as this *new*, minutely differing object is also a nacknick, as my instructions have indicated, *so too* is *another* object that differs from *it*, in the same direction, by at least roughly that same minute amount. It is not hard to see, then, that a sequence of reasoning takes us to the step where an object, only minutely more alike in shape to our "paradigm" nacknick than is our considered non-nacknick, will be declared a nacknick. Then, finally, the object that, we agreed, was not a nacknick will also be a nacknick. According to my instructions, then, there are objects that both are nacknicks and are not. The word 'nacknick', the relevant aspects of which these instructions determine, is an inconsistent expression.

It might be objected against this reasoning that there are sequences of minute differences that will not take us to our agreed non-nacknick, but rather will approach a limit that is safely within the range where proper nacknicks may be recognized. If this is so, the objection continues, then we cannot draw the conclusion that, as the instructions have it, there are objects that both are and are not nacknicks. But unfortunately for this objection, the existence of such limited sequences will not prevent the inconsistent conclusion from being drawn. For our instructions explicitly stated that there is no particular limit on shape for nacknicks, and so they ensured troublesome sequences to be available for our stepwise reasoning. For example, one available sequence is presented when we consider one billion roughly equal steps of difference spanning the range from our paradigm to our considered non-nacknick. This sequence means a long argument for us, if things are spelled out in detail, but the inconsistent conclusion is forced upon us all the same. It is pretty clear, I suggest, that because of our devised instructions, our invented expression 'nacknick', despite its utility and natural appearance, is indeed a logically inconsistent expression.

I shall employ this observation of inconsistency as a premise in an argument, the Argument from Invented Expressions:[2]

(I)   The invented expression 'nacknick' is logically inconsistent.

The conclusion of our argument is to be the proposition that there are no people. To get it from our premise about 'nacknick', we need a good deal more. Most of this remainder will be contained in this second premise:

(II)   The expression 'person' is logically on a par with 'nacknick'; if the latter is inconsistent, then so is the former.

A great deal of this essay will be spent in supplying support for this crucial second premise. There will be great resistance, of course, toward its acceptance. For it is quickly quite obvious that, in conjunction with the eminently attractive first premise, it logically yields the startling conclusion:

(A)   The expression 'person' is logically inconsistent.

Before a lengthy discussion of the claimed logical parity is entered into, a few brief remarks are in order to motivate (II), so that the lengthier, more analytical discussion may appear worth the effort.

Now, as I have set things up here, the only thing important to an object's being a nacknick is the shape it has, though even this matter, of course, evaporates in inconsistency. So, in this regard, our invented word parallels certain ordinary expressions: for example, 'cubical object', in contrast to 'perfect cube'. Further, while I have specified only shape as important for nacknicks, I could have easily specified *additional* requirements for our putative objects, for example, that a nacknick be a certain sort of nicknack. Any such additional requirement could not, of course, have rendered the word consistent: given the determinative instructions regarding shape, nothing could have done that. With only shape in the picture, our example has a certain purity and simplicity. But as regards the basic question, that of inconsistency, our invented word might be the same as expressions that cannot be so neatly described.

---

2. I use the plural term 'Expressions' in naming this Argument because, while I, in fact, chose to begin with 'nacknick', and with certain matters of shape, I could have begun as well with other matters and invented expressions.

Again, our learning situation involved just one paradigm nacknick, imagined or presented, and this artifice also gives our examples a certain simplicity and purity, perhaps one not often found in the more ordinary course of things. But we could have made things more ordinary without importantly altering our examples: For example, originally, I could have asked you to imagine several shaped objects, each to have a quite similar unfamiliar shape. In the second story, I could have presented you with several similarly shaped objects. And, then, when things were to be made explicit, I could have altered my instructions, slightly, to suit. So, whether we have a single paradigm or a multiplicity is not crucial to the logic of the expression learned.

At this point, our second premise will have a certain plausibility at least. As our first premise, (I), is so hard to deny, our conclusion from it and (II), that is, the startling (A), will now also be at least plausible. But however surprising it may be, (A) does not directly concern the existence, or nonexistence, of persons. It is, after all, about an expression, 'person', and is not directly about any putative people. To get a conclusion directly to concern our desired subject matter, however, is now quite easy. We need only add to what we have, this final premise:

(III)   If the expression 'person' is logically inconsistent, then there are no people.

In conjunction with (III), our other premises validly yield our intended final conclusion:

(B)   There are no people.

And, this final premise, (III), really is a logically unobjectionable proposition.

To deny the idea that an inconsistent expression does not apply to anything, one must be involved in a confusion. For what is an inconsistent expression? It is an expression for which the supposition that it does apply leads to a contradiction. But, then, that supposition cannot be true. Thus the expression does not apply. But what confusion might be responsible for such an absurd denial?

The chief culprit, I suppose, will be a failure to distinguish between, first, our using an expression to refer to certain objects and, on the other hand, an expression actually applying to, or being true of, those objects. You and I, for example, may agree to use the expression 'perfectly square triangle', even given what it now means, to refer to such tomatoes as are both yellow and sweet. With normal suppositions in force, including the existence of people, there may well be such tomatoes and we may well usefully refer to them with that expression. But we may be confident that those tomatoes are not perfectly square triangles, even though we refer to them as such, and that there are no such triangles anywhere. We may be just as confident, then, that whatever use we are putting it to, our chosen expression, being inconsistent, is true of no existing entities at all. So much, then, for denials of our final premise.[3]

We have much to discuss, however, as regards our other two premises, in particular, premise (II), where logical parity is claimed for 'person' and 'nacknick'. My support for this idea, which will afford some support to our first premise as well, will come largely in terms of an account of 'person' as a *vague discriminative expression*. On this account, all such expressions, including the invented 'nacknick', are logically inconsistent. Briefly and roughly, we may provide some idea of these expressions: First, in that they are *vague*, these terms contrast with, say, 'inch', which, we may allow, precisely purports to discriminate the inch from all other lengths. Second, in that they are *discriminative*, these terms contrast with the vague expression 'entity', which does not purport to discriminate anything from anything else, supposing that we may allow that anything at all is an entity. And, finally, the vagueness of these terms is essentially *involved in* their purported discriminations. So, they will contrast with 'entity which is less than two', supposing that this expression is about as vague as 'entity,' but that this vagueness does not enter into its purported discrimination (of some numbers from others).

I am about to exhibit my account, which, while it is incomplete, should be detailed enough to indicate that its main lines are adequate. Before I do so, let me remark that I am well aware of a flaw that my account of these expressions is bound to have: If the account is right, then, as 'person' is inconsistent, there are none of us, and so no statements, accounts, or arguments that we produce or understand. The account implies a paradoxical situation. But this paradox, I shall argue, does not nullify the account. Rather, it bespeaks its comprehensiveness and that of "an intellectual need to begin anew."

2. An Account of Some Common Vague Expressions

The inconsistency of 'nacknick' may be crudely characterized as stemming from the following two rough conditional statements:

---

3. My discussion of this matter emerged from conversation with Samuel Wheeler.

> If something differs from a nacknick *minutely*, then it *also* is a nacknick (no matter in what *way* it thus differs).

> If something is a nacknick, then there are things that differ from it in *certain ways* by a *lot*, so much so that they are *not* nacknicks.

If someone, not a philosopher, were asked to express that inconsistency without any specific reference to shape, I think he would express it, well enough for his purpose, in these terms or terms similar to them. Now, if we want, as philosophers, to give a general characterization of the inconsistency, we too shall avoid any reference to any specific property. But we shall try to be a bit clearer about the offending differences than the obscure reference to a *way*. Accordingly, the conditions we should exhibit will not be the sort a typical learner would be likely to articulate. Still, in learning the expression in question, he may learn such underlying conditions.

I shall endeavor, then, to present two conditional statements that characterize 'nacknick', as well as many ordinary vague expressions. The terms I mean to characterize may be regarded as forming an important, but not exhaustive, group among the vague discriminative ones: those that are (purely) qualitative expressions. To indicate these expressions, we may distinguish, well enough for the purpose, between the qualitative or internal properties of an entity and, in contrast, its external properties, or relations. Thus, we shall say that two blue rectangular solids may be the same as regards all their qualitative properties but different as regards certain of their relations, for example, as regards their spatial relations to other objects. Whether an expression is vague or not, we shall say that it is (purely) qualitative just in case it is governed by this following condition: If an entity satisfies the expression, then so too does any entity which shares that satisfier's qualitative properties, that is, which is qualitatively identical with the satisfier. Thus, the expression 'perfect cube', while not vague, is qualitative, as are also the vague expressions 'cubical object' and 'nacknick'.

Among vague discriminative terms, the qualitative ones satisfy this stronger condition: If an entity satisfies the expression, then so does any entity that either (a) is qualitatively identical to that satisfier or else (b) is minutely different from it. It is to be understood, as is most natural, that the minute differences alluded to in (b) are in respect of qualitative properties, rather than relations. As is evident from our previous reasoning, the important problems with these expressions derive from (b); thus, in our subsequent discussion we may in general safely ignore (a), and focus on this problematic aspect.

Focusing on (b), we may present our characteristic conditions as follows, with the help of some terms to be clarified later, namely, *dimensions of difference* and *directions* along them, which are here to concern only the internal properties of the entities involved, as opposed to their external relations:[4]

(1) With respect to any qualitative vague discriminative expression, there are dimensions of difference, with directions along them, such that if some (actual or only possible) entity satisfies the expression, then all *minute* differences from the entity with respect to any one of these dimensions will find *other* (actual or only possible) entities that satisfy, and will find no (such) entity that does not satisfy the expression, providing that such a found entity does not differ more than minutely in any other such regard.

(2) With respect to any qualitative vague discriminative expression, if some (actual or only possible) entity satisfies it, then among the dimensions and directions that suffice for satisfaction under (1), there is at least one dimension of difference and at least one direction along it such that, with respect to these, there are (actual or only possible) entities each of which differs *substantially* from that putative satisfier and each of which does *not* satisfy the expression.

The conditions given in these two statements, along with such discussion as clarifies and supports them, form the heart of my account of vague discriminative expressions. Now this account would, of course, be uninteresting should there be many expressions, but none which are qualitative vague discriminative ones. But this is not so. On the contrary, providing that there are any expressions at all, there are a significant number of this sort, including 'bumpy', 'tall man', 'stone', and 'person'.

The second of these conditions, in (2), is to the purported effect that these expressions are to *discriminate* their satisfiers *from* other entities. This condition, which indicates some objects as *falling outside* an expression's range, we shall call the *discriminative* condition. The

4. I am indebted to several people for help in formulating these complex statements, especially to Terence Leichti. But there have been so many problems with previous versions that I despair that some must still remain. I trust, however, that the reader will not judge my philosophy primarily in terms of formulational details.

first condition is to the effect that, supposing any entity does, various ones together are to satisfy the expression, but no definite bound is to be placed on those to be included. Thus, we shall call this condition the *vagueness* condition for the expression in question.

While both of these two conditions are required to generate our noted inconsistency, it is the vagueness condition over which most discussion is likely to arise. Accordingly, let us first try to get an idea of its import. To do so, we may contrast 'bumpy', a qualitative vague discriminative term, with 'flat' (or with 'absolutely flat') and 'not flat', which are relevantly precise. If a surface is bumpy, that is, satisfies 'bumpy', and is not just not flat, then, just as our condition directs, so too is any surface that is no more than minutely different from it, even as regards shape. If a surface is (absolutely) flat, however, there will be minutely differing surfaces, in shape, that will not be (absolutely) flat. They will have only a few tiny bumps on them, in some cases, but not so much as to be bumpy. Likewise, if a surface is not (absolutely) flat, it will not follow that all minutely differing surfaces are also not flat. Consider a nearly flat surface. There will be a (possible) surface whose shape, while minutely different from it, is different in just such a way that it will be flat. Intuitively, I suggest, of these expressions, only 'bumpy' would be regarded as a vague term. The fact that only it is governed by our first condition, then, helps show the intuitive point of that requirement.[5]

To understand both of our conditions, we should explicate our talk of *dimensions of difference*, for that is a somewhat technical expression whose connection with our ordinary vague thinking cannot be evident. We may begin our explication by noting that things do not just differ as such, but always *differ in* one or more *ways* or *respects*. For example, a heavy red stone differs from things that are not red in respect of *color*, and from things that are not heavy in respect of *weight*. Now, with many such respects, we may, to a certain extent at least, speak comparatively of how much things differ. In respect of color, for example, we say that our red stone differs *more* from things that are blue *than* from those that are purple. In respect of weight, it differs more from things, or at least stones, that are very light than from those of a moderate or intermediate weight. Thus, we think of a *dimension* of color, and also a *dimension* of weight, as a *dimension of difference*. All of this is quite ordinary to think.

5. For an extended discussion of the semantics of 'flat', and of other such *absolute terms*, see chapter II of my book *Ignorance* (Oxford, 1975).

What is less common, but I think still quite available, is the idea that many things vary, too, with regard to stoniness, that is, with respect to how close they are to being a stone, in the case of a certain stretch, or with respect to how good an example of a stone, in the case of another one. Thus, we may recognize such a more complex, less easily described dimension, according to which a very light, blue pebble differs *more* from a similarly light, similarly colored twig, or piece of cloth, *than* it does from a heavy red stone. And, with regard to this same dimension, of *stoniness*, if you will allow that expression, the pebble may differ less from the stone than it does from a boulder, even if the pebble and boulder are in most other respects quite like each other and quite different from the stone. Accordingly, we may say that along *at least one* dimension of difference a red stone differs more from a blue stone than it does from a red pebble, while along at *least one other* dimension, the differences run differently.

What we count as a dimension may include other dimensions, but perhaps in no orderly way. Color, which we have taken as a dimension, is often said to include hue, saturation, and brightness. Perhaps where we spoke of our red stone differing from a blue stone as regards the dimension of color, we might have more specifically said that they differ as regards the dimension of hue. But there is no competition here, nor any need for us to think that there are any ultimate dimensions of difference. Our ordinary thinking does not suggest that, but neither do our two conditions of typical vagueness. For our second condition says, not that there is *one* dimension of difference along which a vague expression will not (any longer) be satisfied, but that there is *at least one* such dimension. Now, my talk of dimensions may harbor a whole host of problems. But that is no fault of it here. For we are trying to reflect the features of our common vague expressions, including whatever problems they may harbor.

Our conditions speak, not only of dimensions of difference, but also of *directions* along these dimensions. What are these directions? In regards to any dimension, say, that of color, we can think of small differences *accumulating* until large ones are reached. This thought of accumulation implies a direction in which the accumulation takes place. Without any direction, such as that *from* red *through* purple *to* blue, there would not be the order among colored things which we suppose there to be. Similarly, a stone differs from a boulder in one direction, while it differs from a pebble or grain in another. We do not always have convenient expressions to label these directions, just as with the dimensions along which they are directions. But it must be admitted, I think, that they do have a place in our thinking with vague terms.

We want our expressed conditions to explain the force of arguments that are forceful.[6] To do this, we must notice that certain of our vague terms are meant to discriminate those entities purportedly falling under them from others that lie only in certain directions, and not in others. For example, the expression 'tall man' purports discrimination of its satisfiers from men who lie, with respect to the satisfiers, only in the downward direction of height, and not in the upward direction. How this means inconsistency for the expression is indicated by considering sorites arguments against the existence of tall men.[7]

In respect of height, here the relevant dimension, two men may differ by a foot and we deem the one a tall man and the other not. For example, one may be six feet six, plus or minus a thousandth of an inch, and the other five feet six, plus or minus that. In the *downward direction*, this difference of a foot would be relevantly substantial; in line with our second condition, the man of five feet six would, thus, *not* be a tall man. In the other, upward direction, no discrimination of the satisfier from anything is purported, and so no problems arise. Just as a man of six feet six is tall, so any man of greater height is a tall man, or so we commonly believe. The substantial difference of a foot, then, means nothing in the upward direction: unlike a man of five feet six, a man of seven feet six is (supposed to be) a tall man.

This purported discrimination in the downward direction is enough to provide an argument that turns on the inconsistency of 'tall man'. We choose a man somewhere down there in height, for example, a man of five feet six, who is supposed not to be a tall man. And, we can show, by the condition of (1), that he also *is* a tall man (if any man is). For if the man of six-six is tall, then so is a man minutely less in height, say, a thousandth of an inch less, plus or minus a small fraction of that. And if he too, then also another, whose height is about a thousandth of an inch less. And, so, by steps, if there is any tall man, then our man of five-six is one of these. But, as we have supposed, he is not. And, while we might seek to avoid the contradiction by saying that, contrary to what we supposed, the man of five-six is after all only a tall one, this is no avoidance but only a futile postponement. For according to our second condition, there must be *some* (actual or only possible) man down there who is *not* tall. But, whomever we choose, our first condition then forces

6. For an alternative interpretation of why sorites arguments are sound, see two papers by Samuel Wheeler: "Reference and Vagueness," *Synthese*, Vol. 30, No. 3/4 (April/May, 1975) and "On That Which Is Not," *Synthese* (forthcoming).

7. In the case of (almost) all the sorites arguments presented in this paper, in regards to matters of formulation, I am indebted to Terence Leichti.

us to draw the opposite conclusion about him as well. Thus, the purported discrimination cannot be made; the expression is an inconsistent one.

There is a potential source of ambiguity which, while I do not think I have invited it, can be placed beyond serious question rather quickly. It might be thought that, according to our second condition, so long as the dimension and direction are appropriate, *any* substantial difference from a satisfier will take us to objects, actual or only possible, that do not satisfy. This would be an unfortunate interpretation, as the following example makes clear: If the difference between a six-six man and a five-six one is substantial, then so is that between a man of eight feet and a six-six man. But, while the latter is, then, a substantial difference, and can be taken in the right direction, it does not take us to a man who, by common judgment, is not tall. But our condition does not say that *just any* entity that thus differs from a satisfier will not satisfy the expression in question; rather, it implies only that there must be *at least some* such. In the present case, there is indeed a plenitude of relevant possible cases. For example, all the possible men with heights less than five feet six will differ sufficiently from the eight foot man. Thus, these men, who are not tall, will allow us to derive a contradiction from the assumption that the eight-footer is a tall man.

In disarming a potential source of ambiguity, we have entered upon the finer points of our account. In this vein, we may notice the final, or 'providing', clause of our vagueness condition. Now, that clause may seem to make matters complex, but it is only a way of providing for what would usually be understood anyway. For we are to understand that such a minute difference, by itself, will not make the difference between satisfier and nonsatisfier, not that the presence of one such small difference will ensure a second satisfier, no matter how different from the original that second entity might otherwise be. By the same token, even with this "providing" clause, our vagueness condition can be applied, in stepwise fashion, any number of times. For while various other differences may add up so that they are eventually more than minute ones, even by common-sense reckoning, in any one step no such large difference will ever be encountered.[8]

Because our conditions do not specify or mention any particular dimensions of difference, or directions along them, but only require, for satisfaction, the existence of some, we cannot state our conditions in a mutually independent form. Thus our reference in (2) to what is

8. On the need for such a "providing" clause, I am indebted to James Van Cleve.

required in (1). We need this to make sure that the differences added up by repeated applications of (1) are comparable to those for which (2) indicates an opposite claim, so that a contradiction will arise, supposing there is any satisfier. With 'nacknick', shape was specified as relevant; by specifying it once in each, independently specified conditions could be given for the term. A similar situation occurs with the ordinary vague expression 'tall man', where we may mention *height* as the dimension, and specify the *downward* direction along it. But oftentimes, we shall be in no position to provide such specific, independently specifiable conditions.

Our conditions make reference to possible entities that may not be actual. By this device, we may explain, for example, our ready judgment that six-inch men would not be tall men, even supposing there are no actual men of that height. For we are very ready to withhold 'tall man' from such an imaginary case. Now, if such an explanatory reference to possible entities is avoidable, then we may just consider it a convenience here, for brevity. If, on the other hand, an implication of such dubious objects is required, that should mean trouble for these vague expressions. But even if such a problem means, all over again, the worst for these terms, I shall not dwell on the matter now. For the same difficulty, if there is one, would appear quite as damaging to various expressions that are not vague: if something satisfies "is not a perfect cube," then there are objects, actual or only possible, that differ from that satisfier in shape, and that, thus, do *not* satisfy the expression. In other words, such problems are not peculiar to our topic.

Let us turn now to discuss some of the limits of our offered conditions, for they are not meant to cover every conceivable topic. We may begin by noting a vague expression that is not governed by our second, or discriminative, condition, namely, the expression 'part of physical reality'. Now, this term is, of course, a qualitative one; if an entity is part of physical reality, then so too is any other qualitatively just like it. And, second, this expression is a vague one; if anything, it is even *more* vague than 'stone'. At the same time, it is governed by our first, or vagueness, condition: If an entity is a part of physical reality, then so too is any other that, with respect to any dimension of difference, is minutely different from it. And, third, the expression is, quite obviously, a discriminative one: it is not to apply to such a putative abstract entity as the number three. But, the discriminations it makes do not appear to *involve* its vagueness, at least not in the ordinary way we have been noticing. For it does not seem that there is any dimension, or spectrum, of graded differences, where parts of physical reality are somewhere to leave off and other entities are to be newly encountered. So, our expression 'part of physical reality' does not seem to be of the sort we have called *vague discriminative*. At the same time, it is not governed by our second condition.

Finally, let us look at some limits of our vagueness condition, and try to see what they may, or may not, mean for us. Toward this end, we notice the contrast between two kinds of vague discriminative expression: those that are (purely) qualitative and those that are not. Only the first of these will be governed by our vagueness condition, in (1), for the notion of *dimension of difference* there employed concerned only differences as regards qualities, or internal properties. Thus, for an easy example, two men may be qualitatively the same, but only one may bear the relation to a woman of being married. Thus, only the other of them is a bachelor. The word 'bachelor', then, is not a qualitative term. As such, it is not governed by our vagueness condition: Scratch the married man alone, so that now he is minutely different from the bachelor as regards his internal properties. But though he is minutely different from an entity that satisfies 'bachelor', this married man does not satisfy the word.

A less obvious example is provided by John Tienson.[9] He points to certain expressions for artifacts, for example, 'table top' and 'door'. Consider two qualitatively identical objects, each crafted in different areas by different people, quite independently. The first is meant to serve just as a door, and does so. The second is meant to serve just as a table top, as it does. It seems clear that, supposing there are table tops, only one of these is that. Scratching one, which means a minute difference between them now, as regards internal properties, will, of course, not alter the situation. Upon reflection, then, it appears that there will be many vague discriminative terms that are not qualitative ones, and that do not satisfy the vagueness condition for our qualitative expressions. Consequently, to have a general account of discriminative vagueness, we need a vagueness condition for these terms as well, along with a matching discriminative condition. But, what does this mean for our main topic?

Even without much thought on the matter, it is quite clear that 'person', unlike 'bachelor' and 'door', is indeed a purely qualitative term. Perhaps some creature qualitatively identical to me, but very far away, might not be a human being should he lack certain relations, causal or otherwise, to all (earthly) humans.[10] But he would still be a person for all that. Consequently, as our chief interest here is in 'person',

9. In John Tienson, "Can Things of Different Natural Kinds Be Exactly Alike?", *Analysis* 37 (1977): 190–97.

10. This is suggested by the main point of Tienson's paper, "Can Things of Different Natural Kinds Be Exactly Alike?"

and in putative persons, it is not much to present purposes to provide such more general conditions for discriminative vagueness as we now, admittedly, do desire.

Still, a suggestion or two seems to be in order, to give some idea of how our account of vague terms might be extended from the purely qualitative ones to cover vague discriminative expressions generally. For a start, we may alter our vagueness condition so that the dimensions of difference involved, and so the minute differences with regard to them, will now concern external relations as well as internal properties. With this alteration we may declare an entity obtained from an alleged door to be a door, should the change be a suitably small one, such as will, in fact, be produced by the net removal of a peripheral atom. For this obtained object's relations to other things will differ only minutely from those of the original satisfier, all things considered, whether or not we regard it as the very same object as that original. But while we thus achieve some added explanatory power, this alteration provides only a rather weak, or unambitious, vagueness condition: Another door, far away from the original, and with internal properties only minutely different, may well not be declared a door. For, all things considered, the external relations of this distant object may be so different from the first, it seems, that no declaration concerning it will be available to us. To group these two doors together, a stronger vagueness condition is needed. A suitable one might be obtained, I suggest, if we do not speak of external relations generally, but limit our reference to those relations the bearing of which, by an object, are relevant to whether or not the object is (supposed to be) a satisfier, for example, a door. If these relevant relations are just the same or minutely different for the two objects, and their internal properties are also the same or minutely different, then they shall be grouped together as well. With these provisos, we may now have a suitable vagueness condition for all discriminative vague terms, as we have been understanding this category of expressions.

For such an extension of our account, I am inclined to think that our original discriminative condition will prove adequate, with its reference to the dimensions in the paired vagueness condition matching things up appropriately. But, if that is not quite right, a suitable matching condition should not be far to seek. These are my suggestions, then, for extending my account from its present exclusive concern with purely qualitative terms to cover vague discriminative expressions generally. Having made them, I shall not pursue the matter here, but will only note that most of the remarks to be made about the qualitative ones will apply as well to the others. Hence, in what follows, I often shall speak indiscriminately of vague discriminative terms, in general, and those of them that are qualitative vague expressions.

3. The Idea of Incomplete Expressions

The main lines of our account are now before us. On this account, vague discriminative expressions are inconsistent terms. Against our account, others may be proposed. Perhaps the most common and appealing alternative will be the idea that these vague terms are *incomplete expressions*. Typically, at least, this idea will derive from the thought that each of our vague expressions has *borderline cases*, that is, cases that neither *definitely* satisfy the term nor *definitely* do not. The reason for these cases, the idea will then go, is that the vague expression says nothing about them one way or the other. This lack of content or commitment is owing to the term's being incomplete, that is, incompletely defined.[11] Now, even if there were something in the idea of an incomplete term, its application to our typical vague expressions would now seem to be quite dubious. For these expressions seem logically on a par with 'nacknick', and that invented expression is (completely) inconsistent, and so is not an incomplete one. But matters are worse than that for our alleged alternative account. For, as I shall argue, this idea of incompleteness is incoherent, as is even the thought of borderline cases, on which it depends.

Let us begin our discussion by seeing that our own account implies the result I seek to establish. Now, on our account, typical vague expressions apply to no cases whatsoever, for they are each logically inconsistent. Hence, we may say all cases are decided negatively by each such term. Thus, no cases are borderline cases, and no expression is incomplete. Here is another way of seeing that, on our account, there are no borderline cases: Any borderline case for an expression requires positive cases, which satisfy the expression. For a case that is (on the) borderline is, on some relevant dimension, *between positive cases* and negative ones. On our account, there are no positive cases; thus, no borderline ones either. So it is amply clear that as our account has it, there are no vague discriminative expressions that are incomplete. In that I shall be arguing for this same conclusion, I shall be reasoning that this result is a virtue of our account.

---

11. Perhaps the most prominent recent exponent of this idea of incompleteness, or of an idea much like it, is Michael Dummett in his unfortunately named "Wang's Paradox," *Synthese* 30 (1975), especially as on pages 309–12.

Let us focus on the notion of borderline cases. These are supposed to be cases to which the expression in question does not *definitely* apply and does not *definitely* not apply. But what can be the proper force of this 'definitely' here? Imagine a typical vague expression and an object. Consider the statement that (1) the expression neither definitely applies to the object nor definitely does not. And consider as well the apparently simpler statement that (2) the expression either applies to the object or does not apply to it. Now, the former statement either is consistent with the latter, simpler one or else it is not. Suppose it *is* consistent with the simpler statement. What the simpler statement says is that each case is one where the expression applies or else is one where it does not apply, and so it leaves no room for any borderline cases. So, for all the statement with 'definitely' then says, there will be no borderline cases. Thus, if our two statements are mutually consistent, the one with 'definitely' cannot coherently indicate any borderline case. Well, then, let us suppose the alternative, that the first statement is *not* consistent with the second. Now, we shall want to notice the logical status of that second statement: it is necessarily true. For this statement is but a special consequence of a quite general necessary truth: with regard to any given object, any relation, and any entity, that object either bears that relation to that entity or does not bear the relation to the entity.[12] Now, if the object is an expression, that cannot change matters; nor can things be altered when the relation is that of application, whatever the entity in question might be. The truth of our simpler statement, (2), then, cannot be seriously challenged. But, if (1), our 'definitely' statement, is not then consistent with (2), (1) will not itself be true, and so it will not correctly indicate any borderline cases. Thus, in either case, that is, in any case, there are no borderline cases.

Our statement with 'definitely', it is true, at first appears to suggest coherently some cases of a third logical kind, though this appearance cannot be borne out. I should try to explain the illusory appearance here. The explanation, I think, falls into two parts: first, talk with 'definite' can be used, coherently, we may allow, to describe certain behavioral situations. And, once that is managed, the description can lead to the incoherent idea that, underlying the described behavior, there are logically borderline cases. Let us discuss the first part, for that is where the trouble starts.

12. As I hope is indicated by the language, this general proposition is not intended to concern future situations. As regards the future, I think there are genuine problems, as made famous by Aristotle and his argument of the sea battle.

With regard to a typical vague expression, a normal person will sometimes be in a state of hesitancy, uncertainty, and, perhaps, even confusion. With regard to certain (real or only imagined) objects, which he may call "borderline cases," he will have no definite disposition or tendency to apply the term nor any definite tendency to withhold it. These objects will contrast with others, for which the person has such a tendency to apply the term, as well as with still others, for which he has a definite disposition to withhold the expression. And, these behavioral contrasts can hold, not just for a single individual at a moment, but for a society during a long period of time. Where such a broadly based pattern of dispositions exists, we may give a certain currency to talk of "borderline cases." But that talk, to remain coherent, must confine itself to reporting upon the behaviors in question; it cannot properly entail, to explain the behavior, situations where an expression does not apply to an object and also does not not apply to it.

The behavioral contrasts just remarked, it may be appreciated, will hold just as well for invented inconsistent expressions, like 'nacknick'. A given individual will be ready to apply "nacknick" to certain objects, and to withhold it from others, but will be uncertain about still a third group. And, should the term gain currency, a more general behavioral pattern to the same effect would doubtless ensue. Objects in the third group might well be regarded, quite generally, as borderline cases. So long as nothing of much logical import is thus implied, such parlance may be allowed. But, clearly, nothing much more than reportage upon these dispositions could be coherently conveyed by such talk of borderlines. For, clearly, 'nacknick' is an inconsistent expression, and actually applies to no cases whatsoever. So it is with all vague discriminative expressions, both invented and inherited.

Except in the irrelevant behavioral sense of the expression, then, there can be no borderline cases. Thus, there are none to threaten our account; there is no competition for us from the idea of vague expressions as incomplete. For any incompleteness will arise only over logically borderline cases, and so the suggestion of incomplete expressions is not a coherent idea. Though we have just made short work of the idea of incomplete expressions, there will be some, no doubt, who will be loathe to part with it. The reason for their reluctance is simple: the idea can be made to appear very attractive. For our reasonings to have maximum effect here, we must consider the motivation from which such an appearance can derive.

The motivation underlying the idea of incomplete expressions is due primarily, I think, to a misplaced analogy between linguistic expressions and mathematical functions. For a mathematical function to yield a value for an object, that function must be defined for, or with respect to, that object. Typically, it will be so defined only if someone, a mathematician, does something, only if he defines it for the object. If nothing is done, then the function is undefined for the object, and it yields no particular value in the case. If one thinks of a linguistic expression as yielding a positive value for those objects it applies to, and a negative one for those it does not, one is well on his way toward applying this analogy.

Like the functions of mathematics, it may then be thought, an expression will yield a value only in the case of those objects for which it is defined. And, it will be defined for an object only if some people *have defined* the expression for the object. Now, this thinking continues, the people may have defined it positively with regard to a certain object: in that case, the value there will be positive, and the expression will apply to the object. Or, they may have defined it negatively: then, the value there will be negative, and the expression will not apply. Or, as in mathematics, they may not have defined it with regard to the object. In this last case, the expression will be *undefined* with respect to the object, it will yield no value there, neither positive nor negative; and, so, it will neither apply to the object nor not apply to it. Rather, it will find a borderline case in the object, thus being an incomplete expression.

According to one way of viewing the matter, a mathematical function that is defined for certain objects but not for others may be completed, so that it is then defined for those others as well. Analogously, the idea of incomplete expressions may be further developed: A vague discriminative expression may be made more precise by completing its definition. So long as the previously positive cases remain as such, and so with the previously negative ones, a completion will be admissible. Thus, for a typical vague expression, there will be a great, perhaps an infinite, variety of admissible completions, none of which violates the meaning with which the expression had been endowed. Any such completion will decide, whether positively or negatively, each of the expression's borderline cases. And, what can determine which completion we fix upon, if ever we desire to make precise a certain vague expression, will be the purposes we then wish it to serve. So, the acceptable completion we choose need not be an arbitrary choice.

The idea of incomplete expressions is thus a very attractive idea. According to it, our expressions are each consistent and more: through their already defined cases, they provide us with stable contrasts, with an intellectual anchor. At the same time, through their borderline cases, they provide us with the opportunity for creative conceptual choice. But, in addition to resting on an incoherent notion of borderline cases, this appealing picture rests upon a weak or misplaced analogy between mathematical functions and the expressions of our language.

What is it, in the special sense intended, for an expression to be defined? Of course, it is not for it to be defined in the usual sense, where a statement is made that elucidates the term's meaning. For, many precise terms, completely defined in our special sense, have never had their meaning thus elucidated and, on the other side, certain vague words have had their meaning made tolerably plain. On the contrary, what is here alluded to is simply this: the expression has been endowed with such meaning that, with respect to some objects at least, that meaning determines whether or not the term applies to those objects. Once we realize that this is what this talk of definition comes to, we can see that the idea of incomplete definition amounts to nothing. For, with respect to any expression, and any object, unless we define that expression with respect to that object, that is, unless society has endowed it with such meaning as determines whether or not it applies to the object, the expression will *not* apply to the object. If we insist that the term's not applying to an object means that it yields a (negative) value for that object, then a (negative) value will be yielded even if nothing has been done to produce such a result. Consider the expression 'ouch'. It has not been defined with respect to the Empire State Building. Yet, it does *not apply* to that entity. If we insist that this means 'ouch' yields a negative value for the Building, then so be it. Of course, one might not insist that 'ouch' yields a value here. But, still, it does not apply to the Building. So, however we describe matters, we cannot coherently apply the offered analogy.

A function, then, if not suitably defined, may yield no value with regard to a certain object, neither positive nor negative. But, whether owing to what is dictated by its meaning or not, an expression will apply to a given object or else it will not do so. Unlike the function, with its values, there is no further course for the expression to take.

The idea of incomplete expressions is itself inconsistent. It can offer no genuine alternative to our account of vague expressions as inconsistent terms. Let us inquire somewhat more deeply now as to the nature of their inconsistency.[13]

---

13. Various remarks in the section just ended are in response to conversations with Terence Leichti and with David Lewis.

4. Vagueness and Groundless Inconsistency

It is easy to assume that any inconsistent expression results from a clash between ideas each of which is itself quite consistent. Our by now familiar expression 'perfectly square triangle' may be reckoned an example of this. As such, that expression may be regarded as governed by two quite precise conditions, which may be expressed as follows:

> (1t)   If some (actual or only possible) entity satisfies the expression 'perfectly square triangle', then (since that putative satisfier is a perfectly square object) the satisfier has exactly four interior angles.
>
> (2t)   If some (actual or only possible) entity satisfies the expression 'perfectly square triangle', then (since that putative satisfier is a triangle) the satisfier has exactly three interior angles.

The clash here is between the idea of having exactly four such angles, which implies having more than three, and that of having exactly three, which implies not having more than three. We might say that the inconsistency in 'perfectly square triangle' is *grounded* in the clash between these two consistent conceptions. It is easy to assume, then, that every inconsistent expression must be grounded in at least one such clash as that. On the contrary, however, it is a feature of vague discriminative terms that their inconsistency is *not* thus grounded, but is relevantly *groundless*. And, it is a virtue of our two conditions for such expressions that they serve to bring out this groundlessness.

The differences that figure in our vagueness condition are referred to as *minute* ones, and those of our discriminative condition as *substantial* in amount or size. Whatever the meaning of 'minute' and 'substantial', we may take it that nothing satisfies both of these at once, whether the thing in question be a slice of meat, a number, or a difference. The terms 'minute' and 'substantial', then, purport to be mutually exclusive in their application; if they have any application, it must respect this condition. It is in virtue of this exclusivity that these terms might appear to underlie successful discriminations purported by our vague discriminative expressions. But 'minute' and 'substantial' are themselves discriminative vague terms. So, both of them are inconsistent expressions; neither has any real application at all, thus none which is exclusive of the other's. Even so, the inconsistency of other discriminative vague terms may be understood in terms of the inconsistency of each of these two expressions. At the same time, their own inconsistency may also be understood in terms of themselves. While these two terms are thus rather deeply placed, they provide no clash between consistent conceptions. Accordingly, the inconsistencies they serve to explain are relevantly groundless.

What is it, after all, for one object to differ minutely from another, in a certain respect, for that difference between them to be a minute one? If that difference is minute, then so is a difference, along the same dimension, which is only minutely greater than it. This leads to the conclusion that a certain difference, deemed substantial, and so *not* minute, must be deemed as well a minute one. Thus, there is no minute difference in the first place.

Let us reconsider our paradigm nacknick and the object we agreed to be so different from it as to be not a nacknick. The difference between these two, we supposed, was a substantial one, and so not a minute difference. But an object that was about a billionth of the way from the paradigm to the non-nacknick differed minutely from the paradigm. If it did, then so did the next object in the considered sequence, for the extra billionth of the way thus added will not mean the difference between a minute difference here and one that is not. But, then, the difference between the paradigm and the still next object will also be a minute one, on the same principle. By stepwise reasoning, we shall thus conclude that the difference between the paradigm and the considered non-nack is a minute difference. This lets us, in turn, conclude two things: first, we may conclude that the supposed non-nacknick is also a nacknick, which helps show how the quantitative term 'minute' underlies 'nacknick'. And, second, we deduce the related contradiction: that the supposed substantial difference, between the paradigm and the agreed non-nacknick, is also a minute one.

In general, we may say that when adding a minute difference to another, the result is a larger difference that is still a minute one. Suppose someone took exception to this generality, thinking that there might be two *big* differences *for* minute ones, so that when *they* were added the result failed to be a minute difference. Let us consider one of these: it is supposed to be large for a minute difference. Let us consider as well a difference, the same in dimension and direction, that is only one *millionth* of *its* magnitude. This latter difference will not be a large one, even for a minute difference; it will be minute for a minute difference. But if it is minute for a minute difference, then so is one that is only two millionths the magnitude of the large minute difference, for the extra millionth cannot mean that we have gotten to a minute difference of some other sort. By stepwise reasoning, we may eventually conclude that our original minute difference, supposedly large for such a difference, is also minute for a minute difference. And, we may do as much for the large minute difference to which it might be added. Adding two such differences, each of which may thus be reckoned minute even for minute differences, cannot, then, yield a difference that is not minute.[14]

The idea of a substantial difference is relevantly on a par with that of a minute one. If a given difference is substantial, then so is one that is only minutely less. But however small we require a difference to be so that it fail to be substantial, we may eventually reach it. Thus, any such difference will be declared substantial, as well as not substantial.

The points we have made about 'minute' and 'substantial' can also be made about other pairs of similar terms, about 'small' and 'large', for example. Each member of such a pair will be a *quantitative* vague discriminative expression; one of them will purport to denote things whose magnitude is *less than* any to which the other can properly apply, the other to denote to opposite effect. Of course, a term may be quantitative in this sense and also be a purely qualitative expression in the sense we previously defined. In every case, I hypothesize, the inconsistency of vague discriminative expressions may be understood in terms of some such quantitative pair or pairs. When a pair is suitable for such understanding, we may call it an *underlying pair* for the expression in question. So, each typical vague expression has at least one such underlying pair.

In giving my conditions, in (1) and (2), for qualitative vague terms, I employed the term 'minute'. This was a measure in the direction of caution. For while a more common word like "small" appears suitable to underlie many such expressions, for which of course "minute" will also serve, there may be some for which only the latter term will prove adequate. It is worth noting, I think, that with many vague terms the sorites arguments that spell trouble can be quite short. For example, I think we regard a man of six-two as tall, but one of five-eleven as not a tall man. But half an inch will not mean the difference between a tall man and not. So, an explicit but quite short argument will yield no tall men at all. I suggest that this helpful shortness is due largely to the fact that 'small' is enough to underlie the first condition for 'tall man'. Consequently, 'minute' here gives us, with a longer argument, a luxury of caution.

---

14. This argument, adapted, shows that there is no genuine dyadic relation of *similarity*. For we can now show that if there is such a relation, then it must be transitive. But, also, quite clearly, if there is such a relation, then it is not transitive. Thus, despite intellectual appearances to the contrary, there is no real similarity relation. (The question of *respects*, and of *degrees*, of similarity changes nothing here.) This point first emerged for me in discussion with Vincent Tomas.

This groundless inconsistency, characteristic of vague discriminative terms, is not to be conflated with the fact that the noted stepwise reasoning exposes the inconsistency of the expressions in question. To clarify this point, we may invent expressions whose inconsistency is exposed in that stepwise manner, but that do not have the feature of groundless inconsistency. In one respect, that of having their inconsistency grounded in precise, consistent concepts, such expressions will be like 'perfectly square triangle'. In another, that associated with the stepwise reasoning, they will be unlike such an obviously inconsistent expression, and will be like our typical vague terms. Because of this latter likeness, such an invented term would, under suitable circumstances, prove useful to many normal people. Let me proceed to invent such a useful expression.

A *tinkergrid*, we might say, is something that one might endeavor to build out of the most typical items found in a tinkertoy set. These items are of two kinds: sticks and wheels. Now, the term 'stick', as well as 'wheel', is a vague discriminative one, and so it has groundless inconsistency. Thus, we do not want our invented 'tinkergrid' to be defined in terms of sticks and wheels, for then the invented term would also have groundless inconsistency. Let us better say, then, that what one would endeavor to build with a tinkertoy set would be, not a tinkergrid itself, but a physical realization of a tinkergrid. The tinkergrid itself would be a mathematical entity, composed of other mathematical entities, which are its *basic parts*: line segments of unit length, which one might use sticks to endeavor to realize, and nodes, where line segments can connect at right angles, for which a wheel might be used. The idea of a tinkergrid, then, is that of a certain mathematical structure. But, of course, there might be no more possibility of such a structure than of a structure that is a perfectly square triangle.

Now, to define the general conception of a tinkergrid, we begin with the more particular idea of a *paradigm tinkergrid*. A paradigm tinkergrid, we shall say, is in the form of a cube, with ten-unit line segments to each of its twelve edges; each edge, then, contains eleven nodes, two at its ends and nine internally. This tinkergrid is composed of a thousand unit cells, each in the form of a cube composed of twelve segments and eight nodes. The cells are arranged in such a way that they do not overlap, but are suitably adjacent, so that the whole tinkergrid is perfectly constituted of them: ten layers each with ten columns and ten rows of unit cells. It should appear clear how, using the standard tinkertoy items, one would try to realize a paradigm tinkergrid. So much for paradigm tinkergrids; what of those that are not paradigms?

As our definition is to have it, a paradigm tinkergrid is but one sort of tinkergrid; related to it are other sorts, which are all suitably related to each other. We shall not put this by means of any quantitive vague discriminative expression for that would involve 'tinkergrid' in groundless inconsistency, which we are to avoid. Thus, we do *not* have as a second clause of our definition any such conditional as this one: If something is a tinkergrid, then anything that differs from it by *a little bit* is also a tinkergrid. Rather, we shall put our second clause more suitably in some such terms as these: If something is a tinkergrid, then anything that differs from it by *the removal or addition of one or two basic parts* is also a tinkergrid.

While we thus move to avoid groundless inconsistency, we have not yet ensured any inconsistency at all for our invented term, but only a certain bizarreness. For without any further clause in our definition, our term allows a tinkergrid to have no basic parts at all. Such a "null tinkergrid" would be a most peculiar entity, of course; still, according to the definition's progress so far, there they will be. But insofar as null tinkergrids are claimed by our invented expression, and no claim is made in the opposite direction, 'tinkergrid' will be quite unlike most ordinary terms. To make it more like them, we add this last clause to our definition: Any tinkergrid is composed of a finite positive number of basic parts. Now, our invented expression will have it that there are no "null tinkergrids," and it will indeed be much more like our ordinary terms. For, with this last clause, we have ensured that our invented expression will be an inconsistent one.

The inconsistency of 'tinkergrid' may be exhibited as follows: First, a paradigm tinkergrid is a tinkergrid, indeed, one having a certain finite positive number of basic parts, say, N of them. But, then, so will be an entity that, may be obtained from it by the removal of one part, which will have N-1 basic parts. By stepwise reasoning, we must conclude that there will be a tinkergrid with N-N basic parts, that is, with none at all. But our expression also requires that any tinkergrid have some positive number of such parts. Thus, this last item, with no basic parts, both is a tinkergrid and also is not one.

While this invented term is thus inconsistent, I have little doubt that it could be easily learned and put to use by many normal people, in various suitable circumstances. In the first place, few would notice that there was any inconsistency here. Indeed, few would notice that, without the final clause, there would be null tinkergrids. Despite the term's having grounded inconsistency, most people would get the idea that a tinkergrid was available only at levels "well above" that where no basic parts remain. So little, then, will these ideas be related to our expression's meaning. And, perhaps more important, even once the inconsistency is pointed out, as we did here, the problem is shunted aside.

Insofar as I have been successful, 'tinkergrid', while inconsistent, has not been defined by using any discriminative vague term in an essential role. Accordingly, the inconsistency thus generated is not relevantly groundless; it is not like that observed with typical vague expressions. Like the inconsistency in 'square triangle', the inconsistency in 'tinkergrid' involves a clash between ideas that are each precise, consistent ones. But of the two, only 'tinkergrid' has grounded inconsistency of a sort that allows for a quite useful expression, potentially, as useful as typical vague ones.

5. Paradigms in Perspective

We began with a putative paradigm of a nacknick, imagined or real, with something that was to satisfy the expression. But as further imposed conditions determined matters, the beginning object could not possibly satisfy the invented term. For, as that expression was thus determined to be logically inconsistent, no object at all could satisfy it. By parity of reasoning, we have suggested that a logically similar situation holds for our ordinary vague discriminative expressions. Against this suggestion, one might try to strengthen the role of paradigms in the learning situations, not only as regards our ordinary expressions, but also as concerns such explicitly invented ones as 'nacknick'. The objection to our reasoning would then proceed along some such lines as these: When I instructed you that any object minutely differing from a nacknick (as regards shape) would also be a nacknick, what you really accepted, and had as a determinant of your new useful expression, was not quite what I instructed you. Instead, it was this rather similar sounding, but logically quite different, condition: If something is (not just any old nacknick, but) a *paradigm* nacknick, then any object differing from it minutely (in shape) is a nacknick. But, the objection continues, this "paradigmatic" condition, even in conjunction with other learned conditions for the term, causes no troublesome inconsistency. As this was the true situation even with 'nacknick', we may be quite confident that this sort of thing occurs with our typical vague inherited expressions. Consequently, the objection concludes, they may be satisfied by their paradigm cases, as well as by various other objects.[15]

---

15. This objection, or one much like it, was offered to me in conversation by Terence Leichti and also by David Lewis. What I go on to say about the matter is indebted to these helpful conversations.

A good deal later on, in Section 9, I shall discuss the question of "what you really got out of my instructions." And I shall there argue that whatever else you may have gotten, one thing you got was the vagueness condition, with no reference to paradigms, that I actually offered to you. And, so, I shall argue, that troublesome condition helped to determine 'nacknick' for you, whatever else may also have played such a determining role. If this is so, then your 'nacknick' will be an inconsistent expression, since you were given our other, discriminative condition for it. For once those two conditions govern a term, that term will be an inconsistent one, however many further conditions may also govern it. But for now, realizing that our recent objection may possibly be deficient in some such other respects as we have just indicated, let us focus only on the condition that it claims is so readily learned. Is this paradigmatic condition quite free from difficulties, and suitable for an objection to our account? I shall argue that, for at least three reasons, it is not: first, it is unlikely that we learn it (unlikelier still that we learn it without learning the simpler offered condition); second, it would involve us in inconsistency anyway, and, third, should the first two reasons be discounted, the condition would have our apparently vague terms be precise and not vague at all.

The first argument proceeds from the recognition that 'paradigm nacknick' will be just as much a vague discriminative term as 'nacknick' itself. Suppose that we have an alleged paradigm nacknick before us. After a while, even less than a second, the object loses some atoms, generally more than any it might have then gained. This will have various effects upon the object. As regards various dimensions, generally including that of shape, the object will be minutely different from the way it was. But despite these minute differences, we regard the object now before us as being a paradigm nacknick. Now, as relevant expressions with the word 'paradigm' will thus also be vague discriminative ones, the sort of condition that is to govern 'nacknick' must govern them as well. To deny this is to impose an entirely *ad hoc* restriction on the situation, and one which, we have just seen, runs counter even to common-sense judgments. So, we must now have this condition as well: if something is a paradigm *paradigm nacknick*, then any object that differs from it minutely (in shape) is a *paradigm nacknick*. But, of course, matters do not rest here, for the expression 'paradigm paradigm nacknick' is also a vague discriminative one. Thus, an infinite chain is established. Do we learn, with 'nacknick', such an infinity of governing conditions? I find the suggestion quite incredible.

On the view I am advocating, each of these infinite conditions does hold true. Indeed, in each case, a stronger condition holds true, from which one of these former may be deduced. For example, I advocate that this condition holds: If an object is a paradigm nacknick, then any object that differs from it minutely (in shape) is also a paradigm nacknick (and so, of course, it is a nacknick). But, on my view, a person, a small child, for example, can learn and understand one of the conditions without having to learn an infinity of them. On the objector's view, infinitely more learning must be done by such a person.

As an addendum to this first argument, we may note that, from an intuitive perspective, this objection gets things backward. The objection would have it that our understanding of 'nacknick', or 'stone', is dependent on that of 'paradigm nacknick', or 'paradigm stone'. But, intuitively, in ordinary situations, the contrary seems to hold. We first learn 'stone' and only then understand longer expressions of which it is a part, like 'expensive stone', 'poor example of a stone', or 'paradigm case of a stone'. Returning to our small child, we can believe that he might understand 'stone' without yet understanding any of these longer expressions. But he could not attach much significance to any of them without first understanding 'stone'.

A second argument is readily at hand should it be needed. Now, for the sake of argument, let us suppose that, for all we have just said, "paradigm nacknick" and its associated infinity may all be learned quite easily even by tiny tots. But even supposing this, we now have to confront the problem of groundless inconsistency. For it seems that if something is minutely different from a paradigm nacknick (in shape), then something which is, in that same direction, only a tiny, minute bit more different, will also be minutely different from the paradigm nacknick. But, by reasoning familiar from the previous section, we shall then have to conclude of any shaped object that it is minutely different from a paradigm nacknick. So, on our new paradigmatic condition, it must be a nacknick. But by our discriminative condition for 'nacknick', some such objects will not be nacknicks. So, our paradigmatic condition will not provide us with a consistent expression.

In reply to this, the objection might have it that a similar paradigmatic condition applies to our underlying quantitative vague expressions, for example, to 'minute'. But is there any plausibility to the idea that we have a paradigm of something minute? What would this putative paradigm be? But, perhaps, then, we should expand the quantitative expression that now is to have a paradigm. What is it to be: 'minutely different', 'minutely different from something as regards shape', 'minutely different from a paradigm nacknick as regards shape', or what? The choice seems hopeless. For there seems no paradigm that we have for *any* of these expressions. Moreover, the expressions that have 'nacknick' as a component seem to get ordinary learning the wrong way round, as before, while those that lack such a component seem too general to have much bearing on the case at hand.

Even if both of the previous two arguments are discounted, and we presume that our paradigmatic condition is both easily learned and also results in no inconsistency, that condition would not seem to serve the purposes for which it was introduced. For, as a third argument shows, the condition would then have it that our apparently vague expressions were actually precise ones, and so not vague at all: We begin by remembering, from Section 3, our truism that a given expression either applies to a certain object or does not apply. This will hold true for 'paradigm nacknick'. Thus, this expression will apply to just those cases in a perfectly definite range, and to any others it will not apply. So, 'paradigm nacknick' will be a precise expression. By the same reason, 'minutely different in shape from a paradigm nacknick' will also be a precise expression. So, both indirectly and also quite directly, we may reason that precisely the same will hold for the simpler 'nacknick' itself: it will be a precise expression and, as such, not a vague one. So, contrary to all appearances, 'nacknick', as well as 'stone', will be absolutely precise, and thus will not be vague at all. This final failure of our paradigmatic condition suggests a thought whose importance goes beyond our interest in rebutting objections to our account. The only way for our apparently vague terms to be vague is for them to be inconsistent. Were they not inconsistent, they should have to be precise, which they are not.

6. Sorites Arguments, Counterfactual Reasoning, and Obscure Dimensions

The stepwise reasoning we have recently gone through, to exhibit the inconsistency in our invented expressions, 'nacknick' and 'tinkergrid', is hardly new to philosophical discussion. Such reasoning is characteristic of *sorites arguments*, which, following the classical case of the alleged heap, or *soros*, seek to show that certain entities, ordinarily alleged to exist, in fact do not. In Section 2, we encountered one such argument, against the existence of tall men. That argument, following tradition, was exhibited in a highly realistic form. With normal suppositions in force, the instances in the sequence over which reasoning ranged were all to be found in the actual world. The realism was available for us, we might say, because of the *relevantly gradual* nature of the actual world. This gradualness, and the attendant realism, is in one way all to the good: It makes sorites arguments hard to dismiss, if not to ignore, by

serious thinkers who encounter them. But in another way, I think, a con-
centration on realistic examples can be unfortunate: it can blind us to the
conceptual basis of the arguments. So, to help illuminate this basis, let us
engage in some suitably counterfactual reasoning.[16] The appropriate
reasoning, as will shortly appear, is more thoroughly counterfactual, or
hypothetical, than that usually encountered in philosophy, as well as
in everyday thinking. It requires us to imagine people living in a world
different from ours who are themselves imagining a world different from
theirs, in particular, a world just like ours. In a way, then, we might think
of this reasoning as doubly counterfactual. But I cannot see that the extra
imagination involved causes any serious difficulties.

Suppose, then, that according to some law of nature, all of the men
who ever lived, and who ever will, were either exactly ten feet in height
or else nine feet, and that they were aware of their heights. Now, let us
suppose as well that, even with this knowledge, these men had the same
expression 'tall man' as we now do, complete with the same meaning;
they might even speak English, or an exact counterpart. Supposing this,
it would be common for them to judge that all men were tall men. And,
supposing them to be aware of the law governing their heights, they
would judge further that all men would always be tall men, as indeed, in
a sense, they must. These men could *imagine* a man of five feet six, of
course, just as we can imagine one of six inches. But for them, such men
would be only imaginary.

Could a philosopher among them, who wanted to construct a sorites
against the existence of tall men, develop an effective sorites? It seems
clear to me that he could do as well as we now can. It is just that his arguments, by our previous suppositions, would be conducted in a counterfactual manner. The philosopher would bid his fellows to consider a
world just like ours in fact is, where the distribution of actual heights
would thus be greatly increased in number and also shifted downward.
They would agree that a man of six feet six *would still be* tall, but a man of
five feet six *would not be*. Our philosopher would then have available a
principle, in counterfactual form, corresponding to our first condition
for qualitative vagueness: If a man of a certain height *would be* a tall man,
then so too *would be* a man whose height *would be* no more than a
thousandth of an inch less. Thus, our philosopher could conclude that
if there *are* any tall men, then a man of five feet six *would be* a tall man
and also would not be one. Since he now could reason that there really are

---

16. For impressing upon me the importance of counterfactual reasoning in relation
to sorites arguments, I am indebted to discussion with David Lewis.

not any tall men in the first place, our philosopher would have constructed an effective sorites against tall men, though he employed counterfactual reasoning in the process. Thus, we have supported the idea that a sorites argument against tall men is essentially a conceptual argument, which fits in so well with our account of vague discriminative expressions.

Just as our account of vague expressions has it, our counterfactual sorites against tall men served to indicate that 'tall man' is inconsistent. Its inconsistency is generated by our two conditions for qualitative vague terms. The second condition says that an expression of that sort will purport to distinguish, with respect to *at least one* relevant dimension of difference, those entities that satisfy it from those that do not. This condition, being quite general, does not specify or characterize the dimensions to be involved. It is up to us in any particular case to pick out a relevant dimension, as a basis for our stepwise reasoning, or else to conduct that reasoning in such a way that, we can be confident, it will cover at least one such dimension. In the case of 'tall man', our understanding of the expression allows us to be confident that height is relevant. With 'stone', as already indicated, no such relevant dimension is ready to be so clearly specified: Size itself is not crucial. If you pour an Alice-in-Wonderland potion on a stone, it will get much smaller, but will still be a stone (if one before). Perhaps, 'size in relation to structure' is more like it, but I cannot say exactly what that means, much less how it is to be treated as a dimension of difference. But we may build confidence, nevertheless, that 'stone' is a logically inconsistent expression.

Toward this end, we may look for a variation or gradation in things that will have associated with it a relevant gradation in at least one dimension that plays a discriminative role with 'stone'. Our actual world, with its considerable divisibility of "material complexes" suggests to us a suitable procedure. By removing a single peripheral atom gently from an alleged stone, and then tossing it randomly away, one will progressively produce a sequence of entities, going down to a single atom, whose properties, with regard to a relevant dimension, will vary quite gradually. With this procedure, we remain quite in the dark as to *what* dimensions of difference (are supposed to) form the basis of our term's discriminations. But whatever ones they may be, we can be confident that at least one is covered by a sequence of entities, many millions in number, obtained in this systematic manner. Let us construct, then, a suitable *sorites of decomposition by minute removals*.

By having relevant properties vary gradually with our minute removals, nature conspires to suggest to us an effective sorites against stones, in a rather realistic form. For it is easy to find acceptable each of these two conditional propositions, at least as true in fact:

(i)   For anything there may be, if it is a stone, then the net removal from it of a single atom, in a way most preservative of there being a stone in the situation, will not mean the difference as to whether or not there is at least one stone in the situation.

(ii) For anything there may be, if it is a stone, then it consists of more than a hundred atoms but of a finite number of them. These two premises, we may notice, will yield us a contradiction from the rather common-sensical assertion

There is at least one stone.

For, consider any plausible candidate for stonehood: That entity will consist of a finite number of atoms, say N, where N is greater than one hundred. That is assured us by our second premise. But, by our first premise we are told that by taking away an atom, we shall still have a stone, now one with N-1 atoms. According to that same premise, then, by stepwise reasoning, we shall have a stone even when what is before us is only an object consisting of ten atoms, or, indeed, even when we have no atoms at all. But this contradicts what (ii) tells us: as there are not more than a hundred atoms there, there is no stone in the situation.

Now, it is, of course, not part of the meaning of 'stone' that any stone should consist of atoms, let alone more than a hundred but some finite number of them. Indeed, so far as I can discern, it is not even required by our term that any portion of a stone should be physically removable from the remainder. Further, providing that some is thus removable, and even removed, there's nothing in 'stone' which says that the rest will not suddenly vanish, or suddenly serve to constitute something utterly different, for example, an exotic plant. That none of these things happen, and that our argument proceed in way of a gradual sequence of suitable entities is, we might say, wholly a matter of worldly, contingent fact. But as presented, our sorites against stones might seem to depend on these suppositions. This appearance is easily dispelled, however. For we may combine the idea of counterfactual reasoning, previously discussed, with the systematic procedure used for obscure dimensions just developed. Without going into much detail, we may imagine a philosopher, with our same language, living in a very different world from ours, where his alleged stones cannot be decomposed. But, if he were imaginative enough, he could contemplate a world just like ours, where stones can be appropriately picked apart. If his world contained stones, then so too would ours, he could reason. Then he could show himself that ours would not and, thus, none anywhere.

We are next to pass to a direct discussion of 'person', and of putative people. Pursuing the ideas so far developed, we shall argue that the expression cannot be satisfied, and that there really are no such entities as people. Before we do so, I should note briefly that many objections have been raised against sorites arguments, even against what might be regarded as the most realistic sort. While I think there is little merit in any of these objections, it is not a main purpose of mine here to meet them. To the extent that my present account is well argued, of course, that provides some support for sorites arguments. Thus, indirectly, the account gives a reply to all objections to these reasonings. But I leave to other places the matter of detailed responses to particular objections.[17]

To give you an idea, however, of what one must accept if one is to reject sorites arguments, I shall just mention two points that I discuss elsewhere.[18] First, to reject our sorites against stones, we must accept this: there will be certain stones, composed of many billions of atoms, whose continued existence, with no atoms replaced, requires every single one of these billions! Can you believe that there are ever any stones whose essence is as refined and tenuous as that? A second thought, on the side of language, mirrors the first: Consider the sentence, "There is a stone before me now," and discount all problems of vagueness except those most directly concerned with 'stone'. With a promising candidate for stonehood before you, imagine peripheral atoms extracted in the style of our sorites. We are to evaluate the sentence after each net removal. We suppose the sentence at first to express a genuine statement that is true. But can a single atomic removal alter the proper evaluation? To suppose it can requires us to suppose an enormous sensitivity on the part of our word 'stone'. This, I suggest, is quite incredible.

7. The Inconsistency of 'Person'

It is now time to extend the results so far obtained to the key expression 'person'. I shall argue that this term is a qualitative vague discriminative

---

17. See three recent papers of mine: "I Do Not Exist," in *Epistemology in Perspective*, ed. Graham Macdonald (London, forthcoming), which is the festschrift for Professor Sir A. J. Ayer; "There Are No Ordinary Things," *Synthese*, forthcoming: "Skepticism and Nihilism," *Nous*, forthcoming.

18. See the three papers cited in the just previous note.

term and, as such, it is inconsistent. Accordingly, as nothing then satisfies the expression, anymore than anything satisfies 'perfectly square triangle', there are no people. Like perfectly square triangles, people are logically impossible entities.

Should we arrive at such a negative result for people, a paradoxical situation will arise. Briefly, if there is not anybody, then there is no one to understand these alleged accounts, arguments, and conclusions to that effect. So, perhaps, these last may themselves be negated or dismissed as "self-defeating." But, if our account is otherwise unobjectionable, we may then employ it again, to complete a paradoxical circle and begin a new one. Now, in the section directly to follow this one, I shall argue that this admitted paradox cannot seriously nullify our nihilistic account. But, first, in this present section, I shall argue that the paradoxical situation cannot be avoided. I shall argue, that is, that our account of vague expressions cannot be brought to rest at some relatively unproblematic stopping point.

The expression 'person' is a vague discriminative term and, as such, an inconsistent expression. To support this thought, suitable sorites arguments shall be sought. Now, as with 'stone', I have no very good idea how to specify adequately those dimensions of difference with respect to which 'person' purports to make discriminations. It is not that I have nothing at all to say on the matter: Perhaps, power of thought, or intelligence, provides one such dimension; perhaps capacity for varied feelings and experiences provides one. But I should prefer to regard these proposals as primarily illustrative, and to construct our sorites arguments on the basis of ideas in which I have more confidence. Toward this end, we recall our experience with 'stone', for we had success there by adopting a procedure that required no specification of dimensions. So, let us look for a sorites of decomposition by minute removals that will work well for 'person'. We may best begin in a moderately realistic vein. Then we can move to the utterly fantastic, so that the conceptual nature of the arguments may be more clearly perceived.

In our common thinking on the matter, though this was not always so, it is supposed that there are some people, if not all, who are composed of many cells, though of a finite number. We distinguish, of course, between a person and his body. But, then, while we think the body to be of a certain weight, and to be composed of such cells, we *also* think the person himself to be. Now, some people, I suppose, do not go along with this idea and think that, whatever might be true of the body, the person himself never consists of any cells, or of any other spatially extended things. But even these people, I imagine, will agree that, in the case of many people, each of whom has a body, there is a certain *close association*, or *intimate relation*, whatever its specific character, between each of these people and his or her respective body. (That intimate relation, for all I am saying, *might* be that of identity.) And, no doubt, they will also agree that there is a close relation, perhaps another one, between each of these people and those cells serving to compose his or her body. So, all of us may agree that if there are any people at all, then some of them, at least, are in a close association with certain cells, or with certain groups or complexes of cells, and that each such suitable group, while containing more than ten cells, has only a finite number of cells in it.

Now, I think that another thing we agree on is this: that if there is a person in a situation, and that person is in some such aforesaid close relation with a certain group of cells, then, if only one cell is removed from the group, and this is done in a *way most conducive* to there being a person in such a close relation with the remaining cells, then there will be a person in the situation after the removal. In certain instances, of course, this *way* will have to include the importation into the situation of certain life-support apparatus, and of certain items for supporting consciousness. For matters with people seem more complex than with stones, however unreal all of these may eventually prove to be. We may say, then, that whatever substances or properties are *supported by* some cells, so that a person is there in close association, they will also be supported, and in sufficient degree, with only one cell less, providing, of course, that the lesser complex is so chosen, and so allowed to function, that it can do as good a job at such supporting as is possible for a group obtained by such a slight removal. Of course, in the cases to be considered, the imported material does *not* replace cells; rather like a kidney machine, it just helps cells, and what they serve to constitute, to function.

These shared suppositions yield a sorites argument to the effect that there are no people at all. For, if any person is closely associated with a certain group of cells, say, N in number, so will one be there with a group of N-1 cells. I suppose that, as matters progress, we shall get down to a brain, in a vat, then half a brain, then a third, and then a sixteenth. In each case, we must say, there is a person in the situation, one who is in a special close association with the remaining cells. Eventually, there are but three living cells in some sort of combination, and it must be said that there is a person there. But we have also agreed that, with no more than ten cells, there will be no such associated person. Thus, supposing there to be a person at the start, there both is and is not a person in close association with our three cells. Of course, this argues that there never are any people in close association with any groups of cells. So, finally, we may conclude, there really are not any people at all.

With an appropriately realistic argument before us, it is now time to reason counterfactually, so as to see the conceptual basis of the idea that there are no people. Let us imagine a world in which there are entities that we should consider persons, and that consider themselves as such. We shall suppose that these putative people have a language just like ours. They are a bit more intelligent than we, but their powers of imagination far exceed our own. Their greatest differences from us, however, are these: unlike us, these people have no physical existence; they have no bodies nor are they in any very close relation with any physical phenomena. Further, as a matter of imagined fact, they are neither divisible, diminishable, nor even susceptible of any major change. Each of them has always existed and always will exist, and always is at or near the peak of his sensibilities and powers. So, these beings are, I suppose, quite as some philosophers have supposed ourselves really to be. Finally, let us suppose that there are no other sentient beings in this world.

Consider a critical philosopher among them. How might he convince himself that his term 'person', which is the same as our expression, is a logically inconsistent term? Now, he has no relevant gradations in reality to help him base a sorites argument. And, we suppose, it is not clear to him either how to specify the dimensions of difference with respect to which 'person' purports to discriminate. Now, what this reasoner should do is try to supply himself with a sequence of imagined entities that differed gradually with regards to at least one such relevant dimension. While by our poor standards it would take a great feat of imagination, how better for him to do this than to imagine a world just like ours is (supposed to be) in fact? In this world, thus imagined by him, whatever features were relevant would be supported by brains, each of which was composed of billions of cells.

Our philosopher, in particular, might imagine someone exactly like you yourself; living, kicking, breathing, and thinking, if anyone ever does, in just such a world as you now find yourself to be. He would think to himself, we may suppose, first, that if *anyone is* a person, then this being like you *would be* a person, for that is our same word, 'person', that is figuring in his premising. What more would that free spirit endeavor to think? Well, we might imagine, he could say to himself that, under the total circumstances imagined, if there is indeed a person just like you, then so too will there by a person when a single cell is removed, most conducively for the continued support of a person, from those that may have supported the original candidate. Far better than we can do, he could imagine in detail the importation of those life-support and consciousness-support systems involved in a most conducive way, so as to establish a suitable sequence of entities. Of course, he can imagine this while starting, not only with an imagined counterpart of you, but with that of any of a great variety of the putative people we suppose to populate our world. For our world, in general, he could then prem-ise that a single cell removed, in such a circumstance and manner, will never mean the difference between at least one person being in the situation and there being none. For he could reason that, in such a world, no one cell will mean a difference, on the dimensions in question, to which 'person' is sensitive. Further, our thinker could say that, in this world, when there were no more than ten cells in a relevant group or complex, then there *would be* no person in the situation. From these premises, by familiar stepwise reasoning, our philsopher would now conclude that if a being like yourself would be a person, then, with ten cells supporting at their best and utmost, there *both would be a person in close association and also would not be.* Thus, he should conclude that the being first imagined, the one just like you yourself, was never any person in the first place. And, finally, by his very first premise, he could now reason that there were not, or are not, any people at all. Thus, without any reality to help him, our imagined philosopher could see for himself that there could never be any people, even while having no clear idea how to specify what dimensions of difference served to determine the impossibility thus perceived.

I have made my imagined philosopher a most pristine soul, a being whose "nature in itself" would seem immune to sorites arguments. Moreover, if he appreciated his nature, that awareness would do noth-ing to suggest our word 'person'. But so long as this being does share our expression, he may reason to expose its inconsistency and, thus, its lack of application. To make these points, I made my imagined philosopher as described.

There is another reason, too, for my giving this being such a logi-cally unobjectionable nature. For philosophers have sometimes sug-gested that our own natures are much as I have stipulated his to be and, what is perhaps more interesting here, even that our term 'person' analytically requires such a nature for its application. Now, let us sup-pose that any being with such a nature as that cannot be dimensionally compared with, or related to, any other being. With these suppositions in force, we may advance, for 'person', a condition of *incomparability*:

(3p)   if an entity satisfies 'person', then there is no dimension of difference such that with regard to it there are entities which differ from that putative satisfier.

According to this condition, there will be no entities that thus differ minutely, or substantially, from a satisfier. So, one might well think that were such a condition to hold for 'person', but perhaps not for 'stone', then, unlike 'stone', 'person' might be a perfectly consistent term after all.[19]

But this supposition of consistency for 'person' would be much mistaken. For as our sorites arguments indicate, 'person' is a vague discriminative expression and, whatever else may be true of it, the term is governed by (1) and (2), our dimensional conditions of vagueness and of discriminativeness. So long as these conditions do govern it, which we have seen no good reason to deny, the expression will be inconsistent. Whatever further conditions may govern it as well cannot erase the two for which we have argued or, then, the contradictions that they serve to generate. This incomparability condition, if there be one governing 'person', will not make matters better for the term. On the contrary, it will serve only to compound the term's troubles. For taken together with either of our prior two conditions for 'person', the incomparability condition, (3p), yields a contradiction from the supposition that any entity satisfies the term. For, by either of the prior two, if there is a person, then there *are* entities that differ *dimensionally* from any satisfier. And, by our new condition, if there is a person, then there are *no* such entities. Hence, if there is a person, then there both are and also are not such dimensionally differing entities, which is absurd. Hence, by (1) and (3p), and also by (2) and (3p), there are no people. Supposing an incomparability condition for 'person', we should say, not that it is a consistent term, but, on the contrary, that 'person' is *inconsistent from multiple sources.*

The inconsistency of 'person' means that no people exist; they can exist no more than can perfectly square triangles. Do I exist, then, but am no person after all? Things would seem otherwise: If I exist, then there is at least one person. So, as there are none, there is no me. This result, paradoxical to say the least, can be obtained as well by sorites arguments where there is a purported direct reference to myself, by means, for example, of such terms as 'I', 'Peter Unger', and so on. The most imaginative of our counterfactual sorites arguments might be out of place with these terms, or at least might have a rather different bearing on the issues. Our more realistic versions, however, will have obviously close parallel arguments. Take away one peripheral cell from

---

19. For discussion regarding an incomparability condition for 'person', I am indebted to James Van Cleve.

Peter Unger, with suitable life-support systems in place, and that will not mean the difference between Unger and no Unger. But, with ten cells there is no Unger. So, there never was that Unger.

The analysis of, or the account of, even the most realistic arguments with such singular terms will require, of course, the presentation of conditions that logically govern the key singular expressions. No doubt, these conditions will be importantly analogous to those given here for qualitative vague terms; perhaps our suggestions for such terms as 'door' will be of some help. But these analytical questions take us beyond our topic.

More to the present point, 'person' is hardly the only qualitative vague expression whose inconsistency means much difficulty for us here. For example, the expression 'entity with a capacity for thought' means similar troubles for us, however that expression may relate to 'person'. For the arguments that point up the inconsistency in 'person' will do as much for this longer expression. Moreover, as this expression is of the purely qualitative sort, even the supporting account of the arguments will be along the same familiar lines. Thus, for quite familiar reasons, it may be concluded that there are no entities with a capacity for thought. As with thought, no capacity for experience could be ours, nor for feeling, nor for anything of importance. As regards each of these negative matters, we have, paradoxically enough, not only adequate arguments, but accounts of how those arguments work adequately. For the key expressions involved are, in each case, vague discriminative terms of the purely qualitative sort.

8. The Inability of Paradox to Nullify This Account

Paradox, already indicated, can easily be made manifest: if there are no beings with any capacity for thought, then no argument or statement can be understood, or accepted at all, and so none to the effect that there are no such beings. So it seems that we are driven back logically to the assertion of our existence, of the existence of beings that can think. Thus, there is next the implication that our expressions 'person' and 'thinking being' do indeed apply. And so, finally, we have the implication that these terms are logically consistent ones. But things do not really stop here, either. For, along lines that are by now familiar, we may in turn reduce these assertions to absurdity. Thus, their negations obtain, including the proposition that there are no beings with any capacity for thought. The reasoning goes around and around. What are we to make of this paradoxical situation? Should we hold onto common sense robustly and say that the only genuine errors are in our account of vagueness and in its connecting sorites arguments? Following this course, we might better try to be comfortable. For then thoughts of absurdity will be harder to keep in mind. But perhaps, "so to try to say," paradox does little to nullify the basic point and value of our radical account and arguments.

In available terms, for want of any better, I have argued that many of our common expressions are logically inconsistent terms, including such key expressions as 'person' and 'entity with a capacity for thought'. Much of my argument began with the invention of a term, 'nacknick', for which inconsistent instructions were given in its very introduction. Then, as our sorites arguments progressively indicated, there appeared no logically relevant difference between 'nacknick' and such common expressions as 'stone' and even 'person'. To be sure, the latter terms are not learned from any explicit instructions at all. But there is still a parity of inconsistency, or at least a very strong suggestion of it, that supports my account of the ordinary terms as logically inconsistent. Despite whatever paradoxes our account may engender, then, how can this apparent parity be rationally denied?

To deny the shared inconsistency, one cannot rationally rely on pointing to paradox. For, let us consider the implications of our lessons with 'nacknick'. Now, as this term concerns only the shape of objects, it is idle to suppose that it might yield the sort of paradox that an expression like 'thinking being' was recently observed to do. What is less idle, however, is to imagine that inconsistent instructions were, at a suitable point, *imposed upon* the learning of such terms as 'person' and 'thinking being'. Let us imagine, then, a society much like ours, with this exception: *After normal early learning had occurred,* explicit inconsistent instructions were given to the moderately young. Thus, children would hear words like these: "Typical vague words that you have learned, like 'stone' and 'person', will now be more clearly revealed to you. To begin with, each of you should know that each of these words serves to discriminate, or distinguish, different sorts of things. So, the word 'stone' distinguishes between the stones and everything else, which differ so from stones that they do not fit the meaning of the word. Of course, this word is a vague one, and you should know this about it too: if something is a stone, and so fits the word 'stone' properly, then anything that differs from it only a little bit will also fit the word, that is, will also be a stone. To be sure, there is no definite limit as to how much something may differ from a stone and for it yet to be a stone. All of this, you are to understand, is part of what it is for the word 'stone' to be a vague word while still allowing us to make useful discriminations with it. And, of course, these points apply just as well to other typical vague words, for example, to such words as 'house', 'person', 'red', 'soft', 'tall', 'running', 'thinking', and so on. Now, none of this should come as a surprise to any of you; in fact, in a way, you have known it already. But it is just as well for us to be explicit about these things, for us to have them out in the open."

What results would such instructions have if they were often involved in teaching routines? As the people in this society are to be much like ourselves, it must be supposed that they will master what they are thus taught, should much training be imposed. Later in life, even, should someone manage to claim some such word to be precise, the people will appeal to the teachings, which they could recite with little distortion. Thus, if someone said that a stone could not be less than one inch in diameter, but that it could be less than one and one millionths inches, he would be accused of violating the meaning of 'stone' just as we should accuse him. Unlike us, however, the people in this other society, to support the charge that such a claim of precision is in way of being an arbitrary stipulation, would appeal to the explicit, repeated teaching routines. They would appear to be in a quite obviously good position, then, to claim that there is indeed a stipulation here and, moreover, one which conflicts with the learned, accepted meaning of the word.

Now, let us suppose that, just as I am doing for our own words, a philosopher in this society puts forward the idea that typical vague terms are inconsistent. This is hardly an arbitrary supposition now, given what we have already imagined. For if I have supposed as much with no such explicit teaching to suggest the thought to me, how much easier it will be for a thinker who is amidst so much apparent inconsistency. Focusing on the teaching, he would point out the inconsistency in the instructions. Now, in that society, since the people are assumed to be much like us, there would be thinkers of a rather conservative bent, who would wish to cleave to the accepted thinking of their culture. How should these conservatives defend that thinking; how should they rationally reply to the nihilistic critic?

Whatever replies may be open to them, it seems to me that *among the least effective* of these would be an appeal to comprehensive paradox. True enough, if such expressions as their 'person' and 'thinking being' are logically inconsistent, as the explicit instructions for them indicate, then they would have to conclude that no one could accept, or even understand, the critic's arguments. But if the matter were allowed to rest there, or even if the burden of argument were thought to be substantially shifted, those conservative thinkers would display terribly little philosophical sense, and virtually no depth of thought or understanding. Generally, we may note that any thoroughgoing radical critique of a language, or a system of thought, conducted in the terms or concepts of what is criticized, must, of course, have this paradoxical quality. But this does not mean that such a criticism cannot be, so to try to say, appropriate to its object. In the society now under consideration, whatever most of its members may think on the matter, such a criticism will be quite appropriate indeed.

Now, it seems clear to me that the situation is not relevantly different in our own case. It is, of course, true that things are not exactly the same with us, for we have had no explicit instructions for our typical vague terms, much less have we any that are inconsistent. But, as our arguments have indicated, what our imagined society's members will have learned explicitly we seem to have learned implicitly. The logic of our expressions is not at variance with theirs. So, it is most unlikely, I submit, that pointing to paradox will be futile against their radical critic but rational against a critic in our less explicit society. As it will not be rational there, so it is not rational here. Pointing to paradox, then, does little or nothing to nullify these present efforts.

The point that paradox cannot nullify our account will stand just as well should we agree that, in addition to the paradoxical situation already noted, various other, perhaps deeper, paradoxes are consequences of our account. For example, it might be held that if there are no entities with any capacity to think, or to use language, then there will be no sentences, or any other expressions. And, it might be held that if there are none of these latter, then there are no statements or propositions, no arguments or accounts of any sort, and not just none that are ever understood or accepted. If this may be maintained, then fuller, or more direct, paradoxes can be added to our account's consequences. But, as our discussion has already indicated amply, this will do little to worsen matters for us. For, *whatever* paradoxes our account should engender will all be rationally treated alike. They all will best be taken, it seems clear, as showing the comprehensiveness of our radical account, rather than its futility.

9. A Reexamination of Our Argument from Invented Expressions

Our account of vague expressions has been provided. It has given support to our Argument from Invented Expressions, support which will not be nullified by any charges of paradox. If we are to maintain common sense still, and hold that there really are people, we must object to one of the premises of that Argument, though few courses for such an objection appear still to be available. To take last things first, there is little to be said against the Argument's final premise:

> (III) If the expression 'person' is logically inconsistent, then there are no people.

For a denial of it, as I have argued in Section 1, will rest only upon a confusion. So, objections must come against its first two premises, for the Argument's form is not faulty. At the outset of our reexamination of them, we note that at this point these premises look well supported. So, now, I suggest, the burden of argument is on any attempted objection. Can this burden be shouldered effectively?

Let us reexamine our second premise, in an attempt to review matters back to our beginning:

> (II) The expression 'person' is logically on a par with 'nacknick'; if the latter is inconsistent, then so is the former.

So far as we have been able to discern, from our early experiments onward, there is indeed this logical parity. If the matter is just an empirical, or contingent, or causal one, to be decided primarily by experiment and observation, then parity seems surely right. For only the most tortuous and forced interpretation of our recent experiments and observations would have things be otherwise. For an objection to (II) to be at all plausible, then, it must be maintained that it is for some conceptual or logical reasons that there is a disparity between our invented expression and our ordinary one. Now, we have already argued that, whatever else may be true of it, 'person' is a qualitative vague discriminative term. As such, it is logically on a par with such other, less central common expressions as 'stone', 'tall man,' and 'cubical object'. So, in effect, what the objection must claim is that there is a logical barrier to a parallel between 'nacknick' and 'cubical object', and even 'object whose shape is quite similar to that of a cube'. But how might the claim of such a logical barrier be rationally supported?

The support required would have to come in the form of 'logical' truths, which would logically yield the statement of no logical parity. But anything that might be even plausibly considered a logical truth appears quite inadequate to provide the needed deduction. Here is an example of the problem, with a candidate for relevant logical truth that is much better than most I have examined: One must understand an invented expression, if one understands it at all, in terms of a set of expressions (each of which is not invented and) each of which is consistent. While it might later be doubted, let us now grant that, in a relevant sense, this is indeed a logical truth. But, even so, of what use will it be in deriving logical disparity between invented and ordinary vague expressions?

We have already encountered an invented expression which, if any ordinary term satisfies this offered condition, quite nicely meets the alleged requirement. That expression is 'tinkergrid', which I introduced and discussed in Section 4. Discounting any minor lapse, I showed there that, unlike both ordinary vague terms and also the invented 'nacknick', the invented 'tinkergrid', while it was indeed inconsistent, had inconsistency which was relevantly grounded. What seemed to hold only between 'nacknick' and the ordinary terms, none of which appear to satisfy our offered requirement, was the *further* parallel of having *groundless* inconsistency. So, even if we grant the offered requirement, the most it could logically yield, it should be clear, is that ordinary vague expressions will differ from 'nacknick' as regards the source or nature of whatever inconsistency they might have. The parity we are concerned with, however, concerns whether, like both 'nacknick' and also 'tinkergrid', typical vague expressions are, in any way, and from whatever source, logically inconsistent. As regards the required disparity, then, the offered requirement, even if logically true, is powerless to yield any result.

While our reconsideration of 'tinkergrid' has shown the offered requirement to be irrelevant, it suggests as well great doubt as to its truth. It seems incredible to suppose that we might have invented a term like 'tinkergrid' to parallel our ordinary vague terms but failed with 'nacknick'. For of the two useful, inconsistent inventions, it is the latter that seems to provide the closer parallel here. So, our problems compound: to have a (logical) truth presented in the first place, we are constrained to weaken our alleged requirement. Perhaps the following has a decent chance for truth: One must understand an invented expression, if at all, in terms of a set of expressions (each of which is not invented and) at least some of which are consistent terms. But, now, we have available to yield contradiction, in addition to the clashes between consistent ideas that 'tinkergrid' displayed, the inconsistency in various vague expressions (which are not invented).

The experience we have just suffered is typical of what I have encountered in my examination of objections to (II), the second premise of our Argument. The more an offered proposition looks like it might be a logical truth, and so suitable for a counterargument in that respect, the less it looks relevant to yielding the required deduction of disparity. No candidate, then, of which I am aware, looks very promising, and no suitable counterargument appears forthcoming. While these matters must, perhaps, always be somewhat inconclusive, it thus seems to me that there is no good objection to the apparent logical parity between the invented and ordinary expressions.

There is only one place left for an objection to be effective against our Argument, namely, in the place of our first premise:

(I)   The invented expression 'nacknick' is logically inconsistent.

This question brings us back to the beginning of our essay. Could we have misinterpreted our little learning experiments, so that the apparently obvious and rational interpretation was really out of place all along? As with (II), if the matter is essentially an empirical, or contingent one, there would be little chance indeed that we have been misinterpreting things, and that some ingenious complicated hypothesis must be preferred. Thus, the objection must be that there is some logical barrier to the truth of our first premise. But how might it be argued that we have been laboring under such an intellectual illusion?

The occurrence of a definite description at the head of our premise, "the invented expression 'nacknick'," may trigger the response that there may in fact never have been any such invented expression. If so, then this premise will fail of truth, whatever other status should then be accorded it. Now, it is clearly no good to deny the thought that if there is any expression 'nacknick', then it is an invented term. But it will also do no good to challenge the premise on the ground that there is no expression 'nacknick' at all. For anything which will serve to argue that much, it appears, will undermine as well the idea that there are ordinary vague expressions, including 'cubical object' and 'person'. The paradoxical consequences of our own account, for example, can be used to this effect against the premise; but they will undermine as well any typical vague expression, including 'person'. So, this is no good way to challenge our premise, as it gets rid of the baby along with the bath water. Similar maneuvers will prove to no better critical effect. For example, it is no good to find 'nacknick' an expression but a meaningless one, for how should 'cubical object' and 'person' then prove meaningful? The only plausible manner of objection, then, will allow 'nacknick' as an expression that either is consistent or else inconsistent.

It remains to object, of course, that this invented expression cannot possibly be, in any sense that it might have, an inconsistent expression. It appears that the teacher, at least, has an understanding of such an inconsistent term, but this appearance, the objection continues, must be an intellectual illusion. How might this be cogently maintained?

I suspect that an idea which might motivate this objection is the by now old one that meaning is use, or is a function of use, though perhaps in one of that idea's newer guises or forms. But, in whatever form, this idea looks quite unrealistic. Even when we consider terms that are not vague, and which may be allowed as consistent, there seems little value in this approach. Consider a surface. With certain purposes in mind, someone may say "This is flat," his idea being that the surface is suitable for those purposes. Weeks later, he may return with other purposes, and say of the same surface "This is not flat," and then turning to another surface may say of it "That one is flat." But, we may suppose, the original surface did not become any less flat, and even may have been somewhat improved in that respect. Weeks later still, with a third set of purposes, the same individual may declare the second surface to be not flat, now declaring a third surface to be a flat one. And, so it may go, half a dozen times or more. How is this most plausibly to be accounted? Surely, the meaning of the words did not relevantly change. And, just as surely, the meaning of 'flat' does not concern anyone's purposes. The realistic explanation, I suggest, involves supposing that *none* of the surfaces here *ever are flat*, and that while actually speaking falsely, the man is informally implying in each case something like this: The currently indicated surface is sufficiently close to being (absolutely) flat so as to be suitable for the purposes the speaker and hearer now have in mind.[20]

If even apparently consistent terms are best accounted by thus distinguishing meaning and semantic application from the uses to which the words are put, at least as much should be expected where the terms appear to be inconsistent expressions. I think we may do well now to consider once again our invented term 'tinkergrid'. This is a term that is to apply only to certain abstract, mathematical objects. To say of a wooden structure that it is a tinkergrid is, just for this reason, a plain failure to speak the truth. If use is to match with truth and meaning here, it will have to come from quarters much further removed from directly observable behaviors and stimuli. Perhaps we might ask various people to try to imagine tinkergrids. Various people, perhaps unaware of any inconsistency, will frequently allege success. They are using the term to describe what they imagine. But, I think we may agree that they can be imagining no such thing, and that a literally accurate description of what they imagine can be given only in some other terms. To go on multiplying examples and considerations would be inappropriate for us now.

20. The points just made were suggested to me by an unpublished paper of John Tienson's, "An Argument Concerning Quantification and Propositional Attitudes." I make some related points in *Ignorance*.

To be sure, it is most unlikely that anything can be said on these matters that will prove absolutely conclusive. But, lacking such certainty, perhaps we may still agree that I have invented some inconsistent expressions, even if those terms are well suited for our use.

At this point, a subtler, and somewhat more plausible, objection may be attempted. The idea here is to grant that 'nacknick' is an inconsistent expression, but to deny it much of a place in our experimental learning situations. It is not obvious, however, precisely how this will serve to challenge our Argument. So, let us discuss the matter.

The attempted objection may take any of several forms, but they are all more or less equivalent to this: our 'nacknick' is a term with two (or more?) meanings. In one sense, which it does seem forced to deny it, the term is indeed an inconsistent one. In this sense, however, the objection continues, the term is not a useful expression. The sense in which the term is useful is another sense, in which the term is consistent. And, what has happened in the learning situation? The teacher has intended by his instructions, to inculcate in his hearers (or readers) the expression 'nacknick' in its inconsistent sense. But what his instructions actually have done is to *suggest* to the hearers *another* sense for the term, a consistent useful one. The hearers then learn 'nacknick' only in this latter sense; the former never gets further than the teacher's sounds or marks.[21]

This objection, we may see, attempts to force an equivocation upon our Argument. Interestingly, the term upon which the equivocation focuses is not a common, accepted one, but is our invented 'nacknick' itself. For the Argument to seem to work, 'nacknick' must have one meaning in the first premise, on which the term is inconsistent, and another meaning in the second premise, on which the term is consistent. As the Argument thus equivocates, it is not a cogent piece of reasoning.

This objection has some plausibility, but it will not bear scrutiny. For it to work, we must suppose that the only way for 'nacknick' to be logically on a par with ordinary vague terms, in particular, with 'person', is for the new expression to be taken in a consistent sense. But, might not there be a deep parallel here between the two, so that 'person' as well as 'nacknick' has an inconsistent meaning? If so, then our Argument will not equivocate, but will concern both terms, as regards their inconsistent meanings. As such, it will be a cogent piece of reasoning, though perhaps a bit limited in its scope.

---

21. This objection, or one much like it, was offered in conversation by David Lewis.

My suggestion of this deep parallel implies that the inconsistent sense for 'nacknick' did get further than my marks or sounds, that it was inculcated in you. What might support this suggestion? We remember our instructive society, where inconsistent instructions for learned ordinary terms became a matter of widespread, repeated scholastic drill. Now, we need only extend our experiments with 'nacknick' to match their drills with 'stone', 'cubical object', and 'person'. So, let us imagine that after I taught you 'nacknick', we went over the instructions so much that you had them down pat. In such a case, there is no plausibility at all in supposing the inconsistent sense got no further than my marks or sounds, and never entered your learning. For, now, you would be confident that the aforesaid instructions governed your 'nacknick', which you had learned from me. Indeed, after you perceive the inconsistency in your term, you will be able to say of other expressions, which are *not* thus inconsistent, that they are thus different from the expression you just learned. Thus, you will say that 'perfect cube' is logically quite different from the term you learned from me. But, of course, you will be ready to use 'nacknick' for many objects anyway and to withhold it of many others. It appears quite easy to tell how our extended experiments will turn out, and what those results show. For what occurs there explicitly also occurs, implicitly, in our original experiments.

Now, none of this is to deny that my instructions may have inculcated in you, in *addition* to 'nacknick' in the inconsistent sense, a consistent sense for the expression. And, it is not to deny that this consistent sense may have been important, even essential, for the term's being a useful one for you. I think these last possibilities to be, in fact, quite unlikely. But there is still some plausibility in the idea of them. What is important for us to notice now is, first, how much less plausible it is to think that with 'nacknick', as well as with 'person', no inconsistent sense ever got to you at all, no matter what else may have gotten to you, and, second, that it is this much less plausible idea that is required for the charge of equivocation to work against our Argument.

To appreciate fully the failure of this charge, we should understand that whatever we may say of 'nacknick' in these regards, we may say with just as much reason, or just as little, in regards to 'stone' and 'person'. Thus, even if it concerns terms only in one, conscious meaning, our Argument will have a second premise suitable to match its first. For example, we may grant that there is an unconscious, consistent sense for 'nacknick' which, in our experiments, you learned and then employed. Then we might say, of course, that you *also* used the term in its inconsistent sense, perhaps doing so in (the process of) using it in its consistent one. But then we might just as well say the same for 'person', or 'stone': We learn two senses and, when we use 'stone' in its inconsistent sense, we do so in (the process of) using it in its unconscious, consistent sense. For another example, we might say that the consciously learned sense is never useful, and that there appears to be a use for 'nacknick' only in this inconsistent sense. But, then, of course, we might just as well say that 'stone' is perfectly idle in its conscious, inconsistent sense, and is used only in that unconscious sense in which it is a consistent expression. Whatever we may say for 'nacknick', we should understand, we may just as well say for 'stone' and for 'person'. So, to repeat, our Argument does not rely upon equivocation, but is an adequate piece of reasoning.

This final objection has failed. But it suggests some ideas, recently considered, that, while they do not constitute an objection to our Argument, may serve to place limits on its application. For, if there may be two senses of 'nacknick', and thus of 'person' also, it might be said that our Argument concerns these expressions in only one of those senses, the inconsistent one. Thus, for all that piece of reasoning says, there may be a consistent sense for 'person', as well as for 'nacknick', and, in *that* sense, there may well be plenty of people. If our Argument is thus limited, then the interest of our conclusion, it might be said, will be equally limited, though perhaps still of some significance. What are we to make of this?

In the first place, we should remind ourselves that the postulation of these additional meanings appears to be quite gratuitous and, if it actually is so, then nothing further need be said. Indeed, can't we leave it at that? For these alleged meanings are not only wholly unconscious ones, but we are to have no clue as to how anyone might ever become aware of them. Of course, someone might take a stab at articulating his putative unconscious meaning of 'person', but how should he ever judge his success, let alone the propriety of extending his suggestion to my own putative unconscious meaning for the term? To my mind, the postulation of these alleged meanings looks to be a desperate pretense.

But suppose we grant that there really are such shared consistent unconscious meanings. So far as I can tell, we still cannot say anything much as to what they are. Unlike the conscious inconsistent meanings, for which we can give at least such conditions as in (1) and (2), these postulated entities are utterly obscure and mysterious. But if we do not have any idea as to these obscure meanings, then we have none either as to what it is for an entity to be a person, or even to be a nacknick. Thus, with respect to any entity whatever, even an alleged shoelace, we have no idea either as to whether it is a person or a nacknick, or both, or neither. In *this* sense of person—and how many others like it—perhaps there may be ever so many people. But now the matter has become utterly mysterious and obscure. If this is all there is to our Argument's being limited, that reasoning seems not to have any serious limitations.

10. Some Outstanding Problems Posed by This Account and Its Relation to Them

Largely by providing and employing an account of typical vague expressions as logically inconsistent, I have argued that there are no people. We have discussed the chief objections to the account, including the charge of paradox, and we have supported the account by answering or disarming them. Thus, paradoxically enough, I suggest that at this point my account is to be accepted, at least as a working hypothesis for certain problems. I should now like briefly to discuss three of these.

A. The Problem of Explanation

If 'person' is an inconsistent term, then *how* are *any* entities able, so to say, to use it as successfully as it appears gets done quite regularly? Indeed, how does this happen with any inconsistent expression? If such an expression is tied to consistent terms, so that it functions in place of them, then the matter is not very problematic. We saw this before, in Section 1, where we discussed a working agreement to use 'perfectly square triangle' in place of 'tomato which is both yellow and sweet', supposing the latter expression to be consistent. But, without any such supposition as that, which is our present problem situation, there is considerable explanatory difficulty.

If our account is right, then any explanation given in available terms must eventually, like the terms themselves, prove logically incoherent. So, we should not expect too much here in the way of valuable results. Nevertheless, it is unhelpful to say nothing more than that there is nothing for us to do. For, even if they are incoherent, the questions that introduced this problem for us appear to point up some puzzling phenomena. So, I shall stick my neck out now and offer the beginnings of an explanatory suggestion.

Perhaps we might understand the role of putative paradigms on the model of an animal's learning to respond to a stimulus. A rat can be taught to press a nearby bar just when a certain sort of stimulus is present, for example, a triangular object. After learning with this stimulus, what happens with rats when, on the next trial, a somewhat different stimulus is for the first time presented, perhaps a more or less rounded triangular object? We may plot measures of response against difference from the original shape, those measures being frequency of any response, quickness of response when one is made, strength of response, such as pressure on the bar, and so on. With such suitable measures, a gradient, or curve, will be established for a rat population and, by extrapolation, for a typical rat member. For almost any rat, the peak of the gradient will center quite precisely on the original shape, the slope away from that varying somewhat from rat to rat. We might say, then, that each rat has his own idea of a *triangular object*, though there is important commonality to their ideas.

I suggest that our conception of a triangular object, and of a nacknick, is similarly based. Much as a rat can be trained to respond to an alleged paradigm nacknick, so I can more quickly learn to respond more flexibly with regard to such putative objects, and with respect to my invented term for them. And, of course, so can you. While our centers will not differ much, though with different people and different individual paradigms *some* difference is to be expected, our slopes may be expected to differ significantly, especially for cases far away from center. Thus, various behavioral borderline cases will arise where you and I are inclined toward disparate judgments. Now, suppose my interior decorator tells me to use a nacknick in a certain place, though any shaped nacknick will be suitable. In a store, I come upon a "borderline case" while shopping in your company. I am inclined to judge it a nacknick, you to judge it not one. Who is right? It would be silly for us, even if we thought there were some nacknicks, to force the issue and to declare that there must be a fact of the matter. Behaving typically, we would not do that. Rather, I suggest, we should treat the matter as a social problem, with each person having a chance to influence the other. Now, to move you to my side, to apply, I will rely on the vagueness condition: Look, this is so like those others, in shape, which you agree are nacknicks; so why should we stop just there, and not here? To move me, not to apply, you will rely on the discriminative condition: But, see here, we have to stop *somewhere*, or just any old thing will do; so why not stop there, which is a perfectly good place to do so? In the logic of the situation itself, there is nothing to settle matters. So, things get settled by further considerations. For example, if you are an architect, and I have no strong interest in conventional shape description, I may well yield to you, expecting like treatment from you in areas where my classificatory interests are the stronger. Of course, if you are a king and I am a peasant, then I may expect to do a good deal more yielding on matters generally. The discriminative vagueness of 'nacknick', as established in our conditions, allows these accommodations to take place with no one getting the idea that he is giving up any truth, or being hypocritical.

Even in one's own case, the matter is similar. If my decorator told me to use a nacknick, and I happen to have a putative borderline case free to hand, while most nacknicks would be quite expensive for me, I might rely on the vagueness condition to allow me to judge it a nacknick, even should I otherwise not be much inclined to do so. I want to follow my decorator's advice, and I also want to use what is free if possible, so as to keep my expenses down. By appealing to the vagueness condition, I can happily satisfy both of my desires.

Now, I do not mean to place much stock in this bare explanatory suggestion. It points up a virtue, though, in our account, and a corresponding problem with other ways of thinking about vague expressions. For people do differ as to how to handle many such behavioral borderline cases, and a given person often differs from himself over time. These do not appear to be matters of losing truth, where thoughts of self-deception should enter, or thoughts of losing one's faculties owing to social pressure. On the idea that 'nacknick' is consistent, and that it actually applies to a whole bunch of things, which are exactly the nacknicks, these bizarre thoughts move to take over. For, as we saw in Section 3, in every case, 'nacknick' either applies or else it does not, so that there are no logical borderline cases. Thus, on this more usual idea, in accommodating, someone will often give up truth (for falsity). But on our account, there are no such strange losses to be further accounted.

In a way, though, the main point for us now is to see how we have succeeded in *avoiding* the complex problem of explanation. We have done so by introducing 'nacknick', and by then formulating our Argument from Invented Expressions. For, just as with ordinary vague terms, with 'nacknick' also we have no good detailed *explanation of how* it might be useful to us even while it is inconsistent. But, we may *accept the idea that* 'nacknick' is both useful and inconsistent, and also that it is relevantly similar to 'cubical object' and to other typical vague expressions. So, even in the absence of a worked out explanation for them, we may accept the idea that our common vague expressions are useful even while they are inconsistent.

Of course, were I able to offer a good explanation of how they were useful, that would offer *more* support for our account of common vague discriminative terms. Similarly, were I able to offer a detailed explanation for 'nacknick', that would further my support for my thoughts about it. In each case, the better the explanation, the more the support we add. But, then, all of this is in the area of adding support to an account which, by other means, is already supported. On the other hand, should no good explanation be forthcoming for any of these terms, that would not, I suggest, detract much from the credibility of my account. For the problem of explanation might just be too difficult for anybody.

B. The Problem of Scope and Comparison

On my account, our language is inconsistent in a certain respect: it is inconsistent in (the fact that it has) its qualitative vague discriminative expressions, including 'being with a capacity for using language'.[22] Already we have found a fair number and variety of expressions to be of this sort. Our success suggests that we inquire as to which other terms can also be thus categorized. This is an inquiry into the problem of the *scope* of our account.

One of the first things we shall wish to examine, as regards the scope of our account, are those expressions that are the negatives of expressions we have already accounted. Thus, we look at such expressions as 'not a nacknick' and 'not a person'. While syntax thus often suffices to spot such terms, we may semantically define a negative of an expression *e* quite simply: *n* is a negative of *e* just in case, with respect to any entity, *n* applies to the entity if and only if *e* does not apply to it. Thus, 'person' is a negative of 'not a person' just as the latter is a negative of the former. We should inquire, then, whether a negative of a qualitative vague discriminative expression is also an expression of that sort. The issues here are, I think, exceptionally difficult and complex. Partly for this reason, I have not broached them in our previous discussions. For now, I think it will be enough to say this: If our negatives are also terms of our key category, that will mean a further source of contradictions and paradoxes.

For consider 'not a stone' and suppose it applies to a certain group of twenty atoms, or to something they constitute. Now, if our first condition governs this expression, we may keep adding suitable atoms, one at a time, and it will apply to the result in each case. But, if our second condition also governs it, we must reach an entity that does *not* satisfy 'not a stone', if not by *that* additive process then by *some* such procedure. But, then, as 'not a stone' does *not* apply to this entity, any *negative* of it *will* apply to it, including 'stone'. Thus, this entity, which by our vagueness condition is not a stone, also is a stone. Thus, 'not a stone'

---

22. Saying that a language is inconsistent is admittedly somewhat unnatural. But if one specifies appropriate respects in which it might be inconsistent, that unnaturalness will be harmless.

does not apply to our original complex of twenty atoms. So, any negative of 'not a stone' applies to that complex. Thus, as 'stone' is such a negative, those twenty atoms constitute a stone! But, then, our familiar arguments show, as well, that those few atoms do not compose a stone.[23]

What we say about our negative expressions, then, will determine whether or not such new sources of paradox and contradiction are upon us. But, even if we eventually say that these negatives are indeed of our typical vague variety, and so have these paradoxes upon us, that will do nothing to discredit seriously our account of them, or of any other terms. For the points we made about paradox before, in Section 8, apply in full generality. Thus, in particular, they will fully cover these present matters.

On a slightly more positive note, another thing we shall want to examine, in connection with the scope of our account, is the logic of vague discriminative terms that are not purely qualitative. For powerful sorites arguments are available to refute the existence of those entities that putatively satisfy 'bachelor', 'door', and many other terms, including arguments of a relevantly counterfactual form. To explain these arguments, we want to exhibit conditions that govern the key terms, according to which those terms are inconsistent. I believe that many proper names will find their logic exposed in this manner, as will various expressions that have been supposed interestingly similar to names. In Section 2, I made some brief suggestions for extending our account to cover discriminative expressions generally. But, we want to go far deeper into the matter.

While there is no real line separating them, we may conveniently move from discussing this problem of scope to examining the related problem of *comparison*. What we want to do here is show that the sort of source of inconsistency so far discussed, which has much to do with vagueness, is not an isolated phenomenon of our language, but is only one of several linguistic sources of inconsistency. As a possible example of another type of source, we may consider the putative expression 'expression that does not apply to itself'. It seems that there really cannot be any such expression, for if there is one, then it applies to itself if and only if it does not, which is absurd. This might be just a surprising case of reason cutting through illusory appearance. But, it may not stop there. For if this alleged expression is really not anything genuine, then,

---

23. If 'not a stone' is indeed a vague discriminative expression, the foregoing argument will go against a good deal of what I said in Section 4 of "There Are No Ordinary Things." But most of what I said there is directed against certain arguments from common sense and, as such, still will stand.

it seems, there will not really be any expression 'expression that applies to itself'. But, if not that, then not either 'expression that applies to something other than itself' nor, then, 'expression that applies to something'. But, if not this last, then it seems there is no real expression 'expression'. And, with this last gone, it seems we must conclude, in fact, that there are no expressions, and so no languages, at all. So, comparative matters merit further examination.[24]

Now, we should notice that the putative expression 'expression that does not apply to itself', supposing it does exist, might well be a vague discriminative expression. If so, then it will yield inconsistency from at least two sorts of source. And, if that is so, then so much the better for our present account.

C. The Problem of Replacement

What I regard as the most difficult problem posed by my account, but also the most important, is that of devising consistent expressions to replace the inconsistent ones that have been prevalent to date. Part of the problem is that it is unclear even in what sense or way the new terms will *replace* the old. But the most dizzying part is that the devising seems to require an indefinite number of choices for us to make, and while these choices look like extremely important ones, they must be entirely arbitrary. While these two parts may not exhaust this problem, it will be enough for us now, in an attempt to understand the problem's difficulty, to focus our discussion upon them exclusively.

In what sense or way is a newly devised term to *replace* an existing ordinary one, for example, to replace 'stone'? Normally, we should think of replacing one term by another where we think of two consistent terms involved. Thus, an old expression may apply to certain cases that we want to capture as well with a new term, but it may include other cases that we want newly to exclude. So, the new term will be defined accordingly. If we then give up the old term, and no other available expression comes near to applying and excluding along these lines, we shall naturally think of having replaced the old term by the new. But, in the present case, each old term is inconsistent, applying to

---

24. The paradox just sketched derives from the Grelling, which in turn derives from the Liar. The Liar is attributed by scholars to the great Megarian thinker Eubulides, who is also credited with inventing the sorites, as well as other important arguments. For some recent research on Eubulides, see Jon Moline, "Aristotle, Eubulides and the Sorites," *Mind* 78 (1969): 343–407. To my mind, it is puzzling how much this great philosopher has been neglected.

no cases at all. So, what does any do that a new term may do with a difference?

A "pragmatic" answer seems the only one relevant. While our inconsistent terms are all logically on a par, different ones serve us differently. Roughly, this difference in service is due to different response repertoires associated with the different terms. Each term has, for any speaker at any time, associated with it a certain pattern of responses to different possible situations. While there is some variation here, there will be, even across many speakers over a substantial period of time, a considerable amount of agreement in response for a term. So, for each inconsistent term, we might devise a consistent one that is to have a rather similar response repertoire. Still, as conflicting responses each has no claim to be (more) in accord with the old term itself, a ruling in favor of some, and against others, will have no basis in the meaning of the common term. But someone's repertoire will suffer should any decision be made. Thus, it is not easy to tell what can possibly count as a successful outcome for such a project.

Let us pretend that, for many vague expressions, this difficulty has been resolved. We are now to replace our term 'person'. For this particular task, we should reflect back on situations we have imaginatively encountered already. For example, when we remove peripheral neurons, one at a time, from an alleged person, there really seems nothing to choose, despite our generous reference to a "way most conducive to there still being a person." Thus, at (virtually) any point, the removal of (almost) any particular neuron does not leave an entity that is, in any acceptable sense, any *less of a person* than would be left instead with the removal of (almost) any other. With nothing for a guide, how are "we" to choose an expression that, unlike 'person', will select certain removals as preferable to others.

To highlight the problem, consider two rather different sequences of removal, each disposing of the same number of neurons, millions of them, where the net result, in terms of eventually supported capacities, is quite dissimilar. Now, in certain cases of this sort, our associated response repertoire may indicate one resulting entity to be preferred as a person over the other. For example, the capacities supported at the end of one sequence may be much greater as regards feelings, while the main advantage resulting from another sequence may lie in the less personal area of physical dexterity. But, in many other such cases, while the net results from the sequences are apparently different in important ways, there seems nothing to choose between them as far as being a person is concerned: suppose one entity is more intelligent and is better able to experience pleasure, while the other is more sympathetic and is more sensitive to varieties of pain. Now, what we are to do, in devising a new term, is to make a choice anyway for even such arbitrary cases, which choice will then be reflected in how the term itself "decides things."

These dizzying matters get far more difficult when the underlying circle of our thought is exposed and appreciated. For, we want our key terms, like 'person', to reflect certain interests, which will favor those entities included under the term over those not so included. But whose interests will these be? They cannot be the interests of any people, since there are not any such things. But, even supposing any of our descriptions to be coherent, should the interests of entities less brilliant than Einstein be accorded in devising a most suitable replacement for 'person'? Should any weight be given to having eyes whose color lies within a certain precise range (of bright blue)? Should entities with a very low degree of musical aptitude be excluded altogether? We have firm ideas and strong feelings on these matters, but who are we to have feelings and ideas that matter? There appears to be an impossible bootstrap operation required of any attempt at replacement to achieve any priority or even significance. Indeed, I cannot see how there could be, in any area of intellectual endeavor, a harder problem than this one.[25]

25. In writing this paper, I have been fortunate in having been helped by many people, too many to thank each individually. However, I should like to express thanks now to three who were especially helpful: Terence Leichti, David Lewis, and Samuel Wheeler.

PART II

Many Material Mysteries: Without *All the Power in the World*

4

THE PROBLEM OF
THE MANY

It is my intention to propose a new philosophical problem which I call *the problem of the many*. This problem concerns the number of entities, if any, that exist in actual ordinary situations and in counterfactual or hypothetical situations. The problem concerns the number even at a given moment of time, and it becomes only yet more baffling when durations of time, and changes, inevitably complicate the issue.

It is a philosophical commonplace to note that, without any further specification, there is no definite finite answer to the question of how many entities a given ordinary situation contains. Considering my own present situation, for example, it might be said to contain a salt shaker, also each of the grains of salt in the shaker, also the atoms that compose the shaker, as well as each of those in the grains, and this is only to begin to enumerate what seems natural. Artificial or contrived entities, so to introduce them, greatly complicate the picture. There is the left half of the shaker, as viewed from right here, and also the right half; there is the scattered concrete entity whose salient parts are that left half of the shaker and the second largest grain of salt inside the shaker; perhaps, there is even relevantly in the situation, the abstract entity that is the set whose sole members are the two concrete items most recently specified; and so on, and so forth.

To illustrate this commonplace is of course nothing new. But it is not even to rehearse any philosophical problem, about numbers of things. For, what is the problem here? On the contrary, it is natural to suppose that once an available category or sort of entities is specified, a definite answer frequently can be given, often in the form of a small positive finite number. Thus, for example, if the question is how many *salt shakers* my present situation contains, the answer is *one*. And, for another example, if the question is how many *human hands* are in that situation, then the answer is *two*. Supposedly without any serious problem, this is what one is given to think. What is new, I believe, is to suggest that even here, with such ordinary kinds purporting to delimit things, no such manageable answers are tenable. And, insofar as there is something to it, this suggestion does mean a problem.

Perhaps "the problem of the many" is a somewhat misleading name for the problem I mean to introduce. Perhaps it might better be called "the problem of the many or the none." For I shall not suggest that various considerations simply lead us to an extraordinarily high accounting, for example, to the idea that in my present situation, in what I take to be my dining area, there are millions of salt shakers. No; what these considerations lead to, I shall suggest, is a difficult *dilemma*: Either there really are no salt shakers at all, or else, in my dining area, there are millions of these things. Insofar as I find the latter of these alternatives rather absurd, I am that far inclined toward the first, to the nihilistic, or Parmenidian, option. But of course most philosophers will wish to avoid both these alternatives. So, insofar as it can be motivated, such a dilemma will be quite a problem for most philosophers.

In addition to informal discussion of it, I mean to motivate this problem in two main ways. First, I shall offer certain *arguments,* whose conclusion is our problematic dilemma, or else a proposition to the same effect, Along this line, I shall suggest that there are no adequate objections to these arguments. I shall try to support this suggestion, in part, by considering what appear the most plausible of objections and by showing that even these miss their mark. In part, also, I shall disarm any objections by examining the implications of my arguments' premises, by trying to understand what underlies them.

These arguments will be presented first in terms of clouds, those putative ordinary things which, so often, seem to be up in the sky. As our problem is one that concerns *vagueness*, beginning with clouds is natural; it should be helpful in promoting some initial understanding, and sympathy, for my argumentation. Later, I shall extend my arguments, in fairly obvious ways, from clouds to many other sorts of ordinary things: stones, tables, hands, and so on.

Although I think arguments are important in philosophy, my arguments here will be only the more assertive way for me to introduce the new problem, not the only way. To complement that reasoning, I shall ask certain *questions*. To avoid our problematic dilemma rationally, these questions must receive an adequate answer. But, it will be my suggestion, there really is no adequate answer to be given here.

Concerning vagueness, as it does, the problem of the many is a problem in *the philosophy of language* as much as in *metaphysics*. Once the problem itself is presented in detail, I shall sketch certain further problems that it implies. While these implied problems also concern the aforesaid two philosophic areas, they do not end there. Rather, they also concern, or give rise to, certain problems in *epistemology*. Accordingly, it is my belief, the problem of the many should prove quite fertile for philosophical investigation.

1. Vagueness and Clouds

Our new problem concerns *vagueness*. Typical vague expressions, such as 'tall man', 'table' and 'stone', purport to discriminate their referents from everything else—the tall men, for example, from the rest of the world. But as is familiar, and as sorites arguments make clear, their vagueness seems to mean a problem for the purported discriminations. Along the dimension of height, for example, where do the tall men stop, so to say, and the other, shorter fellows first come into the picture? With regard to the range of possible heights, at least, "tall man" must have a *boundary*, if we may use this primarily spatial expression, however "vague" or "fuzzy" that stopping place may or may not be. But, it does not seem to have any; or if it does, where the devil can that stopping place occur? So much, for now, for rehearsing familiar problems of vagueness.

For our new problem, the leading idea is to focus on physical, spatial situations where no natural boundaries, no natural stopping places, are to be encountered. Many cases of *clouds* at least appear to provide such situations.[1] Now, when viewed from far away, certain puffy, "pictured-postcard" clouds can give the appearance of rather a sharp clean boundary, a clean end to them, so to say, where the surrounding sky, then, correlatively begins. But many other clouds, even from any point of view, appear gradually to blend into, or fade off into, the surrounding sky. And even the puffy, cleanest items, *upon closer scrutiny*, also do seem to blend into their surrounding atmosphere. For all our clouds, then, this has the makings of a new sort of sorites argument, as

---

1. For the idea that I use clouds to introduce my problem, I am indebted to Ernest Sosa.

to where any one of them could first start, or stop. But we shall not pursue that matter here and now; for our main present concern is to introduce a really new problem, not to discuss any new variation upon an old one.

What we must become concerned with, at all events, is the underlying concrete physical reality, in which any clouds there might be must find their place. Ordinary appearances may be, of course, widely deceptive. Objects that appear to have no natural stopping place may in fact have just that. In contrast, what appears to have such a boundary, e.g., our putative puffy clouds, may in fact have none. We are to consider the reality and not the appearance.

What should reality be like for a cloud to make a clean break with its surroundings? The best possible case or situation is of this sort: The cloud is composed of continuous, relevantly homogeneous matter, or stuff,[2,3] which, relative to each of the "routes into and out of the cloud," just stops at a certain point. Right after any such points, and so external to the cloud, there first begins stuff of another kind, or empty space, or some mixture of the two. The natural boundary, or "break," need not be shaped anything much like it appears, as long as it does have some shape that is suitably definite, or proper. Thus the boundary may appear rather simple and smooth, whereas closer inspection may reveal it to be quite jagged, with bumps on bumps on bumps. But, in relevant regards, a clean natural separation is effected.

In the sort of situation just imagined, which we are confident is wildly hypothetical but which we are supposing to be real, our problem of the many will not readily arise. In such a situation, with the natural boundary remarked, there is just one entity that, in respects relevant to

2. According to certain lexicographers, on the most preferred meaning of 'cloud' such homogeneous clouds are logically impossible. Thus my *Webster's Seventh New Collegiate Dictionary* (Springfield, Mass., 1969) lists for the noun: "1(a): a visible mass of particles of water or ice in the form of fog, mist, or haze suspended usu. at a considerable height in the air. (b): a light filmy, puffy, or billowy mass seeming to float in the air." I am confident, however, that no such ambiguity as the above exists for 'cloud' and that (b), though quite deficient, does more toward giving the only (relevant) meaning than does the ridiculously unsemantic (a).

3. The sort of semantic constraints recently urged by Hilary Putnam and by Saul Kripke for certain terms, e.g., 'cat', do not apply to 'cloud' or to other terms I shall similarly employ later. (Although I was once convinced they were right about 'cat', I now think even that term does not have the constraints they urge for it but is much in the same boat as 'cloud'. For now, this latter issue may be safely passed over.) As regards the putative constraints, see Putnam's "Is Semantics Possible?" and "Meaning and Reference," both available in *Naming, Necessity*, and *Natural Kinds*, ed. S. P. Schwartz (Ithaca, N.Y., 1977), and the third part of Kripke's "Naming and Necessity," in *Semantics of Natural Language*, ed. D. Davidson and G. Harman (Dordrecht, 1972).

being a cloud, far surpasses anything else present. This is the entity composed, or constituted, of all the stuff within the boundary, and not of anything outside (and which, we might add, has the identity conditions over time appropriate to a cloud). So there is no other stuff around, in our specified situation, that is, then and there, suited for constituting any other, second cloud.

In this supposedly real situation, what other entity could make an attempt at being a cloud, so to say, to give some trouble to the unique preferred status of our cleanly bounded item? An artificial or contrived entity might perhaps be introduced. Think of a certain nine hundred ninety-nine thousand nine hundred ninety-nine millionths of our item, all together, and then, also, the remaining millionth "seamlessly attached to" what you first considered. The greater of these two masses of stuff may be regarded, we shall grant, as constituting an entity, one with a much smaller entity seamlessly attached. But is that (greater) contrived entity a cloud, so that we shall have at least two clouds in our supposed situation? I think not. For if anything is a cloud, it must be a *natural* item, with a real, objective place in nature all its own, so to say. So our contrived object cannot ever fill the bill that cloudhood requires. Even passing over this, and doing so very cautiously indeed, whatever claim it might have to be a cloud is *much* worse than that possessed by our natural, cleanly bounded item. If we allow our common-sense belief, that there is *at most* one cloud right there, to have any weight at all, the contrived item loses out to the natural object. So, with this sort of an underlying reality, we might rest happy with the idea that the only cloud we seem to see is, indeed, the only one right before us. Thinking only of such an underlying reality, then, our would-be problem of the many does not seem to have much chance to get off the ground. (But a good deal later on, in section 9, we shall see how the problem arises even in such a clean, sharp world.)

To get our problem going, let us consider a *very* different sort of reality, one in which, I hope, the problem will most clearly emerge. In relevant regards, then, this sort of situation lies at the opposite pole, along a series of "possible real situations," from where we should place the reality just considered. (Later on, we shall consider some of the intermediate cases.) Before, clouds would be *simple* entities, composed only of stuff and *not* of smaller, simpler constituent *things*. So, this time, clouds, if there really are any present, will be relevantly *complex*. Here a cloud will not be composed of continuous, homogeneous matter. On the contrary, there will be present a large number of dispersed items, each much smaller than a cloud, for example, a large number of dispersed water droplets.[4] (So far as currently relevant considerations go, each water droplet may itself be either simple or else it may be complex; either way our problem of the many will be quick to arise. In fact, of course, water droplets are very complex, composed of molecules, atoms, elementary particles, and who knows what else.) The water droplets are separated from each other by relevantly different matter, which is not itself water, or by space, or by a mixture of the two. It matters not precisely how their separation is effected, so long as they may be regarded as relevantly distinct from each other.

So we have many water droplets before us now, and they are suitably dispersed. But, for our problem to meet the eye, what is a most suitable dispersion, or arrangement, for these tiny would-be constituents? Where a normal observer would take a cloud to be, we shall have our droplets closer together. Quite a ways out from that, where it seems clear we are well out of the cloud, well into the surrounding sky, the population is a good deal less dense, the droplets are, on the whole, much farther apart from each other. Moreover, there is no place at all where suddenly, or dramatically, the "denseness" falls off and the "sparseness" first begins. Rather, when we look at things closely, all that is there to be seen is a *gradual transition* from the more dense to the less so. In this reality, which in all relevant regards is the *actual* reality, i.e., really is reality, there is no natural break, or boundary, or stopping place, for any would-be cloud to have. Thus there is none that might give any candidate cloud its own real place in nature. Without this, how are there to be any clouds here, in this actual reality?

If it is anything, a cloud is a *concrete* entity.[5] Further, it is a concrete entity occupying some space, as well as being spatially located, one existing for some time, if only a moment, and one constituted of some matter or stuff. Well, then, what are the concrete things in our real situation? There are, we may allow, things even smaller than the water droplets—but none of those is a cloud; not really. There are the droplets themselves—but neither is any of them a cloud. We may allow, too, that there are many very contrived entities present, for example, a "scattered concrete individual," consisting of a droplet here and three way over there. But those contrived concrete things are not clouds

4. As the previous two notes indicate, this realistic situation is *just one possibility* for clouds, in any relevant use of that thorny term.

5. I cannot offer a good definition of 'concrete', in the sense most relevant to philosophy. Its opposite is 'abstract', which I also will not try to define. By 'concrete entity', I mean much the same thing that many philosophers have meant by 'particular' and that many have meant by 'individual'.

either. Of course, the only likely candidates will be concrete complexes composed, at least in the main, not merely of some water droplets but of a great many droplets that are "suitably grouped together." If *none* of *these* things is a cloud, then, I am afraid, our situation will, in fact, contain or involve no cloud at all. But, of course, perhaps one or more of these most promising concrete complexes is indeed a cloud. And, if so, then all will not be lost so far as clouds are concerned.

Whether or not all is lost, there is a serious problem here, and that is our problem of the many. For it seems clear that no matter which relevant concrete complex is deemed fit for cloudhood, that is, is deemed a cloud, there will be very many others each of which has, in any relevant respect, a claim that is just as good. To perceive this plethora takes a bit of visual imagination, but I am hopeful that you can do it. Think of any given likely prospect and, then, think of the very many similar complexes each of which "overlaps" it just slightly, sharing constituents with it, except for a peripheral droplet or two, here or there. With any given first choice, there are ever so many such suitable overlappers. And, of course, any of them might have, equally, been chosen first. No matter where we start, the complex first chosen has nothing objectively in its favor to make it a better candidate for cloudhood than so many of its overlappers are. Putting the matter somewhat personally, each one's claim to be a cloud is just as good, no better and no worse, than each of the many others. And, by all odds, each complex has *at least* as good a claim as any still further real entity in the situation. So, either *all* of *them* make it or else *nothing* does; in this real situation, either there are many clouds or else there really are no clouds at all. This dilemma presents our problem of the many.

2. An Argument about Clouds as Concrete Complexes

In a manner that was, intentionally, both informal and imaginative, we have begun our discussion of our new problem. Beginning with a wildly hypothetical world, or kind of reality, we moved to discuss the real, actual world. The contrast, informally presented, was meant to help us see where and how our new problem might readily emerge. I hope it was indeed helpful. If the problem is beginning to make some impression, then it may be well to give our discussion a bit more rigor or form. Interestingly enough, it seems that however this is done, the problem, rather than dissolving, or being exposed as some trifling confusion, manages only to impress itself upon us still further.

I shall proceed to present our problem by means of two rather explicit arguments, each quite different from the other, though they will of course be significantly related. In this section, I shall present one of these, which I call the Argument about Clouds as Concrete Complexes. I present it first, because it most directly flows from the discussion that ended the previous section. In the next section, I shall present the other of these introductory arguments.

We have discussed clouds as complex concrete entities, composed of smaller concrete constituents; in the actual world, if there are any clouds, that is what they will each be. Although this discussion served a purpose, it perhaps proceeded a bit too briskly. For as I spoke in quite general terms, someone with a strong aversion to our problem might challenge me with the suggestion of a weird counterexample, or what he would take to be such an example. From this putative challenge, the inspiration for our first argument can be derived.

In our discussion, I have drawn attention to a myriad of concrete complexes, each overlapping many others, which multitude would generally pass unnoticed. I then said, quite generally, that in (any) such situations, there would not be any one complex that had a relevantly and sufficiently better claim on cloudhood than each of many others. But although this is clearly true in most such situations, even a putative objector will agree, there might be a few marginal situations, even some actually in the real world, where among the many poor complexes present, only one just manages to sneak over the minimum requirements that cloudhood sets for complex entities. Here, it is imagined, none of the complexes is well off so far as the criteria for clouds are concerned, and just one is only a bit better off than any of the others. We are to imagine that one to be just enough better off so that it manages to be a cloud, even though a very marginal case of one, while each of its nearest competitors fails altogether. What are we to make of this suggestion?

In the first place, I think it extremely doubtful that, in actuality, such a situation ever really does occur. But, second, if it ever really does take place, then, surely among our real situations, these problematic ones are quite rare indeed. So, certainly, in situations involving dispersions of water droplets, where, in the real world, clouds have their best prospects for existence, it will be at most only *rarely* that we shall *not* encounter our problem of the many or an instance of that problem. Now, these rare situations will be ones where, while we may suppose that there is just one cloud present, the "successful" item is a *very* marginal case of being a cloud. It is not even a pretty marginal case, let alone a fair to middling cloud. Most certainly, this marginal item will be quite far from being a *paradigm* cloud, a *good example of* a cloud or, as I shall most often put it, a *typical* cloud.

To get farthest away from this challenge, whether or not there ever really is any substance in it, we may present our problem in terms of typical clouds. This moves us to the statement of our first argument. As we want the argument to concern all putative real clouds, and not just the alleged typical cases, it is best to begin it with a premise that will ensure such a general result, by having the one stand, or fall, with the other:

(1)   If there are clouds, then there are typical clouds.

Now, this premise, it must be emphasized, is not offered as analytic, or as a necessary truth, or anything of that strong ilk. On the contrary, it is just offered as true, as a true conditional statement (at least supposing there are any true statements about clouds at all). As such, which is all that matters here, it can hardly be denied by one who would avoid our problem of the many. For if there really are clouds around, then a good many of them have been, now are, and will be typical clouds. It is scarcely credible to suppose that, in fact, *all* the clouds in the world are, if not marginal cases, not much better than fair to middling examples.

It is with our next premise that our imaginative powers are called upon for a clear understanding:

(2)   If something is a typical cloud, then *any* situation involving it contains, in addition to itself, millions of other complex concrete entities, each of which differs from it, in any respects relevant to being a cloud, at most quite minutely.

This premise makes the claim, or contains the implication, that any real, actual cloud is a concrete complex entity. This may well call for some further discussion (which will be provided later, mainly in section 6). But, realizing that the premise is put forward merely as a true conditional statement, it is, in this implication at least, no less than extremely plausible. Given this, we move to a more demanding aspect of our premise: Our imagination is called upon to perceive, so to say, all the other relevant cloud candidates. In the argument I shall present next, recently promised, I shall provide a "visual aid" toward this end, for now I rely on goodwill and native ability. Given this, we next face the claim of *millions* of such candidates, as opposed to, say, many. This might appear either excessive or too definite, where no such definite numbers can be gotten. Realizing a gap to be filled here, I pass over it now, postponing this matter, too, for a later detailed discussion (which will be provided mainly in section 5, though certain other sections, in particular 6, will also have considerable bearing on the matter). Finally, regarding this second premise, it is implied that each of these millions of candidates is, if not as well off as the "original choice" mentioned in the antecedent, at least quite nearly as well off, in respect of meeting cloud criteria. So the "claims toward cloudhood" of these overlappers will not be much worse than those of the apparently well-placed original candidate. A detailed discussion of why this should be so will certainly be desirable. I plan to proceed with the matter gradually, through our essay's various further sections. But, even now, the proposition itself is eminently credible.

Our argument requires but one further premise:

(3) If something is a *typical* cloud, then, if there are entities that differ from it, in any respects relevant to being a cloud, at most quite minutely, then each of those entities is a cloud.

This premise, or principle, surely recommends itself to reason. In the first place, it does not even appear to say that any of those latter entities, let alone all of them, will be typical clouds, as is the first. It is content to have them all be only fair to middling cases of clouds, though we ourselves should think a good many of them, at least, to be better placed than that. So, in effect, all this principle is requiring is that the difference between a *typical* cloud and a candidate that fails altogether to instance cloudhood be, in relevant respects, reasonably substantial; at the very least, that it be more than quite minute. Although the credentials of this premise, like its two predecessors, will be furthered by further discussion, the premise, also like them, has every initial appearance of being an entirely acceptable proposition. (We shall find such further discussion in section 8 and, especially, in section 10.)

From these three premises, our problem of the many can be deduced and, thus, introduced. To begin, from (2) and (3), we obtain:

(A) If something is a typical cloud, then *any* situation involving it contains, in addition to itself, millions of other complex concrete entities each of which is a cloud, that is, it contains millions of clouds.

Although this deduction is not absolutely formal, the divergence from that austere ideal is trivial. In like manner, from (A) and (1), we may in turn deduce:

(B) If there are clouds, then there are situations involving typical clouds and, in *any* of these, there are millions of clouds.

Logically speaking, though (B) is conditional in form, it adequately presents our problem. Still psychologically speaking, our problem is in large measure one of confronting a dilemma. So, it is well to have our present argument, which introduces the problem, conclude by offering a disjunction of uncomfortable alternatives. From (B), then, we make our final move to:

(C) Either there are no clouds at all, or else there are situations involving typical clouds and, in *any* of these, there are millions of clouds.[6,7]

With this argument now before us, our new problem has received a somewhat more formal presentation, to complement our initial, more conversational setting for it. At the same time, by focusing on typical cases, the suggestion of certain small logical moves, as to a single present item alone "creeping over the minimum standard," can be seen not to threaten our problem's seriousness or size. For certain readers, however, my talk of overlapping concrete complexes may, perhaps paradoxically, itself "appear all too abstract." So, especially for them, though for the rest of us as well, I shall proceed to offer a second argument, by which our problem may again be given an introduction. Giving "the

6. I offer no definition of 'situation' but use it in much the same way that many philosophers have done. By it, then, I mean much the same thing that many have meant by 'state of affairs'. Situations can encompass more or less space, and so with time. By my stress and placement of 'any', I indicate that even "quite immediate" situations in space (and, of course, in time) will involve so many clouds if any at all. That *some* situations should (even at a moment) involve so many is of course no problem. Consider the present situation of the earth's entire atmosphere. On this matter, I am indebted to Terence Leichti.

7. Following philosophical and logical tradition, I here understand 'there are clouds' to be made true even by the existence of even one cloud. But, of course, this understanding is for me just a convenient pretense, and it is in no wise required for the argument.

For convenience, and *more important to make note of*: Now that this first argument has been presented, in what follows I shall generally omit the qualifying words 'at most' and just speak of entities that differ *quite minutely*. Should they desire to do so, readers may overlook the omission and say to themselves "*at most* quite minutely."

The qualifier 'at most' provides a needed hedge here in at least two (related) ways: *First,* the spotted entities may differ from each other in certain relevant ways by an amount that is *even less* than what should be regarded as quite minute, perhaps one that is only *extremely minute*. But, then, of course, they should still stand or fall, as regards being clods, together with the allegedly typical item. *Second,* there may be certain respects relevant to the kind in which the spotted entities differ *not at all* from the putative typical cloud. Then, too, as far as just being a cloud goes, the typical item cannot thus succeed while the others fail. Once the need for the qualification is noted, it is painfully boring to keep making it.

mind's eye a visual aid," this second argument may help us all get a more vivid idea of our problem of the many.

3. An Argument about Clouds as Bounded Entities

My second argument focuses on the fact that any cloud must be a limited or bounded entity: at least relative to certain routes, traveling from inside the cloud outward, there must be a stopping place for the cloud. Just so, once one is beyond such a stopping place, or group of stopping places, or, as I shall most often say, such a *boundary*, one is outside the cloud, that is, at a place where the cloud is not. This idea makes no great claim for any cloud's boundary, again to use that convenient term.[8] Just as the term 'cloud' is vague, we may allow 'boundary' to be vague as well, at least in our current employment, so that a close connection between the two would not be surprising. But, of course, we are using 'boundary' as something of an abbreviation here, as abbreviating something like 'place(s) of the cloud closest to what is outside the cloud', or like 'place(s) between the place(s) where the cloud is and the place(s) where it is not'. So the vagueness we may attribute to 'boundary', or to our usage of it, will have ample roots in common vague terms: in 'place', in 'cloud', and in lengthier expressions with those vague components. Moving from these linguistic considerations to apparently correlative matters in the extralinguistic realm, our argument will be happy to allow, though it does not require, that clouds have "fuzzy" boundaries with "no determinate width," whatever stricter limits the dictates of reason might, or might not, require.

Just as our boundaries may be treated here in the most liberal, fuzzy manner, so our argument is happy to allow cloud boundaries to have all sorts of shapes and a variety of relations to the clouds they bound. With any typical cloud, I suggest, and any actual cloud in our solar system, the boundary will be fully closed, not "punctured" nor "open-ended." But there may be some possible clouds, I should think them atypical of the kind, with what we may call *open* boundaries. Thus,

---

8. In a recent paper, "Talk About Talk About Surfaces," *Dialectica* 31, no. 3–4 (1977):411–30, Avram Stroll and Robert Foelber argue that the proper application of "surface" is a good deal narrower than one might suppose. I find some of their arguments pretty convincing, and I expect that a similar case could be made for the ordinary word 'boundary'. But I shall use 'boundary' to cover ever so many cases anyway, thus often employing it as a term of art. As the reader can verify, nothing of substance will depend on this eccentricity.

for example, there might be a cloud with an infinitely long, thin tail. Or, for another, there might be one shaped like an infinitely long cylindrical column. Or, at least, our argument will be happy to allow these things and will even be so generous as to allow some such infinite clouds to be typical clouds. But, at all events, with regard to at least some "routes" out of and into the cloud, there must be limits, however fuzzy those may be. This much our argument will require, but so will the dictates of reason. For otherwise there will not be a world with clouds, or even a single cloud, in it, but only a cloudy or foggy world.[9]

With so much disarming generosity displayed, I trust I may begin my Argument about Clouds as Bounded Entities. For similar reasons, it is good to begin here with the very same premise that began our previous argument:

(1)   If there are clouds, then there are typical clouds.

For one thing, as it has already been discussed well enough, we may now immediately move on to add further material.

The second premise of our new argument is a conditional which, for all clouds and not just typical ones, we have just recently provided motivation:

(2)   If something is a (typical) cloud, then there is something that limits or bounds the cloud, that is, something that is the *boundary* of the cloud.

In line with our motivating discussion, we shall continue to be generous with any who might be leery of this premise. We may allow that it is poorly phrased and that, as best formulated, its implications are quite scanty. As far as phrasing goes, for all I know, the required limiting entity, which the premise refers to as a *boundary*, may perhaps not be so called in ordinary usage. And perhaps the verb "limit" also might be somewhat out of place here. But to object to the premise on any such grounds is to quibble beside the main point. For the important thing, as our discussion has indicated, is that with any cloud there will be such a "limiting" or "bounding" *something*, however well or badly I may label it. It should be emphasized, next, that *this premise itself* really makes no great claims for any such boundary; the thing need be neither natural nor conventional, neither salient no indiscriminable, and so on. Further, the

9. On these matters, I have profited from discussion with Jerrold Katz.

premise does not explicitly exclude the boundary from itself having width and thus being rather on a par with a cloud (though, of course, no such thing is explicitly required either). Nor, then, does the premise thus exclude the mentioned boundary from itself having boundaries, which in turn may have various properties, including the having of further boundaries, and so on.

It is with its *third premise* that our Argument first threatens to run up the numbers where clouds are concerned:

> (3)   If something is the boundary of a typical cloud, then there are, in a *bounding envelope* centered on the boundary of any typical cloud, millions of other boundaries of clouds each of which limits, or bounds, a cloud that is different from any cloud thus bounded by any of the others.

Passing over our choice of the phrase "bounding envelope" and other such purely verbal trivialities, there are important substantive and conceptual matters to discuss. In the first place, the function of that chosen phrase is to point out a region that is somewhat thicker than any of the relevant boundaries, but (in case they do have thickness) *not very* much thicker. So, in this region, we may find, side by side, or themselves overlapping, a great many potential boundaries for clouds. Given this, we can see the two key ideas advanced by this premise. The first idea is to focus on the myriad of nearby limiters and, by so doing, on *what they limit,* which then cries out for consideration. Before claiming anything about the presence of clouds, we may notice *that many concrete entities* will be suitably limited: First, each boundary will limit a "region of space" different from every other. Further, in at least many of these regions, the stuff contained will differ from that in many other bound regions. To sharpen the picture, we may note that many of these regions, and their contents, will overlap (slightly) with many others, including (that of) the original typical cloud. In many other cases, there will be no overlap with that original but a rather fine "nesting" between the new candidates and our original item. This first idea is the visual aid, for the mind's eye, that I promised you, in the previous section. So much for the first idea, which brings to our attention many concrete entities, each so similar to our alleged typical cloud, which normally would go unconsidered. The second idea is to judge these newly considered entities with regard to whether or not they are clouds. According to our premise, if our alleged typical item is indeed a typical cloud, then many of these candidates, millions at least, do not fail to be clouds altogether but are clouds of some sort or other. Although antecedently surprising, once the candidates are considered, this judgement seems quite fitting. Indeed, we may say that it even has a certain claim to modesty, or understatement. For, first, this judgement nowhere claims that any but the original choice is a typical cloud, allowing, even, that all the other clouds in the situation are marginal cases. (In contrast, I suggest, our intuitive ideas is that if there are any typical clouds at all, our situation will contain not just one but quite a few clouds that are indeed typical.) And, second, our premise also allows that although many of these candidates are clouds, many of them fail to be clouds, perhaps far outnumbering those whose candidacy is, in any way, successful. (In contrast, our intuitive idea is that not only do many succeed, but none of these "very near neighbors" fail to be clouds.)[10]

Now, our premise mentions *millions* of clouds as present in the typical situation (allowing, of course, that there be an infinity of millions and, thus, an infinity of such clouds). And although we might now agree that many clouds must be present, any such numerical reference as that needs further argument. I shall postpone such argument for the while, until section 5. So our third premise needs further consideration. But, even now, when things are somewhat left up in the air (or sky), this crucial, and most interesting, premise appears at least quite plausible.

There remains but one premise to present for our Argument, and that gap shall now be filled:

(4) If there are, in a bounding envelope centered on the boundary of any typical cloud, millions of other boundaries of clouds each of which limits, or bounds, a cloud that is different from any cloud thus bound by any of the others, then there are situations involving typical clouds, and in any of these there are millions of clouds.

In effect, this last premise adds up, by a procedure that is eminently suitable, only the clouds that we have already agreed to be present and relates the sum to any alleged typical cloud. The procedure is to count the clouds by way of the boundaries limiting them. So where two boundaries limit, or bound, different clouds, there must be (at least) two clouds, and where millions, millions. (We might even *allow* here that

10. I think this intuitive idea is grounded in the adequacy of premise (3) of our first introductory argument. This thought of mine will be developed shortly, in section 4, where I shall discuss some relations between the two arguments.

two boundaries may both bound the same cloud. But even so, the premise's method cannot falsely add to our judgement.)

Although some of our premises may require a good deal of further discussion, we may agree, I believe, that they together adequately yield our problem. Perhaps discounting small points of grammar, by simple logic, our conditional premises yield us, again, this conditional conclusion:

(B) If there are clouds, then there are situations involving typical clouds, and, in any of these, there are millions of clouds.

For many purposes, our conclusion might as well be left in this conditional form. But, as with our previous argument, to heighten the sense of a dilemma, it is well to put matters in the form of a disjunction:

(C) Either there are no clouds at all, or else there are situations involving typical clouds, and, in any of these, there are millions of clouds.

So we have deduced our dilemma now twice over, by our Argument about Clouds as Concrete Complexes and, again just now, by our Argument about Clouds as Bounded Entities. We want to examine these arguments with some care and to investigate the relations between them. For the dilemma they both yield plainly presents a real philosophic problem. Of course, some philosophers, like Parmenides and, in a smaller way, me, too, would be rather happy to accept the first alternative, feeling an absurdity to attend any putatively common particular, such as an alleged ordinary cloud. Perhaps others, maybe certain followers of Leibniz, might be pleased to accept the second. But most will want to avoid both. To do so rationally, they must refute, or properly deny, both our arguments. This, it seems, is not easy to do. Accordingly, there is much for us to discuss here.

4. Some Relations between These Two Arguments

There are, I think, some rather interesting relations between our two offered arguments. As they are not entirely obvious, it will be worth our while to draw them out explicitly. Let us begin to do so now. The first of our arguments, concerning concrete *complexes*, specifies a certain sort of constitution, or composition, for clouds, namely, as involving certain smaller *constituent entities*. This is done by way of the argument's second premise, a statement which is not matched by any premise in our other argument. Indeed, our second argument makes no specification at all as to the constitution of any cloud. For this reason, I believe, our second argument is more *general* than is our first, applying to all the sorts of underlying realities (or possible worlds) to which the first applies, and then to some others as well. Of course, as concerns our actual situation, this logical disparity makes no difference, for the actual underlying reality, the actual world, is quite as our more specific, first argument requires. But for a comprehensive understanding, the more general matter should be investigated.

In section 1, we considered a possible world where the underlying reality involved no tiny things, no dispersal of water droplets, molecules, or atoms, in the morass of which putative clouds would have to find their place. In such a world, clouds would all be simple entities, rather than complex ones: such a cloud would not be constituted of any other distinct particulars. The cloud would be composed of some matter, or stuff, to be sure, but that matter would be relevantly continuous and homogeneous. Now, in that first section, we made a further assumption too: There would be a clean, natural break between (the matter of) the putative cloud and whatever was allegedly external to the cloud. Providing that there are clouds, this assumption really is distinct from that of supposing clouds to be (not complex but) simple. So, while still supposing for clouds the aforementioned material simplicity, let us drop this further assumption now.

What sort of underlying reality, or possible world, will we now be supposing? It will be like this: The matter where a cloud is thought to be will not make a clean break with matter that surrounds it but will gradually blend into, or fade off into, such surrounding matter, at every relevant place. For a heuristic, represent the matter "suited for clouds" in red and that "suited for the surrounding sky" in blue. Now, a very close look at "where the two are adjacent" will reveal no sudden change from red to blue (or equally from blue to red). Rather, it will reveal a *gradual* transition from the one color to the other, with at "suitable places in between" various shades of maroon, purple, and so on. In such a situation, we can now easily see, if there is a cloud, the *kind of matter* in it, of which it is composed, gradually blends into *another kind of* matter, at every relevant place, and the cloud is *not* composed of that other kind of matter.

As any such cloud will be a simple entity rather than a complex one, the second premise of our first argument will not apply to it; so in such a world our Argument about Clouds as Concrete Complexes will not apply. But our *second* argument, regarding bounded entities, can apply to such simple things as well as to complex ones. It does not care, so to say, whether the blending between presumed cloud and alleged environment is accomplished by, or instantiated by, a dispersion of smaller items or whether by a true continuity, as just colorfully imagined. So long as our underlying reality exhibits *any* baffling blend, our second argument is well satisfied.

This may come as something of a surprise. For our second argument, mainly by way of its third premise, provides a sort of "visual aid," whereas our first seems to leave things more indefinite, perhaps even, more obscure. It is the first argument that leaves more for the reader to make vivid and concrete. Yet it is not the first, but the second, that is the more general. But though a surprise, there is of course no real paradox here. For the greater concreteness of the second argument is of an *epistemological* sort, relating to a more concrete *understanding* of whatever situations are to be considered, whereas the greater generality of the argument, and thus, in a sense, its greater abstractness, concerns the *metaphysical characters* of those situations.

There is a second relationship between our two arguments that is even less obvious than the one just discussed. But it is at least as important to consider. It is pretty plain, of course, that there is no statement in the second argument that is quite the same as the third and final premise of the first one. What, then, is the relation of our second argument to our first one's final premise?

This final statement may be regarded as a *principle* that *underlies* the third premise of our argument about bounded entities, which premise is, I suggest, the very heart of that more general piece of reasoning. Indeed, so important, then, is this underlying proposition that we may give it a name to remember it by, *the principle of minute differences from typical cases*; for brevity, I shall sometimes just call it *the principle of minute differences*. How is it that this principle underlies our second, more general argument?

We may regard our second argument's third premise, where so many boundaries are first introduced, as doing *two* things. *First*, it calls to our attention, by way of these boundaries, ever so many (bound) relevant entities, overlapping and nesting in their spatial relations. In some possible worlds, including the actual one, these entities will all be complex; in others, they will all be relevantly simple. In any of these worlds, there will be no clean breaks around, but only relevant gradualness. Just so, *in order for anything* in any of these situations to be properly accounted a cloud, the sorts of entities that overlap must be considered real things. Further, we are supposing, at least for the sake of argument, that in each such situation a certain thing there is even a typical cloud. So we focus on one overlapping thing that is a typical cloud and also, we must then suppose, on at least those many others which, as regards criteria for clouds, differ minutely from a certain typical item.

But are any of these other overlapping entities, which we have had to admit as genuine things, of some sort or other, so much as *clouds* themselves? Giving an answer to this question is the *second* thing done by our key premise: If the presumed item is a typical cloud, our implicit reasoning tells us, then each of the many other entities, so recently focused upon, will be at least a cloud of some sort or other. What is it that guides this reasoning? It is the third and final premise of our first argument, the principle of minute differences from typical cases. Slightly shortened, as per note 7, it reads as follows:

> If something is a typical cloud, then, if there are entities that differ from it, in any respects relevant to being a cloud, quite minutely, then each of those entities is a cloud.

So underlying the key premise of our second, more general argument is implicit reasoning which consists of two parts. And the second part of it is quite explicit in our first, more limited reasoning.

If this is right, then a lengthy argument may be constructed which incorporates material from both the two arguments I have actually offered. The constructed argument will be like our offered second one, except that the latter's third premise, just considered, will be replaced by statements that make explicit the reasoning underlying it. For this replacement, we require but two propositions, which together entail the premise they replace. The first of these is our principle of minute differences, rehearsed in display above. The other statement to be employed will then be this rather complex related proposition, which relevantly states the "first part" of the reasoning that was previously implicit:

> If something is the boundary of a typical cloud, then there are, in a bounding envelope centered on the boundary of any typical cloud, millions of other boundaries of entities each of which limits, or bounds, an entity different from that thus bounded by each of the others, and each of these bounded entities differs from the putative typical cloud in question, in any respects relevant to being a cloud, quite minutely.

With this explicit but complicated conditional, we have an argument of five premises, which is itself, thus, quite complicated indeed. Even so, in relevant regards, this "master argument" is not only *vivid* and *general* but also quite *explicit*. For those who can tolerate complications,

I offer it now, perhaps in place of my original formulation of my Argument about Clouds as Bounded Entities; after all, it is also about these putative objects' having a stopping place, or boundary. But I shall offer nothing in place of my first argument, the Argument about Clouds as Complex Entities. For I have found that although many people are interested in discussing the baffling boundaries I have mentioned, there are also many who want no part of any such discussion. Any mention of boundaries, or of anything of the like, turns them away right away. Our argument about complex entities, of course, makes no such mention at all. And, as might be expected, I have found that it is eminently discussable by virtually everyone with whom I have, in conversation, broached the problem of the many.

At all events, in what follows, it will often prove a convenience to speak of clouds, as well as of various other things, as bounded and to contemplate their alleged boundaries. Those who want no part of such a convenience may cast things in terms where no such speaking occurs, as is done in my first argument. They may, then, take my talk of boundaries as merely suggesting an aid in the task of noting all that is there in the morass of concrete reality. But however one chooses to frame the introductory arguments themselves, it should by now be clear that our problem is difficult and persistent.[11] Indeed, we have already left dangling various puzzling loose ends, some of which I hope to connect with later. And other facets of our problem, at least equally baffling, have not yet been even so much as glimpsed obscurely.

5. On Nearby Clouds and the Mathematics of Combinations

Up in the sky on rather cloudy days, science tells us, there is a dispersion of water droplets. Here, and also over there, the droplets are closer together than in the regions surrounding the here and the there. In those other regions, there are droplets too, but they are less close together. There is a gradual transition from the here, and from the there, to the lesser density in the surrounding regions.

---

11. A good deal later on, in section 10, I shall show how *versions of both* our introductory arguments may be given which make *no* mention of the principle of minute differences. So, although I *think* this principle underlies our arguments, and our problem, I am *not relying* on that idea to get the problem going, or to keep it around. Indeed, then, I am not even relying on it for my *introductory arguments*, let alone in regard to asking relevant *questions*, perhaps the most important route to the problem, which we encounter in section 11.

We are given to think that here is one cloud, there is another, and in those other regions there is no cloud. Just so, we think of clouds as consisting of, or largely of, water droplets, with the droplets in some suitable grouping. As one gets away from here, one gets outside a cloud; one passes a *place*, whatever that is, that is, or is part of, the cloud's boundary.

The "messier" our reality, the better for generating our problem of the many. Our actual reality is plenty messy indeed. In addition to water droplets, clouds may contain impurities (clouds in a smoggy area); the droplets themselves are complexes of constituents (molecules, atoms, particles), and each droplet has its own baffling transitions in store for us. To make our reasoning simple, however, and our exposition concise, I shall discount this extra messiness. For us right now, clouds shall be regarded as being composed entirely of droplets of water.

If a cloud's boundary has thickness, and even "fuzzy" edges, there may be certain droplets whose status as constituents of the cloud is objectively less than clear. (I think this suggestion contains incoherencies, but pass over them now. For, as will become clear, our problem is not helped nor hurt by the suggestion.) If x and y differ in the number of their constituents, they cannot be the same thing, much less, the same cloud. Equally, if x and y differ in the number of their objectively clear constituents, then they cannot be the same complex entity, much less, the same cloud. So, for the purposes of our discussion, it will make no difference, except as regards expository clarity and conciseness, whether we talk of *fuzzy* boundaries and *clear* constituents or, alternatively, and at another extreme, of simple "two-dimensional" boundaries, with no thickness at all, and just plain old constituents. In the sequel, I shall generally speak in the latter idiom, simpler and clearer. For those who must have fuzziness almost everywhere, the translations are easy to make; near this section's end, I shall show how.

In the same spirit, I wish to make one further simplifying assumption: As things have proceeded so far, we must still recognize three, and not two, relations between a cloud's boundary and any of the cloud's droplet constituents. To be sure, there are those droplets, millions of them, within the boundary of any cloud. No trouble there, even for exposition. Also, there are those millions outside the boundary, which likewise present no need for a remark. But there is a third group: the droplets, probably many thousands, at least, that will *intersect with* the boundary of any likely cloud prospect. What of each of these droplets; is it a constituent, or not, of the putative cloud in question? Were we talking of clear constituents, and clear non-constituents, these entities would be assigned, it appears, to some sort of midway status. And, then, we could proceed quickly to our reasoning that would concern only droplets in the clear category. Foreswearing such parlance, I think it most natural to consider these intersected droplets *not* to be constituents of the cloud whose boundary cuts through them. At all events, if I must, then by stipulation I shall now assume as much, since nothing of substance can be lost or gained by so doing. With these simplifications, the key matters emerge without distortion or delay: Our definite claim of *millions* of clouds, in even the smallest typical cloud's most carefully circumscribed situation, is readily at hand, if any clouds themselves ever are. Indeed, as we shall soon see, such a claim is something of an understatement.

Each of the droplets included by a cloud's boundary is a constituent of that cloud and, on our simplifying assumptions, nothing else is a constituent of it. Arbitrarily choose an alleged typical cloud and consider precisely those droplets that its boundary encloses. Now, in close proximity to this alleged boundary, there will be at least one other such boundary, of a *very* similar shape and "size." By only as minimal a deviation from the first as is required for the task, this second boundary includes, in addition to all those droplets just considered, exactly one other water droplet. We may imagine that, except for the slight bulge beyond the first required to include the new droplet, the two boundaries are elsewhere wholly coincident. In any event, this second boundary will include a certain complex entity which, on the relevant reckoning, has exactly one more constituent than does our typical cloud. Its droplets bear to it *very* much the same relation, whatever it is, that the already considered droplets, one less in number, bear to the putative typical item. On the relevant reckoning, then, this second complex entity, larger than the first in number of constituents, and also, we might add, in mass and in volume, is a different entity from our typical cloud. But in any respect important to being a cloud, there is scarcely any difference between the two. So in our situation, right there, there is at least one (concrete complex) entity that is, in those very regards, only *minutely* different from a certain *typical* cloud. By this consideration, it is intuitive, this second entity must also be a cloud, if not a typical cloud, at least a cloud of some sort or other. So our typical cloud's situation, arbitrarily chosen, contains at least two clouds, for it contains two different concrete entities each of which is a cloud.

Let us suppose, what seems very cautious, that the foregoing procedure may be applied distinctly at least a thousand times in the case of any typical cloud. Each application will involve a different single droplet that is very close to, but is external to, our typical cloud's boundary, as well as to the boundaries of every new candidate but one, that single droplet then being a constituent of only that one new candidate. As each candidate has a whole droplet as a constituent that is external to each of the others, each candidate really is a different entity from every other. (With a natural choice of their boundaries, each will slightly "overlap" each of the others, and each will "contain" the original allegedly typical specimen.) As each is only very slightly different from a certain typical cloud, in relevant respects, each is a cloud; so each is a different cloud from every other. Thus, in our situation, in addition to our putative typical cloud, there are at least a thousand clouds. But, of course, what we have just done by "reaching outward," we may do as well in reverse, by "reaching inward." Thus, by similar reasoning, there are at least another thousand clouds, each smaller by one droplet than our original typical specimen.

This rather surprising result, of at least two thousand additional clouds, has been arrived at rather cautiously. For with so very many droplets close to our original boundary, both inside and external, when selecting only a thousand in each direction, we could be very choosey in satisfying cloud criteria, whatever those criteria might be. Given our simplifications, it might seem that if we are to run the numbers up much higher this caution must be sacrificed. For, sticking to our simplified procedure, with whole droplets, it might seem that we should have to extend our boundaries considerably, thus reaching regions where careful selection has been abandoned. But his appearance is illusory. For it results from our overlooking the mathematics of combinations, with its notorious power to escalate.

A boundary that, in addition to the original's droplets, encloses any (combination) of our considered nearby external one thousand, but no other droplets, will enclose a cloud. For, although (most) such enclosed candidates will not be *quite* as similar to our typical specimen as was a candidate with only one differentiating droplet, still, in relevant respects, each will also be only *very* slightly different from a putative *typical* cloud. Now, barring sorites arguments, we may grant that there comes a point where such a slight difference is left behind us.[12] But, surely, we have not even come close to such a point with the variations of boundaries so far envisaged. With just these variations, our previously external droplets produce sufficiently good candidates equal to the number of combinations obtained in taking a thousand items each of the times up to and including a thousand. Each candidate is good enough, that is, not to fail to be a cloud, of some sort or other. And when we include internal selections, and combinations of internal and external,

---

12. *Without* barring such sorites, we get, not only our new problem, but, further, the result that there are no clouds. So I am just being generous here.

we further escalate matters fast, while never straying far from our original bounded paradigm. So if there are any clouds, there are not only millions of them, but, we might say, a problem of *many* millions.[13]

It will soon be my business to extend our arguments from their original exclusive concern with clouds to cover ordinary sorts of things quite generally, including planets and mountains, tables and their legs, human bodies, and so on. Before I do so, I should like briefly to sketch two things: First, as I promised, I would like to show how our discussion can be put in terms that do not imply the fine boundaries we have recently been supposing. And, then, I would like to say a few words about how the entire discussion of this present section relates to our introductory arguments, which were advanced in sections 2 and 3.

First, then, let us suppose that clouds, even typical ones, do not have the "neat and decisive" boundaries we have been discussing but have, instead, "inherently fuzzy" boundaries. Assuming that this idea is coherent, what does it imply? I take it that, according to the idea of fuzzy boundaries, there are things or stuff, whose status with regard to an alleged bounded item, e.g., a certain typical cloud, is *objectively unclear*, or *indefinite*, or *indeterminate*. Despite this rather mysterious complication, however, fuzzy boundaries occasion no great changes in our arguments.

Consider a typical cloud with such a boundary. In addition to droplets with unclear status, there are many further afield that are *clearly not* constituents of the cloud. Third, finally, and perhaps most important, there are other droplets still, closest to hand, so to say, each of which is a *clear constituent* of the cloud. Consider another fuzzy boundary that encloses a space slightly larger than the first. It does that in just such a way that it encloses a complex entity with all the typical cloud's clear droplets as clear constituents for it, too, *plus one more clear one for it*, which had unclear status for the original, typical specimen. What the new fuzzy boundary bounds is a *different entity* from the typical cloud that is fuzzily bounded, for it differs from the latter in *a certain clear component part*. But, all things considered, and in particular as regards any criteria for cloudhood, the difference between these two fuzzily bounded entities is quite minute. As the one is a *typical* cloud, the other, fuzzy boundary and all, is at least a cloud of some sort or other. Thus, with fuzzy boundaries as much as with neat, we must have, if there are ever any clouds at all, at least two clouds in our situation. The reasoning from here to millions, it is plain, will be entirely familiar. What we have just done is quite obvious:

---

13. I do not know how to tote up the numbers, precisely and in detail, but I have been assured that the mathematical results here are *extremely* congenial to our arguments.

we replaced talk of neat boundaries by allusions to fuzzy ones; then we made compensating changes right down the line. As such compensations are always available, it makes no difference to our problem whether we think of a cloud's limiter as neat, even two-dimensional, or as being not only somewhat thick but inherently fuzzy as well.

In this section, we contemplated certain combinations of water droplets. By that means, we saw many millions of clouds where one would normally suppose only one cloud to be. Or better, we saw a dilemma involving such millions. How do these recent perceptions relate to our two offered arguments? The first of those arguments, our Argument about Clouds as Concrete Complexes, mentions millions of relevant entities in its *second* premise. We have now seen why this premise, *apparently the argument's most controversial* one, is actually correct and might even be considered an *understatement.* As concerns our second argument, our Argument about Clouds as Bounded Entities, its *third* premise would, I think, be considered its most controversial one. It is in this premise, after all, where the argument first makes mention of millions of clouds. (In section 4, it will be remembered, this premise is analysed into our principle of minute differences plus a complex statement where millions of bound items are mentioned.) Here, too, our recent perceptions involve us in seeing the correctness of that multitudinous premise. So, by means of the mathematics of combinations, even the "weakest links" in our arguments may be seen as plenty strong enough.

6. Extending Our Arguments to Other Ordinary Things

Clouds, we may say, are *ordinary things* of one particular sort. If things of that sort, clouds, really do exist, then through science we gain an understanding of them as *complex concrete entities*, each composed, largely if not entirely, of many tiny constituents. Now, in addition to clouds, there are, of course, many other sorts of ordinary things about which we appear to think and talk: salt shakers, stones, planets and their mountains, human bodies and their arms, hands, and fingers, trees and their trunks and branches, tables and their legs and tops, swizzle sticks, and so on. Although it takes a bit more doing, science reveals all these things, if they do actually exist, also to be complex concrete entities, with their own tiny components. Through this revelation, I suggest, we may readily apply, or extend, our arguments about clouds to cover all these other ordinary things as well.

If it could be managed properly, the most direct way to do this would be to add to our arguments a premise to the effect that these other sorts of things, typical tables, for example, just are clouds; presumably, they would be clouds of molecules, or atoms, or elementary particles. But although such an idea may be common in trying to view ordinary things scientifically, I should be rather suspicious of any such extension of our arguments. Rather, I am inclined to think that such a characterization is only metaphorical. For it seems to me that, despite the similarities thus alluded to, there remain relevant differences between tables and clouds, that block an identification.

The conditions for the identity of a table through time, for one example, appear to be rather different from those for clouds. A typical table may be readily disjoined into five separated large parts, for instance, its top and four legs. These may later be reassembled or, alternatively, not. Even if never reassembled, there are many situations in which the table would be regarded as existing throughout; the parts might be on exhibit together, to show how such a table looks when taken apart. But no similar strength against separation appears available for the continued existence of any cloud. Now, I am not claiming that, as against the idea that tables are clouds, such considerations are absolutely conclusive. But, surely, they are substantial enough for us to be suspicious of the idea and to look elsewhere for a less controversial means of extending our arguments.

We may do better, I think, by noting that, at least in *those respects relevant* to our arguments, there is *no important difference* between clouds and many other ordinary things. Rather, the relation of a cloud to its constituents is *relevantly the same* as that between a table and what constitutes it.[14] Because of this, parallels to our Arguments may be advanced for many other sorts of ordinary things. For example, wherever 'cloud' occurs in our stated premises, we can put 'table' or 'stone', making whatever grammatical adjustments are then required. In that way, we can obtain arguments, just as good as before, for dilemmas with regard to tables and stones.[15]

14. On matters of physical fact, I have relied on Robert Weingard, a philosopher of physics, and, indirectly, on colleagues of his in the Rutgers University Physics Department.

In section 9, I shall argue that not much depends on the physical facts, anyway. Still, it is nice to have nature, so to say, on our problem's side.

15. Our problem is by no means confined to the putative referents of various common nouns for kinds, like 'table' and 'stone'. If anything, it is even more evident that the problem arises for alleged referents of many ordinary expressions lacking such terms, e.g., 'thing with blue and red stripes', 'delightful gift', 'product of the finest Italian craftsmanship', and so on, and so forth. So, I am just focusing, you might say, on some of the *hardest* cases: If things go badly for common sense *here*, with 'stone', as seems to be impending, an awful lot of "easier stuff" will fall as well.

For specificity, let us focus on our second argument and on how to extend it. What about boundaries, then, for things other than clouds, thus, for typical stones, or tables? Perhaps even more clearly than with clouds, any of these things will have a boundary, which separates it, and its constituents, from whatever is external to it. Centered on such a boundary, there will be our familiar bounding envelope. And in this envelope there will be many other boundaries, each relevantly enclosing a different complex concrete entity.

Regarding small salient constituents, what are the underlying physical facts that ground this plethora of complex candidates? So far as I can gather from reliable sources, the situation here is, in relevant ways, very much like that before with a cloud and its droplets: At any moment, just about anywhere you please along our stone's boundary there will be some atoms, or molecules, whose status, with regard to our typical stone, nature has left unclear; there is no natural break between the atoms of the stone and so very many others that, *ex hypothesi*, are only outside it. But for our argument to be extended properly, we do not even need anything as cloudlike as that which, it appears, nature so generously does provide. Rather, we require only some such extremely cautious proposition as this following one: Even if there are many places along our stone's boundary where a clean break is given by nature, indeed, even if almost all the boundary's places are of this sort, there are at least a thousand atoms (or molecules) of the stone which are not naturally separate from all relevantly similar ones in the stone's environment. The cautious idea here is that with each of at least one thousand different problematic atoms, we may apportion things variously for want of any natural separation.

Where our typical stone's boundary excludes each of these thousand, as may be assumed, a very similar boundary may be described which includes any one or combination of them, as well as all the atoms in the typical specimen, but no other atoms. In this way many millions of boundaries may be described. Cautiously reckoning by atoms, each will enclose an entity that is, in relevant regards, only *minutely* different from a certain *typical* stone. So each will enclose a different stone. Even with such a cautious supposition, and such cautious reckoning, our argument may thus be extended to cover stones as well as clouds: Either there really are no stones at all, or else, in any situation involving a typical stone, there are millions of stones. Dilemmas for other ordinary things, for example, tables, follow in like manner.

Having extended our arguments from clouds to more earthy things, we might ask: Why did we not begin with these latter, "more cohesive" objects in the first place? Logically speaking, we might just as well have done so; indeed, as I shall soon argue, perhaps we might better have done so. But people are not often as logical as they should be. So for psychological reasons, it was best to begin with alleged entities that, *often* in our everyday experience, even seem to present something of a puzzle: Where the devil does one of these things end and where, in contrast, is what merely serves to surround it? This puzzling experience, where reality itself appears to mirror vagueness, opens our minds to "new possibilities." Further, it provides us with motivation to think logically, at length and in complex detail, about what ordinarily passes as being too simple for argument: How many things of such-and-such *ordinary kind are right there now*? Clouds, then, are good food for thought, when one wants to serve up the problem of the many.

Once the introduction has been effected, however, clouds do not seem especially well suited for our problem, after all. For, as I said early on, our problem concerns reality and not, except perhaps indirectly and secondarily, how reality appears to us. Just so, whereas it is at least probably right that a cloud must have a boundary, we may be still more confident that this much is required for a table, or a stone. Why is the latter idea certainly not worse, and perhaps better, founded?

We think of certain things as *concrete* and of others as, perhaps more or less, *abstract*. When a concrete thing is an *ordinary* kind of *spatial* entity, as in the case of a table or stone, it must have a boundary. Consider, in contrast, certain "more abstract" entities, which have their being rooted, so to say, in particular concrete entities. Thus a *swarm of bees* is somewhat abstract, the bees being thought of as concrete. It is somewhat difficult to think of the swarm as really having a boundary: Does the swarm really include as a part a certain (part of the) space that separates the bees? It seems not, but, then again, certain things do point that way. So it is hard to know quite what to think here. No matter: it is not important for us to decide the issue. Rather, my point in mentioning it is this: *Insofar* as we *can* think of clouds as *concrete*, our boundaries for them seem to have a firmer footing.

How, then, *are* we to think of clouds? I think, though I am not very sure of it, that clouds, if they exist, must actually be concrete things. Part of what underlies my thought is that there seems to be the following important contrast between the idea of a cloud and those of such apparently more abstract entities as swarms of bees: A cloud "could be," with no contradiction in terms, composed purely of homogeneous stuff, with no distinct *constituent things* at all.[16] Further, along the same line, it is at least somewhat odd to say of a certain cloud that it is a

16. Contrary to the offerings of certain lexicographers. See note 2.

? *cloud of water droplets* even if the cloud is in fact constituted of just such droplets.[17] In contrast, it is at least false to say, if not utterly nonsensical, that a swarm (of bees) "could be" composed entirely of homogeneous stuff, with no (bees or other) distinct constituent things serving to compose it.

While I believe I have been right in treating clouds as concrete, I am surer of the point where many other sorts of things are concerned: stones and tables, to mention a familiar couple. It is utterly absurd, I feel sure, to talk of a * *stone of molecules*, no matter how many molecules may serve to constitute a given stone. Along with this, so far as the logic of the word "stone" is concerned, all the stones "could be" composed, each and every one of them, entirely of continuous, homogeneous stuff, with no small constituent things at all. So I feel quite sure that stones, if any such things do exist, must be concrete entities. Equally, and perhaps for that very reason, I feel sure that if there are stones, each one must have a boundary. (It is a further question, we may allow, what sort of boundary might prove acceptable for a stone.) By reason of their more evident concreteness, most other ordinary things cleave more surely to our problem than do clouds. Epistemologically and psychologically, clouds do better than stones at getting any problem before us, in the first place; but stones do better than clouds at keeping it there. (Even so, clouds do not do badly at that second stage, either.) As experience with extending our arguments thus serves to confirm, our new problem is not only a very comprehensive difficulty but a particularly persistent one.[18]

At all events, we have done quite enough with clouds, at least for the while. So let us continue to think some more about such more evidently concrete things as stones, and of what this concreteness might imply for them and their situations. A fairly obvious point, but one still worth mentioning, is this: If you are thinking of a stone, you must be thinking of a concrete object. Suppose that an ordinary person, looking at what we take to be a single stone, operated according to the following function: If there is at least one concrete object there before him which "we would all take to be" a stone, he thinks of a *certain abstract object*; otherwise, he does not think of that object. Could this object, about

17. My Webster's also lists under the noun 'cloud', "3: a great crowd or multitude: SWARM." If there is such a sense of 'cloud', then it is different from the one I have been using throughout. In *that* sense, the referents of 'cloud', if any, would *not* be concrete things.

18. On the matters of these last four paragraphs, I am indebted to correspondence with John Tienson and to discussion with Terence Leichti.

which he thus thinks, be the only real *stone* in our story, so that this person might conceivably thus avoid our problem of the many? No, it could not. For since that thought of object is abstract, and not concrete, *it* could *not* be *any* stone at all. For any of those things, the stones, must be concrete entities. Goodness knows what that fellow may be thus thinking of; but we can be sure it is *not* a stone.

Relations of *constitution* may obtain between various sorts of things. Perhaps bees, which are concrete, may constitute a swarm of bees, which is at least somewhat abstract and is thus not concrete. The natural numbers, which are quite abstract, may perhaps constitute the infinite sequence of those numbers which, though not itself a natural number, is also abstract. Various molecules, which are very small concrete things, may perhaps constitute real tables and stones, which are also concrete. Certain stuff, like iron, which is also concrete, may serve to constitute such concrete things as well. (It does not happen, as far as I can see, that abstract things can literally constitute concrete ones.) For our problem of the many it is the alleged constituion of certain concrete things by certain other ones that is of importance.

In any case, no matter what is constituting what, that which constitutes cannot be the very same thing as what is thus constituted; that is, nothing can constitute itself. Now some people will think that by noting the concrete character of a stone, and in promoting our problem of the many, I must be identifying a stone with its concrete constituents, that I must be implying that a stone is "nothing more than" certain atoms, for example. But *nothing* could be *further* from the truth, as my preceding remark indicates. *So far* is it from implying such an identification that the statement that a certain stone is constituted of certain atoms *actually* implies quite the *opposite*: The statement *implies that* the stone is something *other than* the atoms. Still, as my earlier remarks imply, *both* the stone *and* the atoms may be concrete entities; indeed, *if they exist*, they *must* be. Our problem of the many is hardly hindered. In any relevantly typical realistic situation, either there is no stone or else there are so many atoms so arranged that each of *millions* of groups of them has as its members things that constitute a stone, a stone different from that constituted by the members of any other group.

The concreteness of stones disarms thoughts that vagueness might actually enter into the nature of each of these entities itself. And these thoughts certainly should be disarmed. For they can easily lead to others that would seem to produce a solution to our problem. But being as confused as it is quickly effected, such a product would be no genuine solution. According to these thoughts, because stones themselves are vague, or are indefinite things, no particular number of constituents, say, of molecules, can properly be said to constitute any one of them. This, even though stones do exist, as do molecules, and the latter do constitute the former. (Similarly, no particular amount of matter can be said to constitute a stone.) But my bounded candidates for stonehood, it will be pointed out, are definite enough to allow such statements; my complex concrete entities have no inherent vagueness. Hence they are so different from stones that no problem about them need involve other more ordinary, inherently vague objects.

It seems to me that such a common objection, though perhaps well meant, cannot itself be well conceived; rather, it is fraught with confusion. For what can it be for a stone to be constituted of molecules but of no number of molecules? And although in any real situation *we* may have only a *vague idea* as to what is the number, in any given stone, what kind of number can it possibly be if not some particular number? No, either the stone, that presumedly real, typical specimen, is composed of a definite number of molecules, whatever the number may happen to be, or *else* it really is *not* composed of molecules at *all*. But if the putative entity does not number some molecules among its constituents, thus, some particular, definite number of them, it is *not* any real typical *stone* that we are discussing.

As I said, this confused idea about numbers rests on a prior confusion of thinking of stones, of such concrete objects, as themselves being vague or indefinite. The only things that can be vague, of course, are rather more abstract ones: words, statements, shareable ideas, and the like. And although a statement about a stone may be rather indefinite, even, for example, as to the number of molecules in the latter, the stone itself, which is not abstract at all, cannot be in the least bit indefinite. So the vagueness, and any indefiniteness here, will only be a feature of the expressions employed, such as 'stone', the statements made, the thoughts expressed thereby, and the like; it will *not* figure in any *stone* itself. I suggest that, occurring just where it does, the relevant vagueness, far from avoiding or resolving our problem, serves instead actually to generate the problem of the many.

What I have just done, by focusing upon a stone's required concreteness, I am happy to grant, may be regarded as a refutation of the idea that any ordinary thing may have a *fuzzy* boundary. If so, well and good; for I have also argued that such ordinary entities must have boundaries of some sort or other. Thus we may conclude that, if they exist, such things have boundaries that are not fuzzy but that are as neat as you please.[19,20] This conclusion does not, of course, contradict my previously argued claim that even if fuzzy boundaries are allowed, indeed, even if they are required, our problematic dilemma can be generated. On the contrary, either way our problem arises. What we have just argued is this: The more obvious routes to our problem are also, it seems, the only genuine ones. Thus I have just given an argument *a fortiori*.

19. I think this is a good place for me to present an independent argument for the proposition that if stones exist, then each of them must have a two-dimensional boundary, with no width or extent, though suitably curved through three-dimensional space. Consider any alleged stone. With no boundary, or limiting places, one can travel from a point within the stone, in any direction, forever and never get to be outside. But, in that case, we will have a stoney universe rather than a universe with stones. On the other side, with no boundary, from any point outside the stone, and there must be some such, one can travel in any direction forever and never encounter the stone. So, again, nowhere in the universe does the stone exist. The stone has a boundary; but must it be without any width? (I do not care what the ordinary sense of boundary may dictate or allow. If required to do so, I use the term here, as a term of art.) The cloud's boundary must either be part of the stone or else not; we rule out the idea that only part of the boundary is part of the stone. Now, if it *is* part of the stone, then the boundary is *internal* to the stone. But if it has extent, then there must be an "outer" limit to it, otherwise we can travel forever, in any way, and always be in the stone, for being in its boundary. So, it cannot have extent; or, what amounts to the same, whatever limits *that* extent is the stone's *real* boundary and is extentless. All right, now suppose the alternative: the boundary is *external* to the stone itself. If such an external boundary has extent, we can travel through it toward the stone. But unless it has a limit, the *real*, extentless boundary, we shall never get to the stone itself; the stone will not exist anywhere. So, in any case, a stone's boundary has no width at all.

Few philosophers have thought seriously about boundary conditions on ordinary (physical) things. An exception is Ernest W. Adams in "The Naive Conception of the Toplogy of the Surface of a Body," in *Space, Time and Geometry*, ed. P. Suppes (Dordrecht, 1973), pp. 402–24, and in "Two Aspects of Physical Identity," *Philosophical Studies* 34 (1978): 111–34.

20. Perhaps this is a good place to present or sketch a sorites argument, which I call *the sorites of the boundary*. For, otherwise, you might think that I believe in the extentless boundaries lately argued for *on condition*. I have no such belief, for I deny the condition itself; I do not believe in stones. Here, with this sorites, is one reason why: Our gradual, messy world has the atoms of an alleged stone fade off into those merely in the putative surrounding. Take a point "well within the stone" and one "well outside" such that the line joining them by least distance is a problematic path toward, or from, a boundary. (If there is even one such problematic path, the argument goes through. In fact, there are "ever so many.") Take *very* small steps inward, each equal to every other. Chosen small enough, it is quite clear that no step will take you to or across the stone's boundary; none will take you to the stone. So, you cannot encounter the stone that way. If the stone existed, then, even with such a small choice, you could. Therefore, the stone really does not exist.

Both the sorites just given and the argument in the preceding note need further elaboration and defense, which I cannot properly do here. But I have examined them for quite a while. The closer I looked, the better they looked.

7. On Infinities of Nearby Stones and Clouds

The idea of any infinity of stones, or clouds, being right there, ready for you to take in with one quick look, may seem preposterous. It does to me. But, then, I am a sort of Parmenidian philosopher, so to say, who does not believe in the reality of any stones or clouds at all, who opts for the first disjunct of our dilemma of the many. Those philosophers who, like ordinary folks, do believe in stones must allow, as a real epistemic possibility, a nearby infinity of the blamed things; they are faced, we might say, with a problem of the infinitely many. Let us see why.

It is easiest to see how an infinite version of our problem arises when we have in mind a certain possible world, or possible underlying reality, that is quite different from (what we take to be) the actual one. This is the sort of possible reality I discussed in section 4, vividly represented there by a transition between putative red regions (clouds) and their alleged blue surrounding (the sky around them). In such a world, clouds are composed, if they really exist at all, of one sort of matter which, within the cloud, is relevantly continuous and homogeneous. The surrounding, if there really is such a distinct thing, is composed of a matter of a different sort which is "spread throughout it" in the same relevantly continuous fashion. Around where a cloud's boundary is (supposed to be) there is a gradual transition from matter of the one sort to matter of the other. This idea may be immediately extended from clouds to other, more evidently concrete ordinary things, such as stones and tables.

Now, any stone must have a boundary, a place or group of places where it stops, on the other side of which the stone is not; otherwise, we would just have a stoney universe. So, somewhere around the (red) stone matter there is a boundary that separates the stone, the thing composed of that matter, from its surrounding. Especially because it makes no difference to the argument, for simplicity of exposition we shall, as we did before, think of such a boundary as without thickness, as two-dimensional, if you will, though curved through three-dimensional space. This fine boundary includes or limits a certain amount, and indeed even a certain batch, of (red) stuff or matter; it is that very matter which constitutes our putative typical (red) stone.

Think of a second fine boundary that for the most part lies coincident with the first but that bulges slightly outward from it in a certain relatively small area. The relations between these two boundaries are just the same as those between our first and second considered before with respect to a complex stone's nearby, or peripheral, atom. The only difference is in what the boundaries enclose. This time, there is no extra atom for the bulging boundary above to encompass; so what it encloses is not greater by one salient constituent than what the other bounds. But the bulger does include, in addition to all the matter the one does, a certain extra bit or batch of matter, which is not enclosed by the other. Speaking quaintly, we might say the bulger encloses about an extra "atom's worth of stuff." So the bulging boundary suitably encloses a (simple) concrete entity which is, in regard to matter, and also mass and volume, greater than that enclosed by the boundary imagined just beforehand. Thus each of the boundaries bounds a different (simple concrete) entity.

Supposing there to be stones in this world, the first of these bounded entities is so lucky as to be a typical stone. In any respect relevant to being a stone, though, the second differs from it only minutely. So, as is intuitive and as our principle dictates, the second bounded entity will also be a stone, if not a typical one, at least a stone of some sort or other. Or it will if there are any stones. Putting one and one together, we get two: Either there really are no stones in this world, or else our chosen situation contains at least two of those things.

That much is by now pretty familiar. But how to make the step from at least two to *infinity*? It is easy. We need only realize that "between" the two boundaries considered there are an infinite number of others. Starting with the original boundary, each of these others is coincident with it for the most part but makes something of a bulge where our second did. Each one, so to say, makes a slightly greater bulge than the one before it, the maximum being the bulge of the secondary boundary. So we have an infinite number of very similar boundaries there. Each bounds an entity different from that bounded by every other; indeed, they all differ, though very slightly, in mass, in volume, and even in shape. We have here an infinite number of bounded concrete entities. In all sorts of respects, including any relevant to stonehood, each differs quite minutely from the original putative typical item. By our principle of minute differences, if there are stones, there will be an infinite number of them in this very simple situation.

There is another way to "see an infinity of stones" here, which connects more obviously with the original third premise of my second argument (The Argument about Clouds as Bounded Entities.) Centered on our first alleged boundary, and extending just a bit to either side, we may describe a thin "band," what I called a *bounding envelope*. Even sticking with our typical stone's shape, now, we may "see" in this envelope an infinity of similarly shaped boundaries. Each of these bounds an item differing in mass and volume from that bounded by every other; but this time, of course, the shape of each bounded item is the same. From here on, the reasoning is familiar.

It will be granted, perhaps, that if our world were of the sort just mentioned, our dilemma would reach into the realm of the infinite. But our world is not much like that one. On the contrary, over *there* stones are *simple* concrete things; in *actuality*, they are *complex*, each constituted by at least very many distinct smaller things, in particular, of so many atoms. But no actual stone is composed of an infinite number of such atoms. So, *realistically*, where does infinity get a chance to enter our new problem?

One way to try to reach that high is to dig deeply, so to say, into our small salient constituents, into our atoms themselves. But insofar as what we find is real, we appear to be left, at some elementary point, with small units that, in fact, cannot be further divided. We thus encounter, perhaps, combinations of elementary particles. But, while running the numbers up, all such reckoning will leave us in the realm of the finite. Focusing on the most realistic situations, this "descending" line of approach does not look promising.

To give infinity a better chance, let us shift our focus from our atoms, or a cloud's droplets, to *whatever it is that separates them from one another*. What is it that does this? Some other sort of matter; empty space, perhaps? For what follows, any such answer will do as well as any other. The important thing is that whatever its nature, this *separator*, as I shall call it, blend gradually into whatever is found in the putative surrounding. And, indeed, no natural break is ever in fact encountered. Now, then, given this realistic blending, the important issue is whether or not the separator is continuous. If our separator is physically continuous, that is, if it is in reality infinitely divisible, then we may argue to an infinity of nearby stones, and clouds.

So far as science can tell us, the separator of a typical stone might really be continuous. With this prospect before us, it is necessary to inquire about the status of the separator with respect to the stone whose salient constituents it serves to distinguish. Is this separator itself part of the stone, a much larger but less easily noticed constituent than the atoms, and any other things, separated by it? I shall argue that an affirmative answer is available to us here, one that follows from our concept or idea of a stone, providing it applies to such realistic situations at all. Now, ordinarily, no one has any conscious or explicit thoughts about this matter, one way or the other. So we must probe a bit for anything to point the way.

First, we may begin our probe by asking what we should say of a tiny item, perhaps a miniscule space ship, that appeared to travel into a stone, upon learning that, in fact, the item went well in between the atom's (and particles) of the stone, never so much as even touching any such constituent. I am confident that we should then judge, as we did at first, that the item was, nevertheless, actually inside the stone though, with a suitable item, not a part of the stone. Now, someone might of course raise various objections to taking this literally, but I cannot see any of these to have much substance. And it does seem to follow from a literal judgment here that the tiny item must then be surrounded by space occupied by the stone itself. But the space surrounding this tiny thing is all occupied by our separator, for it never so much as touched any small constituent. Given that, the only plausible way for the stone to be in that space is for the separator to be part of the stone. So our miniscule spaceship will be suitably surrounded by, and inside, the stone itself only if the separator is actually part of the stone.

Second, considerations of volume, in the sense of amount of space, lead to the same conclusion. The volume of a typical stone, we should reckon as so many cubic feet, or inches, though perhaps without putting a fine point on things. But much of this volume is occupied only by the separator, and not by any of the stone's smaller, more salient constituents. If the separator is not part of the stone, then either our volumetric judgments are systematically in error, and by quite a lot, or else we must face the mystery of how a volume equal to the separator's may be properly reckoned toward the total for the stone itself. Let us not monger such mysteries, nor torture our thought beyond recognition. Rather, let us explain these matters simply, by means of what may be simply put: Everything within a stone's boundary, as we have described such an encloser, is part of the stone. (Our previous "tiny item" will not be part of a stone even so. How, so? The stone will have an internal (part of its total) boundary, separating it from the enclosed foreign body.)

In the *third* place, if we do not count the separator as part of the stone, we should have to say that a stone is a "scattered" entity, though one which may cease to exist when the arrangement of its scattered components is no longer maintained, e.g., when they get "too far" apart from one another. But it is intuitive, according to our concept of a stone, that if there are such things, they are not thus scattered, being instead relevantly continuous, or at least a relevantly good approximation thereto.

Fourth, and perhaps most important, if the separator is not part of our stone, what are we to make of the stone's boundary? Our idea of a stone has it that its boundary should be a continuous limiter, or at least something much of that sort, and that whatever is just inside of the boundary be, if not the whole stone, then some part of it. However, if the stone's boundary is even roughly where we have been considering it, and the separator is not part of the stone, then much of what the boundary encloses will not be part of the stone but, instead, only a quite alien thing. That is absurd. But if the separator is not part of the stone, what is the alternative? The alternative is equally repugnant: To include just the stone itself, and so no alien thing as well, the boundary will have to be a scattered-sum-of-boundaries of constituent particles. I doubt that such a sum is coherent at all; in any case, it is not the *boundary* of any *stone*. As both of the alternatives to it are absurd, the separator is part of the stone itself. Thus we may reason, at least four times over, that a stone's separator is a genuine, though often overlooked, part of it.[21]

Given this requirement, what transpires if it happens that the relevant space, or whatever separates atoms, is relevantly continuous? What happens is just this: With any nearby typical stone, an infinity of nearby stones will exist. Let us see why.

Supposing things to be continuous, an infinite number of nearby boundaries will each limit a different separator, each thus apportioning a different separator to the stone it bounds. (To see the infinity of boundaries, we just follow recipes for the imagination already given earlier in this present section.) Each of an infinite number of different boundaries will bound different likely candidates for stonehood. If there really are any stones, then, in our situation (at least) one of these is a typical stone. But, in any respect relevant to stonehood, any of the others differs from such a one only quite minutely; quite minutely, indeed! So if there are stones, each of this infinity is a stone, at least a stone of some sort or other. Thus a continuous domain for would-be separators yields an infinite version of our problem: Either there really are *no* stones at all, *or else* there are situations involving typical stones and, in any of these, there is an *infinite* number of stones involved. The reasoning to infinity is quite parallel, I trust, for our old friends, clouds, for tables, and even for human bodies.

---

21. Now, it may also be that an adequate argument, or several, can be adduced to opposite effect, to the conclusion that a stone's separator is *not* part of it. But if there is one, what would it show: It would not necessarily show that our previous arguments were in error. On the contrary, it might show that *in addition to* the requirement on stones that, in these situations, their separators be counted as parts, *there was also a requirement to opposite effect*. Thus it could be that our idea of a stone was *inconsistent*. Reflection on attempts to apply the idea properly to these situations would, in such an event, then serve to reveal the inconsistency. And this, of course, would not avoid our problem of the many. On the contrary, it would not only yield our dilemma but would resolve it in the direction of the first, and the more radical, of its two alternatives.

Not to make things easy for our problem now, we shall assume that our concept of a stone is a consistent one. But then, as we have argued, this means that the *only* relevant requirement regarding the separator is that it *is* part of the stone.

The argument for this dilemma concerning infinity has made a crucial substantive assumption about physical reality: that whatever separates small items, or at least appears to do so, is in fact continuous. Well, what of this supposition; is it true, or not? To get serious about this is to ponder our current epistemological situation regarding the innermost features of physical reality. As a layman, and no scientist, my own position is at a remove. But it seems to me that no one is as yet so very much better off than I am: As of right now, epistemologically speaking, space, or whatever separates, might really be infinitely divisible; so, it might really be that our alternatives are zero or infinity for nearby stones. By the same token, for all anyone can now say, our separators might really not be infinitely physically divisible. For all we can say, it might really be that our alternatives are zero or, not infinity, but a finite number running into the millions. Either way, of course, we have quite a dilemma.

Whether or not our separators are continuous, so whether or not they generate an infinite version of our problem, they will play a part that is quite in addition to everything done by our smaller, more salient constituents. And a realization of the part they play can prove quite instructive regarding the place of ordinary things, like stones, in the concrete complexity of reality. For consider a rather neater world than ours, relevantly possible, in which the arrangement of particles in a typical stone, as well as in other ordinary things, is as neat and regular as you please, both in the interior and even at what we take to be the periphery. And suppose as well that right outside the "most peripheral layer" of atoms, there is a rather spatious vacuum all around, or some undifferentiated field of rarified stuff. Just so, as regards small, salient constituents, there will be no gradual blending here, between those of the stone and those merely in its environment. In a case like this, nature provides a clean break *of a sort*. But is it a break *that will yield exactly one stone* in the described situation? I think not. Confining consideration to small constituents would have things be that way; but we should then miss out on the part played by that which separates them. For even with such a regular arrangement, many different, equally good apportionments of separators are available. One, as good as any, is to take the smoothest outside tangent surface as a boundary; another, just as good, is to take a surface that *barely* encloses each most external particle, then dipping in a certain amount, perhaps the diameter of such a particle, until it is halfway to the next particle, where it then rises, economically to enclose again. And, of course between these two, there are very many (perhaps infinitely many) compromises, each no worse than any other possible boundary for any such stone. Here, then, and *thus also in the actual world*, we shall have *very many stones each having exactly the same atomic constituents as every other*, providing, of course, that, in any world, there ever are any real stones at all.

8. Internal and External Relations

Philosophers have meant various things by *relations*, and there are various philosophic contrasts concerning relations that have been marked by 'internal' and 'external'. Seldom, if ever, have these contrasts been clear ones. So it is with some trepidation that I approach such metaphysical matters here. Still and all, it seems to me that some brief remarks in this regard can serve to make clearer the severity of our problem of the many.

Focusing on salient constituents, say, atoms, we find that those of a certain table bear certain relations to each other, regarding spatial distribution, bonding forces, and so on. It is at least largely owing to these mutual relations, we may call them the *internal relations* among the table's (salient) constituents, that those atoms serve to constitute that table. Ordinarily, we are inclined to think that this is pretty much all there is to the matter of having a table in a common realistic situation. But, on reflection, it seems that, if there are in fact any tables, there are some rather different factors involved that are also crucial. I think that we may fairly say that these factors concern the *external relations* between those constituents of the table and, on the other hand, various other entities that are, quite literally, external to the table, for example, atoms in the table's immediate surrounding. Fortunately for our new problem and, so, unfortunately for our common sense thinking, these relations are, in reality, gradually manifested. Accordingly, a consideration of the complexities they might impose will do nothing to avoid, or to solve, our problem of the many. On the contrary, an appreciation of these external relations will impress upon us all the more the persistent character of this problem.

Consider a table made of iron, an iron table. Now, the internal relations of the table, the relations among its (internal) constituents, are important for the table's being there. But so are the relations to other things in the world, things outside the table. Should "too many" other iron atoms be right up against those of the considered putative table, and be suitably bound together by appropriate forces, we might well have a large solid iron sphere. Well, some such thing as that will be no table at all, let alone the particular table we first supposed. So it is important for the table's being there that the relations of its atoms to those others are as they "in fact" are, and are *not* as we *next* supposed them to be.

Consider a less extreme situation involving our supposed iron table. This time there *would not be so many* additional atoms bound to the first group, to the table's, so many that we should have no table at all in the situation. Instead, there would be only a few new atoms attached to the first group. What of those *first* atoms *now*, when these other atoms are attached to them; would *they* still constitute a table? (Would they, perhaps, even constitute the very same table that they did in the previously mentioned situation?) If the answer is affirmative, then, even sticking just with combinations of atoms, there would be, in this situation, at least two tables present: one would be composed of just the atoms in the first group; the other, larger table, of those plus the few atoms attached to them.

I believe that our thoughts here are in conflict. One thought, quite common enough, is that the first atoms now do *not* any table make, that the attached atoms logically prevent them from constituting a table. So this thought is, in effect, that, in this case, those first atoms would have the wrong external relations, for tablehood, to the world's other atoms. But, I have found, there is another thought that quite a few people have. This *second* thought is that those first atoms *will* still constitute a table. (Indeed, a strong but common version of this thought continues, they will still constitute the first table here mentioned.)

For people who have this second thought (even if they also have the conflicting first one), our problem of the many will have yet another way of arising. For while the first atoms will "by themselves" still constitute a table (presumably, the first table), those atoms *along with* the "newly attached" atoms will constitute another, slightly larger table. And where two tables are thus encountered, many more cannot be far off. But, as I have implied, many folks will resist this second, troublesome thought, or not even have it at all. Let us now suppose, what may be quite doubtful, that they alone are right here. If so, then we might say this, regarding our currently considered situation: With even those few other atoms attached, the *absence* of *certain external* relations prevents the first atoms from constituting a table, hence, from being a problematic factor. By the same token, the *presence* of *opposite* external relations will prevent this trouble here.

But, of course, we have just pretended to think about things in a manner that hardly conforms to the complexities of reality. Even forgetting considerations of the separator, and the complexities that they present, we must have had in mind a very nice regular atomic arrangement, like that mentioned for stones toward the end of the previous section. There, a stone's atoms, here, a table's, were so nicely arranged that "there would be no question" regarding any of them, whether or not it was a constituent of a most salient stone, or table, in the situation. Now, in such a *special* case, the largest group of considered atoms has, as compared with any other group in the situation, some rather special external relation or relations. Surrounded by a vacuum, as we supposed, its members alone would "stand free"; they alone would be a group of bonded entities with no such further entity bonded to them. All the "interior groups," in contrast, have no such special, clean, "free" status. So, in *such* a case (and still forgetting about separators), there *seems some reason* to suppose that *only one table* is constituted. But even when matters of external relations are in the forefront, any *realistic* situations will yield *no* such happy result.

In realistic situations, there is, not the pretty arrangement of atoms and surrounding vacuum lately considered, but a more gradual falling off of the relevant forces and materials, from the central part where stones, or tables, may allegedly be found, to the peripheral areas. Now, it is of *course* true that any selected group of atoms will have external relations, to the other atoms in the world, that are *somewhat* different from those of any other. So this fact of gradualness cannot mean that any group's external relations will be identical to any other's. But if we consider any *such* relation that might, with any shred of plausibility, be of *importance* to any *ordinary kind of object*, to tablehood, or to stonehood, then our gradualness would appear to mean quite a lot. For it appears, there is no *such* external relation which *exactly one* group of atoms will have, in any such gradual, realistic state of affairs. Rather, in such situations, *any* such *appropriate external relation that one* complex concrete entity, or its components, may enjoy will be possessed as well by *plenty of others*, which overlap or nest with it. For example, if one such entity "approximates to standing free to such-and-such a degree," many others will similarly approximate to such a relational status. External relations, then, present only another facet of the problem of the many; they do not present us with any promising way to avoid, or to resolve, that problem.

9. Counterfactual Reasoning, Joined Entities, and Partial Entities

If I am to trust them—and what rational alternative is there for me in the matter—scientific sources have it that typical concrete complexes, big enough plausibly to be tables or stones, do not come with any neat natural boundary. In relevant regards, they present the gradualness we associate readily with clouds: in any such regard, stones are to their atoms what clouds are to their droplets. But, let us suppose, for the moment, that this is not so. Let us suppose that I have been misled by my sources, or that they have overlooked some recondite physical factor that, in a typical realistic situation, sets off just one group of atoms there as suitable for constituting a table or stone. And let us suppose, further, that considerations of separators cannot generate our problem (supposing, perhaps, that our reasoning in section 7 was, somehow, actually fallacious). Would nature then have given us a solution to the problem of the many?

Right off, it seems quite incredible that this problem should arise for some kinds of ordinary things, clouds, but not for others, stones. Intuitively, and as I remarked near the outset, the problem appears to concern the vagueness of so many of our common terms, of "cloud" and "stone" alike. Now, anything is possible, so to say, but it seems quite unlikely, indeed, that such problems as these terms may engender can be avoided, or solved, by happy external arrangements of matter.

This intuitive suspicion, that everything should be in the same boat here, however nature should selectively operate, is confirmed by appropriate counterfactual reasoning. For such reasoning, it is apparent, will exhibit our problem of the many in any case, only casting it in a counterfactual form, while retaining its full logical substance. (Indeed, even if clouds themselves were to have sharp natural boundaries, this point would still hold good.) Consider a situation, then, presumably, only hypothetical or counterfactual, in which a typical stone had a clean natural boundary. Perhaps this stone would be made of homogeneous, continuous matter, which presented a proper two-dimensional surface to empty space outside or to surrounding matter of a radically different kind. Well and good, we may first suppose, for such a stone, or for a table carved from it. We must still reason, however, on pain of intellectual prejudice, about other, then hypothetical situations, ones in which any stones present would be constituted of separated atoms, just as all of our actual stones do seem to be. In these latter situations, now presumed hypothetical, all the relevant physical factors fade off gradually—from presumed stone to required surrounding.

It is absurd to suppose that there would be no stones, and no tables, in the more gradual world but that there would be such things in the naturally cooperative world. To be sure, the stones, and tables, in one world would be radically different in kind from those in the other; in relevant regards, we are considering *two kinds of* stones, and of tables. But this even *implies* that, if there are such things in either world, there are stones and tables in both these worlds. Taking the cooperative world as actual, consider the counterfactual gradual world. In a situation involving a typical stone of that world, how many stones *would* there be? By reasoning that is now familiar, or a counterfactual version thereof, one should have to conclude with our dilemma: In the *gradual* world, either there *would be no* stones at all, or else, in any situation involving a *typical* stone, there *would be millions* of stones. But, as we agreed, there will be stones in the cooperative world (if and) only if there would be stones in the gradual world. So, both our well-placed reasoner and we must conclude: Either there are *no* stones *even in the naturally cooperative world*, or else, in the gradual world, in any situation involving a *typical* stone, there *would be millions* of stones. While this is counterfactual, it is quite a dilemma just the same.

Even if nature did not conspire so that we should *more easily perceive* our problem, the problem of the many would still arise. It certainly looks, then, to be a problem about the logic of typical vague terms. In this important regard, then, our new problem parallels the old sorites problem, which, as I have argued elsewhere, is a problem about the logic of such expressions and, so, would arise no matter how the course of nature should run.[22] At all events, we may now be pretty confident that even if my scientific sources have put me on the wrong track, about the putative boundaries of tables and of stones, our problem of the many will still be with us.

There are other considerations which show that not very much depends on getting the actual facts right about the realistic situations we have had so much in focus. Beginning with clouds, as we did, we have been thinking, implicitly at least, of those very boundaries of objects, including boundaries of tables and of stones, that are, so to put it, exposed to the open air. Although it is common for a cloud to have its entire boundary so exposed, it is only rarely, as far as everyday experience goes, that a stone's entire boundary confronts the air, as happens when a stone is hurled through the air. Normally, the stone is resting on the earth, or upon something that is thus resting, or so on.[23] Therefore, in actual typical situations with stones and tables, in contrast to the case

22. This is a main theme of my paper "Why There Are No People," in *Midwest Studies in Philosophy*, vol IV, *Studies in Metaphysics*, ed. Peter A. French, Theodore E. Uehling, Jr., and Howard K. Wettstein (Minneapolis, 1979):177–222.

23. There are in outer space, I suppose, many stones with such entirely exposed surfaces. But while worth noting, that has little to do with our everyday experience. And, out there, one will find, if any, very few tables, pine cones, and so on.

with clouds, we find a more problematic part of the object's presumed boundary—the part "adjacent to" (part of the boundary of) some other "solid object." Now, even if there were no problem with the more exposed parts of a stone's boundary or surface, these problematic parts would generate the problem of the many quite well enough. For in these areas, at least, there is no natural break of any sort; there is no natural limiting place for an object, where it leaves off and where another object, which it is touching, first begins.

Situations that we describe as those of two objects touching each other, for example, one with an iron table and an iron ball resting upon it, are on a spectrum with those described as involving two objects joined together. It is mainly, we come to suppose about reality, a matter of *how many atoms* or at least, *how much* matter, the two share at the time in question.[24]

Although cases of these objects touching are extremely common, cases of their being joined are somewhat less so. But, of course, very many of these things that are *not in fact* joined, and which *never will be*, are quite *suitable* for certain sorts of joining. Thus almost any two iron objects can be readily joined, by a suitable use of molten iron or of some other metal. Further, a stone, by way of suitable stone material, may be joined to the earth itself, by being joined to a large rock outcrop, which is part of the earth's crust or mantle. Now, we may assume here that the size of the joining stuff is not great: perhaps, even that only a very slender strand joins the putative items. Thus we might best (try to) preserve our idea that there are still at least two objects in the situation, which are joined, and *not* that there is *just one bigger thing*, into which the two objects were so fused that each of them no longer existed.

Where two things are joined, even by a slender strand, part of the boundary of either must "cut through" the joining material. Throughout this material, even if nowhere else, there is, quite surely, no natural break or separation to be found. Not only is the spatial array of atoms in a baffling blend, but any bonding forces are also quite gradually distributed with regard to any candidate boundary. So, regarding either joined

24. These considerations generate a sorites argument in which we gradually increase the size of "the joining part." Such an argument might show, I suggest, that there is no coherent distinction between joining and touching, at least no coherent application of it to ordinary things. But if there are such things, if there are stones and tables, then they must be able, in some possible circumstances, to touch. So such a sorites argument seems an interesting way of challenging the existence of these putative entities and thus of yielding the more radical alternative of our problematic dilemma. But as sorites arguments are, in this essay, always to be in the background, we pass over these difficulties, merely noting them now for work on future occasions.

object, *if any* boundary is proper, there will be *many* that are. With either object, let us assume that the "exposed parts" of its boundary present a clean natural separation. Because atoms are so very small and numerous, however, there will still be, in our one example, millions of iron balls joined to millions of iron tables, and in our other, millions of stones joined, right there, with millions of planets. (With continuous, homogeneous matter, the point is, if anything, more obvious; indeed, in such a reality, infinities are easily obtained.) Each stone, we may assume, can share part of its boundary, the exposed part, with each of the others in the situation, but the parts within the joining stuff, quite sufficient to generate our problem, will differ from stone to stone.

With these thoughts about joined entities in mind, compelling counterfactual considerations favor our problem. Unlike those counterfactuals recently considered, these do not concern any esoteric hypothetical worlds but only small variants upon actual situations. So we may consider a typical iron ball and a typical iron table that have not, are not, and never will be joined or, even, ever be touching. And we may ask: What would the situation be, if, contrary to fact, they were joined by a slender band? If they exist now, they should exist then. If they existed then, there must be a boundary separating at least one table there from at least one ball. But, if so, there would have to be millions of such boundaries; thus millions of such balls and tables. So either such a table *does not in fact exist*, and so with tables generally, *or else* in that situation, there *would be millions* of tables.

A related dilemma may be generated entirely in terms of the actual situations of our world: If there are any tables, then, I am confident, somewhere in the actual world there is at least one typical table at some time joined to some other object, while each must retain its distinct identity. But, with that putative table, there are millions of tables in its "immediate situation," or else it does not exist at all. But as far as tablehood goes, that joined entity is not significantly worse off than any prospect. Hence either there really are no tables or else, in that table's situation, there are millions.

It is now a good time for us to consider these issues as they relate to alleged entities that, so to say, are most naturally, or typically, in a joined state or status. I call these *partial entities* because, as with a leg of a table or a branch of a tree, in this natural or typical state, they are each part of some other, larger entity, the implied table, or the tree.[25] The branch, for

---

25. For the suggestion that I consider such partial entities, which in turn sparked the thoughts of joining recently discussed, I am much indebted to Samuel Wheeler.

example, if it really exists, is joined to, or relevantly continuous with, or "at one" with, the tree's trunk and, indeed, with the rest of the tree. If there really is a branch it must stop somewhere, so that it will not include the trunk or, indeed, the whole tree. But any place that the branch stops cannot be better than all the other available places for its stopping. Rather, realistically speaking, it is no better than many others. And even if, absurdly, just one such boundary, or partial boundary, is somehow the very best one there, in regard to yielding an instance of branchhood, millions of others will still be at least very good, too, in the same regard: At all events, if any boundary yields us a *typical* branch, as we may suppose often happens, each of millions of others will yield a "nearby" entity that is, at least, a branch of some sort or other.

It may be helpful, at this juncture, to consider the "opposite" of joining: the separating or breaking off, of a typical branch from a tree. (The typical or optimal state for our stone and planet, so to say, was to be separate, so we joined them, for our consideration. The typical state for our branch and tree is for them to be joined, or together; so we shall separate them, also for our consideration. Thus we are considering each situation along with its "opposite," endeavoring to be comprehensive.) A certain brach was on a certain tree; now it is on the ground. Let us suppose, for simplicity, that there were no losses or gains in the situation, with regard to atoms or stuff, other than those required for this separation. So the atoms that now constitute a certain branch on the ground used to constitute a branch (presumably, the same one) on a tree. Suppose, alternatively, that a break had occurred along a plane very near to our first, actual break but not so near that the material severed would be exactly the same. With this second alternative, we also would have a branch on the ground. This time the branch would be composed of somewhat different atoms, and stuff, than in what went on before; perhaps we now have a slightly greater group or batch. Well, *these* atoms would *also* have constituted a branch back on the tree. So we must conclude that before either break, and even in the absence of any break, really, *each* of these *two* groups of atoms constituted a branch on this tree, providing of course that there was ever *any* branch in the situation (or, even, any tree). But, then, if there was any branch there, there must have been at least two of them, for at a given moment, one given branch cannot both be constituted of a certain number of atoms and, at that same time, also be constituted of another number of them. Equally, at a given time, one branch cannot be constituted of a certain batch of stuff and also of a lesser batch. The reasoning from two to many more is now rather obvious. So this gives us a handy way to see, all over again, our new philosophical problem.

Near the beginning of section 1, I asked what sort of possible world, or underlying reality, would make things hardest for generating our problem of the many. My answer was that it would be a world where ordinary things, clouds, stones, and tables, were composed of continuous homogeneous matter, which made a clean break with, perhaps, entirely empty space that surrounded the object all over. In such a case, we might say, nature itself provided a definite real boundary and, so, in a given situation, just one ordinary object with a uniquely preferred status. But, as our recent reasoning shows, even in such a world as this, our problem of the many arises: it arises counterfactually, of course; still better, it arises for cases of joining balls to tables; perhaps best of all, it arises for cases involving partial entities, for example, a tree and its branches. For it is hard to suppose that a typical, paradigm tree, which we take to have quite a few branches, but not many millions, somehow does exist in such a world either without any branches or with so many as all that. As I said near the outset, of both section 1, and of this present section, our problem concerns the logic of our ordinary terms and not, or not so fundamentally, the underlying arrangements of matter, in this possible world or that one.[26]

Near the beginning of section 6, where I began to extend our arguments about clouds to other ordinary things, I mentioned several sorts of partial entities among the things concerned. Thus I mentioned along with planets, the mountains "upon" them; along with trees, their trunks and branches; and along with tables, their tops and legs. Most importantly, for us, along with human bodies, I mentioned their arms and their hands and even their fingers. I should now mention a further partial entity, another part of our bodies, in the properly broad sense of that term: human brains. Now, in that I believe our bodies to be relevantly like clouds, I do think that the problem of the many arises for our bodies just as it does for clouds, along lines that are, by now, perhaps boringly familiar. So the problem of the many looks to cut deep, and close to home, on that account. But even if there is no relevant similarity between clouds and our bodies, the problem of the many will still be of great philosophic moment, and not just due to counterfactual considerations.

---

26. If all this is so, and partial entities do everything one might wish for our problem, why did I not just start out with trees and branches, instead of clouds and then stones, and thus wrap everything up quite neatly and quickly? The answer parallels the one I gave for having started with clouds rather than with stones: People are rarely, I am afraid, as logical as they should be; it is hard to get them to ponder our problem unless we start with psychologically gripping cases. I have found, through my own experiences of philosophical conversation, that the order employed in this paper, while logically somewhat roundabout, is psychologically superior to more direct approaches.

For, as a matter of fact, there is no natural separation between any *brain* I have and all of the rest of my body. Since my brain is, I suppose, if not quite a typical one, at least a pretty good example of a brain, this means that my body has, among its parts, millions of concrete complexes, each one of which is a brain of mine. Of course, there is one other alternative, as is characteristic of our problem: Perhaps, instead of having millions of brains, neither I nor you really have any brain at all.

I consider the arguments of this section to be rather important in regard to the problem of the many. But it must be emphasized that their importance is not confined to their providing a hedge against uncertainty, in case my scientific informers have led me astray about the gradualness the real world involves. On the contrary, there are at least two other aspects to their importance. First, because I do believe that my informers are reliable and that our world is relevantly gradual, these present arguments are to be employed, I am confident, *in addition to*, and not instead of, the arguments of previous sections. These present ones, then, are arguments *a fortiori*. Second, and more important, I think, these present arguments, more than those of previous sections, indicate that our problem is one regarding the categories of our own thinking, the logic and meaning of our own terms. The problem is not due to unfortunate circumstances surrounding us, to the messy gradualness that, as it happens, does appear so frequently in the world. That gradualness just helps us to see the problem in the first place; it is no more crucial to the problem itself than is our having started with clouds and not with stones.

10. The Principle of Minute Differences, Exclusion Principles, and Selection Principles

Our discussion has confirmed the intuitive idea that the problem of the many is a problem with our *words*, and with such *thoughts* as those words serve to express. Further, it seems from the *vagueness* of the words involved, though perhaps from other of their features as well. That we have a serious problem here, and even that it involves at least the factors just mentioned, I believe quite confidently. What I am less confident of, but do also believe, is that I can provide an *analysis* of this problem, even with a modicum of illuminating detail. Any analysis I should provide would *begin* with what I have called *the principle of minute differences from typical cases*. I should say that such a principle governs (the meaning, or the logic, of) our words for ordinary kinds of things, like 'cloud', 'stone', and 'table', as well as (that of) many other common vague expressions. What I should then do is go on to analyze this principle itself and to exhibit its relations to other principles that also govern these expressions of ours. This latter task, though it perhaps cannot be fully completed, is, I think, one well worth pursuing. But, for various reasons, including the obvious one of space, I will not do so here.

Especially because of the role I expect it to play in our problem's analysis, I used (an instance of) this principle as a premise, the third and final one, in my first introductory argument. Also largely for this reason, in section 4, I construed the third premise of my other introductory argument as being motivated by this principle; then I developed a lengthened "master" version of that argument where the principle figured explicitly. Finally, I appealed many times, in my discussion of examples, to relevant instances of the same proposition. But I do not think that our problem, the problem of the many, can be avoided even if this principle were to be rejected. On the contrary, as I shall argue in this section, and also in the next one, this persistent problem would still be with us and still be in want of any adequate solution.

In a rather general form (and not just confined to clouds or to stones), the principle of minute differences may be put as follows:

> With respect to any *kind of ordinary things*, if something is a *typical member* of the kind, then, if there are entities that differ from that thing, in any respects relevant to being a member of the kind, quite *minutely*, then each of those entities is a member of that kind.[27]

The kinds of things governed by this principle include, of course, clouds and stones and tables; we need not be precise in delimiting the range. The reason the principle governs the kinds is that it governs the terms the kinds' members must satisfy: 'cloud' and 'stone' and 'table', and so on. The reason the principle governs the terms is that they are vague and, without going into the matter, have their vagueness involved in such discriminations as the terms purport to make.[28]

In almost any context, I have found it very easy to get firm assent to this principle and even to principles that are more ambitious. Indeed, people seem so sure of it that they consider it quite trivial, perhaps a trivial exhibition of the meaning of 'typical' and of its near synonyms, like 'paradigm'. Only in the context where our new problem is introduced have I found any resistance to the principle.

---

27. I discuss principles like this one in "Why There Are No People," *Midwest Studies in Philosophy*, especially in section 5 of the paper.

28. This is admittedly quick, sketchy, and without sufficient argument. For elaboration and argument, see "Why There Are No People"; the elaboration is mainly given in section 2; the argument runs throughout the paper.

Because I have used the principle in introductory arguments, one might think that by rejecting the principle, one could easily reject those arguments and, so, that one could avoid the problems the arguments were used to introduce. But such a thought is *not* correct. In the *first* place, we must notice that the principle is nowhere used in the second of my arguments, the one about clouds as bounded entities. So its rejection would leave that argument just as it is, still introducing our problem. To be sure, in section 4, I advanced the principle as (part of) an *analysis*, or *explanation*, of (part of) that argument. But my explanation of the argument might of course be wrong even though the reasoning to be explained is itself philosophically adequate. In the *second* place, in a manner most harmonious with the preceding remarks, the first of my introductory arguments, about clouds as concrete complexes, may be easily revised, so that the principle is not employed there either. Retaining its first premise, we just compress that argument, so that, instead of its previous (2) and (3), the argument's only other premise now reads like this:

(2′)   If something is a *typical* cloud, then *any* situation involving it contains, in addition to itself, millions of other complex concrete entities, each of which is a cloud.

Regarding our realistic situations, with a plethora of overlapping concrete complexes, what this premise says may be put like this: either nothing there is *so* favored that it is a *typical* cloud *or else* there are *millions* of things there each of which is (well favored *enough* that it is) a cloud, at least of some sort or other. Our principle may be regarded now as an explanation of (part of) the appeal of this very attractive simple premise, (2′). Although I think not, perhaps that explanation is erroneous. Even so, that would scarcely give one much reason to reject (2′) itself, which, in any case, would be very hard to deny in any philosophically adequate manner.

So a rejection of our principle, a dubious move in any event, will fail to solve our problem. That this is so should be rather evident; why it is takes a bit more thought to see. The reason begins to emerge when one asks: If we reject that principle, what should we replace it with, for surely at least something much like it does seem to be required? The answer to be given will be, most likely and most plausibly, a longer, hedged version of the original simpler statement. In the longer version, we begin the same way and, then, tack on at the end an appropriate *exception clause*. Thus we might say that each of those (minutely differing) entities is a member of the same kind *except for those that* share "too much" space, or "too much" matter, with the aforementioned putative typical member.

As reasoning can make clear enough, it is *very* hard to state an exception clause that stands up to any scrutiny. (When we realize that the relevant principle must govern the thinking of many stupid little children, things look better and better for our original simple version.) But with regard to the problem of the many, that great difficulty is a somewhat peripheral matter, which we can well afford to pass over.

The main matter here is this. Such an exception clause will provide, at best, only an *exclusion principle*. This sort of principle says, in effect, that, in those situations it governs, *at most* one entity has the status it accords, for instance, the status of being a cloud or a stone. Such a principle says that there can be at most one winner, so to say, and that any other competitors will then be excluded from sharing the same status. With regard to our problem, it is surprising how much stock philosophers want to place in some such principles of exclusion. When I propose our new problem quite informally, as I did in section 1, many philosophers think they can solve it, and right away, too, by adducing some exclusion principle. Indeed, this has occurred with some very able philosophers. But, nevertheless, it is only an unfortunate error.

A certain philosopher thinks he sees just one table right there before him. He is rather baffled by my suggestion of overlapping complexes fading off into the surrounding. To relieve this puzzlement, he reaches into his bag of tools, or tricks. What might he employ? For a start, he might resort to this old saw: Two physical objects cannot both occupy the very same space at the very same time.[29] This is an exclusion principle. For what does such a principle say? In general terms it says something like this: If two entities both satisfy a certain description or, in a very general sense of the term, both have a certain property, then they cannot both satisfy a certain second description or possess a certain second property; at least one of the two compared entities will be *excluded* from satisfying the second description. What about the saw in hand? So if two entities both satisfy 'physical object', they cannot both satisfy 'occupies precisely all of spatial region R at exactly moment of time T'. So, too, if two entities both satisfy the latter description, then at most one of them can satisfy the former, that is, can be a physical object. (Perhaps one of them will be a shadow, or whatever.)

The exclusion principles employed in an attempt to escape our problem will, experience shows, differ in several ways from the very common sort of proposition just considered. First, instead of speaking

29. For an interesting discussion of such exclusion principles, see David H. Sanford, "Locke, Leibniz and Wiggins on Being in the Same Place at the Same Time," *Philosophical Review* 79 (1970):75–82.

so generally of "physical objects," our objector will mention a specific ordinary kind of thing, for example, chairs, or stones. Second, the concrete complexes we must consider, as the only likely candidates for being stones, or chairs, do *not*, at a given moment, occupy *exactly the same* space as each other; rather, they overlap, or nest, or whatever. So for an exclusion principle that even *seems* to apply, one needs some other description that is a suitable approximation to, and substitution for, one that specifies such exact sameness. Hence, vague and dubious as it may be, some such principle as the following is likely to be adduced: If two entities both occupy *nearly*, or *virtually*, all of the same space, as each other, at a given moment of time, then they cannot both be chairs, or both be stones. Or, perhaps, some near variant will be employed: If two entities both are constituted of *almost*, or of *virtually*, the exact same matter, or (group of) atoms, at a given moment of time, then they cannot both be chairs, or both be stones.

Let us assume, what might be true, that our thinking about stones, and about chairs, is governed by some such exclusion principles, perhaps even analytically so governed. And let us take this supposition a good deal farther: At least one such principle is (coherently and properly) applicable to the bafflingly gradual situations reality so often involves. Without further argument, this is a pretty strong assumption for us to be making now.[30] But let us do so anyway and thus give our stimulated objector what he seems to want. Will such a principle allow him to avoid, or to solve, our problem?

In point of fact, it cannot even begin to do anything of the kind. For what is needed for our problem's solution, if there is any to be had, is a proposition of an entirely different sort, which I will call a *selection principle*. A selection principle, one that is both applicable and correct, will single out, or *select*, from among the entities in a situation, those that satisfy a certain description or possess a certain property (or, in particular, that are of a certain kind). For our problem, if a principle will help, we need such a *selection* principle. Further, we need one that will select *just one* entity, from a nearby multitude, as being of a certain kind, one that common sense affirms. So we require *not* any exclusion

---

30. A main difficulty here is that a sorites argument can be given to question, or undermine, the coherence of the "almost," "nearly," and "virtually" just suggested for stating an apparently relevant exclusion principle. Indeed, I believe that such arguments completely undermine the coherence of *any* available departure from an exact sameness version, thus any available exclusion principle that would even seem relevant to our topic. But, as with so many sorites arguments, I pass over this difficulty now. As the sequel quickly makes clear, I can well afford to do so.

principle but a *selection* principle that will, in realistic situations, *select* just one complex thing, from among all the concrete complexes present, as, say, *the only stone there.*

But of course finding such an adequate selection principle, or even anything that approaches it, seems to be very much harder than formulating exclusion principles or approximations to principles of exclusion. For the former, but not the latter, amounts to nothing less than a solution to our new problem. Just so, as far as all these principles go, we are no better off with our problem that ever we were. The role of exclusion principles, in these matters, is not what some philosophers have expected.

What *is* the logical role, in these matters, of an adequate exclusion principle (if there be any such adequate proposition)? It will say, as we have noted, that in situations where entities compete with each other for a certain description or a certain status, for example, for being a stone, they cannot both achieve it: there can be *at most one* winner. Consider our realistic situation, with all its complex candidates for stonehood. Suppose that an exclusion principle about stones applies, perhaps concerning the sharing of "too much" space or "too many" atoms. What will the principle say, then, about the concrete complexes present? It will say, simply, that *at most* one of those concrete entities is the situation's sole stone. Of course, such an exclusion principle is entirely compatible with any adequate selection principle, but it is *also compatible* with the *absence* of any such principle of selection.

With or without using the principle of minute differences, what our reasoning has *already* yielded is that we have a *dilemma*: In a relevantly typical situation, at any given moment of time, *either* there are many stones there *or else* there are none. Now, our exclusion principle, supposing the most for it, will provide us with this further information, which is entirely compatible with that disjunction: There *are not many* stones there then. So if there is such an adequate exclusion principle, it will, in the absence of a selection principle, "resolve" our dilemma only in a most radical and Parmenidian way. There really are no stones there then, nor any stones at all.

This, after all, is the depressing truth about exclusion principles: They do nothing to escape our problem; rather, given that problem, which has by now been provided from various quarters, they only force us toward the more radical of the two options it poses. Why, then, have philosophers, perhaps in some hurry to escape our problem, assumed that exclusion principles might be of any use? Although it must be somewhat speculative, I think the answer lies along these lines: These philosophers have simply assumed that there really *must* be *at least one* stone in the situation, that this *must* be an *absolute given*, which shall never be questioned, on any account. Now, *given this as an absolute, unmovable dictum*, an exclusion principle *will* yield the result that there is one, and only one, stone present. But, of course, to reach that conclusion in *such* a manner is just to be so deeply in the grip of our ordinary common sense suppositions as to fail, if only temporarily, to consider our problem at all seriously. It is to forget, to ignore, or to misunderstand the problem, rather than to solve it. For if one does think about the problem seriously, one will realize that, in terms of principles, the problem is one of finding an adequate *selection* principle, which is quite a different matter from bringing any exclusion principle to bear. At the very least, we might say, our problem is one of finding, if not the required principle itself, a *philosophically adequate reason* to believe in the existence of some appropriate *selective* proposition, even while no such reason appears anywhere to be found.

Perhaps the most important point of his section is the one just made, a point which, I suggest, is quite important in its own right. This point also has importance, however, for the examination of our principle of minute differences, as I have already suggested. We may see this a bit more clearly now and, partly as a result of that clearer perception, build a case for that principle, in its simple, original version.

As will be remembered, even those who object to our simple principle are wont to agree that something like it governs such typical vague terms as 'cloud' and 'stone' and 'table'. The objectors think, however, that only a more complex (version of our) principle, holds true here, one with a suitable exception clause. Their motivation for that complicating retreat is that they are supposing that such a complicated principle will serve to solve our problem, while retaining what is right in the simple version. As we already saw, that problem can be introduced without employment of *any* such principle, simple or complex; so, for that reason alone, the motivation is undermined. We can now see more clearly that this must indeed be so. Suppose that our vague terms *are* governed by such a complicated minute difference principle, complete with its exception clause. All that such a principle will do, then, is impose on our problem, which is already upon us, a certain exclusion principle, the one stated or implied in that exception clause. Hence, even if it does govern our key terms here, such a principle will only pressure us *from* the many toward the *none*, a most radical result, and will in no wise afford common sense any comfort.

Because I would like my thoughts about our problem's *analysis* to be right, I tend to favor the principle of minute differences in its simple, exceptionless version. But, even apart from this theoretical partiality on my part, I can see no reason to deny this principle, which is as intuitively appealing as it is simple, especially as doing that will be of no use in solving our problem. Nor have I ever seen any reason to accept the more complicated statements, with exception clauses, which are, apparently, as *ad hoc* as they are complex, especially as doing that will, equally, be to no avail here. The point on which I should like to focus now, however, by way of concluding this section, is neither of these two rather evident ideas. Rather, it is a third thought concerning the relation between them, which, while somewhat less evident, is really not a very difficult conception either. It is this: The simple, original principle and a more complex version, with an exception clause, are *logically compatible* with each other. Thus the acceptance of the latter, dubious in any case, *would not in itself rationally require* the rejection of the simple, intuitive principle of minute differences. On the contrary, the two together may hold, both of them governing the vague terms at issue. What would that joint holding imply? It would imply that key vague terms were logically inconsistent expressions, including 'typical cloud' and 'typical stone'.[31] That is, the supposition that anything satisfied these expressions would logically yield a contradiction: certain complex entities that differed minutely from a putative satisfier of 'typical stone' *both would be* stones (by the simple version) and *also* (by the complicated version) *would not* be. For the strongest of reasons, then, there would be no typical clouds or typical stones. As we have already agreed, if no typical clouds, then, in fact, no clouds at all. Hence, with both principles holding, our dilemma would not only be relevantly yielded but, as has happened so many times before, it would be resolved only in movement toward its more radical side.

11. Some Questions for Common Sense Philosophy

Our arguments, I believe, pose a formidable dilemma for common sense thinking. In our time, indeed, since Moore's rejection of idealism, this common thinking has been the cornerstone of the most dominant philosophy, which I call *common sense philosophy*. So our arguments challenge this dominant philosophy as well. They seek to reject, in turn, the ideas of Moore and of his very many followers.

---

31. In "Why There Are No People," I argue for the stronger claim that even such simple expressions as 'cloud' and 'stone' are logically inconsistent. So although I do not see any reason to accept the more complex statement, and thus the route to inconsistency which its addition means, I am of course very well prepared to do so.

However intriguing this may be, few will allow themselves to be convinced, by these or any other arguments. They will assume, instead, that some flaw, no matter how difficult to specify, must always be present. For common sense philosophy is not just another of philosophy's schools. Rather, it does not only rely on, but also advocates and supports, our common sense thinking, which is society's common ground. Consequently, the power of any mere arguments to move us away from this philosophy will be quite limited. Although I should like to pursue our arguments further, I am also anxious for some of this radical movement to occur. So I will now forgo further examination of our challenging patterns of reasoning.

I cannot possibly tell what will prove most effective in getting our problem of the many to be seriously considered as a genuine philosophic dilemma. But it is my hope that *if you ask yourself certain questions*, as I have often done, something toward this end may be accomplished. Now, up until this point, we have often just *assumed* what common sense would have be so: That where people judged, or were wont to judge, that a typical cloud or stone was present, there really was *at least one such* cloud or stone. This assumption led to another implicit in it: *Everything required* for the existence of the assumed cloud or stone, such as a suitable boundary, was in fact there, in the situation. Now, these assumptions are very often made in everyday life, at least implicitly. For the sake of argument, in our philosophic reasoning, we have made them, too, though in a rather more tentative, or even hypothetical, fashion. But let us now become, or at least try to become, a bit more doubtful about these common existential suppostions.

In this mildly skeptical frame of mind, let us seriously ask: What is there in these ordinary situations, with so many small constituents so gradually dispersed about, that could be, or could serve as, the boundary for *any* (typical) cloud or for even a single stone? If you ask this question seriously, and try to think of the underlying situations concerned in all their detail, then, I suggest, you will find no available answer to be very convincing. Nevertheless, as there must be some suitable answer here for there to be any clouds or stones, it should not be hard for you to manage to find an answer that will at first seem a bit plausible. For example, you might hit on the idea that what will do is whatever enclosing curved limiter yields a certain average density throughout a certain more or less well-pictured region. But examining any such answer closely, I suggest, will result in a certain amount of depression; for, in the baffling morass of indicated continuents, there seems no reason to think that our idea of a cloud or of a stone really does require any *given particular* average density, complexity of structures, or whatever, and *not* some *other* one that is only *minutely* different from it. So the result your alleged boundary is to yield seems impossibly arbitrary, rather than well enough determined by real features of the situation. This absurd arbitrariness, and the depression about any allegedly adequate answer, is closely connected with sorites arguments. As we have foreseaken these arguments for most of our essay, so we shall now again pass over these annoying causes of discontent.

We shall still have plenty enough to worry about in thinking over such answers as initially seem even remotely plausible. For we must now ask ourselves the yet more pointed question: What can there be, in these bafflingly gradual situations, that can be the boundary of, not just *a* genuine cloud, or *a* real stone, but the *only* cloud, or the *single* stone, there? To obviate our argument's dilemma, we must find an answer to these questions that is philosophically adequate. But what actual feature can there be, in the baffling morass of separated items, which can select just one complex as uniquely filling the bill? If we take anything that is even remotely plausible as a requirement for a cloud's boundary, like whatever encloses a "largest" complex of just such a particular average density, then there will be very many items that meet it equally well, as our thoughts of overlapping have so often indicated. If we take something even remotely plausible for a stone itself, for example, a "largest" item there that has such-and-such a complexity of structure, overlapping complexes again prevent any answer from adequately bringing forth a uniquely well-qualified candidate. And, as we have seen, looking to "external relations" for help will fail to narrow things down adequately.

No matter what property we pick, to use an available expression, it seems inconceivable that, in realistic situations, there is precisely one entity that possesses it and, *in virtue of that*, is actually the only cloud or stone there present. After this is thought over to any great extent, the idea that there *must be* some answer begins to look badly founded, at least, perhaps even quite absurd. Now, it is no good to say something like "the property of being *the* cloud in the situation," hoping to specify thereby the appropriate uniquely possessed attribute. That would just beg the question here. For you may *readily question* on what real basis, and so *whether or not* at all, *anything does satisfy* the offered *demanding* description. Indeed, we may put the matter in terms of these descriptions themselves, assuming them to be well formulated. For when we ask ourselves what it could be, in realistic situations, that would give such descriptions semantically proper application, we are apt to bounce between two walls: Either we shall think of something that, realistically, is absent altogether, such as certain of those natural breaks in reality which have been previously remarked, or else it will be something, like those features so recently considered, that is many times exemplified. Now, for all our queries and failures, there just might, I suppose, really be something present that we are always overlooking and which, by fortunate circumstance, in many typical situations, always picks out just one (putative boundary as proper, and so with just one) putative cloud or stone. But, unless we can describe or specify it, at least vaguely and obliquely, we should have our doubts. For, otherwise, we should have to assume a great deal. We shall have to assume that, very often, many stupid little children are somehow made to get things right, as to the small number of nearby real clouds or stones, by the operation of some imperceptible, perhaps ineffable, and certainly quite mysterious factor. Unless it is some truly Almighty Father Who so manages things for us all, we may question whether those blissful toddlers are so well placed as common sense would have them be.

In answer to the present line of questioning, certain lines of reply are predictable. Perhaps the chief among these, which I shall discuss as representative, proceeds from a certain view about ordinary vague expressions. On this view, such terms are incomplete:[32] In addition to some cases for which they are positively defined, and also some for which they are defined so as not to apply, there are still others where the matter of their semantic application is *left open*. Thus it will be *up to us*, in certain circumstances, to decide whether or not such terms shall apply. Now, it has been argued elsewhere that this view is actually incoherent and so cannot properly represent the semantics of any expressions at all.[33] But we shall now pass over any such great difficulties. For whether or not those problems prove fatal for the view even quite generally, certain more specific questions may be raised regarding any attempt to apply such a view to the questions that we have been asking.

It is not clear exactly how the intermediate steps should go, but if this view about vagueness is to help us with our present questions, it will at some point have to incorporate an idea at least much like this one: Our language and thinking, on the one hand, and the objective external facts, on the other, all as determinate as they are at the time, together specify *that there is exactly one* cloud or stone in our typical situation; but they *leave open* the matter as to *which* entity in the situation is the unique present cloud or stone, which *further matter* is thus *left open for us* to decide. Looking to preserve common sense, as it does, and offering us the sort of putative logical distinction that might seem to explain some

---

32. I think that in his paper "Wang's Paradox," *Synthese* 30, no. 3–4 (1975):301–24, Michael Dummett presents this view.

33. I argue this in section 3 of "Why There Are No People."

confused questioning directed against society's common ground, this reply is bound to have an appeal for us that is both marked and quite immediate. But if we examine the matter with care, the offered distinction will do little to settle our questioning attitude. For according to what it delivers, which entity in our situation is a cloud or is a stone will be, at least in many cases, a matter of human thought and decision; whereas the truth of these matters is that, supposing there is to be any real stones or clouds, which entities are these is *not* something relevantly dependent upon what we happen to think or decide.

It is, to be sure, a matter of human convention, and so in a way dependent on our thinking, *which things we call 'stones', which 'clouds'*, and which neither, supposing, of course, what we may now allow, that we actually do call some things by these words or names. This is because we have endowed certain sorts of marks and sounds with certain semantic properties, however accomplished, and we may subsequently change these matters by relevantly similar processes. But all of this, as should be obvious enough, is quite irrelevant to the sort of dependency upon our thought required by our considered line of reply. For one thing, with regard to any situation, it is similarly up to us whether we should call *anything at all* a 'stone' or should ever have done so.

In certain situations, it is of course a matter of human action, and its consequences, as to which things present are stones and, in this century, even which are clouds. In the course of events, we can effect the arrangements of matter, so that even which things are plausible candidates for stonehood can be the result of what we do. And since these actions, or many of them, are in turn dependent on our thoughts or decisions, in many cases these matters are correlatively dependent on what we think or decide, or so we may now suppose. But, like the one just previously considered, this is not the dependence required by our reply, for it, too, applies just as much to each branch of the distinction the reply offers. In this sense or respect, it is even dependent on human thought, in various situations, that there is *any* stone present at all.

No, what our reply requires is a good deal more. It requires that even after everything is so specified and determinate, both in our language and in our environment, so that it is *true* that a certain typical situation does contain a *single stone*, it is *still up to us* to decide *which* entity there is the only stone present. And this, I suggest, is to require of a matter that must be relevantly objective, or independent of our thoughts, that it be thus dependent upon our thinking, that it be *only* a quite *subjective* matter *instead*. Now, with various artifacts, for example, chairs, there may be some *shred* of plausibility in claiming that there is no such condition of objectivity. For example, one might suppose that it may be a matter of which of several nearby things certain people right now most prefer to sit upon, or something of the like. And, just perhaps, continuing this line of thinking, this might mean no relevant objectivity for the matter of which of those things is the sole available chair. Now, even here, with such artifacts, the suggestion is *not* very plausible. But with stones and clouds, which entities, if they exist, are entirely *natural* things, the case for any such relevant dependence on our thought appears to have *nothing whatever* to be said for it. So our considered reply, with the distinction it seems to offer, will not answer our baffling questions about clouds and stones. Nor, then, as some *general* answer is presumably required, will it do even for ordinary artifacts.

I have argued that an attempt to reply to our questioning, a rather good representative of such attempts, will fail for an instructive reason. It will overlook, or ignore, a condition governing the terms for the kinds in question, which it must do in order for a distinction it offers to be applicable.[34] In sum, our questions have led to putative replies, and

---

34. A misunderstanding of this error will falsely promise easy answers here. Thus some will suppose, I am afraid, that *in* arguing *for* the condition:

> Clouds and stones (and so on) are things of a sort such that which things are clouds and stones (and so on) is a *purely objective* matter, and so *not* dependent on human thought in any relevant way,

I *must have been arguing* to *deny* the following condition, at the same time:

> Clouds and stones (and so on) are things of a sort such that which things are clouds and stones (and so on) is *not* a purely objective matter, and so *is* dependent on human thought in some relevant way.

And, supposing this, they may think, in addition, that the latter condition may well be correct and, perhaps, even, that arguments based on the considered reply may show it to be so. (I confess that I cannot myself see any strong reason for accepting this latter condition, but we may *suppose* that there is one.) With all this in mind, they may then conclude that my own arguments for the former condition must themselves somehow be unsound, thinking, as they may, that the two putative conditions cannot possibly both hold true together. Although some of this presumed thinking may be quite valid, the first and, particularly, the last of these ideas, each crucial to the conclusion, are surely mistaken. For both the conditions just exhibited can indeed hold true together. What *cannot all be true* is that both of these should hold *and also* that there be clouds and stones (and so on). Should two such conditions as these hold true, as perhaps they might, the relevant expression, say, 'cloud', will be an inconsistent one, logically on a par with, say, 'perfectly square triangle'. (That this should be so would be rather surprising. But, perhaps, it need not be overly so, once we realize that, only with the former expression, and not the latter, will the considerations needed to bring out the inconsistency be quite elaborate and unobvious ones.) At all events, should the latter condition hold true, that will not negate the one for which I argued. Nor will it, then, obviate the dilemma our problem poses for common sense. For if the latter condition holds as well as mine, that dilemma will have been yielded and even, in an unwanted sense, resolved. Indeed, it will have been, still one more time yet again, resolved in favor of the more radical of the dilemma's two alternatives.

these in turn to arguments that the replies are inadequate. It appears, then, that there really are no adequate, unobjectionable answers to be found.

12. Some Implied Problems

The problem of the many poses a formidable challenge, I submit, to our common sense thinking. Were only this by now familiar challenge involved, with no substantial further difficulties as well, our new problem should be of some considerable interest to serious philosophers. But, in fact, the problematic situation is quite the reverse of the isolated conundrum to which I just alluded. On the contrary, the problem of the many implies, for our philosophical consideration, a number of serious further difficulties. In this final section, I shall discuss, very briefly indeed, three (sets) of these. In each case, my discussion will primarily, if not entirely, concern implications of the second, multitudinous disjunct of our dilemma. The reason for this partiality will be apparent: Generally, if the first, Parmenidian situation is presumed to obtain, things will be *so bad* for common sense that there will be little *room left* for any further particular problems to arise. But just as I shall, for this obvious reason, be mainly engaged in disclosing problems in the multitudinous one of our two alternatives, so it will be the other, nihilistic one toward which these implied difficulties will be pointing the way. As will be apparent, in each of these three problem areas, the trouble first arises in what might be deemed a *metaphysical* version; but as soon as one might think to make light of such a problem, an *epistemological* version is right on hand to mystify.

A. The Problem of Having an Object in Mind

We commonly suppose that, regarding various existing ordinary things, several nearby stones, for example, we can think of each of them, or have each in mind. Sometimes, we may think of them all together. But we also presume that often we think of just one of them, individually: Often, if I choose, I can close my eyes and think of just one actual stone. But if there are millions of "overlapping stones" before me, in the manner that our prior reasoning has brought to light, how am I to think of a single one of them, while not then equally thinking of so many others, with each of which "it" might so easily be confused? The presumed *relations* between us, and our minds, and ordinary material complexes look to be in deep trouble.

I look at what I take to be a single stone, right over there. Then I close my eyes and think to myself, "It is quartz." But *what* is *it?* It had better be a stone, at least, or else it is extremely doubtful that, in *this* very common and in *no way untoward* situation, I am thinking of any real object at all. But, then, there are so many stones right there; if any are quartz, they all are. So, being charitable to myself, in any sense or way, will be of no help here. If there is no particular one I have in mind, then what am I doing in conjuring up the sentence subvocally, as I do, "It is quartz." That will not even be grammatically appropriate for expressing any truth that I might be grasping about real objects over there; I should better think, "They are quartz." But, if relevantly more appropriate, that latter thought would be quite disconcerting.

We think it true, and even important, that each of us often does concentrate upon just such a one existing entity, without then and there having to contemplate as well millions of others so very much like it. Indeed, if we *never* do engage in such *individualistic* thinking regarding members of a certain kind of things, e.g., regarding tables or stones, it might well be doubted that we ever think *at all* of any real things of that kind. So this problem is rather serious. But how is it to be resolved? I suggest that up until now, at least, not one of us has ever really thought of any existing stone or table or human hand.[35]

Supposing there are stones, there are millions right there now. How should I individuate in thought any one of them, so that I might contemplate it alone, without the confusion, or intrusion, of so many competitors for my attention? Any mark I could observe would be shared by so many; so would be any description, or property, I should have even the slightest reason to think is exemplified there at least once. I could, of course, *formulate* a demanding description that *calls* for unique satisfaction, e.g., 'the largest stone over *there*'. But as just indicated, there is no reason whatever to suppose such a description to be satisfied. With all that overlap going on, it is far from clear that there is a single largest stone there, whether in mass, in volume, or whatever. What might be largest in one regard might well not be in another. And who knows how many "regards" there are here? But even if, perhaps by God's design, there were one, clearly and univocally, largest stone right there, it seems incredible that I should have *it alone* in mind just by my thinking of those quoted five *words*. Rather, there should be some real *connection* between

35. I have no theory of *thought about objects* or, as some philosophers say, of *de re* thought; nor do I know of any wholly convincing view. For an interesting and well-argued account, however, I can suggest Stephen R. Schiffer's "The Basis of References," *Erkenntnis* 13, no. 1 (July 1978):171–206. On Schiffer's account, our problems emerge quite strikingly.

me, and even those demanding words of mine, and, at the other end, the single stone there that is the real object of my thought. With so many stones there, however, what connection could, appropriately and uniquely, link me, or my words, to just the single stone I am supposed to be contemplating?[36]

Perhaps there is some special *causal* connection between me, or my thoughts and words, and a single nearby stone that is to be the sole object of a certain salient idea of mine? Putative causal accounts of things are now much in vogue. This is particularly true as regards a person's thoughts about a given existing concrete entity and as regards such language as may be most appropriate to that thought or to its expresion. Finding the notion of causation itself at best obscure and suspecting it to be even semantically inapplicable, I find little illumination from these fashionable accounts.[37] But even discounting any such general suspicion, an allusion to causal processes would seem futile for the particular problem at hand. For consider two very similar, barely overlapping quartz stones over there. Whatever causal relations the one beares to me are *very* closely matched by those the other bears. How, then, is just one of them to be causally connected to me so that I am thinking now only of

36. There are *two* related problems here, which we may distinguish. *First* is the problem of finding, or of finding adequate reason to suppose the existence of, a connection that has actually, with some considerable frequency, been there to serve me in the past. Such a connection has, presumably, even been enough to get many stupid little children thinking individually of stones nearby them. This is the problem of accounting for actual individualistic thought; if it cannot be solved, then our common sense thinking is in very bad trouble. A *second* problem is this one: Especially assuming the first problem finds no adequate solution, how can one, by whatever strategy necessary, get oneself to think, at a certain time, of just one real nearby stone? With this second problem, it is obvious, we may employ many more assumptions than a proper solution to the first will allow. I will make things easier for myself, now, and focus on the first of our problems. But my reasoning about it will, I suggest, indicate that even the second problem may well be beyond any adequate solution.

37. First, of course, there are the doubts one feels upon encountering Hume's writings on the subject. But I am thinking more of certain other problems with *causation* that closely *parallel* those we have been discussing here regarding *ordinary things*. In my paper "The Uniqueness in Causation," I argued that any particular thing (event, or whatever) can be caused by *at most one* entity. But in our messy, gradualistic, complex world, no one candidate entity, be it object, event, or whatever, seems relevantly better suited than ever so many very similar alternatives. Since it is arbitrary and, hence, false, to say of any one that it causes the event in question, there is *nothing* that *causes* the given particular. As I argued, this uniqueness is not a peculiar nuance of 'cause' but holds for any available locution that would seem, at first, suited to describe the relevant "interactions." The present radical extension of those ideas is, of course, very sketchy and needs much further development. But, for now, I mean only to be raising some doubts. The mentioned paper appeared in *American Philosophical Quarterly* 14, no. 3 (July 1977):177–88 and is reprinted in *The Philosopher's Annual*, vol. I—1978 (Totowa, N.J., 1978), pp. 147–71.

it, and not of the other, whose causal credentials seem so relevantly similar?

Whether it involves causation or not, *perception* might be thought to provide the link from my thought to its sole relevant object. Normally, of course, we suppose that this is how most individualistic thinking gets started. But then, normally, we suppose that a person can, and often does, *perceptually discriminate* a certain stone from its background and from whatever other stones might be nearby. However, given our prior reasonings, it seems that such perceptual discrimination never does in fact place, and that our common, sanguine idea that it does is but a comfortable illusion. Indeed, rather than solving our problem of individualistic thought, reflections about perception now mean further problems for us there, as well. For if we *do not ever* perceptually discriminate one stone from millions of others, it is *doubtful* that we ever *perceive* stones at all. What, then, *if anything, do* we actually perceive? This is a question I suggest, that we should take quite seriously. Just so, we should not assume, at the outset, that any affirmative answer, especially one congenial to common sense, will prove philosophically impeccable.

Largely owing to work of Kripke and of Donnellan, *ordinary proper names*, of individual people, places, and things, have recently been the focus of much discussion.[38] Accordingly, we might expect some philosophers to think that by an *act of naming* one might bring before one's mind just a single ordinary concrete entity, just one real stone, for example. Frankly, following the tradition of Russell and Quine, I cannot see how having such proper names around, like 'Plymouth Rock' or 'Felix', can yield solutions to *any* fundamental philosophic problems. But even if one doubts the generalization, in regard to the particular case at hand the negative point is plain. Especially with no help in sight from causal or perceptual processes, how am I to name just one stone here 'Plymouth Rock' or 'Oscar' or 'Felix', while leaving its overlappers quite anonymous? There seems no more prospect of bringing this off than of individually thinking of just one nearby instance of stonehood. So, again, rather than solving our problem, the appeal to a familiarly presumed activity calls that activity itself into question. It is doubtful, then, that we have ever named any ordinary thing without at the same time naming so many others much like it (whatever the situation with regard to naming people). But it is also hard to believe that we have, in

---

38. See Saul A. Kripke's "Naming and Necessity" in Davidson and Harman, *Semantics of Natural Language*, and his "Identity and Necessity" in Schwartz, *Naming, Necessity, and Natural Kinds*. See Keith Donnellan's "Proper Names and Identifying Descriptions," in the former volume, and his "Speaking of Nothing," in the latter.

some happy act, actually named millions of things each 'The Rosetta Stone' or each 'Plymouth Rock'. So we have another problem to take seriously: Have we ever really *named* any *ordinary things* at all?

If I have never thought individually of any stone, or any other common object, then it seems doubtful, to put it mildly, that I have ever thought of any such things collectively either. Accordingly, it may well be that I have never *thought of* any real stones at all, or tables, or even human hands. If that is so, then it would seem that *a fortiori* I do not *know* anything *about these entities*, however commonly I might otherwise suppose. In discussing this (complex of) problem(s), I have been sketching, then, a new route to a view of epistemological skepticism, concerning much, if not all, of our alleged knowledge of the external material world. The alternative of the many, we may say, means many problems for common sense. What of the none, our first, Parmenidian alternative? Well, if there are no real stones or hands, then it is as clear as reason's light that no real hand or stone will be the object of my thought, nor within the scope of any human knowledge.

B. The Problem of Identity through Time

Throughout this essay, our focus has been upon situations at a given moment, or instant, of time. Such a moment may be conceived as without duration altogether or else, for any who are squeamish of such a fine idea, with only such extremely short duration that any changes taking place therein would be negligible with regard to our problem. In reality, however, time goes on, and various significant changes do occur with respect to any of the putative ordinary things that have been our concern. In particular, with any significant lapse of time, these things, stones, for example, lose some of their salient constituents, some molecules or atoms. (They also gain some such constituents; typically, they lose "a lot" while gaining "a few.") It is commonly supposed that an ordinary thing can survive the loss of some such constituents, even without replacement, providing that their number, and their role in its structural arrangement, is not "too great."[39] I think that this is right and, indeed, that some such condition governs the logic of vague terms like

---

39. This is one of the most conspicuous places for sorites arguments to operate against the alleged existence of stones and other presumed ordinary things. I have in mind the *sorites of decomposition by minute removals*, especially as presented in section 1 of my paper "There Are No Ordinary Things," *Synthese* 41, no. 2 (June 1979):117–54. Also relevant are *the sorites of slicing and grinding*, in section 2 of the paper, and *the sorites of cutting and separating*, in section 3. For those of you who think those arguments to be mere fallacies, the present paper's problems may well help you think them over again.

'stone', at least 'typical stone'. But if we consider our new problem's implications, there is a lot of trouble here.

Consider an atom or molecule that leaves its place within the boundary of a typical stone, stone B, and travels outward a very short distance, so that it is now alongside, perhaps even "nosing ahead of," one of those atoms which, just before, was right outside, and very close to, that aforesaid boundary. In reality, if there are stones, this happens with any one of them, during any hundredth of a second (and, generally, a lot more happens, too). Before the movement of this atom, there were at least two stones in our situation, B and a slightly larger stone, C, which, at our outset, contained all B's atoms plus that one, just mentioned, right outside B's initial boundary. Now, what are we to think once the movement has taken place?

To simplify matters, but not in any way that these present difficulties require, we shall think of stones as distinguished by those atoms which compose them. We ignore, for example, possible infinities that separators might impose. (This mirrors our earlier thinking of clouds just at the level of droplets.) Given this, and even with only the one small movement to consider, it seems there is an impossible problem for the continued existence of stone B, thus for the identity through any significant time of any real stone. We may call this problem of identity, which is of course not confined to stones, *the problem of competition for parts*. The propriety of this name will become apparent soon enough, as we consider along with B and C, a third stone, A, smaller than either of them, and as we then notice the struggles between stone B and each of the two others.

Before the traveler's journey, *the atom that it is now alongside*, or just nosing out, *used to be* a constituent (of stone C) *necessary and sufficient to distinguish C*, the larger of our first two stones, *from* B, the smaller. Given this, can B survive the journey of that traveling atom? Common sense, of course, says "yes." But an affirmative answer leads to a dilemma. This is how the dilemma begins: *The traveling atom, itself*, also before its journey, *distinguished B*, the smaller of our two stones, *from A, a smaller stone still*. That smallest stone of these three had *all the atoms of B*, the middle stone, *except for the to-be-traveler*. So for B to remain distinct from such a smaller A, *B must retain the traveler*. Otherwise B will cease to exist (or else B will entirely coalesce with A so that, *from that time ever onward*, the two will become objectively indistinguishable, which is hardly a serious option). This is the first horn of the dilemma. Let us see the second.

If B, the middle stone, is to *retain* the traveler, then its boundary must move outward, so that that atom is still internal to it and not external. Such an adjustment, however, means that the alongside, or nosed-out, atom will also be within B's boundary and so part of B itself.

This means, in turn, that the largest stone of the three, stone C, must now cease to exist (or else C entirely coalesces with B, from then ever onward, those two becoming forever indistinguishable, again not a serious alternative). But the relation of the smallest to the middle, of A to B, is relevantly the same as that of the middle to the largest, of B to C, so that there is nothing to choose between the two horns of our dilemma here. First, it is arbitrary, and so not true, to think that, while losing the traveler, B, but not A, continued to exist. And second, it is just as arbitrary, and so just as false, to think that, while retaining the traveler, B, but not C, continued to exist. As those are the only options for B's continued existence, and neither holds, the traveler's little journey means an end to B's existence.

Like our stone B, any typical real stone can be treated as the middle member in a trio of the kind just considered.[40] Just so, with any such stone, the loss of a tiny peripheral part means an end of it. But such losses occur in any hundredth of a second. So a typical stone, if it exists at all, does so for no more than a hundredth of a second. This result does three things. *First*, it makes the second disjunct of our original problematic dilemma yet more unpalatable: (at any time) in any case involving a typical stone, there are millions of stones, and all of these last for no more than a hundredth of a second. *Second*, again assuming that there are stones, it makes it even more doubtful that we ever have a single one in mind. And, if anything, it is more doubtful still that we ever perceive any stone, much less that we should gain knowledge of any. For not only is any putative one so difficult to discriminate from many others, but, if it exists at all, any stone is so soon gone that we never get much of a chance even to try. Nor are we much better off with any other sort of ordinary material thing. So our epistemological problems, having already been bad enough, get even worse.

Third, and finally for now, we should notice that the argument just sketched does *not* contradict the common sense assumption that, at least in realistic situations, any typical stone can survive the loss of a tiny peripheral part. For *that* assumption does not itself imply the existence of any typical stones. Rather, it says:

(cs)   If there are any typical stones, then, in realistic situations, each of them can, and, given science, even will, survive the loss of a tiny peripheral part; that is, such a stone will still exist, whether or not it is still a typical stone.

40. With *certain marginal cases* of stones, such trios may be unavailable. But if they do exist, such trivial exceptions scarcely affect the present argument.

What we have argued for is a conditional with the same antecent and a consequent to opposite effect. Thus, joining our recent conclusion with the entirely plausible statement (cs) yields, instead of any contradiction, the result that there are no typical stones.[41] And this, in conjunction with the all but indubitable idea that if there are stones, then some (in fact) are typical ones, yields, in turn, the consequence that there really are no stones at all. So, three times over, considerations about time pressure us to our problem's nihilistic, or Parmenidian, side.

C. The Problem of Minds and Bodies

A person's presumed body, just like its supposed salient parts, is susceptible of our problematic dilemma. Even brains, as we saw near the end of section 10, bear the brunt of our problem. And whereas the numbers, in the second disjunct, might not rise quite so high so fast, individual cells, including neurons, would each also present a momentary overlapping multitude. When changes through time are considered, as sooner or later they must, no typical human body, or any such part of it, would seem to last long enough to be of any use. (Or else, what is less plausible, though hardly less troubling, there will be with respect to any such body, or relevant part, very many indistinguishable from it at any time.) If this is our physical situation, what is one to make of one's own nature and, then, of one's relation to any other sentient beings?

　　Whether or not he is a physical entity, a person, if a real existent at all, must be an utterly concrete individual and in no wise any mere abstraction. But if one is a physical entity, then, it is only plausible, one should be a rather complex one and not some elementary particle, or atom, or whatever. Granting this, a physical nature will imply for oneself, and for people generally, our problem of the many: Either one does not exist, and there are no people, or else in any case of any typical person, or even of any pretty good example, there are, right then and there, millions of people present. And then, of course, further problems will arise: No typical real person will last for even a hundredth of a second, your alleged self included, not long enough to formulate, or to understand, even a rather simple thought or idea. (Or else, and less likely, right where you are now, there are many objectively indistinguishable people: So, who can you be, anyway?)

　　At first blush, then, our problem would give comfort to dualistic views regarding the mental and the physical: I am a concrete entity that

---

41. So, of course, our argument, together with the commonsensical (cs), *does* contradict *another* common sense assumption, namely, that *there are* typical stones. It is easy to conflate these two common sense assumptions, but that is a temptation to be resisted.

is *only* mental or spiritual in nature and *not* physical or material. So that I might be distinct from other entities, and last long enough to think, I would lack spatial extent altogether. But although such a move might formally avoid those difficulties we have been disclosing, it leaves one, to put it mildly, with a very puzzling epistemological situation. For one assumes that each of us knows about various other people, whom one distinguishes each from the other. But, given our prior reasoning, no such knowledge seems possessed by anyone.

If I ever am successful in distinguishing one person from others, so that I might know something about him, then at least sometimes I do this by distinguishing a particular body from others, which body I take to be *his* body. This involves the thought, on my part, that this particular body is the body of a single person and that this person has no body but this one. But our problem pulls the ground out from such common implicit thinking. For either there are not any human bodies, in which case this presumed way of distinguishing people is without any real substance, or else there are so many bodies there to go on that the associated thought of other persons runs wild. Given the latter option, we should ask: Are there millions of people right across the way from me now, where there "seems to be just one, or two"? And, if so, who's who?

Even in my own case, trouble is very near. Either I have no body at all, even none as a useful shell or appendage, or else there are millions right around where I take mine to be. The former alternative is obviously troubling, but the latter gives one troubles too. With all these bodies about, and so very many brains as well, how many are really mine (even for a moment)? How can I possibly know? Might there not be, instead of just me with millions of bodies and brains, millions of people "right here now," each "with much of my perspective on things" and a slightly different body and brain (momentarily) to employ? How is *anyone to know* what is going on here, *myself included*? Unless they are extremely skeptical, then, metaphysical dualists, regarding mind and body, can take only cold comfort from our problem. In the associated epistemological area, they face a very severe form of skepticism, a very severe version of the problem of other minds.[42]

42. It is, I believe, interesting to compare what I have been doing in this essay with what was done by my erstwhile tutor, Professor Sir Peter Frederick Strawson, in his very interesting book, *Individuals: An Essay in Descriptive Metaphysics* (London, 1959), especially in chap. 1 and 3. Roughly, beginning with certain epistemological requirements, assumed to be met, the tutor derives our common sense metaphysics. Just as roughly, the pupil, by first questioning certain metaphysical assumptions of common sense, now goes on to question associated epistemological suppositions.

13. Brief Concluding Polemic

Once the problem of the many is appreciated, the choice we face is clear. First, one may try to break the dilemma posed, in a manner that is, of course, philosophically adequate. But as most of our essay has strongly indicated, perhaps especially our asking of questions in section 11, the prospects here are dim indeed. Second, one may accept the alternative of the multitude. But as the discussion of this present section has begun to indicate, this is only a way of compounding and proliferating problems. What we want, of course, is to find a way that is relevantly free of such difficulties. This leaves the third and final alternative, the way of Parmenides, of the other Eleatics, and of the Megarians: There really are not any of those putative ordinary things we think there are. Within this final option, further more specific routes may be sketched. With the ancients, we may think that "thought mirrors reality"—so that we have been discovering the Oneness that is the Only Reality or have been taking steps toward that philosophical ideal. On the other hand, we may, at this late juncture, finally part with our Parmenidian company: Perhaps there is no available thought that is adequate to concrete reality, and what passes for that is really as to nothing. Here the idea is to strive to find something that is relevantly adequate, before making claims "in its terms" as to what obtains in (perhaps the complex of concrete) reality. This, indeed, is the position I favor. According to it, we must set our sights in wholly new directions, that being the true lesson of our failure to find a proper course between the many and the none.[43,44]

43. The arguments of this paper are meant to complement those offered in several other recent papers of mine. I have already cited "Why There Are No People" and "There Are No Ordinary Things" I should now mention as well: "I Do Not Exist," in *Perception and Identity*, ed. G. F. Macdonald (London, 1979: 235–51), which volume is a festschrift for Professor Sir Alfred Jules Ayer, and "Skepticism and Nihilism," *Nous*, forthcoming.

The epistemological problems raised in this last section, an outcome of considerations from metaphysics and the philosophy of language, should be taken as complementary to the universal skepticism for which I argue in my book, *Ignorance: A Case for Skepticism* (Oxford, 1975). In "Skepticism and Nihilism," I discuss certain other connections between skepticism (in epistemology) and radical views in those other areas of philosophy.

44. In coming to appreciate the many facets of this problem, I have had helpful discussions with many people. In addition to those already cited, all of whom were quite generally helpful, I should gratefully mention: Tamara Horowitz, Sidney Morgenbesser, Thomas Nagel and Stephen Schiffer.

5

THE MENTAL PROBLEMS
OF THE MANY

Many years ago, I blush to recall, I published some arguments against the existence of all sorts of commonly supposed entities—against rocks and desks, plants and planets, stars and salt shakers, human brains and bodies, and, perish the thought, against us human thinking experiencers, including even the one who's me.[1] By contrast, now I'm trying to

1. In chronological order, the most directly nihilistic of these papers are: "There Are No Ordinary Things", *Synthese*, 41 (1979): 117–54; "I Do Not Exist", pp. 235–51 in *Perception and Identity*, ed. G. F. MacDonald, London: Macmillan, 1979; and "Why There Are No People", *Midwest Studies in Philosophy*, 4 (1979): 177–222. The main thrust of these papers is the articulation of a nihilistic approach to various *sorites* arguments. Typically, these arguments trade on the (for all I really know perfectly correct) idea that an extremely minute difference between two ordinary entities—minute as regards propensities as well as all sorts of other things—will never mean the difference between one of them being a rock, for example, and the other not being a rock, or the difference between one being a thinking being and the other not being a thinking being. Less directly nihilistic are a few other papers, including "The Problem of the Many", *Midwest Studies in Philosophy*, 5 (1980): 411–67. In this paper none of the key ideas has anything much to do with any sorites arguments, or with "discriminative vagueness", though a casual glance at these key ideas may often give such an erroneous impression. Right now, I'll warn you against conflating these two very different sorts of nihilistic reasoning. And, in the bargain, I'll warn against mistaking, for any sorites argument, or any reasoning at all concerning discriminative vagueness, the trying thoughts I'm about to supply in this present essay. Finally, I signal that, while several of this essay's key ideas do arise from issues central to "The Problem of the Many", some of these presently central ideas go, in various important respects, far beyond anything considered in that old paper. (While there are great differences between the thoughts of this new essay and the ideas of the

develop, in a book I've been long writing, a humanly realistic philosophy, wherein my existence, and yours, has the status of a quite undeniable philosophic datum.[2]

As it seems to me now, certain *trying ideas* then deployed in such nihilistic reasoning may bear importantly on the question of what sort of a humanly realistic view we should adopt. These are ideas to the effect that, where I'm apt first to think that there's just this one human body, "my body", seated in just this one chair, "my desk chair", there are, more accurately, many billions of human bodies, each seated in many billions of chairs. And, where I'm first given to believe that there's just one healthy active brain, "my brain", promoting someone's mentality, there may be many billions of brains, each of them largely overlapping so many of the others, and each serving, quite equally, to promote a thinking, experiencing and choosing human being, or human self. Maybe each brain promotes the very same mind, or self, as do each of the others, in which case there's just one self promoted (rather redundantly?) by them all; or maybe each promotes a numerically distinct conscious individual, in which case many billions of experiencers may be, in my situation, simultaneously promoted. Right now, these remarks should seem no better than cryptic comments; but, in the course of this essay their import should become clearer.

These *trying ideas* might provide, I'll be suggesting, much force against the Scientiphical View that each of us is a highly complex wholly physical thing, with each of our powers just some sort of (physically derivative) physical power; or, on a less popular version of Scientiphicalism, each of us is epiphenomenal on, or supervenient on, a highly complex wholly physical thing.[3] And they might also provide much force against a related Emergentist View, on which each of us is a physical-and-mental complex.[4] Without further ado, let's encounter these trying ideas.

---

older one, an attempt to detail the differences looks to be more distracting than instructive.)

2. Still in progress, the book is entitled *All the Power in the World*, to be published by Oxford University Press.

3. Spelling it differently, as "Scientificalism", I first sketched this View, which is our dominant metaphysic, in "The Mystery of the Physical and the Matter of Qualities", *Midwest Studies in Philosophy*, 23 (1999): 75–99. Using philosophically more suggestive spelling, I discussed it further in "Free Will and Scientiphicalism", *Philosophy and Phenomenological Research*, 65 (2002): 1–25. One of the main aims of *All the Power in the World* is to explore, very critically, this Scientiphical Metaphysics that, for several decades at least, has been the dominant worldview among prominent mainstream philosophers, as well as many others.

4. There's a discussion of this Emergentism in my "Free Will and Scientiphicalism". The excellent suggestion that I treat this view very seriously I owe to Dean Zimmerman.

1. Recalling the Problem of the Many

In a paper called "The Problem of the Many", I introduced a problem for our everyday thinking, distinct from all sorites problems and, indeed, quite different from problems of "discriminative vagueness". Much as I found it useful to do then, let us start by considering certain cases of *ordinary clouds*, clouds like those we sometimes seem to see in the sky.

As often viewed by us from here on the ground, sometimes puffy "picture-postcard" clouds give the appearance of having a nice enough boundary, each white entity sharply surrounded by blue sky. (In marked contrast, there are other times when it's a wonder that we don't simply speak singularly of "the cloud in the sky", where each visible cloudy region runs so messily together with many other cloudy "parts of the sky".) But upon closer scrutiny, as may happen sometimes when you're in an airplane, even the puffiest, cleanest clouds don't seem to be so nicely bounded. And this closer look seems a more revealing one. For, as science seems clearly to say, our clouds are almost wholly composed of tiny water droplets, and the dispersion of these droplets, in the sky or the atmosphere, is always, in fact, a gradual matter. With pretty much any route out of even a comparatively clean cloud's center, there is no stark stopping place to be encountered. Rather, anywhere near anything presumed a boundary, there's only a gradual decrease in the density of droplets fit, more or less, to be constituents of a cloud that's there.

With that being so, we might see that there are enormously many complexes of droplets, each as fit as any other for being a constituted cloud. Each of the many will be a cloud, we must suppose, if there are even as many as just one constituted cloud where, at first, it surely seemed there was exactly one. For example, consider the two candidates I'll now describe. Except for two "widely opposing" droplets, one on one side of two overlapping cloudy complexes, way over on the left, say, and another way over on the right, two candidate clouds may wholly overlap each other, so far as droplets goes. The cited droplet that's on the left is a constituent of just one of the two candidates, not a component of the other; and the one on the right is a component of the other candidate, not the one first mentioned. So each of these two candidate clouds has exactly the same number of constituent droplets. And each might have exactly the same mass, and volume, as the other.

Now, all around the outer portion(s) of a supposedly single cloud, what obtains is a gradual change of droplet density, along ever so many paths, from the considered cloud's central portion(s) to what is merely its droplet-infested environment. In actuality, there's not just one "problematic pair of opposing droplets". Rather, there are very many such *distinct* pairs, that is, many pairs of peripheral droplets each of which has no droplet in common with any of the other pairs. So there's certainly nothing special about the opposing pair that, above, fueled some peculiar thinking. Indeed, any droplet from any one of the many opposing pairs might be coupled equally well, instead, with at least one of the two droplets from (almost) any other one of these very many pairs. This being so, the mathematics of combinations will have it that, in the situation where one first supposes a single concrete cloud, there are *very many millions* of clouds present. Each of these many millions of cloud candidates has precisely as many droplets as does each of the others. And, in every way plausibly deemed relevant for cloudhood here, each is the exact equal of all the others. By contrast with considerations central to sorites arguments, here there is *no* difference at all between any one of these complexes' current cloud credentials and the credentials of any of the millions of others.

Though it's not needed to generate our problem, it's sometimes fun to combine what's just been offered above with some considerations concerning vagueness. So, in the case we've been considering, the extremely good cloud candidates are not limited, of course, to the exactly equally good ones that differ only as regards two such opposing peripheral constituent droplets. In addition, there's a candidate that's plenty good enough for current cloudhood that *lacks not just one but both of* the peripheral "opposing" droplets first considered. If there are any real clouds here at all, this will be a cloud that's just one "droplet's worth" less massive than either of our first two candidates, and just slightly smaller in volume, too. And, there's another perfectly good candidate that *has not just one but both of* those peripheral droplets as constituents. As regards both mass and volume, it will be just two droplets' worth larger than the candidate considered a moment ago, and just one droplet larger than each of the two complexes we first considered above. With even just this much thrown into our cloudily explosive mix of considerations, our situation's recognized cloud population rises enormously.

While there should be limits to how far such "numerically differential shuttling" can be taken, lest sorites arguments here lead to nihilistic ideas, we won't be anywhere close to approaching those limits with differences of just two peripheral droplets in the cloudy complexes we're considering. Indeed, even with differentials of *five* such peripheral droplets, even five on *either* side of our initially chosen "tied clearest current cloud case", we won't be anywhere close to threatening any such limits. Now, these matters concerning vagueness have been, as I predicted, some fun to consider. But, they themselves are peripheral to what are here the main issues, to which we now return.

Even as concerns the main issues, there's not an absolutely perfect parallel between a common cloud and its constituting droplets on one hand, and a water droplet and (at least some of) its constituting molecules, or atoms, or elementary particles on the other. But there's no important difference between the two. We may grant, if needs be, that there are routes from a drop's center into its mere environs with breaks that are quite clean. Even so, there'll be many others that are very much messier, quite messy enough to allow for "opposing" pairs of plausible enough constituents. With these opposing pairs of "particles", we may reason, in a relevantly parallel fashion, that there are many millions of water droplets where at first there would seem to be just one. And, as it is with water droplets, so it is also with rocks and desks, planets and plants, and human brains and bodies.

Where at first there seems to be just a single human body, here, which is just "my body", there may really be vastly many human bodies. And where I take your single brain to be ensconced in your one head, there may be very many human brains (each equally "yours"), all similarly ensconced in vastly many human heads (each "yours").

All this sounds very strange. But, maybe there isn't anything in it that should be very disturbing. So long as we're clear as to what are the relations among which brains, and which bodies, maybe there needn't be any serious problem. For instance, we can be clear enough about what we may correctly express when saying that none of your brains is in, nor are any of your brains a part of, any of my many bodies. And, we may be similarly clear about saying that each of my brains is in, and is a part of, all of my bodies. And, even as many of your brains each overlap with many other brains that are yours, none of your brains overlap with any of mine, of course. At the same time, it's also clear that none of my many bodies ever nest in, nor do any ever greatly overlap with, any one of your many bodies.

Now, even on the face of things, the problems of the many just canvassed, or rehearsed, concern nothing of much greater moment, or depth, than what's commonly found with many merely semantic issues. There seems nothing of much metaphysical moment in these problems with common thoughts about quite grossly complex physical entities. (Nor does there seem any perplexing problems of moral moment, or any deep difficulty concerning rational concern.) Should every "problem of the many" be no worse than these noted problems—about many overlapping clouds, and brains, and human bodies—there may be no very serious philosophical problem to be found along these lines. Is there, perhaps, such a relatively untroubling situation happily in the cards for us here?

2. The Experiential Problem of the Many

Maybe so; but maybe not. Indeed, matters may start to get much worse, I'll suggest, should we be unable to quash the thought that, in what I take to be just my own situation, there are really very many experiencing thinkers, each promoted by a different one of the very many brains that, above, I bid us recognize as "my brains".

But, can anything much like *that* be right? In addition to me myself, whose conscious metaphysical struggles are, apparently, producing these awkward sentences, are there many other thinkers, too, each similarly responsible, and maybe each of us then just barely responsible, for producing these strangely disquieting philosophical utterances? Right here and now, "in my situation", are there vastly many experiencing thinkers, each with a protracted illusion of being, in this very present situation, quite singular and unique? While anything's possible, as we say, the idea that there are, along with me, so many distinct like-minded experiencing thinkers is incredible.

Am I being, perhaps, overly self-centered here? I don't think so. In fact, when I consider a similar "experientially explosive" suggestion about you, and about the many bodies and brains "in your situation", I find the thought of billions of like-minded experiences just as incredible as in my own case. Whether it's for my own case or for yours, with our Experiential Problem of the Many there's a very serious issue of credibility.

Just a few sentences make clear how very much such an experientially explosive supposition flies in the face of our commonsense thinking about ourselves. Possibly excepting what happens when certain rarified metaphysics is done, each one of these many supposed billions thinks that, at least among all the people on earth right now, he alone is experiencing—immediately, complexly, and totally—in the precise way or fashion that, at the moment, he manifests, or exemplifies. As I take it, you're not experiencing in a way that's precisely like the way I'm experiencing right now, even though we may be near each other in the same room. For one thing, I have a tingling condition "in my left foot" that, I believe, is quite different from any felt condition you now suffer. For another, my perspective is different from yours, which almost certainly means a notable difference in our visual experiencing. Obviously we could go on and on; but, just as obviously, that's enough.

Matters quickly go from bad to worse; incredible thoughts compound incredibly. Am I to think that, with vastly many experiencers promoted by vastly many brains "in my situation", each may be communicating his innermost thoughts to all of the enormously many other experiencing thinkers, across the vastly many tables between us, promoted by the vastly many brains "in your situation"? Such an idea is, I think, patently absurd.

Something has gone badly wrong here. And, as we are now dealing with human thinking experiencers, with the likes of you and me, what's gone wrong concerns what's central for any humanly realistic philosophy.

Indeed, whatever philosophical projects one may find interesting, this present matter presents an issue that one should recognize as philosophically puzzling and disturbing. Part of what makes the matter so puzzling may be that it concerns what has been called, in recent years, the "subjectivity of experience". This so-called subjectivity is closely related to—and it may even be the same thing as—what was called, in earlier years, the "privacy of experience". Very sketchily put, that is indeed my partial diagnosis. In a way that may resonate intuitively, I'll try to amplify on this diagnostic idea.

The thought that there are, "in my situation", vastly many individuals each similarly experiencing the sweet taste of chocolate is, to my mind, a very disturbing suggestion. It is far more disturbing than the thought that, in this situation, there are vastly many complex entities each of whom is chewing a sweet piece of chocolate, or digesting a sweet piece of chocolate. A digesting of the sweet chocolate that's very much like my (body's) digesting it may as well be ascribed—quite indifferently, tolerably, and readily—to each of however many human beings (or human bodies) may very largely overlap me (or mine). This contrasting thought concerning digesting is far less deeply puzzling, and far less disturbing, than the thought concerned with experiencing.

With the digesting of the chocolate, the situation seems far more relaxed than with the experiential tasting of anything. With so much more relaxed a matter, it seems little more than a matter of choosing what forms of words to use. Following common sense, even if perhaps speaking loosely, we may say that there's just one process of digesting now going on "in my situation". Or, paying less attention to common thought, and maybe more to certain principles of differential constitution, we may instead say that, with many similar overlapping entities each engaged in a very similar digestive process, there are many similar overlapping digestive happenings. As it seems, this latter description is only somewhat less intuitively palatable.

Not so, it seems, with my experiencing as I do. Rather, it seems, my power to experience will be radically different from my power to digest (or, perhaps better, from my very many bodies' powers to digest.) The latter is just a highly derivative physical propensity; it's a metaphysically superficial power ascribed, perhaps properly enough, to many such ontologically superficial complexes as are typical human bodies, or entirely physical human organisms. By contrast, a power to experience may be a radically emergent mental propensity, in no wise any mere physical power, neither derivative nor non-derivative. For some, this contrast will be both evident and even profound. But, for others, further discussion may be useful.

For the sake of the argument, or the diagnostic exposition, just suppose, for the moment, that a Substantial Dualism holds. And, further, suppose that I causally interact, quite equally, with each of very many overlapping complex physical bodies, each of which thus may be called, properly enough, one of *my bodies*. Must there be very many other Cartesian thinkers, in addition to myself, who also causally interact, quite equally, with (so many of) these same physical complexes—so that (many of) my bodies are also *their bodies*? Certainly not. Indeed, it may be a great advantage of this Dualism that its most plausible versions won't have things turn out this way. As a matter of metaphysical fact, all the bodies "in my situation" serve to promote only myself, and not any other sentient self. On such a Substantial Dualistic View, there may be much reason to take each of these many bodies to be one of my bodies, but not to take any of them to be anyone else's.

Even as I may have so many human bodies, none of which are anyone else's bodies, so I may then also have very many *digestive systems*, many of them greatly overlapping many of the others, while each such system has a slightly different group of basic physical constituents from all the rest—perhaps an "extra" electron here, or one less hydrogen atom there. To be sure, this sounds like it's squarely against common-sense thinking, and ordinary biological thinking. And, very possibly, it is. Still, there's nothing that is all that disturbing in any of it. Indeed, there's nothing very disturbing, either, in going on to think many further thoughts, elaborations on these materially explosive ideas. For instance, without very much disturbance, we may think that each of my many digestive systems may undergo, or be engaged in, a process of digestion—a digesting—that's ever so similar to the digestive processes undergone, simultaneously, by ever so many overlapping digestive systems. Readily enough, I trust, we may accept the idea that all these systems are mine, and mine alone, and all these digestings are mine, and mine alone. Though it's somewhat unnatural for us to say such profligate things, there's no grave philosophical error, I'll suggest, in being so liberal about these metaphysically material matters.

For the same reasons that I might be said to have billions of digestive systems, I may also be said to have vastly many *nervous systems*, each largely overlapping very many others, and each having slightly different physical constituents from all the rest. Indeed, it seems established that *my* causal interaction with all these systems is much more direct than *my* interaction with any of my digestive systems. Anyhow, much as we might readily tolerate the thought that my many overlapping digestive systems may be engaged in many overlapping digestive processes, so we might also easily tolerate the thought that my many overlapping nervous systems may be engaged in many overlapping neural processes.

But, may we similarly tolerate the idea that each of these many nervous systems may undergo, or may be engaged in, a process of *experiencing* that's quite simultaneous with, and ever so similar to, the experiencings undergone by ever so many other largely overlapping nervous systems? I certainly don't think so. More cautiously, may we fairly happily think that, even as each of very many particular experiencings may occur during exactly the same time as ever so many others, each may occur in very much the same place as so many others? May we think this nearly as happily, at least, as we may think parallel thoughts about my digestings? Again, it certainly doesn't seem so to me. By contrast, this following seems a much more intuitively congenial expression of what's apparently happening experientially. More *directly* than any other comparable part of my body, or parts of my bodies, each of the many nervous systems now in "my situation" physically *promotes just a single (total) process of (total) experiencing*, which is just *my experiencing*, even as I myself am the single experiencer that's physically promoted by (any of) the nervous systems now in this particular situation. Briefly put, here's a reasonably plausible way for how all that may be so, even if it is also a rather nicely amazing way. In whatever serves to constitute my nervous systems, there's a propensity to the effect that there will be a limit placed—(almost always) a limit of just one—on how many experiencing particulars may be promoted by the optimally arranged basic physical constituents—optimally arranged, that is, for the promoting of any experiencing individuals. In the same way, we may hypothesize that each of my simple physical constituents—every single one of them—has a marvelous propensity with regards to how it may interact with very many others, so that, in optimal arrangements for promoting consciousness, there's an effective *singular resolution* as to what experiencer they promote. And so also is there a singular resolution of what experience, or what experiencing, is then promoted by them.

In the last several paragraphs, we've been supposing that the correct metaphysical view is a Substantial Dualism, not terribly different from the classical view of Descartes. Now, let's drop that supposition and, to the contrary, suppose that a more materialistic view of mentality is correct—maybe some form of materialism itself, maybe some more relaxed version of our Scientiphical Metaphysic, as with a suitable Scientiphical Epiphenomenalism. Or maybe what's correct is something as moderately different from Dualism as the Emergentism that, in this is paper's preamble, I mentioned so briefly. Now, on this Emergentist View, there are radically emergent mental powers, all right, but they all inhere in physical complexes, in the very same complex objects that also have so many physically derivative physical powers.[5] *Insofar as* we may maintain one of these more materialistic views, quite comfortably and intuitively, we may not find it disturbing, at all, to think that, in my situation right now, there are billions of experiencing thinkers. But, then, *how far is it* that, all the while doing it quite comfortably and intuitively, I actually can sustain the thought that, in my situation right now, there are billions of experiencing individuals, each enjoying his very own experiencing, numerically distinct from the similar experience of all the others? Not very far at all, that's for sure. And, as I suspect, pretty much the same is true of you.

For most of us, all this should be fairly intuitive, maybe even highly intuitive. For that reason, all this should be, for most of us, a point in favor of Substantial Dualism—as against the Scientiphical Metaphysic and, as well, as against the Emergentism lately noted.

3. The Experiencing of Split-Brain Patients Underscores This Disturbing Problem

The previous section offered a fairly succinct presentation of the Experiential Problem of the Many. Now, I aim to amplify on that. With the further considerations I'll discuss in this amplification, we may see that this problem provides a more clearly forceful point in favor of Dualism, even if, perhaps, not yet any point that's enormously forceful.

At all events, it's extremely interesting to think about human "split-brain" patients—epileptics whose main neural connection between

5. As noted earlier, I discuss this Emergentism in my "Free Will and Scientiphicalism".

their two cerebral hemispheres, their corpus callosum, was severed so that they might gain relief from frequent severe seizures. When these patients are placed in certain specially designed experimental setups, as some of them actually were, in many cases their behavior almost cries out for exotic psychological interpretation.

Here's a simple case, contrived for illustrative purposes, that's relevantly similar to striking actual cases. Our psychological subject, a cooperative split-brain patient, is asked to handle some regularly shaped solid figures, each object being either a cylinder, or a cube, or a pyramid, or a sphere. And, right after handling a solid object, our subject is to write down the sort of object she just handled, inscribing just one of these four common words for shapes, the one that seems suitable to her: "cylinder", "cube", "pyramid", and "sphere". Now, none of these objects is ever seen by the subject; the solids are all behind an opaque screen that obscures even the surface of the table on which they rest. Usefully, the screen has two holes in it, while each hole has an easily movable but always visually obscuring flap. At all events, our subject places her left arm through the hole on her left, and her right arm through the one on her right. So her left hand can handle objects on the table's left side, from her perspective; but, it can't handle any on the table's right side. Why not? Well, protruding upward from center of the table's surface, there's a large solid barrier, which precludes any left–right, or right–left, crossover. In this way the right hand is conversely limited; with her right hand she can handle only the objects to the right of the barrier.

That's our experimental setup. Now, we suppose that, within about a minute of putting her arms through the appropriate holes, her right hand grasps a cube, and no other regular solid object, while the sole object her left hand grasps is a sphere. For a few seconds, she holds the two objects like that. Then, she withdraws her hands from the holes, as instructed. And, then, on the near side of the screen, she places her hands on two pieces of paper and is given two pencils, one placed in her left hand and one in her right. Then our ambidextrous subject, who can readily employ both hands at once, is asked to write, on each of the pads, just one of the four words: "cylinder", "cube", "pyramid", "sphere". Something quite amazing now happens. With her right hand, she writes "cube", while with her left hand, she writes "sphere". In this strangely diverse writing activity, our subject evinces no hesitation, conflict, or ambiguity. Rather, as far as her behavior seems to indicate, (it's as though) "a part of her" experienced a cube tactiley, and not any sphere, while at the very same time "another part of her" experienced tactiley only a sphere, and no cube at all.

Many actual cases are, as I said, very like this contrived example.[6]
They strongly suggest that, in many actual experimental setups with
split-brain patients, the subjects become involved, at once, in two quite
separate experiencings, or "streams of experience". Of course, these
split-brain episodes are very unlike what we imagined above for our very
many "largely overlapping experiencers". With those very many overlappers, each of *very many millions* of experiential streams was supposed
to be *qualitatively extremely like* each of the others; with our split-brain
subjects, by contrast, each of *just two* presumed experiential streams is
qualitatively very *unlike* the only other.

What's going on here, with a split-brain patient in a dually productive setup? To provide a sensible answer to this question, we first put
to one side all our problems of the many. That done, what's going on
seems to be this: along with a good deal of the subject's nervous system
that's not cerebral—her brain-stem, for example—one of her hemispheres serves (most directly) to promote one sort of experiencing that
the subject's written answer indicated she enjoyed—say, her tactile experiencing as of a cube. And, in a relevantly complementary way, the
other hemisphere serves (most directly) to promote another sort of
experiencing, a tactile experiencing as of a sphere, and not as of a cube.
Now, except as regards cerebral hemispheres, a big exception here,
what's promoting the one experiencing, is the same entity—presumably
the same physical complex—as is promoting the other; or, at the very
least, the one precisely coincides with the other. In exactly the same way,
the physical complex (most directly) promoting one of these experiences has a promotionally important part that is the same as, or that
coincides with, the physical complex that's (most directly) promoting
the other experience. And at the same time, of course, each complex
lacks a promotionally important part, a whole hemisphere, that is a
crucial part of the other.

Far be it from me to think that in these cases everything is readily
amenable to our customary ways of thinking about human experiencers
and our experiencings. On the contrary, the apparent simultaneous
"contrary" experience is very puzzling. Here's just some of what's so
puzzling. With each numerically different total momentary experiencing, there is a numerically different experiencer—or so we're strongly
inclined to believe. So, in the case that's in focus, we have a certain

6. For a nice presentation of some of these actual cases, along with an interesting
discussion of what might be much of their philosophic import, see Thomas Nagel, "Brain
Bisection and the Unity of Consciousness", *Synthese*, 22 (1971). This essay is widely reprinted, notably in Nagel's *Mortal Questions* (Cambridge University Press, 1979), pp. 147–64.

inclination to think that there is one experiencer who writes only "cube" when reporting her experiencing, and another who doesn't write "cube", but writes only "sphere", when reporting her tactiley very different simultaneous experiencing. So, intuitively, there's a certain difficulty here for our thinking that in this experimental situation there's just one single experiencer.

But, that inclination isn't our only proclivity here. Can there really be two human people in this situation? Can there really be, in this experimental setup, an experiencing writer who is not a human person? As it certainly seems, there's *also* a difficulty for our thinking that in this setup there's *not* always just one experiencer. Indeed, there might be an even greater difficulty here.

For the moment, though, suppose there's not just one, but two experiencers here, each tactilely experiencing quite differently from the other. Well, what happens when these two experiencers are removed from the artificial setup, when each hemisphere again gets very much the same stimulation as the other? Do we have only one experiencer once again, the same single person who went into the experiment (say, about a year after she had her split-brain operation)? That suggestion seems strangely implausible. Where was she in the intervening period, this one experiencer, when (as we're supposing) there were the two simultaneous different experiencers? Was she just a certain one of these two? That seems quite absurd. Did she go out of existence altogether, just when the experimental setup was introduced, and then come to exist again, just when the differentially stimulating setup was removed? This suggestion also seems unsatisfactory.

As a still further alternative, there's the conjecture that, not just during the experimental setup, but ever since her operation first affected how she experienced, our split-brain patient was engaged in not one, but two experiencings. Quite dramatically, during the differentially stimulating setup of the experimental situation, her experiencings were qualitatively very different, and not just numerically distinct. Less dramatically, before the post-operative patient was introduced to this setup, her two (streams of) experiencings were qualitatively very alike. (But, for all their qualitative similarity, these experiencings were numerically different from each other.)

What are we to make of these conjectures? And what are we to make of various further proposals, which may also be, at once, both somewhat attractive and somewhat problematic? I do not know. It is all very puzzling; and, it seems, quite *deeply* puzzling. But even in our deeply puzzled ignorance we might make, I think, some useful comments.

Let us meanwhile continue to suppose that, during the puzzling middle period of the experimental setup, a certain apparently exclusionary diversity of experiencing is all at once promoted. And let's suppose, just a little explosively perhaps, that then there is not just one sentient being, but *two experiencers*. Though that thought is somewhat uncomfortable, it's not nearly as disturbing as the thought that there are *many billions of human thinkers experiencing* as of a cube; nor is it nearly as unsettling as the thought that billions are each tactiley *experiencing only spherically*. (Far more disturbing yet is the thought that there are billions experiencing tactiley only in the first way, and billions only in the second way.)

However, unless we believe in a naturally resolving limit on the experiencers promoted, how are we rationally to reject the thought that, with so very many exceptionally similar complexes of matter, there are, right then and there and all at once, so very many experiencers as *that*?

Recall the speculation that, before and after the experimental setup with our patient—or with our two "neighboring" patients—there may be two quite parallel experiencings promoted. Supposing that's really so, a somewhat plausible explanation will run rather like this. One of these parallel experiencings is promoted by a neuronal system featuring only the left hemisphere as its distinctively highest region or part, and the other by a nervous system that, lacking the left, similarly features just the right hemisphere. Whatever one thinks of this speculation—I myself don't think it's all that plausible—there's nobody, I trust, who thinks there are many billions of experiencings physically promoted largely by the left hemisphere, and billions more promoted largely by the right. But, to avoid such a numerically explosive idea, in a properly principled fashion, we must accept, again, that there is a resolving limit on what, by way of experiencers and their experiencings, is physically promoted by various mentally productive arrangements of physical constituents.

Almost everything we've been discussing in this section strikes me as not only puzzling, but *deeply* puzzling. Far from being concerned only with semantics, or with the application conditions of some concepts, these puzzles seem to concern, beyond all that, metaphysically deep considerations. And, if that's right, they may point to some matters of much metaphysical import. Below, I'll try to make these points more clearly vivid.

Recall our remarks as to how we might take it upon ourselves to say that, "in my situation", there are many different digestive systems, each involved with a different simultaneous digesting. While that's a rather unnatural thing to say, and while the motivation supplied for saying it may be somewhat puzzling, there is nothing in it that's *deeply* puzzling. Nor is there any deep puzzle concerning whether we should continue always to think that, "in my situation", there's always just one digester, presumably a certain human organism, or whether there are very many digesters, most of them largely overlapping many others. So, here again, we find an intuitively striking difference between our experiencing and, on the other side, such evidently physical processes as our digesting. This difference may indicate something deep metaphysically.

4. Might the Singularity of Common Experiencing Favor Substantial Dualism?

To deal effectively with our deep puzzles about our experiencing, perhaps we might accept, if only very tentatively and somewhat skeptically, a certain Substantial Dualism. Central to this Cartesian doctrine is the thought that each of us is a non-physical experiencer, though an experiencer who (causally) *interacts with* certain physical things.

With such a suitable Dualistic doctrine, there may be a singular resolution for our Experiential Problem—featuring just a single experiencer "in my situation" that isn't so horribly arbitrary as to be terribly incredible. Well in line with this Dualism, we can conjecture that "in my situation" very many overlapping physical complexes—physical brains, perhaps—may altogether serve to promote, causally or quasi-causally, a single non-physical experiencer, or a singular mind, or exactly one individual soul, even while each of the complexes may do its promoting in what is really a quite derivative sense or way. In the case of each mentally promoting physical complex, the derivation will proceed, of course, from the basic (enough) physical components of the very complex in question, and from the physical relations obtaining among its particular components, to the complex's being a (derivative) promoter of just a single sentient self. And so, in each of very many worldly derivations, it may be the very same sentient self, or experiencing mind, that the complexes in question each serve (derivatively) to promote. In a happy enough sense, then, the (physically derivative) promoting of this single mind, *by any one of* these physical complexes, will be a *causally redundant* promoting. Of course, there won't be any complex that's doing any of this (derivative) promoting without there being, all at once, a great many each doing it rather redundantly.

In any very direct sense or way, it will be this promoted single non-physical mind itself—just me myself—that has a power to experience. So, it will be only in a very attenuated sense or way that an experiential power will be possessed by any of the concrete physical complexes that serve to promote the experientially powerful non-physical being.

Nowadays, it's very hard for respectable philosophers to believe in mentally powerful non-physical beings. But, even for us now, this may be *less* incredible than the thought that *just a single one* of our considered physical complexes itself has this power—with all those other slightly overlapping complexes being quite powerless experientially, even all of those others that, in mass, in volume, and in number of basic constituents, are each precisely the same as the supposedly sole experiencing physical complex. And it's *also* less incredible than the thought that just a single one of the basic (enough) physical entities here—say, a certain particular quark—has the power to experience richly—with all the other quarks "in my situation" being quite powerless in such a mentally rich regard. And it's certainly less incredible than the thought that some mere abstraction from what's physical, and nothing concrete at all, should be the sole entity, "in my situation", with the power to experience, a power that's manifested, this very minute, in *my presently experiencing* precisely as I now do.

As easy as it is for us to think, quite rightly, that each of us is a concrete being, not a mere abstraction, or abstractum, it's equally hard for us, in this present day and age, to believe that we are not spatially extended beings. Indeed, it's enormously hard to believe anything about ourselves that's very different from how our Scientiphicalism has us be. What's more, it's hardly ever that I manage to get further from the Scientiphical Metaphysic than the nearby Emergentism that I've been trying to take very seriously. Yet, as this essay has been suggesting, this Emergentism is deeply embroiled with the Experiential Problem of the Many, as deeply as Scientiphicalism itself.

Among the metaphysical options not so embroiled with this apparently deep problem, Substantial Dualism is, so far as I can tell, the available view that departs least radically from our dominant Scientiphical Metaphysic. It's a much less radical departure, certainly, than is any fundamentally mentalistic metaphysic, whether such an exhaustively mental view be called "idealism", or "phenomenalism", or, as seems more fashionable nowadays, "panpsychism". Wishing not to be radical metaphysically, I'll suggest that, in the face of the Experiential Problem of the Many, we take Substantial Dualism, in its most coherent and tenable forms, rather seriously; or, if that is not yet psychologically possible for us, at least we should take it rather more seriously than almost all prominent professional philosophers have done in recent decades.

Professionally socialized as I am, even this much is very hard for me now to do. Apparently, I need a good deal more help, psychologically, than what's afforded by the Experiential Problem, to give any very sub-stantial departure from our dominant Scientiphicalism, even so much as just a very moderately serious run for the money. So in the following section I'll try to provide some potentially liberating thoughts, perhaps novel enough to help us get beyond the circumscribed bounds dictated by our unquestioning allegiance to Scientiphical thinking.

5. The Problem of Too Many Real Choosers

For the Scientiphical view of ourselves, and for our noted Emergentism, too, there's a mental problem of the many that's yet more disturbing, and far more baffling, than the disturbingly baffling Experiential Problem of the Many. It's the Problem of Too Many Real Choosers.

In order that our metaphysical meditations could begin most man-ageably, we haven't yet addressed issues concerning the choosing of our thinking experiencers. But now it's high time to explore them. When exploring these issues persistently, we may find it absolutely incredible that there should be, "in my situation", very many experiencing choosers, rather than just me choosing all alone.

As with everyone else, there are some sorts of things I'm far more prone to imagine than things of some other sorts. For example, I'm far more prone to imagine a pretty woman than an ugly plant. But, with regards to many (other) things, there's no great difference in my imagi-native proclivities. For example, this may happen with my imagining a horse, or else a cat, or else a dog, where each of the options is to exclude each of the others. Equally, it may occur with my imagining something wholly red, or else something wholly blue. With many groups of real alternatives for imagining, then, I have no enormous disposition toward just one of the mutually exclusive options for me.

What's more, even with something I'm strongly prone *not* to imag-ine, (not always but) often I can choose to imagine it experientially nonetheless. I have just done some demonstrative imagining. Counter to my proclivities, I chose to imagine an ugly plant. And because I chose that option for my imagining, I actually imagined a pathetic weed, very dry and brown. What's the moral of this little exercise? Dramatically put, the point is this: the domain of my power to choose encompasses a very great deal of the domain of my power to imagine experientially. Often enough, I can choose to imagine experientially even counter to my quite strong imaginative proclivities.

Having taken note of my power to choose even contrary to my strong proclivities, we turn to an easier case. Here, I'm to choose among roughly equal options for my imaginative activity, where my proclivities for each option are about equally strong. And so, just for the sake of it, I'll choose to imagine experientially either a horse, or else a cat, or else a dog. And, just for the sake of some potentially instructive reasoning, let's now suppose that the experiential imagining I'm about to perform will be a *purely mental* act of mine, entirely isolated from the world's physical realm. Not only will this imagining not be anything physical, but we suppose it to lack any real physical cause. And, both concurrently and in the future, it will have no physical effect or manifestation. (Later we'll drop this pretense of mental purity; but not just yet.)

All right, I'm now imagining just one of the three mentioned sorts of very common domesticated animal. Make a guess, please, as to which of the three I'm imagining. You might guess, I suppose, that I'm imagining a cat. Or you might guess that it's a dog I'm imagining. Or you might guess it's a horse. Whatever you may have guessed, I'm now done with that bit of imagining. Now, as you'll recall, I said that my chosen imagining won't have any physical manifestation, not even in its future. Sticking with that supposition, I won't ever communicate to you, in (physical) writing, what sort of animal it was that I actually did just imagine.

For the sake of instructive reasoning, let's make the *supposition* that it was a cat I just imagined. And let's proceed to reason from that supposition.

When I put the question of this three-way choice as a little exercise for myself just now, did billions of very similar people, all of them "in my situation", each similarly put the question to himself? And, when I made a choice among my three specified options for imagining, each an alternative excluding the others, did each of them also effectively choose? How many of them effectively chose to imagine a cat experientially, the alternative we're supposing that I effectively chose?

If there really are vastly many people in my situation, then the only plausible thing to suppose about them is that, like myself, each of them has his own power to choose. And, since this is a real power to choose fully, and freely, *each* of these thinker's powers to choose is relevantly *independent of the power of each of the others*, including, of course, my own power to choose. So it's only plausible to suppose, further, that, when I made my effective choice to imagine a cat experientially, each of them made an equally effective choice to imagine that was independent of my choice, and also independent, of course, of the choice of each of the others.

That being so, it would be an astounding coincidence, and not a credible occurrence, if all these billions of people should also imagine a cat, each freely choosing to imagine the very sort of animal that, of the three exclusive options, I freely chose to imagine. (After all, we've been properly supposing that, just as with me, none of these billions of "overlappers", each so similar mentally to me, *is not much more* prone to imagine a cat than he is to imagine a dog, or a horse.) Indeed, it would be extremely unlikely that there should be, among the billions of choosers "in my situation", fewer than ten million real choosers who imagined a dog, when I myself was imagining a cat. And, equally, it would be extraordinarily unlikely that should there be, among the billions with independent powers, fewer than ten million who would choose, quite effectively, to imagine a horse experientially. With *any less* diversity of chosen animal images than *that*, among my overlapping physical-and-mental cohort of independent full choosers, there would be *far* too little qualitative experiential diversity, among "the population in my situation" for an outcome that's even the least bit credible.

The point here is, in its essentials, quite the same as a point about choice concerning me and you, and billions of other relevantly independent choosers, thinkers who *aren't* largely overlappers, thinkers who *aren't* "in numerically the same situation". For this case of "spatially separated choosers", or choosers with spatially separate bodies, and brains, we may playfully consider the most suitable two billion subjects, for a very widespread but temporally tiny psychological experiment, selected from among the world's current population, which numbers a bit over six billion. Now, as we may similarly suppose here, very few of these two billion have a tremendous proclivity toward imagining cats, as against horses or dogs. The great majority have a roughly equal propensity in each of the three specified directions. So, if fewer than ten million of us choose, freely and effectively, to imagine a dog, while almost all of us choose to imagine a cat, that is an unbelievably great coincidence. I myself would not believe in such an outcome. Rather than accepting that overly coincidental nonsense, I'd go back and question various propositions that we were supposing to hold true. Was there, perhaps, mass mesmerization going on globally, so that almost all of us were made to imagine a cat, with few really able to exercise his power to choose?

Whether overlapping or not, it's just incredible that billions of real choosers should all choose to imagine a cat experientially, with hardly any opting for a dog or a horse, when those two are, quite as forcefully, presented as appropriate alternatives. But at the same time it's not really credible, either, that there really was, in my situation, truly substantial diversity in experiential imagining, when I was (supposedly) just imagining a cat. So it's just incredible that, overlapping with me right now, there are many other complex entities, many physical-and-mental beings, who really do choose.

In one of its endless variations, that is the Problem of Too Many Real Choosers. Maybe I'm being overly quick about the matter, or even simply quite dense. But, in any case, I suspect that this problem may be an insuperable difficulty for the dominant Scientiphical Metaphysic. And, as I also suspect, it may undermine the Emergentist View.

6. This Problem and the Emergentist Idea of Physical-and-Mental Complexes

On the Emergentist view we've been exploring, each of us is a physical-and-mental complex. By contrast with our severe Scientiphical View, which has all our power as physical propensities, whatever the details of their physical derivations, on this Emergentism each of us will have, in *addition* to ever so many physical proclivities, various non-physical radically emergent mental powers. Yet, on the Emergentist View, any being that has such radical mental powers must be, at the same time, a complex physical entity. Indeed, it is precisely this aspect of our Emergentism that has it as a *more conservative* departure from Scientiphicalism, or *less of* a departure, than a Cartesian View, or any Substantial Dualism concerning mind and body.

In my "Free Will and Scientiphicalism", I argued that Scientiphicalism is, in several ways, incompatible with our thought that we really choose from among real alternatives for our thoughtful activity. And after offering those arguments, I observed that, so far as any of us could then tell, this fairly conservative Emergentist View might be as free of such Scientiphical Incompatibilisms as is Substantial Dualism. Our Emergentism *might be* tenable, but only insofar as a complex physical being's real physical features are no obstacle to her having, as well, many non-physical mental powers, saliently including a radically emergent purely mental power to choose. And, as it was then suggested, that might be quite far indeed; for, as it then appeared, there wasn't any such obstacle; there wasn't any real philosophic difficulty. Well, that was then; and, this is now.

In the light of our current discussion, there does appear to be a very real philosophic difficulty. In the first place, it appears that, "in your situation right now", there are very many different physical-and-mental complexes (each greatly overlapping with many others)—supposing, of course, that "in your situation right now" there's at least one complex physical entity with radically emergent non-physical mental powers.

Though it may be logically possible that there is a great plurality of spatially extended real choosers, each of whom may share much of your space with you now, this is a proposition that defies belief. Indeed, this conflict becomes quite unbearable when we reflect, as we have, that the almost perfectly certain consequence of this is that, from time to time, there'll be great qualitative diversity in the chosen mental lives of the largely overlapping physical-and-mental beings.

Nor is there, on our Emergentist View, a credible way out of this philosophic difficulty. In a "messily gradual" world like this actual one, with very many very similar physical complexes to be found "in the situation of" any alleged physical-and-mental complex being, there's no credible resolution as to *which one*, among all the very many overlapping complexes, alone has the power to choose. Nor is it credible that, while each of the many complexes has a power to choose, there's somehow just one physical-and-mental complex, among the billions overlapping, that, at any given moment of time, gets to exercise his power. Nor is there any other credible way to offer a suitably singular resolution of the matter. But the only alternative, we have just observed, is an incredible diversity of choosers diversely choosing experientially. So, at least in any world much like our messily gradual actual world, the Emergentist View is not a credible alternative to our besieged Scientiphicalism.

7. A Singular Physical Manifestation of the Power to Choose Underscores This Problem

To make the presentation of the problem both vivid and manageable, the initial offering of the Problem of Too Many Choosers featured just such choosing as might be considered quite purely mental activity, and even quite isolated from all physical happenings. It may now profit us further, I imagine, to explore cases of choosing an imaginative option where the agent, just before she starts to imagine as she chooses to do, communicates to others what she's imagining, presumably via an appropriate physical sign or signal.

As before, again I'll now imagine either a horse, or a cat, or a dog. And, while I'm imagining it, I'm going to produce a physical signal of what it is that, because I just chose to imagine it, I'm now imagining experientially. (Pretend that I'm communicating by writing on a pad in plain view, or by an electronic instant messaging system.) Anyway, with this very physical sentence that I've just produced and that you're now reading, I tell you that it's a dog I'm now imagining, not a horse or a cat.

In producing that writing, I made a certain change in physical reality. And this change was a real result, of course, of the choice I just effected.

Putting aside our previous worries, maybe we can somehow make it palatable to ourselves that, this time "in my situation", there are millions of people choosing to imagine a horse, quite effectively, and millions of others choosing to imagine a cat, as well as the millions who, like me, were imagining a dog. Each of the people, though overlapping ever so many others, chose quite independently and very effectively, with each managing to alter his own imaginative experiencing just as he independently chose freely to do. Well, maybe that's too far-fetched really to be palatable. Even so, let's *suppose* that there are all these overlapping choosers, independently and effectively choosing images of striking qualitative diversity. If, quite fantastically, that should be true, will it help our Emergentism?

No, it won't. Even if we allow ourselves this supposition, there will arise, or will remain, this parallel problem: with each of our three animal options chosen by many millions, each of them an independent chooser though overlapping so many other free choosers, *how is it that just those who chose to imagine a dog* managed to produce an intended (revealing) signal change—but not those millions who imagined a horse, or imagined a cat? Here's one specific suggestion. Maybe it's a matter of the numbers, as with a voting procedure; and maybe more chose to imagine a dog than chose a cat, or a horse. But, though that idea may occur more obviously than most of its equally specific alternatives, it's no less absurd than so many other terribly incredible thoughts.

All this just brings home to us how incredible is the idea that, in my situation, or in yours, there are very many real choosers. Indeed, it's absurd for us to believe anything in the neighborhood. It's absurd to think that there are many overlapping people here—but only one of them has the power really to choose. It's also absurd to think that there are many with this power—but at any one time only one gets to exercise the power; and, so on, and so forth.

8. Does This Problem of Real Choosers Favor Substantial Dualism?

Recall our remarks about how *each of many* overlapping nervous systems, "in my situation", might be one of *my* nervous systems. In what serves to constitute my overlapping nervous systems, there are propensities to the effect that there's a limit to be placed—a limit of just one—on how many experiencing particulars may be promoted by these overlapping systems. How so? Here's a way. Each of a system's simple physical constituents, as with each of its constituting quarks, has marvelous propensities regarding how it may interact with very many other simple physical things, so that, in their optimal arrangements for promoting experience, there's an effective *singular resolution* as to what experiencer they may promote. And, because there's that singular resolution, there's also a nice singular resolution as to what experiencing may be promoted by them all.

It was hard to believe, we said before, that the single experiencer thus promoted should be a complex physical thing, whether or not the complex should have radically emergent purely mental powers. For, as it surely appears, no good candidate for being the single experiencing complex, "in the situation", is any better a candidate than each of very many extremely similar and massively overlapping others. It's hard to believe that, somehow or other, *just a single* one of these should have the power to experience richly, while all the others should be perfectly powerless in this salient regard. (Yet it's *also* hard to believe that, running very much in parallel with me, there are *vastly many* highly similar distinct experiencers promoted, rather than just me experiencing here alone.) Indeed, if a certain one of these physical complexes should somehow be the sole experiencer here, what happens when it loses one of its peripheral constituents, as will surely happen quite soon? Does this sole experiencer go out of existence? That's incredible. Does it, rather, come to coincide with a just slightly smaller complex, previously "nested" in it, while having only one fewer simple component than just before the slight loss? Will there be, then, an experiencing complex that's materially coincident with an insensate complex? That too is incredible. Will there then be, alternatively, two experiencing complexes, one previously experiencing and one just now newly experiencing? That's also incredible. Is a further alternative markedly more credible than these patently fantastic claims? I can't see any further alternative to be much more credible. In line with our Scientiphical Metaphysic, or even in line with our noted Emergentism, there's no credible resolution, I submit, to our Experiential Problem of the Many.

So, for folks so accepting of Scientiphicalism, myself included, there's a disturbing problem with the Experiential Problem of the Many. But, as I've lately been arguing, we may find the Problem of Too Many Choosers to be still more disturbing. With that Problem, there's the following dilemma: on the one hand, it's blatantly absurd to think that there are *very many* real experiencing choosers "in my situation", sometimes many choosing in a certain experiential way and many others choosing in a very different experiential way. This is yet more disturbing, I think, than our thinking there to be, "in my situation", very many experiencers, where it may always be that each of them experiences, immediately and totally, in much the same way as all the others. But on the other hand, and just as with the Experiential Problem, it's also absurd to think that there's a single *complex physical* being that's the only real chooser here; rather, any promising candidate for being such a choosing complex appears no better at all, not even the least bit more qualified or promising, than each of very many extremely similar, and massively overlapping, complexes.

Well, then, are there other alternatives for the Scientiphically inclined to favor here, evidently less absurd for us to accept? While there are other logical possibilities, I suppose, I can't see any that are notably more credible options. Certainly not that *I'm a simple physical* thing. So far as I can tell, there are ever so many quarks, or maybe superstrings, each of which might be a simple physical thing. But, then, it's not at all credible that *I'm* a quark, or whatever. (The matter can't be improved by suggesting I might be a simple physical-and-mental thing. For, any such entity must be a simple physical thing, of course, whatever else also might be true of it.) And, not that I'm a complex spatially extended entity that's not physical, with substantial simple spatial parts that aren't physical parts. Nor is it at all credible that I'm any other, still different, sort of spatial or physical thing.

Now, remember, I'm an independent real chooser, a conscious being who, at least from time to time, chooses fully and freely his own conscious activity. So, I'm not any mere epiphenomenal being, nor anything that merely supervenes on a base that's fully physical. In all of our Scientiphicalism, there's nothing that does much justice to my being a real chooser.

While still believing in a vast heterogeneous physical reality, what are we now to think ourselves to be? Among the traditionally available options, the least implausible view may be a Substantial Dualism, rather like the Cartesian View noted earlier. As I'm suggesting, then, maybe we should think that our mental problems of the many, especially the Problem of Too Many Choosers, mean a point in favor of such a Dualistic Metaphysic. (This may be so, of course, even if these problems also favor views that depart still further than does Dualism from the Scientiphical Metaphysic now so widely accepted, as with many Idealistic worldviews.)

I myself cannot yet believe in a metaphysic that departs even as much as a Substantial Dualism departs from our standard metaphysical conception. For one thing, I can't believe that I really haven't any spatial extension; at least, not yet I can't. And, as I suspect, you're in the same commonsensical boat. So, what are we to do?

Three main courses strike me as available.

First, we may go back over what our investigation has so far offered, and look for serious errors. Then, we may come to think, perhaps quite rightly, that there's no mental problem of the many, nor any other difficulty, that's truly a serious problem for our widely accepted Scientiphicalism. I hope that you will try this very seriously. And, whether successful or not, I hope you may be so good as to tell me what you find. As for myself, however, at this point in time this option has been exhausted and, in the wake of my laborious struggles, is not widely available. So, for me, right now, that leaves two courses.

Second, we may ask ourselves what are the most disturbing aspects of a Cartesian View. And, after trying our best to articulate them well, we might then endeavor to show how they might really give far less cause for intellectual disturbance than at first they appear to do. Yet, this has been often tried before, by many others. So, while I think I should try to do something here, I have doubts as to how much I might accomplish in this way.

Third, and finally, there's a more novel and speculative approach, though it's not wholly divorced from the Dualistic course just noted. Perhaps, in addition to many physical and spatial parts, many of them overlapping many others, I might have a single non-physical non-spatial part. And perhaps it may be that it's only in this non-physical part of me, in my "soul", that I'm mentally propensitied and empowered. It's through my exercise of certain powers inhering in this soul, my soul, that I may perhaps choose various aspects of my mental life, and sometimes even choose how it is that my body moves.

Though it's pretty speculative, so far that's not novel, but just old hat. In bare and sketchy terms, here's something that, far from being so old hat, is even more strangely speculative: though this non-physical part of me—my mind, or my soul—may *not* have any *spatial extension*, at least not in any strict or narrow sense of the terms, perhaps it may *have* some *non-spatial spacelike extension*. In what's only a very schematic way indeed, I'll try to say something about the general tenor of this strange speculation.

Now, as it *seems* to me, *space* is the *only clearly non-temporal dimension of concrete reality* in which I exist. But that appearance may be an illusory appearance. As it might really be, space is but one of the clearly non-temporal dimensions in which I exist; as I'm speculating, there's at least one other such dimension in which, quite equally, I also participate—in which I also exist. Even as my many substantial physical parts exist in space, I may have another enduring substantial part (or maybe more than one) that *does not* exist in space itself. This non-spatial part of me, this soul of mine, if you will, may exist in some other clearly non-temporal dimension (or in more than one) that is *extended*, all right, *but not spatially* extended.

No easy matter; it remains for us to suggest for these speculative ideas some helpfully more concrete terms, not so abstract as those I've just employed or offered. Since they require our engagement with the most profoundly radical sort of imaginative thinking, we may need to connect the offered abstract speculations with some of our (more nearly) experiential thinking, or at least with some thinking of ours that's more experientially informed. With no great confidence that I'll have much success in any such positive effort, I postpone this for another occasion. Anyway, and as with almost everything else in first philosophy, here too it may be that only the problems rightly last long with us, while our attempted resolutions are all fleeting, fashionable, and, maybe, flat-out futile as well.

6

THE MYSTERY OF THE PHYSICAL AND THE MATTER OF QUALITIES: A PAPER FOR PROFESSOR SHAFFER

1. Introduction: A Russellian Respect for the Mystery of the Physical

For some fifty years now, nearly all work in mainstream analytic philosophy has made no serious attempt to understand the *nature of physical reality*, even though most analytic philosophers take this to be all of reality, or nearly all. Whereas we've worried much about the nature of our own experiences and thoughts and languages, we've worried little about the nature of the vast physical world that, as we ourselves believe, has them all as only a small part.

In 1995, David Lewis dedicated a paper to Professor Jerome Shaffer, his undergraduate philosophy teacher, for the occasion of Jerry Shaffer's retirement from teaching philosophy: "Should a Materialist Believe in Qualia?" *Australasian Journal of Philosophy*, Vol. 73, 1995, 140–44, and *Faith and Philosophy*, 1995, 467–71. Now, I much more belatedly dedicate this paper to Shaffer, who was also my undergraduate philosophy teacher. Not only for his understanding and encouragement, but especially for that, I'll always be grateful to Jerry Shaffer.

For many years, Shaffer's thought hard about the relation between the mental and the physical. Now, I try to write usefully about part of what may be sustaining his thinking.

In this central respect, we've been very different from the man emerging as the century's preeminent analytic philosopher, Bertrand Russell. Although Russell thought hard about the things that have preoccupied us, *he also thought hard about the nature of physical reality.* Why has there been such a great disparity?

By contrast with Russell, most contemporary workers in core analytic areas just assume that, largely as a legacy from the physical sciences, we have been granted a happily adequate conception of physical reality: Thanks to physics, we have a pretty good understanding of physical reality, even if there may be some serious deficiencies in our understanding.

When in this frame of mind, we philosophers aren't moved to think hard about the nature of physical reality, even if we believe it to be all of reality. Rather, we're much more moved by thoughts like this: "Let's leave such terribly large matters to so many successful scientists, and to the few philosophers so concerned to interpret the work of the many."

Just so, when we trouble ourselves about what's what with things grossly physical, or with physical reality that's extralinguistic, and extramental, and so on, our concerns are with quite superficial matters. For example, we may reflect on the apparent fact that, if an ordinary rock should be split down the middle, with the two resulting "halves" never even coming close to being rejoined, the rock that was split ceases to exist, while two substantially smaller rocks then begin to exist. And, then, we may reflect on the apparent fact that, when a rock that's as famous as Plymouth Rock is similarly bisected, there's still that rock that's then in two salient pieces, whether or not there are also two smaller rocks then coming into existence. Based on these two reflections, we may aspire to a complex theory that "capturing intuitions" about both cases will serve to illuminate the "persistence conditions" for rocks in general, both the famous and also the obscure. But won't such a theory reflect our own interests more than it will tell us about the nature of physical reality? At all events, it won't deliver anything very deep, or very illuminating, about physical reality.

With this effort, help came from many others: In the fall of 1997, it was discussed by those regularly attending the graduate seminar I gave at New York University with John Gibbons. In addition to Gibbons, I gratefully thank Mark Bajakian, David Barnett, Geoff Helmreich, Peter Kung, Brian Leftow, Barbara Montero, and Sebastien Pennes. Grateful thanks also go to Robert Adams, David Armstrong, Gordon Belot, Michael Della Rocca, Hartry Field, Kit Fine, Brian Loar, Michael Lockwood, Barry Loewer, Graham Priest, Michael Rea, and Galen Strawson. For almost incredible efforts, very special great thanks go to John Carroll, John Heil, and C. B. (Charlie) Martin.

Even while knowing all that very well, we still don't trouble ourselves to be more searching. Rather, we're still affected by thoughts like, "Let's leave such terribly large matters to so many successful scientists, and our few colleagues who know their science." Especially in this fearfully complacent philosophical day and age, we do well to remember what Russell counseled: About the rest of concrete reality, we don't know anything nearly so intimately, nor nearly so fully, as we know our experience or, maybe better, as we know the phenomena apprehended in experience. (This remains true, of course, even if what we know most fully, and intimately, might be known less fully, and less intimately, than it can often appear.) And, we do well to recall that Russell did not exaggerate much, if at all, when, in a generally robust epistemological spirit, he said, "as regards the world in general, both physical and mental, everything that we know of its intrinsic character is derived from the mental side."[1] Nor did he exaggerate very much when, in a specifically materialistic spirit, he said, "we know nothing about the intrinsic quality of physical events except when these are mental events that we directly experience."[2]

· If there's to be appropriately ambitious analytic philosophy done any time soon, then we'd best pay heed to such Russellian reminders. And though our philosophical efforts might diverge from his in many respects, they should be guided by the same realization that so greatly moved Russell: Except for what little of the physical world we might apprehend in conscious experience, which is available if materialism should be true, *the physical is mysterious to us.*

So we should wonder: To what extent, if any at all, do we have a philosophically adequate conception of physical reality? Do we have a conception well enough related to the human mind for it to ground a metaphysic in terms of which physical reality can be understood, at all well, by us very limited human thinkers?

Inspired by Russell and others, I'll try to give decent answers to such daunting questions. In the course of the effort, I may do more

1. Bertrand Russell, *The Analysis of Matter* (London: Kegan Paul, 1927), 407. My own copy of the work is a reprinting by Dover Publications, New York, 1954. In that, see p. 402. Anyway, the quoted words are from the book's penultimate sentence.

2. Bertrand Russell, "Mind and Matter," in *Portraits from Memory* (Nottingham, England: Spokesman, 1956), 153. Until recently, truths like those just quoted were, for centuries, influential with serious philosophers. For a seminal example, "the father of modern philosophy" advances some in Descartes' *Principles of Philosophy*, part 1, paragraph 11: "How our mind is better known than our body," as in *The Philosophical Writings of Descartes*, trans. J. Cottingham, R. Stoothoff, and D. Murdoch, Vol. 1 (Cambridge: Cambridge University Press, 1985).

toward raising further questions than toward giving decent answers. But if they are fresh questions, that might be all to the good.

2. A Brief Exposition of the Scientifical Metaphysic

As a first step in this effort, I'll sketch, very briefly, what I take to be the metaphysical worldview that, for several centuries and with no letup anywhere in sight, has been the dominant metaphysic of the highly educated in cultures much affected by the development of the natural sciences. It will be useful to have a memorable name for this dominant worldview, but not a name loaded with positive connotations, like "the scientific metaphysic," or with negative ones, like "the scientistic metaphysic." For a name that's reasonably memorable and neutral, I'll introduce a word that's meant to parallel "philosophical" and, with it, I'll coin the naming phrase "the *scientifical* metaphysic."

Though various modifications of it appear required by certain twentieth-century scientific developments, notably, by quantum mechanics and relativity theory, the heart of our scientifical metaphysic is, apparently, essentially the same as before the advent of the twentieth century. So, even if folks versed in contemporary physics would rightly prefer esoteric analogues of the ordinary terms I feel most comfortable using for the job, for my main philosophical purposes the following few paragraphs may serve to express our dominant worldview.

First, differently distributed in space at different times, there is physical stuff or *matter*. Placing aside the thought that this matter may have been, very long ago, created by some Extraordinarily Powerful Mind (or Minds), and placing aside thoughts of how such a SuperMind might, even nowadays, occasionally affect matter, this matter is *independent of minds:* To exist, the matter needn't be sensed by, or be thought about by, sentient beings.

Second (again placing to the side all such "theological" ideas, which from now on will generally be done only implicitly), insofar as it's determined by anything at all and isn't merely random, the distribution of this matter at any given time is determined by the distribution of the matter at earlier times, with the determination proceeding in line with our world's basic natural laws, which are physical laws.

Third, owing to the variety in these material distributions, at certain times some of the world's matter, or possibly much of the matter, is configured so as to compose various complex material structures and systems, ranging from the slightly complex through the fairly complex to the highly complex. Among the more complex of even these highly complex material structures and systems are living entities, or those serving to constitute living entities.

Fourth, among the more complex of even these living material entities, and possibly even among some (very distant) nonliving material complexes, there are those that are thinking, feeling, experiencing physical entities. Or, more cautiously, complexly composed of some matter, there are the living physical bodies of such thinking physical entities.

Fifth, there are certain properties that are the *naturally important* properties of matter, both matter that's involved in composing a highly complex material system and, equally, matter that's never so interestingly involved. To date, it's mainly been the work of physics to discover what actually are these properties.

Sixth, beyond what physics aims to discover, there are other naturally important properties. The most salient of these properties are to be found in a most intimate connection with the minds of the sentient beings of the world: These salient properties will qualify the conscious immediate experiences of these beings; or, if not quite that, they'll qualify whatever it is that such beings most immediately experience, perhaps manifolds of qualia. So, these properties will include (absolutely specific) phenomenal color properties and, just as well, (absolutely specific) phenomenal pain properties. None of these properties are, of course, even remotely like mere powers of material bodies to promote, in finite minds, any sort of experience. Because they figure prominently in my inquiry, I'll refer to the phenomenal properties as the *Qualities*, which capitalized term I'll reserve for them and only such other properties as are strongly and deeply analogous to phenomenal properties.

Seventh, the six preceding paragraphs are to be understood as implying that our scientific metaphysics conflicts with many traditional metaphysical systems, even though it's not in conflict with many others. Thus, whereas Berkeley's subjective idealism conflicts with our scientifical metaphysic, other metaphysical views comport with it well. For example, Descartes' dualism, or at least a view much like the Cartesian metaphysic, provides a consistent line for further specification of our scientifical metaphysic. And it appears a materialistic worldview provides a quite different consistent line.

Although I've sketched the main thrust of our scientific metaphysic in the seven paragraphs just preceding, I've ignored some very large matters. For example, I've offered nothing about what this metaphysic might say, or might not say, regarding questions of genuine choice, or free will. Still, even with only as much of the scientific metaphysic as what's been presented, there may be raised questions of philosophical importance. In this paper, we'll explore some of them.

3. This Metaphysic, Three Kinds of Property, and the Restriction of Qualities to Minds

For a discussion that we may hope to be as profitable as it's protracted, I'll move deliberately toward displaying a doctrine that's assumed true by most who embrace the scientifical metaphysic, even if it might not be so much as actually implied by the dominant worldview. Toward succinctly presenting this popular proposition, which I'll call the *Restriction of Qualities to Minds*, it will be useful to notice *three categories of basic natural property* (of whatever entities, or entity, might serve to constitute physical reality).

First, I'll take note of what might be called the purely *spatiotemporal* properties or, for short, the *Spatiotemporals*. Central to this group are, with one exception, what Descartes regarded as "the primary or real properties of matter . . . shape, size, position, duration, movability, divisibility and number. This list we can immediately diminish by one, because it is clear that *number* is an interloper here."[3] As concrete reality might have very many dimensions, this group may include, in addition to geometric properties, topological properties and, perhaps, other such "mathematically recognized" properties. Of course, even such determinables as Descartes' are just a starting point here; more to the concrete point are such absolutely specific determinate properties as, say, *being perfectly spherical*.

As I'm understanding the Spatiotemporals, even absolutely empty regions will, at least when limited in some dimensions or respects, have Spatiotemporal properties whether at an instant or over time, even if they might be devoid of all other basic properties. And, at least in many possible worlds, there's nothing more to the having of Spatiotemporal properties than what a perfectly empty region has, at an instant or over time.

As I'm painfully aware, the scientifical metaphysic *might not* help provide us with any understanding of concrete reality that's even modestly adequate. But, if it does profit us in that large regard, then we must think of very much of this reality, even if not absolutely all of it, as having spatiotemporal properties. Indeed, though I'm far less confident of it, I suggest that we should accept even this much more ambitious proposition: For the scientifical metaphysic to do much *for our understanding* of concrete reality, there must be *some* truth in the thought that

---

3. The quote is from David Armstrong, *Perception and the Physical World* (London: Routledge and Kegan Paul, New York: Humanities Press, 1961), 184. For Descartes's list, Armstrong refers us to "the second paragraph in the Fifth Meditation, and elsewhere."

much of this reality has the three-dimensional nondirectional spatial structure, and the correlative one-dimensional directional temporal structure that, in our conscious perception of reality, are spatiotemporal properties that physical reality appears to have. For although such perception might provide us with only a *very partial perspective* on reality, and with a *quite superficial* perspective, still and all, unless there's *something about physical reality* in virtue of which it has these familiar spatiotemporal properties, the scientific metaphysic will, I think, do far more toward providing intellectual illusion than toward giving us even a very modestly adequate understanding of reality. But in the present essay, I will rely only on less ambitious propositions. At all events, so much for my first category of basic natural properties, the Spatiotemporals.

Second, I'll notice what, for want of a better expression, I'll call the *propensity properties* or, more briefly, the *Propensities*. Often, these properties, or some of them, have been called "powers"; but inappropriately for us, that term connotes positive force. Others have called the properties "dispositions"; but despite the valiant efforts of C. B. Martin and others, that term has been so badly abused that it will arouse, in the minds of too many, undue confusion.[4]

Now, at least for the meanwhile, we'll understand the Propensities as being distinct from, even if they might be importantly related to, the Spatiotemporals. On this understanding, regions of absolutely empty space, or perfect vacuums, can have spatiotemporal properties; but as it at least appears, no such physically empty regions will themselves have any powers or, as I'll say, any Propensities. By contrast with such vacuums, we may envision a finite spatial region that's precisely occupied by an electron, where our supposed electron is well suited to making true an early theory of such supposedly simple physical things. Then what's in that small finite region will be something that has, in addition to its spatiotemporal properties, *unit negative electric charge*. Its having *that* property is, we may suppose, the electron's having a certain complex Propensity or, perhaps the same, its having a cluster of simpler Propensities. The complex Propensity of our electron will include, for salient examples, its Propensity to repel any other electron with such-and-such a force in so-and-so a direction, and its Propensity to attract any proton with such-and-such a force in so-and-so a direction. As with

4. Though some of Martin's writings on this subject are very hard to understand, others are helpfully clear. For work that helps clarify the fact that *dispositions are as categorical as anything*, see C. B. Martin, "Dispositions and Conditionals," *Philosophical Quarterly*, Vol. 44, 1994, and Martin's contribution to D. M. Armstrong, C. B. Martin, and U. T. Place, *Dispositions: A Debate*, ed. Tim Crane (London and New York: Routledge, 1996).

any entity's having any Propensity, the electron's having this one is not dependent, not even in the minutest degree, on there ever actually being any protons, or there being any other electrons. In contradistinction to there being any *chance for* the Propensity of our electron to be *manifested*, which does require there to be things external to it, the electron's *just having* the indicated Propensity doesn't depend on there ever being *any* such external entity.

Third, and last, I'll notice what I call the *Qualities*, a group of properties whose most accessible members are the phenomenal properties available in our conscious experience. But the Qualities may also include other properties: Beyond the properties experientially available to us, and even beyond those available to any of the world's finite minds, there may be properties that are *deeply analogous to* at least some of the phenomenal properties. Through *extrapolative analogical thinking*, perhaps we might get some grasp as to the nature of some of these farther-fetched properties, even if, perhaps, never a grasp that's very rich, firm, or clear.

So on the one hand, consider those phenomenal properties best suited to filling space, or to being spread through space. Here, we may consider a perfectly specific sort of translucent red, and an equally specific "colorless transparency," as with what's apprehended in experience of, say, a typical windowpane, and an equally specific "silveriness," as with what's experienced in, say, seeing some shiny silver. Since they're so well suited to filling space, we'll call these *Extensible Qualities*. Now, and on the other hand, consider some phenomenal properties that seem *unsuited* to filling space. Here we may consider a perfectly specific sort of taste of sweet chocolate, and a perfectly specific sort of pleasant sound, as with what's apprehended in one's experience of, say, a certain rendition of a favorite song, and a perfectly specific sort of elation, as with what's experienced upon, say, hearing some wonderful news. Since they're so unsuited to filling space, suppose, we'll call them *Nonextensible Qualities*. Now, we can have a conception, it appears, of properties that, though they're *not* available in experience to the world's finite minds, are very much *more like each* of our indicated Extensible Qualities than they're like *any* of our indicated Nonextensible Qualities.

The qualities we're analogically contemplating are very much more like our indicated Extensibles than our indicated Nonextensibles both overall and, as well, in those respects, whatever precisely they may be, that have our Extensibles be so very much more suited to filling space than are our Nonextensibles. By way of such extrapolative analogical thinking, I'm suggesting, we may have a contentful conception of (even if not yet any reason to believe in) a world featuring many instantiations of Extensible Qualities that can't, at least as a matter of natural fact, be experienced by any of the world's finite minds. In parallel, we can also conceive of properties that, though they're likewise unavailable to experience, are much more like each of our indicated *Nonextensible* Qualities than they're like any of our indicated Extensible Qualities. Here, too, there may be properties that, though they're not properly phenomenal properties, are among a world's farther-fetched Qualities.

In marked contrast with how things were fifty years ago, nowadays it appears almost universally believed by analytic philosophers that the phenomenal properties are properties of, and only of, conscious experiences; and, rather than being any mere contingent truth, this belief runs, it's conceptually and necessarily true that the phenomenal properties are all properties of, and only of, the mental, and even just the experiential. Let's suppose this belief is correct. Then it might be that, though the phenomenal color properties *seem well suited* to filling space, that's an illusory appearance. For as far as any of us can tell, it might be that conscious experiences can't literally occupy spatial regions.

Let's further suppose that, whether or not for that reason, none of the phenomenal properties are actually Extensible, are Qualities well suited to filling space. Well, even in such an event, it's still true to say this: The phenomenal properties may be peculiarly helpful leads for our only quite partially grasping, through extrapolative analogical thinking, Qualities whose instances *are* so prevalent in our mind-independent spatiotemporal reality.

Having said that, I'll also say this: Apparently against almost all other contemporary analytic philosophers, I *don't* believe that the phenomenal properties are features only of conscious experiences. Rather, I'm quite agnostic. Toward explaining this unfashionable agnosticism, in the next section I'll offer two sorts of consideration. Here it suffices to note that the present project doesn't depend on what's the best approach to this interesting issue. To indicate what's much more relevant, I display this from Russell:

> To assert that the material *must* be very different from percepts is to assume that we know a great deal more than we do in fact know of the intrinsic character of physical events. If there is any advantage in supposing that the light-wave, the process in the eye, and the process in the optic nerve, contain events qualitatively continuous with the final visual percept, nothing that we know of the physical world can be used to disprove the supposition.
>
> The gulf between percepts and physics is not a gulf as regards intrinsic quality, for we know nothing of the intrinsic quality of the

physical world, and therefore do not know whether it is, or is not, very different from that of percepts. The gulf is as to what we know about the two realms. We know the quality of percepts, but we do not know their laws so well as we could wish. We know the laws of the physical world, in so far as these are mathematical, pretty well, but we know nothing else about it. If there is any intellectual difficulty in supposing that the physical world is intrinsically quite unlike that of percepts, this is a reason for supposing that there is not this complete unlikeness. And there is a certain ground for such a view, in the fact that percepts are part of the physical world, and are the only part that we can know without the help of rather elaborate and difficult inferences.[5]

At all events, at least for the meanwhile we may understand the Qualities as being distinct from, though perhaps importantly related to, both the Spatiotemporals and the Propensities. On this understanding, whereas the spatiotemporal properties can be possessed by regions of absolutely empty space, it is at least somewhat doubtful that any of the Qualities, including even any of the Extensible Qualities, can be possessed by an *absolutely* perfect vacuum. For now, that's all for this last sort of basic natural property.

With this threefold classification providing the context for it, I can briefly display the doctrine that, at this section's start, I said was assumed by most who hold with the scientifical metaphysic, even if it's not actually implied by the dominant worldview:

> *The Restriction of Qualities to Minds.* Unlike the Spatiotemporal properties and the Propensities, which are so widely instantiated in what's physical, there are not (any instantiations of) any of the Qualities in physical reality, with the possible exception, at any given time, of such a small part as may subserve the minds of sentient beings.

According to the *Restriction*, to use this doctrine's short name, all the world's matter, or almost all, has no Qualities, whatever might be its Spatiotemporal properties and its Propensities.

Though they need fleshing out if they're ever to be of much philosophical interest, here are a couple of questions that, I'll suggest, may already be of some interest: If we *add* the Restriction to our scientifical metaphysic and, thus, obtain a *deeply segregated* worldview, what will be, for us, the advantages of, and the disadvantages of, such a view of the

---

5. Bertrand Russell, *The Analysis of Matter* (London: Kegan Paul), 1927. My copy is a reprinting by Dover Publications, New York, 1954. In this reprinting, see pp. 263—64.

world? On the opposite hand, if we add the *Denial* of the Restriction to our scientifical metaphysic, obtaining a *deeply integrated* worldview, what will be the advantages and disadvantages?

4. Might Phenomenal Qualities Outrun Experience?

Before inquiring into the implications of the Restriction, which will soon be my main order of business, I'll offer two groups of ideas, each complementing the other, that serve to motivate this pretty unusual philosophical stance of mine: Apparently against almost all my analytically philosophical contemporaries, I *don't* believe that the phenomenal properties are possessed only by experiences. Rather, I'm agnostic about the matter. Though providing motivation for this unfashionable stance isn't crucial for my project, my doing that will help contemporary readers appreciate, rather well, what I mean to say about the implications of the Restriction.

For the first group of motivating ideas, I'll quote at length from Michael Lockwood's wonderfully stimulating book, *Mind, Brain and the Quantum:*

> I find it plausible to suppose that the phenomenal qualities themselves are less fickle than one's attention, and may persist even when one's awareness of them lapses. On this view, phenomenal qualities are neither realized by/being sensed nor sensed by being realized.... The realization of a phenomenal quality is one thing, I contend; its being an object of awareness is something else, ...
>
> At first hearing, the present proposal may seem wildly eccentric....
>
> But now consider the following example. Suppose we have three colour patches projected close together on to a screen; call them *L* (left), *M* (middle) and *R* (right). Suppose, further, that in the absence of *R*, *L* is indistinguishable from *M*, and that in the absence of *L*, *M* is indistinguishable from *R*. *L*, however (in the presence or absence of *M*), *is* distinguishable from *R*. ... So what are we to suppose happens if we start with a screen containing only *L* and *M*, which are *ex hypothesi* indistinguishable, then add *R*, so that all three patches are present, and finally remove *L*, leaving *M* and *R*, which are likewise indistinguishable?
>
> There are only two possibilities, surely. By far the more plausible, to my mind, is that the phenomenal colours corresponding to *L* and *M* are distinct, even in the absence of *R*: there *is* a phenomenal difference here, but one too small to register in consciousness, no matter how closely the subject attends. Adding together two phenomenal differences of this magnitude does, however, produce a difference

that registers in consciousness; hence the subject's ability to distinguish L from R. The only alternative is to suppose that the effect, either of adding R or of removing L, is to induce a qualitative change in the phenomenal colour corresponding to one or the other of the remaining patches. But it surely won't *seem* to the subject that this is what happens. So on this supposition too, there would be phenomenal differences—or at least, phenomenal *transitions*—that defied conscious detection.

Not only, in such perceptual cases, does the phenomenal character of what one is immediately aware of outrun one's awareness of it; it actually seems to do so. . . . What I am suggesting, in effect, is that we should allow phenomenal qualities quite generally to outrun awareness. Those who think they understand what it is for phenomenal qualities to inhere in portions of their visual field of which . . . they are not currently conscious, now have a model for what, . . . the unsensed portion of the physical world is like in itself, quite generally—even in regions beyond the confines of the brains of sentient beings, where awareness, as far as we know, never intrudes.[6]

These passages provide extremely suggestive argumentation, even if no decisive argumentation, to the effect that there are instances of phenomenal color qualities that outrun experience (and also *fairly* suggestive reasoning that these Qualities outrun even nonconscious mentality).

Much as the quotation from Lockwood indicates, insofar as philosophers now think they have difficulty understanding the suggestion that phenomenal qualities may outrun mentality, it's generally because they think they have difficulties with the suggestion that phenomenal qualities might ever outrun *conscious* mentality. But what's just been quoted serves to confute the latter thought. So most of these philosophers should reject the former as well.

While many may still find it hard to *believe* phenomenal properties outrun all of mentality, myself included, by now few should have trouble with the thought that the suggestion is a *coherent* proposition. With that said, there's enough from the first group of motivating ideas.

For the second group of ideas, I'll relate the results of some bouts of phenomenological thinking, and some analysis pertaining thereto: When lying still in silence and darkness, sometimes I vividly experience my body as filling space. Then, it appears, I apprehend *Qualities felt as suffusing space*. Naturally enough, I'll call these Extensible Qualities the *Felt Bodily Qualities*. Now, with the Felt Bodily Qualities I can conceive *only* of there being such instances as are *experienced*; indeed, with *these* Qualities, I conceive only of such instances as are *experienced as extending through space occupied by (some of) a being that experiences them.*

By contrast with the Felt Bodily Qualities, it seems clear, I can conceive of there being instances of *color* Qualities that *aren't* ever experienced; indeed, I can do that about as well, it appears, as I can conceive instances that *are* experienced. (To me, this has been intuitive for as long as I can remember, long before any encounter with *arguments* in support of such an idea, like what's just been displayed from Lockwood.)

In marked contrast to the phenomenal colors, it appears, the Felt Bodily Qualities are *essentially mental* Qualities, which can be instanced only when they figure in experience. By that same contrast, the phenomenal colors, and the Extensibles strongly analogous with them, *aren't essentially mental* Qualities, and can be instanced *even when they don't* figure in experience. So as it appears, we have tolerably clear conceptions of two quite different sorts of Extensible Quality. Considerations like these serve to motivate my agnosticism as to whether the phenomenal qualities may outrun experience, or even mentality.

Having had both groups of motivating ideas presented, perhaps readers will be sympathetic to the idea that the phenomenal qualities can outrun experience. And with that reasonably open-minded stance, perhaps they'll appreciate, rather well, what I'll now say about the implications of the Restriction. At all events, it's high time for that main order of business.

5. The Restriction, Particles in Space and Spaces in a Plenum

For the scientifical metaphysic to provide us with a reasonably adequate view of our world, do its bare bones need such Qualitative flesh as can be had only with the Denial of the Restriction? My conjecture is that the question receives an affirmative answer.

Toward motivating this conjecture, I'll *suppose that the Restriction holds* and, in terms of the scientifical metaphysic as thus limited, I'll begin two *extremely simple attempts to characterize* our world. (Toward the Restriction's being fully in force, I'll stipulate that both are mainly aimed at characterizing the world well before there were any [finite] minds.)

First, and familiarly, I'll begin an attempt to characterize physical reality in generally Newtonian terms: Moving about in what's otherwise uniformly empty space, there are many particles of matter, grandiosely labeled Particles, whose motion is governed by physical laws. In that we're supposing the Restriction to hold, we must suppose that, in this *Particulate World*, the laws concern only Nonqualitative properties that the Particles might have, not Qualities.

Second, and unusually, I begin this attempt to characterize physical reality: In what's otherwise a continuous material plenum, or a continuous field of matter, there are little perfectly empty spaces, or absolute vacua, or *Bubbles:* As regards both shape and size, each Bubble is precisely similar to a certain Particle, its *counterpart* Particle, in the Particulate World. And, wherever there's a Particle in our Particulate World, there's a counterpart place with a counterpart Bubble in this *Plenumate World*. So, if there are eight spherical Particles arrayed in a quite cubical pattern in a certain region of our Particulate World, then in the counterpart region of our Plenumate World there'll be eight such Bubbles arrayed in just such a pattern.

Even as various Particles may instance certain physical properties that will have them be suited for governance by certain physical laws, so various regions of a physical Plenum may have certain correlative physical properties that will have them be correlatively suited for governance by apt parallels of, or nice inversions of, the Particle-governing laws. So, in a nice parallel with the law-governed behavior of the Particles in our Particulate World, this Plenumate World features laws governing the distribution of its Plenum throughout all its time. And, since its Bubbles always *are* at just the places in the World where there *isn't* any Plenum, this World's laws also serve to determine the distribution of all its *Bubbles* over time. So, our Plenumate World's Bubbles will move through its material field along trajectories that, over time, perfectly parallel the trajectories of the Particulate World's Particles through its empty space.

Always supposing the Restriction holds, I'd make two extremely simple attempts, it appears, at starting to characterize our world. Before concluding the section, it may be useful to comment on what may be the two most salient respects in which my attempts were so simple.

First, there's the point that my attempts were conducted in the general framework of classical physics, with its quite intuitive conceptions of space and of time, rather than the framework of more recent physics, with its quite *unintuitive* conceptions, like the notion of *space-time*. One reason for this, I blush to confess, is that I know precious little about contemporary physical science. A more important reason is that I'm engaged in an endeavor that's meant to transcend the differences between classical physics and more recent scientific developments. And it's perfectly possible, it appears, for there to be an endeavor that succeeds in being that comprehensive: Since recent scientific developments make no Completely Revolutionary Break with earlier science, what's new in the recent scientific conceptions doesn't affect the question of how we might, with the Restriction fully in force, ever have an intelligible worldview that, far from being any sort of idealism, is an adequate specification of the scientifical metaphysic.

Apparently with complete sincerity, that's what I've been told by philosophers knowledgeable about contemporary physics. So apparently, my employing the framework of classical physics means no loss of generality for these philosophical exercises.

Second, there's the point that, in trying to characterize a Particulate World, and also a Plenumate World, I forswore saying anything about complex material structures or systems, much less anything about any minds that any material complexes might subserve. That was done for several reasons, the most important being that such a simplification would be helpful toward having the Restriction be fully in force. Even if it might be unnecessary, I'll again implore my readers: When trying to think of a Particulate World, *don't do anything even remotely like*, say, thinking of *light grey* spheres moving through a *dark grey* space or field; and, when attempting thoughts of a Plenumate World, don't do anything even remotely like thinking of dark grey spheres moving through a light grey space or field!

For holding to this supposition, it will be useful to discuss some relations regarding the scientifical metaphysic, the instantiation of Qualities, and "the place of mind in the world order," or, as it might turn out, what just appear to be some such relations: Even while they try to have the Restriction be in force, some may have these following thoughts regarding the scientifical metaphysic. As our dominant metaphysic seems fully to allow, where and when a World features creatures with conscious minds, there and then there'll be someplace in the World for Qualities to be instantiated. So, if we should endeavor to characterize, say, a Particulate World, at greater length, then, as we may make specifications for complex living material creatures, and so consciously experiencing creatures, we may thus characterize a part of the world in which Qualities will be instanced, even while supposing the Restriction to hold. So, if we just go further in our attempts to characterized Worlds, even while supposing the Restriction, won't we do quite a lot toward characterizing a Particulate World, and also a Plenumate World?

No, we won't, for the situation is this: Whenever there's something that seems to characterize an experiencing creature as constituted of many Particles, there's also something, in correlative Plenumate terms, that seems to characterize that creature, with just as much propriety, as not being so constituted. Let me explain.

In an attempt to characterize an experiencing creature that features a body as well as a mind with *Particulate* terms, we may say this: Ever so many material Particles, perhaps billions and billions, serve to *constitute* the material creature with a mind. Or at the very least, they all serve to constitute the body of the creature; and because so many of this body's Particles are going through an appropriately complex sequence of arrangements, this body, it may then be said, subserves the creature's mind. When the duly constituted creature has experiences, Qualities are, through or in the creature's mind, instanced in the Particulate World.

But using *Plenumate* terms, we can say *this* about any materially realized experiencing creature: Ever so many Bubbles in the Plenum, perhaps billions and billions, serve to *institute* the physical creature with a mind, to coin a euphonious Plenumate term. Or at least they serve to institute the body of the creature, which body subserves the creature with a mind. When the duly instituted creature has experiences, Qualities are, through or in the creature's mind, instanced in the Plenumate World.

In this section, serious questions were raised about any attempt to contemplate physical reality within the confines of the Restriction. Initially, it may have appeared that each of my attempts to characterize physical reality, one with Particulate wording and one with the Plenumate terms, clearly contrasted with the other. But mightn't it be that I actually made just one extremely insubstantial start twice over, first using one mutually connected group of terms, the "Particulate terms," and then using another, the "Plenumate terms"? Mightn't it be that, as long as any attempt to conceive of our world is limited by the Restriction, it will be doomed to futility?

6. When Limited by the Restriction, How to Conceive a Particle's Propensities?

In my two attempts at characterizing Worlds, I tried to attribute Spatiotemporal properties to the objects of the Worlds. For example, I said that, in one sort of World, there are spherical Particles and, in the other, there are spherical Bubbles. By contrast, I did little, or nothing, as regards the other basic natural properties of the intended objects, the Propensities and the Qualities. Of course, as the Restriction was fully in force, it was forbidden to attribute any Quality to a Particle or to a Plenum. But what about Propensities?

On this we can hardly do better, I should think, than to consider what, historically, appears the propensity most saliently proposed for philosophical consideration, the supposed *solidity* of things material. And, on that, we can hardly do better than to begin with book 2, chapter 4 of the *Essay Concerning Human Understanding*, which is "Of Solidity," in which Locke aims to present an "Idea" that serves to distinguish material Bodies from the mere Space they may occupy:

> That which thus hinders the approach of two Bodies, when they are moving one towards another, I call *Solidity*. . . . but if any one think it better to call it *Impenetrability*, he has my Consent. . . . This of all other, seems the *Idea* most intimately connected with, and essential to Body, so as no where else to be found or imagin'd, but only in matter: . . . the Mind, . . . considers it, as well as Figure, in the minutest Particle of Matter, that can exist; and finds it inseparably inherent in Body, where-ever, or however modified.
>
> This is the *Idea*, belongs to Body, whereby we conceive it *to fill space*.[7]

As with other passages, we should understand Locke here as assuming, if not affirming, that the Restriction holds. Even as Newton's physics ignores Qualities, Locke excludes them from the world's vast material realm, restricting them to our Minds *(Essay, 136–37)*.

For Locke, solidity is impenetrability. But, with the Restriction in force, what can such solidity do for our conception of a Particle? An excellent discussion of the question can be found in John Foster's terribly difficult but at least occasionally brilliant book, *The Case for Idealism*. According to Foster:

> Locke . . . thought that the nature of solidity is revealed in tactual experience. . . . But in this Locke was clearly mistaken. . . . The tactual experience of solidity is no more nor less than the experience of voluminous resistance, and, in so far as our concept of solidity is acquired through tactual experience, the specification of matter as solid is opaque. All it adds to the specification of matter as a voluminous substance is that there is *something* in its intrinsic nature (it does not say *what*) which makes material objects mutually obstructive.[8]

---

7. In P. H. Nidditch's edition of John Locke's *An Essay Concerning Human Understanding* (Oxford: Oxford University Press, 1975), the quoted words can be found on p. 123.

8. John Foster, *The Case for Idealism* (London: Routledge & Kegan Paul, 1982), 63. By contrast with the passages from it that I'll cite, much of the book is written in a very difficult technical style. From the parts I've managed to understand, I'm convinced that the work deserves serious study. A few of its last words convey the thrust of the courageous book: "I hope one day to . . . make the case for mentalism irresistible. But until then, I must be content with a Defence of idealism in its anti-realist and phenomenalist forms."

With his paper, "The Succinct Case for Idealism," in H. Robinson (ed.), *Objections to Physicalism* (Oxford: Oxford University Press, 1993), Foster gives an overview of the difficult work.

Now, I do not know that Foster is right in his suggestion that Locke thought that solidity was not a Power of material objects. More likely, it seems to me, in "Of Solidity" Locke was involved in muddles: How could *Impenetrability*, which Locke says is the very same as Solidity, *not* be a Power of resistance on the part of Impenetrable Bodies. But philosophically, there's no more to be gained from Locke here than what Foster contends, nothing much at all. Indeed, insofar as Foster's reading of Locke may be mistaken, his error will be, apparently, *undue charity* toward the old philosopher.

At all events, where Foster is most helpful is in his own discussion of the quite general question of the "Powers of Material Bodies." This occurs in an appendix to chapter 4 of the book. As Foster's thinking there is so very helpful, I'll quote this appendix at length:

> The only properties of fundamental particles which can be transparently specified in physical terms are (1) spatiotemporal properties, such as shape, size and velocity and (2) causal and dispositional properties, such as mutual obstructiveness, gravitational power and electric charge. From this, I have concluded that . . . the intrinsic nature of the particles can, in physical terms, only be specified opaquely, as that on which their behavioural dispositions and causal powers are grounded. But, is this conclusion justified? An alternative would be to say that . . . each particle is, in itself, no more than a mobile cluster of causal powers, there being no "substantial" space-occupant which possesses the powers and on whose categorical nature the powers are grounded. Such a thesis has been endorsed, in different forms, by a number of distinguished scientists and philosophers. [Here, Foster has a note naming such intellectual heavyweights as Leibniz, Boscovich, Kant, Priestley and Faraday.] If it is coherent, this thesis certainly has some appeal. . . .
>
> But is the powers-thesis (PT) coherent? The main problem is that if all the fundamental particles are construed in this way, there seem to be no physical items in terms of whose behaviour the content of the powers could be specified, and consequently, it seems that, in the last analysis, there is nothing which the powers are powers to do. Let us begin with a concrete example. We will assume that the atoms are the only fundamental particles and that all atoms are of exactly the same type. Now each atom has a number of causal powers. It has a power of resistance, whereby any two atoms are mutually obstructive. It has a power of gravitational attraction, whereby, between any two atoms, there is a force of attraction inversely proportional to the square of their distance. . . . And it has a number of other powers which we need not list. For PT to be true, it is necessary some subset of these powers constitutes the essential nature of an atom. Let us suppose, for

simplicity, we select the power of resistance as the only (putatively) essential atomic power and leave the other powers to depend on the contingent laws of nature governing the behavior of atoms. Thus each atom is construed as a mobile sphere of impenetrability, the behavior and causal interaction of these spheres, apart from their mutual obstructiveness, being governed by additional laws. The problem arises when we ask: "To what is a sphere of impenetrability impenetrable?" The answer is: "To other atoms, i.e., to other spheres of impenetrability." But this means that the specification of the content of the atom-constituting power is viciously regressive: each atom is a sphere of impenetrability to any other sphere of impenetrability to any other sphere of impenetrability...and so on *ad infinitum*. From which it follows that the notion of such a power is incoherent, since there is nothing which the power is a power to do....

The problem is not avoided if we include further powers in the essential nature of the atom. Thus we might take the atomic nature to combine a power of resistance with a power of attraction, so that each atom is constituted by a mobile sphere of impenetrability surrounded by a more extensive (perhaps infinitely extended) field of gravitational potential (the field being structured, in accordance with the inverse-square-law, around the centre of the sphere). We could then try to specify the content of the power of resistance in terms of the behavior of gravitational fields or specify the content of the power of attraction in terms of the behavior of spheres of impenetrability. But neither specification blocks the regress, since it merely specifies the content of one power in terms of another. The only way of avoiding the regress, it seems, is to construe at least one of the powers as a power to affect the behavior of some...space occupant...with an intrinsic nature independent of its causal powers and dispositions. But such occupants are just what PT excludes. (67–69)

My conclusion, therefore, is that the powers-thesis is incoherent. And consequently, I stand by my previous conclusion that, apart from their shape and size, the intrinsic nature of the fundamental space-occupants (assuming there are occupants at all) cannot be empirically discovered or transparently specified in physical terms. (72)

Now, I'm not sure that the considerations Foster marshals show that the powers-thesis is so much as *incoherent*. But, it does seem clear that they show there to be grave difficulties, perhaps even insuperable ones, with the thought we can understand certain regions of space, or certain entities occupying the regions, to have just so many Spatiotemporal properties and Propensity properties without their having any Qualities at all.

To take full advantage of them, I'll conjoin Foster's ideas with some complementary considerations. Toward setting out these considerations,

I'll quote from "Of the Modern Philosophy," a marvelous section of Hume's *Treatise*:

> The idea of solidity is that of two objects, which being impell'd by the utmost force, cannot penetrate each other; but still maintain a separate and distinct existence. Solidity, therefore, is perfectly incomprehensible alone, and without the conception of some bodies, which are solid, and maintain this separate and distinct existence. Now what idea have we of these bodies? The ideas of colours, sounds, and other secondary qualities are excluded. The idea of motion depends on that of extension, and the idea of extension on that of solidity. 'Tis impossible, therefore, that the idea of solidity can depend on either of them. For that wou'd be to run in a circle, and make one idea depend on another, while at the same time the latter depends on the former. Our modern philosophy, therefore, leaves us no just nor satisfactory idea of solidity; nor consequently of matter.
>
> Add to this, that, properly speaking, solidity or impenetrability is nothing, but an impossibility of annihilation,...An impossibility of being annihilated cannot exist, and can never be conceived to exist, by itself; but necessarily requires some object or real existence, to which it may belong. Now the difficulty still remains, how to form an idea of this object or existence, without having recourse to the secondary and sensible qualities.[9]

We should now understand Hume, like Locke before him, as assuming the Restriction to hold. And as these passages then serve to show, in fixing on solidity, or on *what's left of that notion when the Restriction has been supposed*, Locke found nothing to distinguish adequately between Particles of Matter and Bubbles in a material Plenum.

Now, right before the quote just displayed, there are these sentences:

> The idea of extension is a compound idea; but as it is not compounded of an infinite number of parts or inferior ideas, it must at last resolve itself into such as are perfectly simple and indivisible. Those simple and indivisible parts, not being ideas of extension, must be non-entities, unless conceiv'd as colour'd or solid. Color is excluded from any real existence. The reality, therefore, of our idea of extension depends upon the reality of that of solidity, nor can the former be just while the latter is chimerical. Let us, then, lend our attention to the examination of the idea of solidity. (228)

9. David Hume, *A Treatise of Human Nature*, book 1, part 4, section IV. My copy of the *Treatise* is the P. H. Nidditch edition, based on L. A. Selby-Bigge's earlier edition, from the Oxford University Press (Oxford, 1978). In this edition, the quoted words are on pp. 228–29.

As Hume's here suggesting, without phenomenal colors available, or any similarly helpful Qualities, we'll lack the resources for an adequate conception of something's being physically solid or impenetrable. As Hume also seems rightly to suggest, the same pertains to any other alleged physical Propensity. (Except that Locke fixed on solidity as his favorite, there's nothing very special about that candidate, as the passages from Foster can be seen to show.)

In light of what's been presented in this section, we may be able to make useful comments concerning the questions that, at the just previous section's end, arose for my attempts to characterize a Particulate World, and also a Plenumate World: Though it may have appeared that each of my attempts to characterize physical reality, one with Particulate wording and one with the Plenumate terms, clearly contrasted with the other, mightn't it be that I actually made just one extremely insubstantial start twice over, first using one mutually connected group of terms and then using another? Indeed, it may now be so plain that those questions have affirmative answers that the whole matter's no longer interesting.

What may still be interesting, I think, is to notice these further points: With those attempts, even my *very talk of particles* may have been badly misleading, as was my *talk of a plenum*. As I'm suggesting, it may be that something's *being a particle* isn't ever a completely Nonqualitative matter, and the question of whether there's *a plenum* might not be wholly Nonqualitative. With the *Restriction in place*, it may be that we're unable to think of a World as containing any *particles*; when supposing the Restriction to hold while trying to think of a "Particulate World," perhaps the most we can do is think, very abstractly indeed, about a physical World where "Quality-purged correlates of true particles" are to play a certain role in the history of the World. And, with the Restriction in place while trying to think of a "Plenumate World," perhaps the most we can do is think, just as abstractly, about a World where "Quality-purged correlates of a true plenum" play a perfectly parallel role, or maybe even the very same role, in the history of the World. With thoughts so abstract, perhaps there's no significant difference between what we're thinking at the one time and at the other.

7. Extensible Qualities and Intelligible Propensities

With the Restriction in force and no Qualities available, we'll have no adequate conception of physical reality. By contrast, with Qualities having "real existence" in the physical realm, we may have a systematically rich

variety of physical conceptions, perhaps far beyond anything imagined by
Locke or Hume. Directly, I'll explain.

Whether or not we scientifically educated philosophers now can
believe that any matter is a certain Qualitative color, say, that it's a certain
Absolutely Specific shade of phenomenal red, it certainly seems that we
can *conceive* of there being matter, even perfectly insensate matter, that's
entirely just such a red, and that has no other Absolutely Specific
Quality. As I'll say, we're to contemplate matter that is *Red*.

It may also be helpful to have our considered stuff be, through and
through, *pretty highly phenomenally transparent* (and *somewhat phenomenally translucent*). As with any Quality our matter may have, it's (degree
of) transparency must be Absolutely Specific. So, it's Red Transp-Taso
matter that we're to conceive. For easy exposition, we'll call our matter
just by its first name, Red.

Though it might not be believable for you and me, it's perfectly
conceivable, even to us, that all of a World's matter be Red. In particular,
it's conceivable that all of a World's matter be distributed so as to comprise eight Red congruent material spheres, each separated from the
others by Qualityless empty space, and with nothing else in such a region having any Qualities, while what's where any sphere is has just the
color Quality we're contemplating.

Consonant with such a conception, there may be clear content in *each
of several different ideas of impenetrability.* For just one salient way of cutting
the conceptual pie, we may have clear content both in (1) the idea of a
sphere that's impenetrable to, or by, *all* the matter that's external to it
and in (2) the idea of a sphere that's impenetrable to *some*, but *not all*, the
matter external to it. In turn, I'll illustrate both ideas.

(1) We may think of an infinity of Red spheres each of which is
    absolutely impenetrable to every other, with the matter of these
    spheres comprising all the matter of the World in which there
    are the spheres. When two such spheres collide, then each di-
    rectly recedes from the other, without either making any in-
    trusion into the bounds of the other.

(2) In addition to all our Red spheres, we may contemplate an in-
    finity of spheres that are each an Absolutely Specific shade of
    phenomenal blue and a certain Absolutely Specific phenomenal
    transparency, an infinity of *Blue* spheres. Now, just as each Red
    sphere is completely impenetrable to all other Red spheres,
    each Blue sphere is impenetrable to all other Blue spheres.
    More interestingly, each *Red* sphere will be *perfectly penetrable* by
    any *Blue* sphere, and *vice versa*; so without even the least resis-

tance or temporal delay in trajectory, Red spheres and Blue spheres will pass through each other, as will parts of such Qualitatively different spheres. To conceive such a "perfect passing" most vividly, we may think of a region where a Blue and a Red sphere overlap as suffused with a certain Absolutely Specific transparent purple, as being *Purple* regions.

As this discussion of impenetrability suggests, any intelligible conception of physical Propensities, and any adequate conception of physical entities, has a central place for Extensible Qualities. At the same time, there's an abundance of such good conceptions that do that.

It's not surprising, then, to observe that, just as thought of Extensible Qualities allows us to have intelligible ideas of physical objects, variously distributed through spacetime and disposed toward various possible interactions, so it allows us to make intelligible specifications of Particulate Worlds, and clearly contrasting characterizations of Plenumate Worlds.

With attempts at Worldly characterization, we'll now have there be instanced some Extensible Quality *wherever there is matter*, from the minutest particle to a material expanse infinitely extensive in all directions. And, it's *only where* there's matter, or only where there's physical reality, that there'll be Extensible Quality instantiated.

In a Particulate World, there'll be Extensible Quality where, and only where, there are Particles, these being relatively small bounded regions of materially filled space, or spacetime. Each suffused with Extensible Quality, each particle is surrounded by a region that, as it's completely devoid of Quality, will also lack any real physical Propensity.

In a Perfectly Plenumate Physical World, Extensible Quality is instanced everywhere, and always, in the whole space (or spacetime) of the World. And, this Qualified space will be equally pervaded with physical Propensities; so, then, the World is filled with matter.

In a Plenumate World with Bubbles, finally, such well-Qualified materially filled space won't exhaust the space of the World. Rather, with each separated from the others by well-Qualified matter, there'll be many regions without Quality, and without anything of physical reality.

8. Intelligible Physical Reality and a Principle of Contingency

In terms of our three kinds of basic property, what's required for there to be a humanly intelligible mind-independent *physical* reality, whether or not it's the World's only realm of reality? Without much detail, I'll try to give the question a serviceable answer.

First, some words about some necessary relations: For a World to feature *physical* reality, it *must* include at least one entity such that (1) it has *some* Spatiotemporal Properties—even if it may be, in a quite extreme case, only the property of being, in all directions, infinitely extensive, and (2) it has *some* Extensible Qualities—even if it may be, in a quite extreme case, only the property of being, everywhere and always, the very same Quality, and also (3) it has *some* Propensities—even if it may be, in a quite extreme case, only the Propensity to exemplify, in each place at each time, exactly the same Quality it exemplifies right there at the just previous time. The necessity just stressed is the same as with this more familiar proposition: As does any Euclidean geometrical closed solid, a physical entity precisely bounded by such a figure *must* be such that (1) it has *some* shape and also (2) it has *some* size.

As far as its being required of a physical entity that it instantiate some Extensible Quality, we need only recall the discussion of the previous section. As far as its being required that it instantiate some Spatiotemporal Property, we need only note that, for any thing to exemplify any Extensible Quality, there must be some space (or spacetime) that's occupied by that thing and suffused with that Quality. And as far as its being required that our physical entity instantiate some Propensity, we've already observed the point to hold even in the extreme case of a physically homogeneous reality.

Second, some complementary words about some contingent relations: Even with regard to something that's a *physical* entity, there is *no necessary connection* between (1) *which* Spatiotemporal Properties the thing has, and (2) *which* Qualities the thing has, and (3) *which* Propensities are those of that physical thing. The *lack* of necessity just stressed, and the *contingency* just indicated, is the same as with this proposition: As is true of the Euclidean closed solid figures that precisely bound them, physical entities precisely bounded by such figures *may* be a certain given *shape* even while being *any* one of *numerous distinct sizes* and, equally, they *may* be a certain given *size* even while being *any* one of *numerous distinct shapes*. As seems fitting, I'll call the proposition this paragraph aims to express the *Principle of Contingency (of Relations among the Basic Properties)*.

For an easy appreciation of this Principle, recall the most recent remarks on characterizing Particulate and Plenumate Worlds. Perfectly in line with them all, for each of numerous Particulate Worlds, for example, there may be specified distinct exemplifications of Extensible Qualities. Even with a World specified as being "fully monochromatic"

in Extensible Quality, there are numerous Particulate Worlds to countenance: Some are some Worlds where all the Particles are Red; others
have all Blue Particles, and so on. Equally, just as there are Plenumate
Worlds where the Plenum is Red, there are others with a Blue Plenum,
and so on.

For ease of exposition, we'll focus on Particulate Worlds, and we'll
narrow the focus to Worlds whose Particles are like the Newtonian
entities familiar from the quote from Foster. In these Worlds, each of
enormously many Particles has the same "mass" and the same "amount
of matter," and each will attract the others with a force that varies inversely with the square of the distance between the centers of the interacting Particles. In some of these monochromatic Newtonian Worlds,
all the Particles are Red; in others, all are Blue Particles, and so on.
Whereas that's old hat, we newly notice this: In *Tutti-Frutti* Particulate
Worlds, many Particles are Red and many others Blue, with yet many
others being Yellow, and also Green, and Brown, and Grey, and Silvery,
and Goldenish, and so on. (Along with such Qualitative variety, in many
Tutti-Frutti Worlds there's also much Qualitative stability; there, any
Particle that's Red will always be Red, and it will never have any other
Quality, not Blue, not Yellow, and so on.)

Our supposition of Tutti-Frutti Worlds is as perfectly intelligible as
it's vividly imaginable. So, as I'll suggest, our Principle of Contingency
may be both perfectly intelligible and entirely unobjectionable.

9. Qualities as a Factor in the Development of Physical Reality: A Problem

As it often appears, the Qualities of physical things won't be much of a
factor in determining the development of any physical reality. The
problematic appearance is most acute with physically well-behaved
Worlds that, while otherwise heterogeneous, lack Qualitative variation,
as with many monochromatic Worlds. What are we to make of this appearance? This question poses the *Problem of the Roles for Qualities (in
Physical Reality)*.

Without thinking long and hard about the possible relations
between physical entities and Qualities, there's little likelihood of encountering this Problem. So, as I expect, most contemporary philosophers will find this to be their first encounter with it. But many may
quickly come to appreciate the puzzle quite well.

To that purpose, we'll focus on the comparison between a monochromatic Newtonian World and, on the other hand, a Tutti-Frutti

Newtonian World. Except that the first has no Qualitative variety and the second has a great deal, the two Worlds may be exceedingly similar. So the behavior of the Tutti-Frutti World's Particles may precisely parallel the behavior of the Particles in the monochromatic World. And then all its Qualitative variety will make no difference to the physical development of the Tutti-Frutti World. But, then, are there *any* Worlds where Qualitative variety means much more than that for the development of the World's physical reality? All too often, it seems there are none. So, our Problem often appears acute.

To appreciate this Problem properly, however, it's also important that we not overestimate the apparent predicament: Our Problem is *not* to show how it might be true that, in *every* World with physical reality, all the Qualities of physical things are very significant factors in the physical development of the World. Nor is it to show even how it might be that, in every such World, *at least some* such Qualities are such significant factors. Indeed, it follows from the Principle of Contingency (of Relations among the Basic Properties) that there's no more chance of doing such a thing than of drawing a perfectly round square. Rather than any of that, our Problem asks us to show how it might be that, in *some* Worlds with physical reality, some Qualities of physical things are quite significant factors in the development of that reality.

10. The Problem of the Roles for Qualities in Physical Reality: A Solution

At least since Galileo, physics has made great progress by ignoring, it appears, thoughts as to Qualities. Because we're so impressed by that, when we contemplate physical Propensities such thoughts are excluded from our consideration. For progress with the Problem of the Roles for Qualities, we must rectify this intellectually restrictive situation.

To that end, I'll first characterize a World whose salient Propensities we find it easy to take seriously. Using this *Size-Propensity* World as a model for further characterization, I'll then characterize various *Quality-Propensity* Worlds, whose quite different Propensities we can also take seriously. When we fully acknowledge these Quality-directed Propensities, perhaps we'll have found a solution to our Problem.

First, we'll contemplate a monochromatic Particulate World: Whereas all the World's Particles have the very same Extensible Quality, perhaps *Grey*, these spherical Particles come in ten different Sizes, with many Particles of each Size. As regards both its volume and its "amount of matter," each of the smallest Particles is one-tenth as great as each of the largest Particles; each of the next smallest is two-tenths as great as a largest Particle, and so on. Now, each Particle has the Propensity to attract each of the others, and to be attracted by each of the others, with a force that varies directly with its Size (and, say, inversely with the square of the distance between its center and the centers of the each of the other Particles). It's easy enough to take seriously the thought that a World might work in that way.

Next, we'll contemplate a *multichromatic* Particulate World: Whereas all this World's Particles have the very same Size, perhaps the Size of the smallest Particles in the foregoing monochromatic World, these spherical Particles come in ten different "Achromatic Colors," with many Particles of each such Color. The lightest Particles, each of them Snow White, each have one-tenth "the amount of matter" of the darkest, each of which is Jet Black; each of the next lightest Particles, each of them Very Light Grey, is two-tenths as "massive" as the darkest, and so on. Here, each Particle has the Propensity to attract each of the others, and to be attracted by each of the others, with a force that varies directly with its *Qualitative Darkness* (and, say, inversely with the square of the distance). Though there might be *no good reason for it*, as I'll suggest, it may be quite hard to take seriously the thought that a World might work in *this* way.

To make progress on our Problem, we must overcome this difficulty. We must take seriously not only the thought that physical entities have Qualities, but also the thought that, at least in some Worlds, such entities have Propensities *with respect to Qualities*. In other words, we must adopt a *more inclusive mode of thinking* than the one that, apparently, proved so successful for Galileo and so many successors. For adopting such more inclusive thinking, what's most helpful, I imagine, is more experience with such thinking.

Accordingly, we may do well to contemplate a different contrasting pair of Particulate Worlds, again one a Size-Propensity World and the other a Quality-Propensity World. In both of these Worlds, there are four sorts of spherical Particles: Each exactly the same as the other in Quality, there are Large Red Particles and Small Red Particles, with the former being ten times the Size of the latter. And, each of them having a Quality very different from that of any Red Particle, there are Large Blue Particles and Small Blue Particles, the former being exactly the same size as the Large Red Particles and the latter the same as the Small Red Particles.

Now, in the first of our two Worlds, each Particle will have a Propensity to attract any Particle that's different from it in Size, and a Propensity to repel any Particle that's the same Size. In this World, the Large Red Particles and the Large Blue Particles will repel each other, as will the Small Red and the Small Blue Particles. And the Large Particles, both Red and Blue, will attract, and will be attracted by, the Small Particles, Red and Blue. As I'm envisioning this World, when Particles attract, or repel, other Particles, it's *because* the former have Propensities *with respect to the very Size* the latter possess.

In the second World, no Particle will have any of those Propensities. Rather, each will have a Propensity to attract any Particle that's different from it in *Quality*, and a Propensity to repel any Particle that's the same Quality. In this World, the Red Particles, Large and Small, will attract, and will be attracted by, the Blue Particles, Large and Small. Far from repelling each other, here the Large Red Particles and the Large Blue Particles will *attract* each other. As I'm envisioning this other World, when Particles attract, or repel, other Particles, it's *because* the former have Propensities *with respect to the very Quality* the latter possess.

Toward gaining comfort with the good thought that, in addition to their having Qualities, many physical entities have Propensities *with respect to Qualities*, I've considered a couple of relevantly contrasting pairs of Particulate Worlds. Although the job is a tad more complex, we can do as well with, say, apt pairs of Plenumate Worlds. But even without actually encountering such a variety of illustrative examples, we see how the Qualities of physical entities can be a very significant factor in the development of physical reality.

11. Concluding and Continuing Questions

In comparison with most recent papers in philosophy, this one has been quite ambitious. But it is not nearly so ambitious as might appear. So it might sometimes seem that I have attempted an argument, very largely a priori, to the effect that, in this actual world, certain sorts of properties are basic properties, to wit, Spatiotemporals, Propensities, and Qualities. But of course, it's futile for anyone to argue, in such an a priori fashion, to any such substantial effect. And of course, I haven't really attempted anything like that much.

Much more modestly, I've argued only for conditional propositions. Conspicuous among them is this: If the scientifical metaphysic provides us with a tolerably accurate understanding of this world, then, as basic properties instanced in the actual world, there are Spatiotemporal Properties, and Propensities, and also Qualities. As we should bear in mind, it *might* be that this dominant worldview provides us with no such thing.

When the limits of the present essay are appreciated, we see large questions for future inquiry. Salient among them is this: If the scientifical metaphysic should be inadequate, then what might we best suppose are the basic properties of concrete reality? As a first pass at this fearful question, I hazard the conjecture that we should still countenance Qualities and Propensities, and perhaps Temporal Properties but no Spatial Properties.

In the present climate, I may be a greater friend of qualities than any other admittedly ambitious metaphysician. Yet I have doubts about that. Now, especially as this essay is dedicated to Jerome Shaffer, for a most salient example of work that fuels these doubts it's especially fitting to consider work from a most salient student of Professor Shaffer's. So, I ask: What does David Lewis denote with "qualities" in this schematic metaphysical passage?

> Many of the papers, here and in Volume I, seem to me in hindsight to fall into place within a prolonged campaign on behalf of the thesis I call "Humean supervenience." ...
>
> Humean supervenience is named in honor of the greater denier of necessary connections. It is the doctrine that all there is to the world is a vast mosaic of local matters of particular fact, just one little thing and then another. (But it is no part of the thesis that these local matters are mental.) We have geometry: a system of external relations of spatio-temporal distance between points. Maybe points in spacetime itself, maybe point-sized bits of matter or aether or fields, maybe both. And at those points we have local qualities: perfectly natural intrinsic properties which need nothing bigger than a point at which to be instantiated. For short: we have an arrangement of qualities. And that is all. There is no difference without difference in the arrangement of qualities. All else supervenes on that.[10]

Though Lewis clearly uses "qualities" for *some* metaphysically basic properties, it's not clear what these properties are. Are his qualities much like our Qualities?

Following Russell, who followed Hume, in characterizing the Qualities I wanted there to be *some* connection, however indirect and tenuous, between the properties targeted and what we might experience, if only with the experience enjoyed in imaginative understanding. Without *any* connection to *any* such aid to intelligibility, what are we humans

---

10. David Lewis, "Introduction," *Philosophical Papers*, Vol. 2 (New York: Oxford University Press, 1986), *ix*.

to understand by *anyone's* metaphysical reference to qualities? So it is that, in trying to say *something intelligible about what are* Qualities, I referred us to phenomenal qualities. Anyway, as Lewis's qualities are absolutely basic in his metaphysics, it should be asked: In humanly intelligible terms, what's there to say as to *what are* these items on whose arrangement, perhaps, all else supervenes?

This paper serves also to raise questions about the work of other students of Shaffer's, including the work in this very paper itself: When I said that, if the Extensible Qualities don't include phenomenal colors, then they should be strongly and deeply analogous to such colors, what sort of analogy could I sensibly have had in mind? More specifically, *in what respects* are such Extensible Qualities to be so analogous to phenomenal colors?

The previous section's discussion promotes the appearance that, for an intelligible conception of the actual world as comprising a heterogeneous physical reality, we need only a very few Qualities, and these may bear very much the same relations to each other as obtain among a *very few achromatic* phenomenal colors, perhaps much as obtain between just a certain Light Grey, say, and a certain Dark Grey. So, perhaps we can do a fair amount to sharpen our questions, and even to place limits on the range of sensible answers: What is it about the relations among, or even between, a few colors that, at least to a quite significant degree, must find a parallel in relations among Extensible Qualities, if thinking in terms of these Qualities will do much toward our having an adequate conception of physical reality?

As I've just observed, there's been the appearance that an adequate conception of what seems most of our world requires us to conceive only a very few Qualities as basic properties, perhaps just two Extensible Qualities. But that appearance might be illusory. To do justice to even just the Qualities apparently available in, or through, our immediate experience, perhaps we must regard as basic all the known phenomenal qualities, both such as seem Extensible and such as seem Nonextensible. Now, insofar as it may come to seem that the truth lies in such a more expansive vein, then, however restricted the academically respectable options of the time, serious philosophers will have to confront such extensive considerations as this final question: Might it possibly be that, rather than with the scientifical metaphysic, only with a more mentalistic worldview, maybe one where neither the physical nor the mental is most basic, will we have anything like an adequate conception of what's actually concrete reality?

PART III

Defending and Transcending
Identity, Consciousness and Value

7

PRÉCIS OF *IDENTITY,*
CONSCIOUSNESS AND VALUE

While it concerns other large issues as well, a single question *focuses* the inquiry of this book[1]: What is involved when an actual person, like me, survives until some future time, like a century from now? To this question, *some* seek a *completely general* answer. Even if *Berkeley* should be right and there is no physical reality, *their* (desired) answer is to inform us about our survival. Although *pretty* ambitious in the matter, I'm content to settle for a *lot* less than that. For me, it's enough to give an answer that articulates, along lines *general enough* to prove philosophically interesting, *our deep beliefs about* the conditions of our survival. There's a good reason for this: By disclosing our deep *beliefs* about our survival, I *indirectly* articulate what *are*, as we most deeply *believe*, some quite general *conditions* of our survival. How do I detect these deep beliefs? Doing informal psychology, I uncover them by noting people's responses to examples. But many examples have contexts where responses are misleading. And, even in revealing contexts, some examples promote responses that are best explained away, as arising from sources other than our deep beliefs about ourselves. Still, often, we may sensibly avoid all the pitfalls. In chapter 1, I describe and defend the aims and methods of the inquiry.

After a lot of methodical looking, what do I find to answer our question about survival? First, some bad news: In chapter 2 I find that,

---

1. Peter Unger, *Identity, Consciousness and Value*, Oxford University Press, 1990.

despite their undeniable *initial* appeal, there's no lasting credibility in dualistic views and in subjective (or transcendental) views. In chapter 3 I find that the same holds for the *psychological approach*, the governing paradigm that's dominated the literature for decades.

Then, some good news: In chapter 4 I come upon the *basis* for a good answer, the *physical approach*, whose two key ideas are these: (1) For your survival, the causal furtherance of your *distinctive psychology* is of *no* importance: Against the psychological approach, we may ignore your personal memories, your constellation of intentions, your peculiar character traits, and so on. All that counts is the causal furtherance of your *core psychology*: Consisting only of things like your capacity for conscious experience and your capacity for *very* simple reasoning, your psychological core is exactly like that of even the dullest amnesiac moron. (2) For your survival, the *way* the core is causally furthered is *all-important*: For you to exist at some particular future time, there must be the *sufficiently continuous physical realization* of a core psychology *between* the physical realizer of your core now (your brain) and the physical realizer (whether brain or not) of someone's core psychology at that future time.

What is meant by this continuous physical realization? Mainly, I tell you in three ways: First, and right from page one, I exhibit scads of helpful examples; both lots of positive cases and many negative ones. Second, in section 5 of this fourth chapter, I tell you about *very high standards* for, and about *lower standards* for, the *attribution of* psychological capacities to people. Unlike almost everywhere else in our context-sensitive discourse, here it is the *everyday* standards that are the *higher* ones, and the theoretical standards that are the lower. On high (everyday) standards, we say people in "irreversible" coma no longer have even their basic mental capacities; on the lower standards more appropriate to philosophizing, we attribute *many* mental capacities to these unfortunates. Third, in sections 7 to 11, I discuss four of the *aspects* of physical continuity: gradualness of material replacement, constitutional cohesion, systemic energy, and physical complementarity. Rather than just explaining one technical idea by means of several others, these aspects are used to *organize* still further examples. In these three ways, you get quite a serviceable idea of physically continuous realization. As this idea fits well with a *contextually sensitive semantics*, as shown in section 3, it is true to say that, for you to survive, there *can't be any interruption* in the physical realization of the central psychology that you now have.

As our intuitions regarding myriad cases attest, this physical approach provides an answer that's better than the others currently on offer. Yet, as we notice in chapter 5, even when well endowed with constraints against unwanted cases of branching, it is not quite good enough. Perhaps there are two troubles. A small trouble is that distinctive psychology *never* counts. More plausibly, a *tiny* loss in the core might be offset by physically good furtherance of *loads of* distinctive psychology. So, in moving toward the *physically based approach*, first we allow for such trade-offs.

The *big* trouble concerns *assimilation*, the main focus of the fifth chapter. Toward your seeing this trouble, I'll actually *present* you with a couple of cases. *First* case: Suppose that four non-overlapping quarters of my brain are, in sequence, replaced by their respective "duplicates," each replacement starting five minutes after the previous one was completed. Taking about one minute to occur, each replacement may itself be very gradual; only one percent of it's done during each successive half-second. Hence, in the original body, there's always at least 99.75% of a whole healthy brain. For good measure, *assume that every step in the process is part of a "statistical miracle," uncaused by any (relevant) event.* As part of this miracle, anything replaced is trashed. (By the miracle's end, *all* the brain matter in the skull is new stuff.) Finally, *between* replacements, an emerging person will think and act quite normally for about four minutes. Now, in this situation, there is a *great* deal of physically continuous realization even of *all* my psychology. Yet, as most intuitively respond, *by the end of* these minutes, *I* do *not* exist. Why is that? A *second* case suggests an answer: Suppose that the period *between* quarterly replacements *is a full year*; between replacements, an emerging person always will engage in *much* normal thought and action. As we respond to *this* case, *I will survive.* So, what's the difference between the two cases? Roughly, it's this: In the first case, further new realizing parts *enter well before previous newcomers have done enough in my life.* In the second case, well before I take on *yet another* of them, the *earlier* central additions have been assimilated into me.

Now, the *various factors* of assimilation are themselves pretty complex matters, as chapter 5 details. But this proves no obstacle to the physically based account's being *quite a good* answer to the book's leading question, *perhaps much* better than the available alternatives.

Related to the leading question, I address several other issues: As early as chapter 2, I articulate *six metaphysical doctrines* that, as I argue, underlie the appeal of transcendental views, and of dualistic views, of our survival. The three *most* appealing of these concern *conscious experience*:

(1a)   Experience is all-or-none.

(2a)   Experience is completely private to a single subject.

(3a)   Experience is absolutely indivisible.

Deriving appeal partly from their connection with these doctrines are three others, concerning the *subjects that experience*:

(1b)   A subject is all-or-none.

(2b)   A subject is completely separate.

(3b)   A subject is absolutely indivisible.

By confronting them with numerous thought-experiments, in chapter 6 the appeal of these doctrines is dispelled: Insofar as there is *any truth* in the displayed *sentences*, that is owing to *conventions of language*, or to certain un-problematically *natural facts*, or to a combination of the two. Briefly, the *most positive* results of the encounter are these: We subjects ourselves are wholly objective entities, mainly or wholly physical, and *our experiences* are wholly objective processes, mainly or wholly physical. Moreover, in an important sense, we are *conventionally demarcated* entities, and our experiences are conventionally demarcated processes.

Drawing on material from the first six chapters, in the last three the focus is on some main questions of *our broad ego-centric values*: As argued in chapter 7, by itself my survival has *no* value. Rather, it is a *pre-condition* of certain things that I (rationally) value, like *my* leading a long happy life. Equally, my survival is a pre-condition of certain things that I (rationally) *disvalue*, like *my* being severely tortured for the next ten years. Similarly, *my son's* survival is a pre-condition of certain of my *other* broad ego-centric values, like *his* leading a long happy life. Partly owing to confusions about all this, and partly owing to confusions over various uses of expressions like "what matters in survival," strange views have recently dominated the discussion about the relation between (strict) survival and our values. Against these views, I argue for a *realistic compromise view of what matters*: (1) In the relevant *prudential use* of the term, "what matters," what matters in a given person's survival *basically* is only that the person himself will still exist. (2) Also, certain continuities do matter, but they matter only *derivatively*. (3) Now, as happens in the middle of certain *physically well-based spectra* of examples, these continuities *may* have great *independent* importance: Regarding what matters, *some of* these cases of *non*-survival are "pretty nearly as good as" cases of strict survival itself. (4) But, this derivative

independent importance will *never* be as great as that basic importance: Concerning what matters in survival, *any* case that *lacks strict
survival* will be worse than *every* case in which the person himself *does
survive*. Closing with an argument from a *spectrum of assimilation*, the
case for this view is multi-faceted.

Chapter 8 starts with a *clarifying* discussion of *fission*. Because the
existing literature on these matters appears nearly as confused as it is
engaging, such a discussion is worth some effort. Anyway, increased
clarity yields a double payoff: First, even as we find it's *not* (determi-
nately) *true* that one survives fission, we find yet more reason to endorse
the realistic compromise view of what matters. More important, we
uncover a previously unnoticed basic (pre-condition of) broad ego-
centric value: the *focus of a person's life*.

In the final chapter, I undertake an *appreciation of our actual values*.
Because you are pretty normal, among your *strongest* (broad ego-centric)
values are these: Certain particular people—you yourself, *your* lover,
your children—should lead long and pleasant lives of a *certain complex
character*. In your life, you should have close personal (developing) relations with *these* people, not changing (mid-stream) to precisely similar
relations with precise duplicates of them. Further, and as is *pretty* obvious, you should have pleasant and interesting *conscious experience*. Less
obvious, this experience should *not just happen* to give you an accurate
idea of what is actually going on between you and your loved ones.
Rather, much of this conscious experience should be experience *of* those
people, and experience *of* your intentional behavior with regard to
them, and experience *of* the effects of your actions upon them, and
experience *of* their resulting behavior toward you, and so on.

For these values to be fulfilled, it is argued, there must hold, between the active lives in the world and your own conscious experience,
the "right sorts" of *causal relations*. Now, while we'll allow *some* slack about
which causes count as being of the *right* sorts, still, as *further* arguments
show, we're pretty *inflexible* in this regard. By contrast, and as *still further*
reasoning shows, we *don't* require that *sublime metaphysical* ideas be satisfied: Quite rightly, we regard these strong values as *very* well fulfilled
even if the world should be wholly deterministic—with no transcendental free will, and, more to the main topic, even if the world should be
fully physical—with no immaterial souls.

REPLY TO REVIEWERS

1. Reply to Sydney Shoemaker

Strangely, Sydney Shoemaker's most provocative remark concerns merely *terminological* matters: Most conspicuously, he says it's curious that, although I oppose "the psychological approach," my own account is straightforwardly a version of the psychological account of personal identity. What are we to make of the strange swipe at my book's coherence and newsworthiness?

Coherence: In chapter 3 I *specify* the psychological *approach*. As specified, the approach has *two most distinctive aspects*: (1) *Positively*, for my survival until some future time, *it's required* that, at least within suitably short relevant causal chains occurring between now and then, *much distinctive psychology* should be causally furthered. (2) *Negatively*, it's *not* required that *any* psychology be causally furthered by *just certain* effective causal routes; *any* route will do. Since my *own* account *contradicts both* propositions, there's nothing at all incoherent in, or even *at all curious* in, *my opposition* to the psychological *approach*.

Newsworthiness: Why bother to specify *that approach*? Well, when one opposes a number of closely related positions, as I do, it's useful to articulate a paradigm *around which* these positions cluster. Maybe David Lewis' view clusters closest, but a Widest Psychological Criterion that greatly interests Derek Parfit is very nearby, and others are also near.[1] So, philosophers as real as they are able find views *much like* my paradigm *very appealing*. Further, when I notice *nine motivations toward* the approach—like its *apparently* good fit with common ideas about who deserves reward or punishment, and with common ideas about the value of survival (74–97), then I notice there's a *very* good *explanation* of this appeal.

Consider Shoemaker's words "the psychological continuity account of personal identity." Supposing them to have a referent, it's *some* such thing as *this*: A single view *around which* the ideas of such noted philosophers most closely cluster and, less centrally, *toward which* the noted motivations most strongly point. So, supposing there's a referent here, at the very least it's a great deal *like* my paradigm. And, just as the book *very* effectively argues against the *paradigm*, so, *at least nearly that* effectively, it works against *the psychological continuity account of personal identity*. Thus, for able real thinkers, the work may be *all too* newsworthy.

That being an ample reply concerning terminology, let's now discuss more *substantive* issues. Now, just two substantive disagreements with me dominate this large part of Shoemaker's comments. I'll take them in turn.

First, there's his complete *denial* of a "requirement of strong physical continuity": For me to survive until a future time, there must be, from now until then, continuous physical realization of my basic mental capacities. With only *minor* qualifications, I *accept* it. Based on an example of mine (126–27), Shoemaker offers an argument against (anything *even much like*) the requirement. As he concisely puts the example, "my brain is superfrozen, then divided into quarters that are temporarily scattered, then recombined and thawed and reembodied in such a way that the resulting person is pretty much as I was before." Now, he'll *agree* that, here, I *survive*. As he then rightly notes, since I accept the disputed requirement, I *must also* hold that, here, there's physically continuous realization of my basic mental capacities. And, I certainly do think that. Not only does Shoemaker *disagree* with my thought, but he says it "is extremely implausible on the face of it." But, actually, the thought's extremely *plausible*.

As a *help* in seeing this, here's a *relevantly analogous* case that's both a bit *simpler* and a bit more *realistic*: Did I tell you about my *self-starting*

---

1. See David Lewis's "Survival and Identity," in his *Philosophical Papers*, I, Oxford University Press, 1983, cited and even *quoted* on my page 93, and section 78 of Derek Parfit's *Reasons and Persons*, Oxford University Press, 1984, as (only!) cited on my page 71. Indeed, as I construe him in *Personal Identity*, Basil Blackwell, 1984, at *that* time, even Shoemaker's own view was *fairly* close to my specified approach.

Saab, complete with an internal timer and aimed at many mattresses some blocks away? Well, when the timer goes off, then, typically, the car starts and hits the mattresses at over 80 mph. So, surely, this car has the capacity to go 70 mph. Now, sometimes my car is taken apart in such a way that there are four *important* parts separated: The motor is *here*, the whole "wheel-assembly" is *there*, etc. And, later, the parts are reassembled just like they were. Well, *one* obvious truth is this: The *original* car existed *all* the while. And, (while my view of *car*-survival *doesn't require me* to hold it,) *another* evident truth is this: Even in the middle, and realized in those four parts, *there was that car's capacity to go 70 mph*. Now, because the parts were then separated, this capacity was *very far* from being *exercised*. But, so what?

When disassembled, my special car does have the *capacity* to ("start up" and) go 70 mph. When disassembled, it's just that she's "in no shape for" that capacity to be *exercised*. Put her back together, and she'll *exercise* the capacity. For similar reasons, when my brain is quartered, then *I'm* "in no shape for" *my capacity to think* to be exercised. But, realized in those quarters, there still is that capacity of mine. Put *me* back together, and I'll exercise *it*.

Having gained clarity, we see a red herring: Considering *four* quartered (people or) brains, Shoemaker *irrelevantly enlarges* on my personal example. Considering *four* self-starting Saabs, I may likewise enlarge on my automotive example. In *my* enlargement, *each car's* capacity to go fast is realized just in *its* separated parts, *not* in *any* parts from any *other* car. In *his* enlargement, *each person's* capacity to think is realized just in *his* separated (brain) parts; *not* in any parts from any *other* person, or brain.

Shoemaker then brings up the standard case of informational "teleportation." (My book argues I can no more survive such a process than can my car.) As he suggests, and as I agree, in *this* case there's *no* continuous realization of mental capacities. In effect, he then challenges me by asking: Between this case's radio waves and the brain quarters from before, *what important difference can there be*?

Well, each hard to state both briefly and well, there are several. Fortunately, and easy to see, there's *no need* to give a good statement of *any* of them. For, with a parallel case of "teleporting" my Saab, two central ideas stand out. First, the parallel point can be made about there *not* being the continuous realization of *its* noted capacity. Second, and *just as impotently as before*, the parallel question can be asked: Between this case's radio waves and the quartered car parts from before, *what important difference can there be*? Here, too, it's tough to give a good brief statement of the differences. But, who cares? As is *very* clear, in *both* matters, there *are* important differences between the cases. And, because *that's* so clear, it's clear that Shoemaker hasn't located any trouble for the requirement he fully denies.

Looking to find trouble elsewhere, Shoemaker comes to the site of our second big substantive disagreement: Here, he considers the question whether, in a battle over survival, physically well continued core psychology will trump a "causal succession" of (core and) distinctive psychology that lacks physically continuous realization. As he suggests, on my view the core will win. Indeed; on *my* view, it's *no contest*! By contrast, and based on the "too storylike" example of Brainland, *his* discussion sees a triumph for distinctive psychology. Before going to Brainland, it's useful to consider an example the presentation of which does less to generate contexts where misleading tendencies have much force.

A small variant on old standbys, here's the helpful case: A machine records the exact nature of, and relative arrangement of, all your atoms. The information is then sent to a companion device that, from new matter, makes a qualitatively identical person. Now, instead of destroying anything much, as in the old standbys, the very process by which the information is recorded also *immediately* does this: It effects your *brain* in such a way as to make it the brain of an amnesiac moron. As is *very* clear, you survive, just becoming such a moron; it's *someone else* who now has the (sort of) distinctive psychology that, before, only you had. A moral certainty: Between these two sorts of causal chain, when it comes to our survival, it's no contest.

Brainland. Pace Shoemaker, this storylike example is *not even remotely like* a best case for testing the claim about trumping, as the just previous example certifies. Anyway, in order to learn as much as we can from Brainland, we'll take his statement of Brainland at face value: Core psychology always stays realized in each head, while distinctive psychologies are *variously realized*, in different heads, in accord with the noted *intentions to move* (and the natural laws constraining such various realizations.) About this case, *my* intuition is that, *the people stay put*: Unable to *fulfill* a confused intention to move, when a *given person forms* one, and the situation is ripe for an "interesting event," then, causally related, these two things happen: (i) That person becomes an amnesiac moron. (ii) An adjacent person comes to have distinctive psychology of precisely the same *sort* that, just before, was realized in the head of the "frustrated" intender.

Sometimes with conflict, many will share my intuition and many others will share his. As I think, only those sharing my intuition will make a response *mainly generated by their deep beliefs about the general conditions of our survival.* Then, how am I explain the responses of those others? Well, in much the same ways that, in the book, I explain parallel responses to old parallel cases. A salient old explanandum: The common but misleading response that, in informational "teleportation," there's the movement of someone—*and also of the hunk of mud he's holding*—from where scanning occurs to where, from new matter, *just such a* person—holding *just such a* hunk—is configured. Often, the single biggest explanatory factor is this: Being good audiences, especially to more storylike examples, we have a tendency to respond along lines that, even if misleading for philosophical inquiry, make for a better story. Old hat: As we realize, stories about space explorers coming back with hunks of rare minerals are much better than those where they die and are replaced with duplicates holding precisely similar hunks. New hat: As we also realize, stories where people go for strolls and discuss philosophy are much better than those where nobody has any stroll or any good discussion. Unlike many of us, in responding to storylike examples, many others are *much* affected by this philosophically misleading tendency. So, just as surely as *hunks of mud* can't move like *that*, all of us, but especially they, should focus on less storylike cases.

Chapter 3 presents many arguments that such "teleportation" doesn't involve the movement of people—or mud. Several of these involve examples *highly similar to storylike* cases, but with features *nicely discouraging* our taking *these* examples as (bits of) good little stories. Easily, properly, and tellingly, all this further exposes Shoemaker's claims for Brainland. A tiny sample from the battery: In Lag Brainland, the intender's brain *keeps distinctive psychology for seconds after* the adjacent brain comes to have such psychology. Now, we have the *very* strong *first-order intuition* that, in *Lag* Brainland, folks *don't move and just become morons*. And, we have the *very* strong *second-order intuition* that, as to who's who, things in *Brainland* are *just* as in *Lag* Brainland. Bad news, the intuitions *together strongly tell us*, for the prospects of anyone's strolling in Brainland.

In sum: Just as no trouble's been found in my choice of terms, so no problem's been found in my substantive view.

2. Reply to Peter Strawson

It's pleasing when Strawson says that, in the main, he agrees with my account of our survival. It's strange when he says that he has *a few* doubts about my book's stand on questions of choice, preference and value. For, with only *one possible* exception, there's no disagreement with my views, but only misunderstanding of what I said.

Strawson considers "the Avoidance of Future Great Pain test, seen simply as a test for whether" one believes that one survives a certain process. While he describes much of this test correctly, he omits a crucial part. When I introduce the test (27–34), I give this key instruction (28): "...in applying the test to yourself, successful application requires that, in contemplating the person before the process and the person after, your main basic attitude will be one of self-concern." And, when I provide a more sophisticated treatment (225–33), I say (225): "In choosing whether to make the sacrifice, I am to proceed wholly from my concern for a particular being, in the simplest instance, from my concern for myself."

Pace Strawson, the test is *not* held to show the great importance each of us attaches to whether the emerging person will be himself; nor is it held to show how much identity matters to us. Far from all that, the situation is this. To *apply* the test *to one's own case*, a person's *choice* must be *based on* his concern to avoid *his own* future great pain, *not* on any of his *other* concerns. That is why *my choice* to undergo lesser pain now, just to spare the *emerging* person torture, (presumptively) indicates *my belief* about the identity of the emerging person: *that* person is *me*.

Strawson's remarks about his Complacent Egoist, and about his Self-sacrificing Altruist, also express misunderstanding, not disagreement. With the Altruist the point is simplest. Of *course*, there are people who are willing to undergo pain for the sake of others. They are willing to do this if they are, *and even* if they are *not*, facing impending extinction. In fact, I myself am one of these *myriad* people. But *none* of that has *anything* to do with *this test*. Look: Suppose that a certain process will grind me up and, using all my matter, will then produce a *million* nice tiny people. Making a choice based on *all* my concerns, I choose even to undergo some considerable pain now so that (each of) the *million* not suffer *slightly lesser* pain later. So, *surely*, I choose present pain so that the million not suffer *enormously greater* pain. Of course, this does *nothing* to suggest that, as I believe, *I'll be* all of, or even any of, those million people. And, clearly, my use of the test implies nothing of the sort. Rather, the situations is just this: When *I apply* the test to my *own* case, I *don't* choose on the basis of my *altruistic* concerns. Choosing *only out of my self-concern*, I choose to forgo the smaller pain and let the million suffer torment. According to the test, this suggests that, as I *believe*, *I won't* survive that process.

It's nearly as easy to get clear on the Complacent Egoist. We suppose: (1) The emerging person is an amnesiac moron; (2) just as you believe, he's you; and (3) because *almost* all of them are so very vapid, you care nothing for *almost* all his interests. Then, to further his *typical* interests, you may very well choose *not* to undergo even *very mild* pain now. Now, this just *recalls* certain reasons against using the "more positive" tests I discuss (30–32), and *for* using but the Avoidance of Great Pain Test. Basically, the main idea here is this: Unless you're *very* weird, there's at least *one* interest that, even with respect to impending moronhood, *will* carry great weight, namely, your interest *in avoiding protracted torture*. Duly impressed with *this* interest, you'll choose mild brief pain now over getting, when such a moron, years of excruciating torture. Since your choice is based only on your interest in being at the *low end of this enormous difference in pain*, and (presumably) you're not *very* weird, you can use the test to get clear that you'll survive becoming an amnesiac moron.

Along the way, Strawson *suggests* that I hold something like this: Necessarily, we attach enormous value to the bare fact of our continued existence. But, my *actual view* is *nothing like* that. Indeed, even when I first broach the subject, this couldn't be clearer, "While we would be delighted to be around a hundred years from now, delight in such a prospect is not unconditional ... there is no good, for us, in being alive many years in a wholly non-conscious state ..." (7). More elaborately (212–17), I hold that my survival is only a *pre-condition* of *some* things that I (rationally) value and, equally, of some *other* things that I *abhor*; "... my survival is as much a precondition of my being terribly tortured as it is of my being happy" (212).

There remains to discuss the one area where, as it appears, there might actually be disagreement. In Strawson's comments, this comes with the speculation that he soon might be annihilated and, in a few minutes, be replaced by a precise duplicate. Now, because they may obscure the main issues, I'll place to the side the stuff about knowledge of, and ignorance of, when this will happen. Anyway, the main issues concern how we view, and how we rationally ought to view, two things: (a) our having certain *prospects* and (b) our having certain *pasts*. Since it's clear that the issue regarding the prospects is far more relevant to the topics my book addresses, I'll first try to get clear about that.

Toward this end, we'll suppose that, whoever's there—me or my duplicate, he'll be leading a *happy* life. Well, what about the two prospects? Contrary to what Strawson says, I should *not* view with *equanimity* the prospect that, say, in a month I cease existing and my duplicate begin. Rather, I should, and I do, view that prospect *very negatively*. After all, in *that* event, *I won't* have (an expected) forty more years of happy life. As I'm sure, my very negative view is fully rational. Now, of course, my mentor is much older than I. Still, we may *suppose* that, *unless there's replacement*, Strawson may expect *at least ten* more years of happy life. Now, if the "complete equanimity" with which he views replacement next month is anything very like *indifference* between the two prospects, then the view he professes is *wildly* implausible. Indeed, it's *so* wildly implausible that, *despite* what he *says*, I doubt that his actual deep view of that awful prospect is really the one he professes.

We turn to our pasts. Now, since my book says *little about* our pasts, there's not much here *with which* Strawson might *disagree*. But, anyway, based on suggestions from Keith DeRose, I'd like to express an idea on how our (rational) views of "possible" pasts *may* differ from our views of prospects. Now, it may be only within certain limits that the idea applies. So, *outside* these limits, the "retrospect" of my having thus replaced someone only a *minute ago* seems *about as awful as* my having come into being a minute ago *where before there never was anyone very like me*. And, a few minutes of emptiness seems awful. But, *within* limits, perhaps things may be much better: Where the envisioned replacement takes place a *month* ago *and* occurs in *well under a millionth of a second*, my situation *doesn't* seem *so terribly* awful; it seems *a lot better than* coming into existence *a minute ago without replacing*. While I'm unsure of it, maybe this is a site for uncovering some interesting (rational) attitudes we have toward our lives.

Anyhow, pretty completely, I agree with Strawson's closing paragraph. And, if he'll allow that the elucidation of a common concept needn't be (even very like) the articulation of an ordinary term's meaning, I'll agree with it all.

3. Reply to Richard Swinburne

Richard Swinburne offers a variety of objections to my book. As is clear, none are sound. Rather than cursorily pointing up inadequacies in them all, I'll focus on just two main lines of his criticism. Why? Well, trying to make this symposium most worthwhile, I'll reply to them in a way that encompasses some very broad issues.

A. Objection Putatively Based on Epistemological Argument

Reacting to my statement that the physical approach isn't offered as anything analytic or conceptual, Swinburne offers an epistemological argument that's *meant* to ground his first main objection. Put roughly, the argument's main premise is this: As is rational, we *believe that (a)* each of us goes where her healthy brain goes *because we inductively correlate* (*b*) the continuity of memory and of characteristic behavior *with* (*c*) the careers of (most of) the brains that, in each instance, are causally responsible for those continuities. But, even granting the adequacy of such a simple epistemological framework, it's crystal clear that *that's* not *at all* what's going on. So, with most of it still waiting in the wings, this objection is a non-starter. Let me explain.

Following Swinburne's lead, we'll *suppose* that, as we amazingly discover, when a certain tiny bit of my brain is removed, then there's "total discontinuity of memory claims and behavior." Now, for this discovery to be *relevant to our topic*, there must remain *someone* where most of the brain remains, not just, e.g., a lot of living but non-thinking meat; for the discovery to be relevant, it must leave only the question of *who is* that (idiotic amnesiac) person remaining there. Further, and as is rightly clear from Swinburne's context, there's *no competition* here; that is, there *isn't anybody* where there's just that little bit of brain removed. Indeed, to make things *clearest*, we may suppose that the tiny bit is removed by being ground into *pulp* and then *drained*. At all events, what a relevant discovery will yield is just this: Exactly one amnesiac moron, a person whose brain, while realizing no distinctive psychology, continues to realize my core mentality.

Well, with this being what we'll relevantly have discovered, what should we conclude about the key question of my survival? Far from concluding that I won't exist anymore, as Swinburne would have it, we'd rightly conclude that this pathetic imbecile is *me*. Intuitively, this is very compelling. So, even as things still look good for the physical approach, right off the *bat* they look just awful for Swinburne's prime premise.

In a last little section of this reply, very hesitantly I'll have a go at speculating what it might be that, with its (putative) epistemological basis so hopeless, is left waiting in the wings. For what will emerge as very good reasons, right now I'll pursue a line of thought that's already underway.

It's very easy to elaborate on the hardships of Swinburne's false prime premise. Is that *just* beating a dead horse? No; for, *this* flogging can be conducted *instructively*. So, seeking instruction, we consider a closely related, more elaborate case: (1) While that horrible surgery is performed on me, over in Oxford parallel surgery is performed on Swinburne, turning his brain similarly moronic there. (2) The respective *removed* bits are subsequently *joined* with the *opposite* weak brains. (3) As a result of that, (a) the whole new brain *here* generates thoughts previously typical only of *Swinburne* and *this* body evinces behavior before characteristic only of him, while (b) the *opposite* happens over *there*.

As most respond, it's as clear I survive here as that I make it through the simpler example: Just as it's perfectly clear that I'm in New York *right* after the bit's removed, so it's *just* as clear that I *remain* here after it's *later* placed nicely in someone's head over in Oxford. For his part, it's perfectly clear Swinburne stays in Oxford. Even while no one moves, it's just that, by the case's end, *he* acquires distinctive psychology precisely like *I* used to have and *I* get distinctive mentality just like *he* had.

Suppose it turns out that we're *all* susceptible to such transplants. Then, in high tech terms, what we discover is this: What makes each human person psychologically different from others is realized in a tiny (physical) *module*; but, of course, the continued presence in someone of her module is *not* required for her very *survival*.

B. Physical Cores and Non-physical Distinctive Realizers

Before proceeding, a clarification: Though he calls me a *physicalist*, in fact that's only *partially* correct. Beginning at least as early as page 7, many pages other than 36 indicate this very clearly. Just so, while being very sympathetic to the idea that my experiences of color and of pain are wholly, or are mainly, physical, still I'm very unsure whether that's really so. On the other hand, I am confident that, along with my other mental capacities, *my capacity to have such experiences* is realized in structures that are wholly, or are mainly, physical structures.

Anyway, while they *haven't required* any strong physicalism to be true, so far the *examples have been wholly compatible with* such views. Seeking to address some broad issues, I'll now change the situation. So, let's allow that, quite coherently, we may make these new suppositions: (1) As with other human people, although my *core* psychology is realized only in my *wholly physical brain*, that's *not at all* true of my distinctive psychology; rather, even while it *never* realizes any *core* mentality, there is, in intimate causal relations with my brain, a *non-physical* entity in which my *distinctive* psychology is wholly realized. (2) There are natural laws governing the intimate relations of these non-physical realizers such that, upon my completing this reply, these things happen: (a) *for the next hour*, where before there were two very thoughtful people, in both places there are merely amnesiac morons, and (b) *after that hour's end*, instead of there being any morons in the works, where Swinburne first was there's someone with distinctive mentality just like I first had and where I was there's someone with distinctive mentality just like he had.

What happened to Swinburne and Unger; did they *cease to exist*? As most respond, it's *not at all* like that. Rather, each first became a moron and, then, Swinburne acquired precisely "Ungerian" distinctive psychology, while Unger came to be, psychologically, just like Swinburne was at first. The intuition here is *just as* in the previous case, with the little *physical* modules. So, our equine flagellation pays off: On our deep beliefs about the conditions of our survival, *non-physicality* carries no more weight, and perhaps even less, than does distinctive psychology.

C. The Question of a Wholly General Account

As further examples eventually show, in rough, in brief and in sum, the general situation is this: In judgments about our survival, great weight is carried by *whatever* continuously realizes *core* psychology, whether the realizer is physical or not. Now, this *tempts* me to advance a certain *wholly general* account of our survival conditions, labelled *GA*. While having various complexities, GA's leading idea is that I'll survive where there's the continuous realization of enough of my central enough mentality, whatever the *metaphysical* status of what's realizing. Though a friend of analyticity, I resist the temptation to offer GA. Why the resistance?

Well, let's look at a paradigm sentence *for* analysis, "I am the same person as that person later," which I'll label *FP*. Now, for one thing, FP *doesn't entail* that there's even anything *like* a temporal *continuum*; for all FP says, there might only be two times in the world's history, now and later. For another, FP *doesn't entail* that there's *anything in which* any capacities *are realized*; for all FP says, I might *just have* the capacity to think. And, certainly, there are various other difficulties. Thus, just as it's only relative to the truth of the *general* outlines of our accepted world view that my physically based position is advocated in the book, so it would be only relative to truth of the *very, very general* outlines of our world view that I'd ever advocate anything even a lot like GA.

D. Objections Based on Semantic Claims

While putting things in this larger perspective, I've already said enough to undermine, en masse, most of Swinburne's remaining objections. These are meant to be based on sound semantic points—points about conventions, paradigm cases, logical rules, and so on. Thinking it helpful to go into some particulars, I'll briefly do that.

We begin with paradigm cases. Well, just as Johnson couldn't touch Berkeley's philosophy by kicking a paradigm stone, so pointing to paradigms here—whether of people, ships or stones—won't do anything to undermine, or to support, any interesting account of survival—whether the putative survivors be people, ships or stones. If this isn't already as clear as can be, it will soon enough become so.

In an attempted contrast with a term like "people," with regard to "ships" and "stones," Swinburne says they have "logical rules connecting (of logical necessity) sameness with extent of physical continuity—e.g. that ships are largely the same if they are made of largely the same material put together in roughly the same way." But, even if we grant that what is meant here is *informal* logic, still, nothing even remotely like that can be any logical rule. Indeed, as each of two very different considerations establish it, the point is *overdetermined*.

(A) Let's suppose that, in fact, *Berkeley* is right. Then, the survival of ships will have *nothing to do* with *physical* continuity. Rather, and again as a matter of general fact, the situation will be something like this: "This ship now is the same one as that ship at that future time" is true if, and only if, {from now till that time, there first are minds having *Ship-Perceptions* that are *Indicated* with the relevant use of "this ship now," and, then, some of these minds, or some suitable succession of them, continuously have suitable *Ship-Perceptions* including, at that future time, some *Indicated* with the relevant use of "that ship at that future time"}. Now, there's a clear lesson here: Just as my book's account of *our own* survival is true only *relative* to the general truth of *our accepted* world view, and *not Berkeley's* view, so, the *same may be said* for standard accounts of the survival of unthinking *ships*. Taking physical continuity accounts of ship survival *sensibly*, they are *no more* a matter of *logical rules*, and they're no more a purely conceptual matter, than what I offer regarding our own survival.

(B) Just as is almost certainly true, let's now suppose that, about the quite general way of things, Berkeley's wrong and we're right. But suppose, as well, that we're badly wrong about whether stones and ships think and feel: Unlike lava and lakes, stones and ships *do* think and feel. As is clear, there's nothing in the *semantics* of "stone" or "ship," nor of anything in their neighborhood, that contradicts the supposition. Now, regarding questions of ships and time, in such an event, a certain *non*-logical condition will be a philosophically *instructive* condition. Roughly put, the condition is this: For a certain *ship* to survive from now until some future time, there must be, from now till then, the continuous *physical* realization of *its* basic *mental* capacities. So, again, when *modestly taken*, some available physical continuity account of ships' survival may be taken as (near enough) true; in particular, it may be true even while saying *nothing* about any realization of any mental capacities. But, when the idea is that the account will be true by virtue of (anything even much like) *logical rules*, as Swinburne would have it, then, again, truth is left far behind.

E. The First Objection Revisited?

Offered with a vain hope of an epistemological basis, Swinburne's original non-starter still waits in the wings. Since it's so terribly unclear what that objection actually is, it's only *very hesitantly* that I venture, at all and at last, to trot out even a semblance of it. Anyway, as far as I can make out, if there really does remain any argument there, it's not much better than this:

    (1a)   It's *not analytically* true that I'm a physical entity. So,
    (1b)   it's *not necessarily* true that I'm a physical entity. So,
    (1c)   I have, as an *essential* part, something *not physical*.

Now, while (1a) is quite acceptable, the inference from it to (1b) is at least *somewhat* dubious, since there *might* be here, something I *never deny* in the book, namely, an *a posteriori* necessity that's *not* an analytic necessity.[2] But, what's sure as shootin' is that, *especially* if this first inference is allowed, and, really, even in *any* case, the inference from (1b) to (1c) is just hopeless. If this isn't already perfectly clear, directly it will become so.

As the previous section shows, just good as (1a) is:

    (2a)   It's *not analytically* true that my *ship* is a physical entity.

And, just as good, or just as bad, as going from (1a) to (1b) is the inference from (2a) to:

    (2b)   It's *not necessarily* true that my *ship* is a physical entity.

Finally, *just as enormously unacceptable* as going from (1b) to (1c) is the inference from (2b) to:

    (2c)   My *ship* has, as an *essential* part, something *not physical*.

Like you, I'm *ever* so confident that (2c) is *false*, that no ship on earth has *any* part, essential or not, that's non-physical. While I'm *not that* confident that I myself have only physical parts, this *difference* in

---

    2. For a *conventionalist* account of how there *might* be *a posteriori* necessities, see Alan Sidelle's fine book, *Necessity, Essence, and Individuation*, Cornell University Press, 1989. By my lights, this is far more plausible than what we find in the celebrated and stimulating, but essentially mysterious, essentialist works of Kripke (and Putnam).

confidence, a *fairly* moderate one, certainly *isn't* due to *anything* in Swinburne's remarks.

4. Reply to Stephen White

Especially since he speaks well of my book, it's unpleasant for me to point out even a few of the flaws in Stephen White's comments. But, unless I do that, readers will be badly served.

Partly because he fails to distinguish between a merely floated view, the *slightly modified physical approach to our survival* (139–43), and my actual view, the *physically based approach* (147–52), White wrongly takes the former, simpler view to be my account of our survival. Consequently, he very inaccurately *states* my view of our survival and, after that, he *even more* inaccurately *characterizes* my position.

As White states it, on my view, for a subject's survival the following is not just necessary but is also a sufficient condition: (SMP) With a bar on bad branching, there is sufficiently continuous physical realization of enough central enough aspects of that subject's psychology. But, of course, SMP is just (the condition of) the slightly modified physical approach, floated but never endorsed. Now, taking things *modestly*— see my reply to Swinburne, I'm content to say that SMP *is a necessary* condition. But, very clearly, my view *denies* that SMP is (even close to being modestly) *sufficient*. As I even repeatedly argue, in many cases *assimilation* must be given its due (147–62): From the précis, recall the *first* case of replacing my brain quarters. While (1) each of the replacements proceeds in a *smoothly gradual way*, still, (2) they are all made *in very short order*. Now, because each replacement *proceeds so gradually*, there is even *highly* continuous physical realization of even *nearly all* my psychology. But, just as is intuitively compelling, my account has it that I *don't* survive: Because the relevantly central replacements *occur in such short order*, there's *hardly any assimilation* of the central parts. So, White gives a very inaccurate *statement* of my account.

Next, while citing passages from Parfit, White *even more* inaccurately *characterizes* my account: "Unger's theory of personal identity, then, is a version of the traditional physical criterion."[3] (Bad as this is, still, it's *not nearly as* inaccurate as *Shoemaker's* characterization of my view as "straightforwardly a version of the psychological continuity account

---

3. For White's citation, see the first note to his comments.

of personal identity.") But, why do I say that White's *characterization* of my account is even more inaccurate than his *statement* of it? Well, *not only* does my account happily differ from previous physically oriented views in that it recognizes assimilation, but, in *addition*, it nicely differs from them in *other* ways. For just one thing, and even as Parfit there indicates, *those* views typically require that, to survive, a person must retain enough of her *brain*. But, as I argue, nothing even much *like* that will figure in an *adequate* view (103–6). Largely, that's why, in presenting *my* view, I bother to say a lot about (*successions of*) *physical realizers* (106–12). So, while it's of *course* true that there are *some important similarities* to previous physical approaches, it's just *awfully* inaccurate to say my account is "a version of the traditional physical criterion."

In order to distinguish my view from more orthodox physical accounts, then, there's certainly *no need* for the next thing White offers, namely, a certain unobvious, novel interpretation of concepts central to my account. Further, when White claims that, in *defending* my view of survival, I'm *committed* to strange construals of its key concepts, he makes a claim that's incorrect. (To be sure, White *doesn't base* this false claim on his statement of, or on his characterization of, my account. Still, *motivation to take an interest in* the claim, White seems to think, may derive from some such quarters.)

To support this claim, what does White offer? First, if not foremost, we find this: As directly relevant to personal identity and to associated special concern, he attempts to distinguish two different senses of "survive," his *survive1* and *survive2*. Clearly, this attempt is futile. At least in uses directly relevant to my main topics, "survive" has just one sense, nearly as clear as it's simple. For its having this simple sense, nearly all "survive" does is provide us with a handy way to speak of a *single* person *existing* at *different* times. Thus, roughly, I *survive* (all of) a temporal period if, and only if, (1) I *exist* when the period *begins* and (2) I *exist* when, or even after, the period *ends*. So, at least for my topics, it's White's survive1 that, near enough, is the only sense in which to use "survive."

What are we to make of survive2? As White has it, this is a sense of "survive" that generates *substantive implications* about (a) rational motivation and (b) kinds of sacrifices. Being competent English speakers, we know that, relevant to my topics, there really isn't any such sense of "survive." Being charitable readers, we must take White to be *introducing a new* sense for "survive." But, what can *that* do? One of the myriad things it *can't* do is (help) show I'm saddled with peculiar commitments.

To be sure, and as White next notes, I accept that there *are examples* of a certain interesting sort: Found both with *physically well-based* fission and with the mid-range of certain *physically well-based* spectra, these are cases in which, although *I myself don't exist*, there *is someone* who is an *appropriate object* of a slight, natural, and rational *extension of* my concern for *myself*. But my acceptance of these cases, even as just described, *doesn't* derive from *my account of our survival* or, indeed, from *any account* of mine. Rather, it derives only from my being, like *many others*, a sensible and open-minded person. And, of course, *that* doesn't commit me to any *unusual construal* of any *concepts* at all.

Allowing for rough statements, White's next thought *seems* to be a certain "weirdly wondering challenge": Even while *granting* that my view of our survival is *correct*, he gives importance to this claim: That it remains *open* why I *should* (rationally) endure pain to avoid terrible torture, occurring in the future, to the person to whom I'm connected in the way this correct view specifies. Well, given *only* the correctness of my view that does remain open. But, of course, in *any sensible* discussion, that proposition will have some company. At the very least, we'll also be given, or we'll take, these thoughts: Just as is most rational, *I greatly care that I won't get* terrible torture. And, even as I rationally believe that (admittedly) correct view of my survival, I rationally believe that a person who'll be connected to me in *its* ways will be *me*. So, when we *sensibly combine* all the *relevant* propositions, then it *doesn't* remain *open* why I should (rationally) endure the much lesser early pain. For an awfully simple reason, the case is *closed*: I should endure it just so that, later, terrible *torture* won't befall *me*.

Unfortunately, similarly unsettling thoughts occur to many philosophers—in his comments, Swinburne, too, appears to be among them. Moreover, the *central* aspect of these thoughts isn't peculiar to matters concerning *our survival*. Rather, it just concerns looking at something in an unaccustomed, roundabout way, and then thinking that the thing seen is itself peculiarly remote. A simple example makes the *highly general* matter pretty clear: As you already know, of course, there are some people who just *love* cats, all *sorts* of cats. Now, I'll tell you another thing about these folks, *ever so closely related to* what you know already about them. They love *those entities that semantically satisfy our word "cat" and, as well, that satisfy the linguistic conventions that serve to determine the satisfaction-conditions of that word*. Well, the unsettling thought may occur, aren't *these* folks *mighty* peculiar! Unless they're somehow involved in a *rewarding language fetish*, one centering upon a certain *English word* and certain *linguistic conventions*, why should *anyone*, rationally, care about *those* entities? Well, despite some appearances to the contrary, these folks are perfectly normal. The reason they care about those unusually *specified* entities is as mundane as it's simple: Although *referred* to in a very roundabout way, *those entities*, every last one of them, are just the *cats*.

White's next attempt to help his claim is this: Even while noting my denial of any commitment to a coherence account of rational values, White says that, in large parts of my project, I (must) assume such a position. But what reason is there to think that? Although, doubtless, there's a *good explanation of why* White believes it, I'm confident that there's *no good reason to* think any such thing.

As I'm afraid, much of the explanation may lie with (some of) my own *presentation*: In trying to gain *wide acceptance* for certain of my arguments, I presented things in a certain *ecumenical way*. Just so, in the book I said things like this: Suppose that there are people some of whose key concepts, beliefs and values are quite different from ours, but whose whole psychology is just as coherent as ours. For example, coherent with the rest of their mentality, they prefer cheap, quick purely informational "teleportation" over expensive, slow, ordinary travel. Seeking *wide agreement on some* matters of rational choice and value, I then *granted* that, for *those* people, such a preference *might be* rational. But, as I thus ecumenically argued, *even if* that *might* be so—and I *never said* that it actually *was* so—nonetheless, for *us*, such a preference is *not* rational. For, *at the least*, there is clearly *this difference* between us and them: By contrast with the noted preference that *their* totality of attitudes might "indicate" for *them*, our *own different* total psychology will "indicate," for *us*, a quite *opposite* preference as most rational, namely, the preference for the expensive and slow, but genuine travel.

As I suspect, there are certain semantic facts that enabled my presentation to be widely appealing. Briefly and roughly, they're these: Owing to a certain *flexibility in the semantics* of "rational," we may employ the term to set contexts where the satisfaction of *lenient* conditions suffices for its *correct* application and, as *well*, we may employ it to set *stricter* contexts. Properly setting a lenient context, we can have it so that the satisfaction of certain *(quasi-)formal* conditions by a person's attitudes may suffice, near enough, for his desires, values, choices, etc. correctly to be called rational. In making my ecumenical presentation, perhaps I set a context where such a lenient use was in effect.

Of course, there's the other side of this story: Though not useful for my book's ecumenical presentation, there's *also* room to use "rational" more strictly, and *that* room is helpful for certain *other* things. For example, when used more strictly, often the term is employed to get "the authority of reason" behind values, etc. that the speaker *recognizes to be good* ones—or, for those less objectively inclined, behind values, etc. that the speaker *endorses*. Two simple examples clarify my point: (1) At least when I'm the one speaking, even on a very strict use, a person's deep basic desire for *loving relations* with others *is correctly* called rational. (2) But, at least when I'm speaking, on such a strict use, someone's basic desire to spend his life *collecting string* is *not* correctly called rational, no matter *how* well it may cohere with the rest of his psychology.

By now, it should be amply clear that, whatever my *presentations* of various arguments, there's nothing actually in my *view* of our survival, or in *any* of my *philosophical views*, that presupposes coherentism.

Having already taken so much space, I can't talk much about White's three offered flexibilities. Being *desperately* brief, I'll say this: By writing in a *certain sketchy way*, White makes it somewhat appealing to think that, even complying with all the dictates of rationality, there's quite a lot of leeway, for us, regarding our concepts, values, desires, choices, etc. Not being moved by his sketchy invitation, I say this: Concerning the *flexibility regarding the survival of others*, it's only if we agree to use "rational" most *leniently* that I'll agree that there is any such thing. Concerning the *flexibility regarding our future survival* and the *flexibility regrading our present survival*, I deny the existence of them both, just as White suspects. Why do I decline White's invitation? Is it because I'm *stubborn*; or is it because I hold certain *philosophical* views? Neither of those, it's just because, like you, I'm a pretty sensible guy.

Seeking to fill in details for White's sketchy invitation, I'm directly led to ask many questions. A few of them go like this: Given the impending radiation, if I resist the impending conceptual change and, consequently, I don't go in for the *taping with transplantation* itself, then, in good health, how much time will I have left? As against my actually expected forty more years, will it be only, say, *two weeks* that I'll have; or will it be, say, *twenty years*?

If it's *just two weeks*, then, very rationally, I'll opt *for* the taping, and so I certainly *won't resist* any changes of thought that *help* lead me into it. But that's *not owing* to any interesting feature of my *concern for myself*, *nor* to anything interesting about when it's rational to go in for *conceptual change*. Rather, it's just because, very rationally, I greatly care about certain *other* things, each as philosophically boring as this: I'm concerned that, largely deriving from my own current ideas and intentions, a very big book on ethics, which I've been working on for a couple of years, be completed and, then, that it be read, and enjoyed, by quite a few thoughtful people.

If it's *a full twenty years* that's left for me, then, along with resisting such changes of concepts as will help lead me into the fatal process, I'll very rationally resist the taping. Again, that's *not* because I greatly hate changes in my central concepts, nor anything like that. Boringly obvious, it's because, *very rationally indeed*, I greatly prefer to live to be at least a *fairly* old man than dying when just forty-eight years old.[4]

4. To my benefit, I've discussed all four comments, and my replies to them, with several people. In particular, I'm especially grateful to Keith DeRose and, above all, to John Carroll.

8

THE SURVIVAL OF
THE SENTIENT

1. Introduction: Ourselves and Sentient Others

In this quite modestly ambitious essay, I'll generally just assume that, for
the most part, our "scientifically informed" commonsense view of the
world is true. Just as it is with such unthinking things as planets, plates
and, I suppose, plants, too, so it also is with all earthly thinking beings,
from people to pigs and pigeons; each occupies a region of space,
however large or small, in which all are spatially related to each other.
Or, at least, so it is with the bodies of these beings. And, even as each of
these *ordinary entities* extends through some space, so, also, each endures
through some time. In line with that, each ordinary entity is at least very
largely, and is perhaps entirely, an *enduring physical* entity (which allows
that many might have certain properties that aren't purely physical
properties). Further, each ordinary enduring entity is *a physically complex*
entity: Not only is each composed of parts, but many of these parts,
whether or not absolutely all of them, are themselves enduring physical
entities, and many of *them* also are such physically complex continuing
entities.

When an ordinary entity undergoes a significant change, then, at
least generally, this change will involve changes concerning that entity's constituting physical parts, whether it be a rearrangement of (some
of) these parts, or a loss of parts, or a gain of parts, or whatever. Often,
the entity will still exist even after the change occurs. As we may well

suppose, this happens when, from two strokes of an ax, an ordinary log loses just a chip of wood. As we may then say, such a change conforms with the log's "persistence conditions." Somewhat less often, such an ordinary entity undergoes a change that means an end to it: When a bomb's explosion makes our log become just so many widely scattered motes of dust, the log will no longer exist. Such a momentous change *doesn't* conform with the log's persistence conditions.

Insofar as we may learn which changes involving a particular log conform with its persistence conditions, and which do not, we might learn a fair amount about what it is for a physically complex enduring entity to be that log. Perhaps pretty similarly, insofar as we may learn which changes involving *you* conform with *your persistence conditions*, and also which do not, we might learn a fair amount about what it is for a physically complex enduring entity to be *you*; and, presumably in parallel, we might learn what it is for *another* such complex entity to be *me*.

This learning is clearly a possibility for us, I'll suggest, should materialism be true, and should a weak form of dualism be true, where some concrete individuals, at least, have not only physical properties, but also some nonphysical mental properties. And, it may also be possible, I'll suggest, should the truth lie, instead, with a more substantial dualism, rather like Descartes' view, but one allowing, perhaps, there to be nonphysical minds that aren't personal minds, as with porcine minds, and canine, and feline.

Whatever the metaphysic we might favor, when inquiring into our persistence conditions we should seek to appreciate what's involved in a *philosophically adequate concept of ourselves*. As I'll even now suggest, such an adequate concept must be well suited for engagement with our central prudential thoughts and concerns, with what, in my *Identity, Consciousness and Value* (henceforth ICV), I called our *(broad) egocentric values*.[1] And, it must be well suited for engagement with our morality. Our appreciation of that may help us see, better than I saw in ICV, that an adequate concept of ourselves must be a psychological conception, perhaps the concept of a being who'll exist when, and only when, his mind does. This may be so *whatever* worldview may be true, whether materialistic, or dualistic, or idealistic, or what-have-you.[2]

---

1. In ICV, see pages 212–217. Henceforth, ICV's numbers will be (bracketed) in the text.

2. Owing largely to considerations concerning agency and the will, I'm now far more inclined toward a substantial dualism than when I wrote ICV and when, a couple of years later, I replied to a prominent dualist, Richard Swinburne, in a Book Symposium on ICV; see Swinburne (1992) and Unger (1992). Detailing these considerations would be the

A prompting cause of the present effort is the appearance of Eric Olson's valuable (1997) book, *The Human Animal: Personal Identity without Psychology* (henceforth THA). Using the label "The Psychological Approach" very broadly, Olson has it cover all the views on which our persistence is tied to the continuation of our psychology. In opposition to all such views, he forcefully advocates a Biological Approach:

> In place of the Psychological Approach I propose a radically nonpsy-chological account of our identity. What it takes for us to persist through time is . . . biological continuity: one survives just in case one's purely animal functions—metabolism, the capacity to breathe and circulate one's blood, and the like—continue. I would put biology in place of psychology, and one's biological life in place of one's mind, in determining what it takes for us to persist: a biological approach to personal identity.[3]

In much of what follows, I'll be arguing that, with the Biological Ap-proach, there can't possibly be any philosophically adequate view of our existence or persistence: As any conception of ourselves that's a bio-logical concept isn't (primarily) a mental conception, it won't comport well with central prudential thoughts and concerns, and also with our moral thinking. Even as either failure shows the inadequacy of a Bio-logical Approach to ourselves, with both there's an overwhelming case for a Psychological Approach.

In parallel, I'll argue that it's only a Psychological Approach, and not a Biological Approach, that's adequate for those *nonpersonal* sen-tient beings whom, in the normal course of events, will be found with typical living animals: Even if they be subpersonal entities, still,

---

work of another essay, much longer than the present paper. Due to the complex con-siderations, I'm now *at least somewhat* more inclined toward *any* view on which I'm not wholly constituted of parts each ontologically more basic than myself. So, it's important to me now that, for the most part, this paper's thoughts comport well with very many metaphysical conceptions.

3. THA, pages 16–17. [As with ICV, often THA's page numbers will be (bracketed) in the text.] Though failing to notice the intriguingly allied work of W. R. Carter, Olson does usefully observe on page 19 that, in recent decades, such a biological view, or a position much like his, has been advocated by at least these other able authors: Michael Ayers, Paul F. Snowdon, Judith J. Thomson, Bernard A. O. Williams, and Peter van Inwagen. Yet, on that very page, Olson says, "The Biological Approach has been strangely neglected in the literature (sic) on personal identity." If, along with the five philosophers he there notes, we count Olson himself, who'd already published several papers to this effect, and Carter, with even more such papers then published, we find at least seven able and active advocates in the recent literature. (Mentions of their relevant works constitute most of the present paper's References.) By my standards, this Approach has been *very* strangely neglected!

a philosophically adequate concept of such nonpersonal beings my feline pet, Felix, and your canine pet, Oscar, must closely parallel an adequate concept of ourselves.

Toward the essay's end, I'll float an extremely general thought about our commonsense metaphysic, about our ordinary ontology: Though this ontology recognizes many entities whose mentality is essential to their very existence, it recognizes *none* whose biology is truly essential. Perhaps there are *no ordinary entities*, I'll conjecture, for which the Biological Approach provides an adequate account.

2. Questions of Strict Survival, Vegetable Cases and Transplant Cases

After the book's Introduction, the body of *The Human Animal* (THA) begins with this paragraph:

> The topic of this book is our identity through time. What does it take for you and me to persist from one time to another? What sort of changes could one survive, and what would bring one's existence to an end? What makes it the case that some past or future being, rather than another, is you or I? (7)

As an early step in advocating a Biological answer to these opening questions, in the book's first section Olson presents a relevantly puzzling pair of cases. Apparently favoring the Biological Approach, there's first a "Vegetable Case;" and, apparently favoring the Psychological Approach, there's then a "Transplant Case."[4]

To do justice to the intriguing Vegetable Case, I quote Olson at some considerable length:

> Imagine that you fall into what physiologists call a persistent vegetative state. As a result of temporary heart failure, your brain is deprived of oxygen for ten minutes—... by which time the neurons of your cerebral cortex have died of anoxia. Because thought and consciousness are impossible unless the cortex is intact, and because brain cells do not regenerate, your higher mental functions are irretrievably lost. You will never again be able to remember the past, or plan for the future, or hear a loved one's voice, or be consciously aware of anything at all, ...
>
> The subcortical parts of the brain, however, ... are more resistant to damage from lack of blood that the cerebrum is, and they sometimes hold out and continue functioning even when the cerebrum has

---

4. The Vegetable Case is first presented on pages 7–9, the Transplant Case on 9–11.

been destroyed. Those ... sustain your "vegetative" functions such as respiration, circulation, digestion, and metabolism. Let us suppose that this happens to you. ... The result is a human animal that is as much like you as anything could be without having a mind.

The animal is not comatose. Coma is a sleep-like state; but a human vegetable has periods in which. ... It can respond to light and sound, but not in a purposeful way; it can move its eyes, but cannot follow objects consistently with them. ...

Neither is the animal "brain-dead," for those parts of its brain that maintain its vegetative functions remain fully intact. ... The patient (sic) is very much alive, at least in the biological sense in which oysters and oak trees are alive.

How can we be sure that the patient (sic) in this state has really lost all cognitive functions? ... there may be room for doubt. So imagine that you lapse into a persistent vegetative state *and* that as a result your higher cognitive functions are destroyed *and* that the loss is permanent. (THA, 7–8)

... My question in the Vegetable Case is whether the human animal that results when the cerebrum is destroyed is strictly and literally you, or whether it is no more you than a statue erected after your death would be you. Do you come to be a human vegetable, or do you cease to exist ... ? (THA, 9)

Both among people and within folks, there are conflicting responses to the Vegetable Case. Of most interest for Olson, there's the reaction that, even at the Case's end, you'll still exist (albeit as a "human vegetable").

When confronting a relevantly similar case right on the heels of the Vegetable example, we'll be pretty primed to respond to it, too, along a similarly Biological line.[5] And, it's right on those heels that Olson offers us his Transplant Case:

... Imagine that an ingenious surgeon removes your cerebrum ... and implants it into another head. ... Your cerebrum comes to be connected to that human being in just the way that it was once connected to the rest of you ...; and so it is able to function properly inside its new head just as it once functioned inside yours.

The result is a human being who is psychologically more or less exactly like you. ... On the other hand, she does not remember

5. Here, I may well rehearse these words from page 92 of my (1996): "Long examined by psychologists, but longer ignored by philosophers, the response someone makes to a given example can be greatly influenced by (her memory of) responses made to cases previously encountered. And, since folks want their responses to seem consistent, often the influence is greatest when the present case seems "essentially the same" as the just previous example."

anything that happened to the person into whose head your cerebrum was implanted, nor does she acquire anything of that person's character (at least at first).

The puzzle, as you have no doubt guessed, is what happens to you in this story (call it the "Transplant Case"). Are you the biologically living but empty-headed human being that has inherited your vegetative functions? Or are you the person who ends up with your cerebrum and your memories? (Or has the operation simply brought your existence to an end?) (THA, 9–10)

(Now, for such a Transplant Case to be most instructive, what's extracted from [the head of] the body must be fit for subserving what's central to mentality. But, as science seems to show, your upper brain, by itself, can't subserve conscious experience; rather, there must be some neural interaction between your upper and your lower brain. So, the presented example will be suppositionally enhanced; as may be safely done in the current context, we suppose this scientific appearance misleading and, in fact, your cerebrum's sufficient to subserve all your mentality.) Even though it's presented right after the Vegetable Case, most respond to the Transplant Case by thinking you are "the person who ends up with your cerebrum and your memories."[6]

With our responsive tendencies to Olson's two main cases being such a perplexingly messy batch of proclivities, there's much reason to think hard about the examples. What's more, we have yet more reason to think hard when we ponder passages in W. R. Carter's valuable recent (1990) paper, "Why Personal Identity is Animal Identity," which boldly begins:

6. Though it seems recently to have gone into a great and welcome decline, at least for several decades and right up through the 1980s, all too many philosophers have championed the view that, when thinking about hypothetical cases that are more than just quite modestly hypothetical, we'll be (almost) doomed to promote far more confusion than philosophical insight. Toward showing the prominence of that protracted pessimism, on page 200 of his (1984) *Reasons and Persons*, Derek Parfit presents this passage from W. V. Quine (1972): "The method of science fiction has its uses in philosophy, but . . . I wonder whether the limits of the method are properly heeded. To seek what is "logically required" for sameness of person under unprecedented circumstances is to suggest that words have some logical force beyond what our past needs have invested them with." But, such very wholesale pessimism has no real basis. Indeed, soon after offering the quote from Quine, Parfit makes quite a good case for the truth that there's at least as much to be lost from a great aversion to using far-fetched cases as from a dogged reliance on such examples.

Let me close this note with the observation that in my (1996) I give a great deal of thought, and space, to making the case that, though very far from always, quite often our responses to cases, including even actual cases, do more toward engendering confusion than providing instruction. So, I'm no friend of an *uncritical reliance* on cases, not even on *actual* cases.

We start with two felines, Felix and Jefferson, say, who are treated by the same veterinarian. A bizarre surgical blunder occurs and Felix's brain winds up in Jefferson's head. The resulting cat, call him Felixson, *looks* for all the world like Jefferson but *behaves* exactly like Felix (and not at all like Jefferson). The situation is complicated by the fact that Felix's debrained body is provided with enough transplanted tissue [tissue that does not come from Jefferson] so that it continues to live and function in feline-like ways. (Let's call this cat Felixless.) We are confronted here by certain questions of feline identity. To my way of thinking, these questions have rather obvious answers. It is true that Felixless is (=) Felix. Accordingly, it is false that Felixson is (=) Felix. My guess is that this assessment of the matter will encounter little, if any, serious resistance. This is surprising (to me), since many people take an entirely different view of a similar situation involving human rather than feline subjects.[7]

As we'll eventually see, the questions Carter thinks "have rather obvious answers" are actually subtly difficult questions. Now, we'll see these related words from Carter's paper:

... a psychological continuity account of feline identity looks so utterly implausible. Why is this? Well, perhaps it is because it is clear (isn't it) that cats are (attributively) *animals*. ... Since the term "Felix" refers to the animal..., and the term "Felixless" refers to the animal..., there is no denying that Felix is identical with Felixless. Accordingly, Felix is not identical with Felixson.... And why should the situation be different when we turn from feline identity to personal identify?

With at least some force, Carter *challenges* the thought that, in the Transplant Case, you are the being who ends up with your mentality, even as he *provides at least some* plausibility for the idea that (before getting new brain tissue) *you are* the (temporarily) mindless being that's inherited your vegetative functions, much as you (permanently) might be in the Vegetable Case.

Much more than favoring any particular Approach to ourselves, this section supports this importantly more general proposition: Whatever the right approach to the general conditions for the existence and persistence of Peter Unger, the personal sentient being, it will be, in all

7. For the quoted opening passage, Carter (1990) has two notes; the first just specifies salient ways in which Felix and Jefferson are qualitatively different, and the second just says what I've above place in [square brackets]. Right after the quoted material, Carter places in display a quote from page 78 of Sydney Shoemaker's contribution to Sydney Shoemaker and Richard Swinburne (1984), rightly acknowledges Shoemaker's seminal influence for our topics.

essentials, the same as the right approach for Felix Unger, the *nonpersonal* sentient being.

3. Thoughts and Concerns about Particular Sentient Beings: Avoiding Great Pain

Whatever else you may be, you must certainly be whatever it is that you think about when you think about *yourself*; if you're not *that*, you're nothing at all. Likewise, you must be whatever it is you *care* about when you care about *yourself*. On a most natural and central reading of these sentences, both are, of course, quite platitudinous. Yet, the second sentence, concerning your concern for yourself, might serve as a helpful reminder and guide, helpful toward our appreciating our deepest beliefs about ourselves. For, it may help us bear in mind these related sentences: When you truly care about yourself, then, whatever else may concern you, you must certainly care, and care very greatly, that *you'll not experience protracted excruciating pain;* when just *that* concern of yours is quite fully in force, it's from a *strictly egoistic* perspective that your concern flows. Conversely, and maybe most instructively, if there's someone that, from a strictly egoistic perspective, you *don't* care whether she'll experience such horrible great pain, then, as far as you can tell or believe, *that* person *isn't you*.

A concept of ourselves that comports well with these points concerning self-concern might be a philosophically adequate conception, as with, perhaps, a concept that's central to a Psychological Approach. By contrast, any concept that comports *poorly* with them, as with, perhaps, concepts central to a Biological Approach, can't be an adequate concept of ourselves.

The sensible thoughts just proposed may be sensibly generalized from us people to all sorts of sentient beings: So, flowing from a concern *for Oscar*, there might be no concern on your part whether a certain canine sentient being will feel great pain. But, then, as far as you can tell or believe, *that* sentient being *isn't Oscar*. And, any concept that comports poorly with *this* point, as *might* be true of any central to a Biological Approach, can't then be a philosophically adequate concept of Oscar, or of any canine sentient being.

Guided by this section's reflections, I'll look to use a "philosophical tool" first employed in ICV, the Avoidance of Future Great Pain Test.[8]

---

8. In ICV, it's first used in section 10 of chapter 1. Much later, in "How Presumptive Tests for Survival Beliefs May be Improved," which is section 5 of chapter 7, the avoidance

Eventually, I'll apply it to Olson's Vegetable Case, or to a most suitable enlargement of that example, and to Carter's Feline Transplant Case, or to a most suitable enlargement of that related example. By the time all that's done, few should be friends of a Biological Approach to the existence and persistence of any sentient beings, ourselves included, and many should favor a Psychological Approach. First, let's look at a case where it's easy to observe the test to be quite well employed.

To begin, suppose that, for no good reason, a bad surgeon replaces your heart with an artificial blood-pumper. About the person who has only such a plastic "heart," our central question is this: Is the person emerging from this operation *you*? For a most convincing answer to the question, we may employ our Test: With the choice flowing fully from your purely egoistic concern, will you choose to (have yourself) suffer *considerable pain* right before the operation takes place, if your *not* taking the bad hit up front will mean that, soon after the procedure's over, the person emerging from the operation then will suffer *far greater pain*? Yes; of course, you will. This response indicates that, as your strongest beliefs run, *you'll be* that person. Now, I'll try to use our Test to make progress with this essay's philosophically far more interesting questions.

Following Sydney Shoemaker's early work on the subject, in recent decades the literature on personal identity has seen many cases where there's the exchange of two people's bodies.[9] Much as was done in ICV, let's consider such a case involving you and, not someone qualitatively quite unlike you, but, rather, your precisely similar twin.[10] At this case's end, do *you* still exist? And, if so, *who are you*? Toward answering these questions reasonably, we may employ the Avoidance of Future Great Pain Test. Indeed, we may employ it twice over.

First, about the person who ends up with your original brain and a new body, we ask this question: With the choice flowing fully from your purely egoistic concern, will you choose to (have yourself) suffer

---

of future great pain test is refined. But, for most of what's to be done in the present essay, the refinements are more distracting than enlightening.

9. For the exchange case that starts this flurry of examples, see pages 23–25 of Shoemaker (1963). As he plainly realizes that case is very naturally regarded as a materially robust version of a famous case in Locke. Indeed, just before presenting his own example, on page 22 Shoemaker quotes Locke's remark that "should the soul of a prince, carrying with it the consciousness of the prince's past life, enter and inform the body of a cobbler, as soon deserted of his own soul, every one sees that he would be the same person with the prince, accountable only for the prince's actions," appending a footnote for Locke: *Essay*, I, 457. (In a footnote on his page 14, Shoemaker cites Locke's *Essay*.)

10. On page 103 of ICV, there's an exchange case that's thus qualitatively symmetrical. In some notable respects, the qualitative symmetry provides a useful purification.

considerable pain right before this case's wild processes begin if your *not* taking the bad hit up front will mean that, soon after all its processes are complete, the person then with your brain, and thus with your mind, will suffer *far greater pain?* Yes, of course, you will. Though not completely conclusive, this strongly indicates that, as we most deeply believe, throughout this case you're the person with your brain.[11]

Second, and yet more tellingly, we ask the parallel question: With the choice flowing fully from your purely egoistic concern, will you choose to (have yourself) suffer considerable pain right before this case's wild processes begin if your *not* taking the bad hit up front will mean that, soon after all its processes are complete, the person then with your body, but with your twin's mentally productive brain, then will suffer *far greater pain?* Not at all; from an egoistic basis, that's a *poor* choice. Though this response might not be absolutely decisive, it's quite conclusive enough. So, we conclude, well enough, that *you haven't even the slightest belief that here you're the being (with your healthy old body) who's inherited your vegetative biological functioning.*

At least as regards our commonsense view of ourselves, about the general conditions of our existence and persistence, this negative response may be indicating a very bad fate for the Biological Approach, in any of its versions. As well, it may also be indicating doom for any view on which the survival of our *bodies* is central to our own survival.

With parallel moves, we may see some indications that a Biological Approach might be no better for canine sentient beings than it is for personal sentient beings: We may see this with a slight variant on the case just considered, in which each occurrence of you is replaced by Oscar, each occurrence of your precise twin is replaced by an occurrence of his twin, and so on. About the canine being who ends up with Oscar's original brain and a new body, we ask this question: With the choice flowing fully from your *concern for Oscar,* will you choose to have him suffer considerable pain right before this case's wild processes begin if *his not* taking the bad hit up front will mean that, toward the end, the being then with his brain, and his mentality, will suffer *far greater pain?* Yes, of course, you will. And, this strongly indicates that, as we most deeply believe, here he'll be the being with his brain. Second,

11. What I've just been saying *doesn't* imply that, throughout all conceivable cases, or even all nomologically possible cases, you will be wherever your mentally productive brain will be. Indeed, in ICV there's an entire section, section 6 of chapter 5, that's devoted to providing argument for the contrary view, those arguments providing an affirmative answer to the section's interrogative title, "Might We Survive Brain Replacements and even Brain Exchanges?"

and again far more tellingly, we ask the parallel question: With the choice flowing fully from your *concern for him*, will you have him suffer *considerable pain* near the start if *his not* taking the bad hit up front will mean that, toward the end, the being then with his body, but not his mind, then will suffer *far greater pain*? Not at all. So, again well enough, we can conclude that *you haven't even the slightest belief that Oscar is the being (with his healthy old canine body) who has inherited Oscar's vegetative biological functioning.*

4. Can There Be an ENORMOUS Separation of Strict Survival and Relevant Concern?

For clear thinking about (our deepest beliefs about) the conditions of our existence and persistence, the points observed in the preceding section are, I think, of great importance: Where there is a being that's the proper object of your full-fledged egoistic concern, just there you yourself will be. And, most crucially, where there's no such "properly protected" being, there's no being that's you. But, some able philosophers have even so much as denied that importance, and many, I think, may fail to appreciate it.[12] Why?

In recent thinking about the relation between our transtemporal identity and our egoistic concern, there's much confusion engendered, I believe, from encounters with some salient and seductive hypothetical examples. Most salient among them may be a certain physically robust case of "symmetrical fission." Toward dispelling the confusion, and toward furthering clarity, let's now most thoughtfully encounter just such an example.

Suppose, now, that each half of your brain can do all that the whole does, as far as subserving mentality goes (and, we may now add, as far as sustaining biology goes). Further, suppose that, when we extract your brain from your body, and we nicely slice your brain in two, we'll have two new people, each relevantly just like you were right before this two-sided fission occurs. (Each of them may then be given a new body, each precisely like the old was at the time of extraction.) Further still, we'll agree that you're not either of the two who are so new.

From a rational concern for yourself, how much should you care about each of the two resulting people? Well, as we've agreed, neither is you; so, from just that concern, you shouldn't care a fig. But, then,

12. In section IV, chapter 3 of THA, Olson conspicuously denies this.

closely related to your purely egoistic concern, you might have other rational attitudes that are quite small and natural extensions of self-concern. And, then, we may ask: Flowing from at least some few of these related concernful attitudes, how much should you care about one of your fission descendants?

As it has seemed to many philosophers, you should care just as much as, even in the ordinary case of your own day to day survival, you today should care for yourself tomorrow. And, as it has seemed to some of these many, the salient lesson to be learned from that first thought is this second proposition: Questions regarding someone's strict survival can come apart from questions regarding his egoistic concern, and also his closely related concerns, quite *as far as you please*.

Even should all of the prior paragraph hold true, a thought that seems nearly as absurd as it's extravagant, there still might be no reason whatever to think that these questions can come apart so enormously that, from concerns much like purely egoistic attitudes, it may be natural, or rational, for us to care about beings with whom we have no substantial mental connection. But, what's needed to give some plausibility to the Biological Approach is precisely some reason to think just that. And, as it certainly seems, the prospects here are as bleak as can be.

Suppose that, flowing from your own egoistic concern, or even from any relevantly small extension thereof, you haven't even the least concern whether a certain being will experience terrible pain. Well, while that being might then be a certain horse, perhaps somewhere in Australia, or even a certain person, perhaps a young girl in Africa, one thing of which we can be quite confident is that, as far as you know or believe, *that* being *isn't you*. Perfectly parallel points hold for other sentient beings: Suppose that, flowing from your concern for *Oscar*, you haven't even the least concern whether a certain being will experience terrible pain. Now, while that being might then be the President of France, we can be quite certain that, as far as you know or believe, *that* being *isn't Oscar*.

5. A Complementary Pain Test Confirms Our Avoidance of Great Pain Test

Because we're hardly omniscient, and we're not even close to being perfectly logical or rational, it's good to see that, as a check on our results with the Avoidance of Great Pain Test, we may appropriately employ a logically related test, even a *complementary* test, and observe the results that then obtain. Just so, we'll now look to apply, most relevantly, a philosophical tool that may well be called the *Sparing from* Future Great Pain Test.[13]

So, let's return to consider the body-exchange (or, as the Biological Approach would have it, the brain-exchange) between Oscar and his precisely similar twin. As we've supposed, at this case's end there'll be one canine being with Oscar's original brain and mind, though little of his biological structures and processes, and there'll be another with another canine being's original brain-based mentality, and a great deal of Oscar's biological structures and their continuing processes. About all of that, you've never had even the least choice or influence.

In application to such a nicely relevant case, our Sparing from Future Great Pain Test directs that, always to be flowing (as closely as possible) from your concern for Oscar, your choice is to be just this choice: Shortly after awakening from the operations just envisioned, one of the two canine beings will experience much excruciating pain and the other will be spared from feeling even any pain at all. You are to choose, perhaps even before the operations are performed, which of the resulting beings suffers such great pain and which of the canines is spared. Very rationally you will choose for the canine with Oscar's original brain, and Oscar's canine mind, to be spared, and for the torture to go to the other resulting canine. For, your reasoning, evidently, is every bit as appropriate as it's simple: The former canine is Oscar, the being about whom you're here so especially concerned; the latter is another sentient being.[14]

With simple variations, we may strengthen the probative value of our Sparing Test. For example, we may suppose that your choice is between (1) sparing the being with Oscar's old brain the infliction of severe pain for a certain significant period and letting the being with his old body suffer *far more* severe pain for a *far greater* period and (2) sparing the being with his old body that *far worse* severe pain and letting the one with his old brain suffer that *far less bad* pain. With the concern being for Oscar, this great imbalance of pain makes no difference; just as surely as before, you choose (1), sparing the one with

13. In ICV I used this test rather rarely. Thus, till now, it's been anonymous.

14. Though the examples are pretty far-fetched, it's very clear, and it's perfectly determinate, what is the truth of the salient matters in these cases. Indeed, the salient matters are very nearly as clear as with cases of *heart*-exchange: When there's the exchange of hearts between you and a qualitatively identical other person, it's extremely clear, and of course perfectly determinate, who's who throughout and, in later stages, who's acquiring which heart. And, that's hardly any clearer right now than it was years before the first (successful) heart transplant operation, when it was (already) very clear, and perfectly determinate, who'd survive in the event of such a (successful) operation.

Oscar's brain-based mind. So, this now seems very clear: It's just that canine being that, as far as you really believe, is actually Oscar.

Now, if we were perfectly logical and rational, it would be a foregone conclusion that these responses with the Sparing Test would comport with those previously elicited with our Avoidance Test. But, of course, we're not perfectly logical or rational. So, while the observed agreement was at least somewhat to be expected, it wasn't a foregone conclusion. Thus, the results obtained with our truly complementary test confirm those obtained with our previous philosophical tool. So, in our inquiry, we'll employ them both.

6. Clear Moral Thinking about Particular Sentient Beings

Early on, I said that, just as much as for engagement with our central prudential thoughts and concerns, a philosophically adequate concept of ourselves must be well suited for engagement with our morality. In a brief treatment of the issue, I'll show why that should be so.

As the progress of our project suggests strongly, many of our moral thoughts regarding you and me will regard, just as well, Oscar and Felix. Then, at a bare minimum, an adequate concept of ourselves must engage morality in the way that's well done, as well, by a philosophically adequate concept of a particular sentient being.

Suppose that I've solemnly promised *you*, a moral agent, to look out for (the well-being of) your son, Al, who's another moral agent, and also to look out for (the well-being of) your sentient canine pet, Oscar, who's not a moral agent. Then, in the normal run of things, I'll have incurred a moral obligation, first, to look out for Al, and, second, to look out for Oscar. Let's focus on this second obligation.

Going philosophically hypothetical, suppose that some dastardly superscientists have produced a precise duplicate of Oscar, one Oscarnew, and, shortly thereafter, they've taken Oscar's brain and nicely placed it in Oscarnew's debrained body, and vice versa, with the philosophically expected result. Finally, we suppose that they force, on me, this instance of our Sparing Test. I must choose between (1) having terrible pain inflicted on the being with Oscar's original brain—still subserving Oscar's mind—in Oscarnew's original body and sparing from pain the being with Oscarnew's brain—still subserving Oscarnew's mind—in Oscar's body and (2) having terrible pain inflicted on the being with Oscarnew's brain in Oscar's body and sparing the being with Oscar's brain in Oscarnew's body. Flowing from my obligation to keep my promise to you, what should I do? As we deeply believe, I morally must choose (2) over (1). What does that suggest? Contrary to the Biological Approach, it suggest that, as we deeply believe, Oscar will be where his original brain is still subserving his mind.

As it is here with Oscar, so it is with Al. And, so it will be with us, too. As with any sentient beings, a philosophically adequate concept of ourselves, one well suited for engagement with morality, must be, primarily and essentially, a psychological conception. So, as those suitably sensitive to moral matters should agree, a Psychological Approach is very far superior to a Biological Approach even for the likes of Oscar and Felix, let alone for you and me.

7. Properly Painful Problems with Human Vegetables, and with Feline Vegetables

As I'm suspecting, by now most will indeed agree that, at least for such personal sentient beings as ourselves, a Psychological Approach is quite as appropriate as a Biological Approach is irrelevant. But, even if there's very widespread agreement on the matter, it's still well worth resolving, I think, some problems, or puzzlement, whose treatment we've deferred. Among this unfinished business, perhaps the most salient task is to provide a satisfactory treatment for Olson's intriguing Vegetable Case. Anyhow, to that task, we'll now turn.

As with other examples relevant to our central topic, for a treatment that's revealing we should use one of our Pain Tests. But, as a being in persistent vegetative state hasn't any capacity to feel any pain, how can we apply even our Avoidance of Pain Test? Initially at least, that seems a tall order. As things turn out, the job may be done rather well.

Toward that end, we make these suppositions: Within the next month, you'll have just such a horrible temporary heart failure that, as your brain will be deprived of oxygen for ten minutes, your cerebral cortex will die of anoxia; consequently, you'll "become a human vegetable." As you also know, there'll then be extracted, from the head of the "vegetative animal," its dead (upper) brain. And, into the continuously living "debrained body," there'll be well implanted a suitable living (upper) brain: Perhaps even coming into existence via a "statistical miracle," but, in any case, this will be a brain made of matter quite distinct from any that ever served toward constituting you. At the same time, this implant will be precisely similar to your (upper) brain, as it was when last it subserved your mentality. By the end of this sequence, there'll be a person with your original body, who's inherited your biology, though there'll be nobody who's inherited your mentality. While this person's mind will be precisely similar to yours, in its last moments of existence, it will be a numerically different normal mind. As with anyone with a normal mind, this person can certainly suffer terrible pain.

With such suitable suppositions made, there's an Aptly Enlarged Vegetable Case. And, with this Enlarged Case, there's ready to hand, I think, a revealing employment of our Avoidance of Future Great Pain Test: From your egoistic concerns, at the beginning you are to choose between (1) your suffering some significant pain, before a human vegetable's in the situation, so that, near the sequence's end, the person with the new (upper) brain suffers no pain at all and (2) your suffering no early pain and having it that, near the end, that person suffers terrible torture. Rationally, you choose (2) over (1). This choice shows that, as far as you know or believe, you *won't* be the entity that's inherited your biology.

It's still a "logical possibility," let's agree, that, after the anoxia but before the implantation of a new living upper brain, you were an insensate human vegetable. Then, just with that vegetable's receiving just such a new brain, you ceased to exist. But, really, is any of that even the least bit plausible? Are we really to believe that, though it's possible for you to come to have *no* mind, what's impossible is for such a mindless *you* to survive your coming to *have a mind*? Such a suggestion as that, I'll suggest, is quite an absurd idea.

From Human Vegetable Cases, there's really no case to be made for a Biological Approach to *ourselves*. And, from Feline Vegetable Cases, as may happen with my sentient Felix, there's nothing to be gained for a Biological Approach to *nonpersonal sentient* beings, as an Aptly Enlarged Feline Vegetable Case can help us easily see.

Sensibly, we may extrapolate from our recent experiences: The more we're free from confusions about sentient beings, saliently including ourselves, the less there'll even seem to be said for a Biological Approach to beings that must have minds.[15] Nor will there seem anything significantly favoring a "Bodily Approach" to ourselves, or to

---

15. As our treatment of Vegetable cases also shows, there's also precious little to be gained from hybrid approaches that feature biological continuity as an even reasonably central element. For example, we might consider a "closest continuer" view according to which, whenever suitable psychology is present, the mentality dictates the conditions of our survival, but, when it's absent, biological continuity might suffice for our survival. What we just said for the Biological Approach itself, we may say, apparently with equal justice, for such hybrid approaches: The more we're free from confusions about our existence and persistence, the less there'll even seem to be said for them. For the main point of this note, I'm grateful to Kit Fine.

nonpersonal mental others. Now, without going hypothetical in a way that's utterly wild, it may be impossible to take a case with a *completely dead* human, wholly devoid of life as well as mind, and to enlarge it so that our Pain Tests can be revealingly applied. But, so what: If a *living* mindless human body won't ever be one of us, and won't even ever subserve one of us, a *dead* mindless body will hardly do better. And, again, what's true of you and me also holds for Oscar and Felix.

By this point, we've seen more than enough, I think, to do a good job with what may be the sole remaining salient piece of unfinished business, namely, the provision of a satisfactory treatment for Carter's Feline Transplant Case. For, what does this case involve, if not a feline vegetable, an insensate Felixless obtained from the sentient Felix, by the extraction of that feline being's (upper) brain? According to Carter, though he has no mentality at all, still Felixless is (=) Felix, because the mindless entity's inherited the biology that supported, or subserved, the sentient being. But, Felixless really isn't Felix, as our recent reasoning revealed.

We've just taken good care of what might well be called "the harder of the two main halves" of Carter's Transplant Case. The easier half concerns what we are to make of Carter's Felixson, a feline being who results from transplanting Felix's brain into the debrained body resulting from extracting a feline brain from one Jefferson; at the case's start, this Jefferson is another normal feline sentient being, who's wholly distinct from Felix. In either of two ways, our Avoidance Test can show that (as far as we know or believe) Felixson is Felix (and he's not Jefferson). To the most energetic reader, I leave all that as an exercise.

8. People and Seople

On our "scientifically informed" commonsense view of things, your psychology is realized in, or it's at least subserved by, your brain: If there's someone else who's physically precisely similar to you, then *his* mentality will be realized only in *his* brain and *yours* will be subserved only by *yours*. There will be this numerical difference of the two mentalities, of the two minds, even if the distinct brains that subserve the two are precisely similar in every detail. And, if your mentality ceases to exist, then you yourself will cease to exist, even though your "duplicate" may continue to exist.

Equally on this commonsense view, though quite completely against the "vivisectionist" view of Descartes, the brain of Oscar, your beloved canine pet, realizes *Oscar's* psychology, or at least it subserves the mentality of that canine sentient being: If there's a canine who's physically precisely similar to Oscar, and wholly distinct from Oscar, there will be a numerical difference of the two minds, even if the canine mentalities are qualitatively quite the same. And, if his mentality ceases to exist, then Oscar himself will cease to exist, even though his "duplicate" may continue to exist.

Now, even while our commonsense view has these parallels be quite deep commonalities, our common language might lack a sortal common noun that serves nicely to highlight them for us, so that, for such central issues as this essay's main questions, we're prompted to take an essentially parallel approach to all sentient beings, us people being just some among many. In what's meant to be a sensibly progressive spirit, let me introduce a new English sortal noun, "serson," whose meaning is the same as the phrase "sentient being," and whose most colloquial plural is "seople." (As well as having such new nouns, we may have correlative new words, saliently including new quantifier words. For example, even if "everyone" doesn't include, in its proper reference, Oscar and Felix, we may have "everyane"—pronounced EVERYWANE— properly include them, just as properly as it will include you and me.)

With these terms, we may progressively express propositions that, even as they concern our main topics, feature centrally in our commonsense view of things: Every earthly serson, and not just every earthly person, has both a body and a mind. And, while it's *not* true that an earthly serson will exist just exactly in case her body exists, it *is* true that any serson at all, whether earthly or not, will exist when, and only when, her mind exists. Following from the foregoing, some such sentences as these should be treated more as commonplace thoughts than contentious ideas, both by materialists and by commonsensical dualists: If there's only a barely developed organic body extant, and there's not yet any mind even so much as barely subserved by the body, as with an early fetus, then, in such a mentally insignificant situation, there's really no serson existing, neither personal nor even nonpersonal. [In ICV I left it as an open question whether there might have been an (earlier) time when I wasn't a person and, even, when I lacked all capacity for thought and feeling. (5–6) In THA Olson argues that, given my book's main views, there's no good way for me to have us people, or any seople, be (identical with) any such wholly mindless things. (81–85) Agreeing now with Olson, in the present essay I no longer leave that question open; on my present position, a more complete view, I never was any mindless early fetus, nor was sentient Oscar ever any mindless canine fetus.] By contrast with such wholly mindless early episodes, if there's a more developed body that's subserving a mind, even a quite rudimentary mind, then there'll be a serson. And, if it comes to pass that there's only our serson's body extant, with the mind no longer existing, then this serson will no longer exist.

When a serson is alive and well, what's the relation between the serson himself and, on the other hand, his body?

On what I take to be a pretty appealing substantial dualist view, but a view that might be at least as troubling as it's appealing, a serson's body will causally support, and subserve, the serson's immaterial mind. What's more, and what may be metaphysically even a bit more basic, just when providing just such support, the serson's body will support the immaterial being that's the serson himself. Further, Oscar won't have any spatial extension and, perhaps, that immaterial being won't even have any spatial location. In ways we might never well understand, immaterial Oscar may be, nonetheless, quite directly affected by, and he may quite directly affect, certain physical entities, perhaps certain parts of a certain brain.

On what I take to be a pretty appealing materialist view, but perhaps also a view as troubling as it's appealing, a serson and his body will be spatially coincident entities; with each in the very same space as the other at the very same time, the very same matter will serve to constitute each of the two distinct material entities. So, even as Oscar may now be alive and well, he and his body will be different material complexes, though each is composed of exactly the same matter, and each occupies precisely the same space. On a pretty commonsensical materialist view, a rather plausible reckoning of such ordinary entities will have that be so, even if, perhaps, that reckoning is hardly free of difficulties. How, or why, will that be so? As with you and me, Oscar's *persistence conditions* differ from those of his body. To see what that rather technical sentence says, I'll aim to display its main implications, in the next section, while providing the sentence with intuitive support.

9. A Serson and His Body Are Distinct Entities

Even if it subserves mentality, as it now does, your brain is just one of several salient organs in your body that, together with various other bodily parts, serve to constitute the body as a whole. Accordingly, whether your body's dead or alive, in this regard, at least, the relation between your brain and your body is very like that between your heart and your body, and very like that obtaining between your liver and that whole human body. It's no surprise, then, that, if any single one of these organs is removed from the bodily whole, and then is even annihilated, your body will still exist. Of course, the same holds for other serson's bodies, as with Oscar's.

Along with some philosophically familiar thoughts, and some ideas here previously presented, those intuitive propositions suggest a certain pair of cases. While each example is but a slight variant on the other, the lesson that one suggests is, in an obvious way, quite the opposite of, and quite a nice complement of, the lesson we may learn from the other.

Continuing to employ the suppositions that have served us so well so far, we'll start with the Brain Explosion Case: Right out of sentient Oscar's skull, some strangely fanatical scientists remove his (upper) brain, and they place it in the philosophically familiar stimulatory vat. While in this vat, that living brain will subserve just as rich a stream of conscious experience as ever it did when in the serson's head. At the same time, and still lying on a laboratory table, (the rest of) Oscar's body, as it's placed on a highly effective life-support system, remains alive, though it can't, of course, subserve mentality.[16] For a while all is pretty peaceful, until an exploding bomb destroys the brain in the vat, the vat itself, and even the building in which the vat is housed. In this explosion, the matter that served to compose Oscar's brain is so utterly wrenched apart, and the tiny bits are so fully intermingled with so much other dust from the explosion, that there's not even any significant chance of anything like a relevant reversal ever occurring. Meanwhile, (the rest of) your canine serson's body remains intact, and even alive.

At the end of this Brain Explosion Case, Oscar, the salient serson, no longer exists. (On a materialistic metaphysic, and on plausible forms of dualism, that will be so.) At the same time, Oscar's body continues to exist. On the most relevant understanding of the terms employed, it's most reasonable to accept both sentences. So, Oscar's body can survive the termination of Oscar himself.

It's time to turn to the complementary example, the Body Explosion Case. From the example's start right up to the time when "all is pretty peaceful," things are just as in the previous case, with Oscar's brain in a vat in one area and, at a distance, his living body on a lab table.

---

16. When the serson's active brain is way over there and (the rest of) his healthy body is right nearby here, is the serson simply over there, a quite cohesive entity, or he is partly there and partly here, a rather scattered entity? And, what of his body? In this essay, I mean to leave open what are the answers to these questions.

As I'm inclined to believe, the serson himself is, in the envisaged situation, a quite cohesive entity that's just where his mentally productive brain is, way over there. As I'm also inclined to think, the body is also quite cohesive, but it's right nearby here, not at all where the brain is. But, to support these inclinations, at all well, rather complex arguments may be requited. So, in this essay, I set them both aside.

Then, an exploding bomb destroys (the rest of) the body on the table, the table itself, and the whole lab building. In this explosion, the matter that served to compose (the rest of) Oscar's body is so utterly wrenched apart, and the tiny bits so fully intermingled with so much other dust, that there's not even any significant chance of anything like a relevant reversal. Meanwhile, your canine serson's brain continues to subserve his mind.

At the end of this Body Explosion Case, the salient serson's body no longer exists. At the same time, Oscar himself continues to exist. On the most relevant understanding of our terms, Oscar can survive the termination of Oscar's body.

Now, if Oscar could survive the cessation of his body, but Oscar's body couldn't survive Oscar's own cessation, then, while we should think the two were different, we might well think that, while Oscar himself was a genuine entity, his body had some lesser ontological status. And, in such an event, perhaps we shouldn't think that, with Oscar and his body, we have two distinct entities. But, as we saw just before, Oscar's body *can* survive Oscar's own cessation, just as Oscar can survive his body's cessation. So, apparently, we do quite well to think that, inasmuch as each has persistence conditions so utterly different from the other's, sentient Oscar is one being and, though spatially and materially coincident with him, Oscar's body is quite another entity. Apparently and intuitively, even if we should accept a most materialistic version of our common-sense metaphysic, we should think that much to be true.

A. Finessing Questions about Materially Coincident Entities

At least to my mind, sometimes it's puzzling, to put the point mildly, how there could be two quite different entities each composed of the very same matter, in the very same space, at the very same time, and not just one entity that we may think of in two quite different ways. But, for two related reasons, this paper's not the place to dwell on any such puzzle.

First, and as was stated at its outset, we're here just assuming that, for the most part, our "scientifically informed" commonsense view of the world is true. And, in dwelling on our puzzle, we might well be calling into question what's here our working hypothesis, rather than seeing what work we can do within the compass of what seems the accepted view.

Second, and as is familiar in philosophy, the puzzle about the possibility of materially coincident entities is a quite general puzzle, hardly peculiar to questions about embodied seople and their bodies: In illustration, consider a certain ball, we'll call it "Barry," and a certain spherical piece of brass, we'll call it "Patty," each composed of the very same brass, in the very same place, throughout all the time of their existence. (The brazen alloy first comes to exist in the very form in which it composes Patty and Barry and, later, it ceases to exist suddenly, suddenly composing neither.) Yet, even as Barry and Patty have quite different persistence conditions, there are here, it seems, two quite distinct entities. So, on the one side, if the brass were forced through a wire extruder, that brass would come to compose a long thin brass wire and no ball at all. In such an event, it seems, we'd have the same *piece* of brass as before, and Patty would still exist, but Barry wouldn't exist. And, on the other side, we might have gradually replaced our ball's brass, bit by tiny bit, by congruous bits of gold, widely scattering all our brass. In such a very different event, it seems, we'd have the same *ball* as before, and Barry would still exist, but our piece of brass, our Patty, wouldn't still exist.

As is proper with this quite modestly ambitious essay, we leave for other inquiries such a general problem as the puzzle about the possibility of materially coincident entities. As is also proper, we set aside other puzzles, more or less related, that may similarly seem to call into question, more or less effectively, our commonsense view of the world.

10. Reference and Existence, Appearance and Reality

For what's really a very bad reason, many of my paper's points might be denied by philosophers, perhaps especially by materialists, who may be unduly impressed by what sometimes seem plain expressions of common sense in ordinary discourse. For example, after my mind no longer exists and there's only my living body in a vegetative state, someone may point at what's in that state and say, apparently with complete propriety, "There's Peter Unger." Doesn't that serve to indicate that, even if my mind no longer exists, I can still exist? And, isn't that a strong point in favor of a Biological Approach to my existence and persistence?

Well, quite the same may be done, apparently, when there's only my dead body in the situation. So, such apparently ordinary and proper episodes won't provide any strong points, it seems clear, in favor of a Biological Approach to me. But, then, mightn't they provide a strong point in favor of a Bodily Approach to my existence and persistence, on which I may still exist not only without my mind, or any mind, but also without my biological life, or any such life? No; it does not.

Very often, we refer to one entity, conveniently, obliquely and indirectly, by more directly referring to another, with which the first is, especially in the context of the current discourse, readily associated. Now, sometimes the discrepancy between the two referents is blatantly obvious. This happens when we say of a bus driver that she's over fifteen feet high, and unable to get through a certain tunnel, referring not only to her but, less directly and more truthfully, to the bus that she drives. Now, when the discrepancies are that blatant, there's little tendency to take our direct remark, about the driver herself, to be a literal statement that's really true; rather, it's only some implied statements, like the statement that a certain bus is over fifteen feet high, that we take to be true.

Other times, however, the discrepancy is less blatant. That happens, I'll suggest, with (standard uses of) sentences like "As Uncle Joe is dead, we should get him off the floor and out of the house, so that we can put some nice big potted plant right where he is" and "As Oscar is dead, we should get him off the floor and out of the house, so that we can put some nice big potted plant right where he is." Though not so blatantly obvious, in these sentence's closing clauses there's reference to more than just the relevant seople themselves; rather indirectly, there may be a reference to the seople's bodies, or to their remains, or to both of the foregoing, or to yet something else that's fit for spatial removal. And, while the standardly expressed statement about the moving of the seople themselves might not be true, there may then be such suitable implied statements, about the moving of their bodies, and about the moving of their remains, that are perfectly true. And, the discrepancy just stressed will be made yet more evident when we observe such closely related sentences as "Billions of years after Uncle Joe's death, he'll be interstellar dust" and "Billions of years after Oscar's death, he'll be interstellar dust."

What is more, paralleling the "apparent facts of reference" regarding ourselves, there are such apparent facts regarding our bodies. Thus, after I'm dead, you may point at my corpse and say "There's Peter Unger's body;" and, not only may what you say be in perfect conversational order, but, as well, it may be perfectly true. Now, a sentence like "Billions of years after it decays, Unger's body will be interstellar dust" also looks to be in perfect order. But, when standardly uttering such an orderly sentence, will you be saying what's true? Of course, not.

Now, suppose that, after I die, my corpse is placed in a spaceship and, when the ship is somewhere between Mars and Jupiter, the spaceship explodes, along with all its salient contents, including my body. Pointing at an apt place between Mars and Jupiter, when night next comes you may say "There's Peter Unger's body;" and, what you say may be in perfect conversational order. But, is what you say really true; does my body really still exist? Not a chance. By contrast, it might well be that my *remains* still exist and, mainly between Mars and Jupiter, they're widely scattered.

Over a wide range of referential discourse, what may first look to be plain facts may come to look, much more realistically, to be nothing factual at all.

11. Seople (Conceptually) Can Survive the Loss of Their Biological Lives

Absent sufficient psychological continuity, biological continuity isn't sufficient for the continued existence of sentient beings, neither people, like you and me, nor nonpersonal seople like Oscar and Felix. But, is biological continuity *necessary* for our survival? Well, insofar as it's needed for subserving the serson's mind it may be necessary. But, then, this biology's needed only causally, or quasi-causally; it's not most basically necessary, as the persistence of the serson's mind is necessary, for the survival of the sentient being.

As a philosophically adequate concept of the sentient canine who is Oscar centers on his sentience, it follows that the concept won't place any biological requirements on Oscar, provided only that there's no entailment from his sentience to anything biological. And, as it certainly seems, there isn't any such entailment. To confirm this appearance, it may be useful to reflect on an example that's just an adaptation, to the canine situation, of a case concerning people that, perhaps a bit too timidly, I offered in ICV. (122) So, suppose that very gradually, over the course of a year, the neurons of Oscar's brain are replaced by inorganic entities, but always in such a way that, from one day to the next, there's precious little effect on his thought and feeling. (If the supposed proposition conflicts with actual natural laws, then, suppose that there's a change in the laws so that, in consequence, there's no longer any conflict.) During the year, there's a serson whose brain, partly natural and organic, and partly artificial and inorganic, continues to subserve Oscar's mind, including his conscious thoughts and feelings. By the end of this year, there's a serson whose entirely inorganic brain, we're supposing, still subserves the nonpersonal mind of sentient Oscar. Finally, suppose that this mentally productive brain is transplanted into a suitable inorganic "canine" body, so that the nonbiological whole is able to engage with his environment, and experience this active engagement, just as effectively, and just as vividly, as the original organic Oscar ever did.

From your concern for Oscar himself, supposing that also to continue, you choose lesser early pain for Oscar, even though he's then organic, rather than much greater later pain to be inflicted on the inorganic being we've just been supposing. As this indicates, we take this later being to be the very same sentient being that was sentient Oscar at the case's start; though he's no longer biologically alive, your nonpersonal serson survives.

12. Are There Any Ordinary Entities That Can't Survive Losing Their Biological Lives?

On our ordinary metaphysic, many of the things we recognize are in fact alive; they all share the property of *being alive*, we may say, where that property's understood to be a purely biological attribute, a property without any psychological implications. And, among these living entities, there are many that, so far as we know and believe, haven't even the least capacity for thought or experience. These insensate ordinary entities include many organisms, as with a tree outside my window that we may conveniently call *Trudy*, as well as many that are far from ever being organisms, as with a skin cell of yours that we may call *Sylvia*.

As has happened with ever so many trees, some day Trudy will die. When that happens, we may agree, Trudy will no longer be alive; but, will Trudy no longer exist? On our commonsense metaphysic, at least, it seems that Trudy may still exist, even as, on this common view, there may exist, on earth right now, very many dead trees that were once alive. (Now, when a dead tree undergoes a great deal of decay, and almost all its matter becomes widely dispersed, then, in the typical case, at least, the tree will no longer exist. So, should *all that* happen to Trudy, and not just the cessation of her (biological) life, then Trudy will no longer exist. And, should an exploding bomb blow our living Trudy sky high, as we lately imagined happened with Oscar's living body, then, again, Trudy will no longer exist. But, then, apparently, it will not be simply by ending Trudy's (biological) life that the bomb will end Trudy's existence.) Perhaps it might be that, on our common metaphysic, Trudy's being alive isn't essential to Trudy's existence, no more than it's essential to the continued existence of Oscar's body that it remain alive.

As has happened with ever so many cells, some day Sylvia will die. When that happens, Sylvia will no longer be alive, we may agree; but, will Sylvia no longer exist? Perhaps it might be that, on our commonsense metaphysic, Sylvia will still exist, even as it seems that, on your feet right now, there really are many dead cells that were once alive.

Without having confidence in the proposed propositions, I've suggested some thoughts for the serious consideration of contemporary philosophers. Continuing to assume our commonsense metaphysic is

generally correct, I'll just as neutrally propose a few further propositions.

First, there's this quite general statement: With *being alive* not essential even for the likes of Trudy and Sylvia, there *aren't any* ordinary
things, or things (of a sort) ordinarily recognized by us, for which
having that property is crucial to their existence.

Second, and more cautiously, there's this more specific statement:
It's not essential to the continued existence of any *animals* that they
continue to be alive.

For the moment, let's suppose that this second proposition is true.
Then, even if it may be easy to distinguish conceptually between sentient
Oscar and his body, it might be impossible to distinguish between Oscar's body, which might also bear Oscar's name, and a certain canine
animal, which might *also* be an Oscar. So, then, it just might be that,
while there's one Oscar who's so much as a sentient being, there's another, materially coincident with him, that's both a canine animal and a
canine body. On the other hand, it may still be possible to distinguish
between Oscar the canine body and Oscar the canine animal, even if, as
we're supposing, neither need be alive. Then, there'll be (at least) three
materially coincident Oscars, the serson, the animal and the body.
Sometimes inclined even toward this somewhat suspicious last alternative, I leave further thinking on these matters to future investigations.

13. Maintaining an Adequate Philosophical Perspective on Ourselves

When attempting ambitious philosophical work, we may fail to maintain
an adequate philosophical perspective: For example, we may come to
think that, when properly concerned for ourselves, what we should be
most concerned for are certain bodies, or animals, or organisms, that
may have not even the least capacity for any thought or feeling at all. Far
from bettering our understanding of ourselves, we've then quite lost
sight of ourselves. To better our understanding, we must, at the very
least, maintain an adequate philosophical perspective on ourselves.
And, for that, we must continue to think of ourselves as being, most
essentially, thinking and feeling individuals.[17]

17. Many people have been helpful toward getting this paper to be more useful and
less riddled with error. Very helpful indeed have been David Barnett, John Carroll,
W. R. Carter, John Gibbons, John Heil, Peter Kung, Jeff McMahan, Michael Lockwood,
Eric Olson, Michael Rea, Sydney Shoemaker and, most especially, Mark Bajakian and Kit
Fine. To such helpful sentient beings, I'm duly grateful and thankful.

References

[1] Ayers, Michael. 1990. *Locke*, Vol.2. London: Routledge.

[2] Carter, William R. 1980. "Once and Future Persons," *American Philosophical Quarterly* 17: 61–66.

[3] ———. 1982. "Do Zygotes Become People?" *Mind* XCI: 77–95.

[4] ———. 1988. "Our Bodies, Our Selves," *Australasian Journal of Philosophy* 66: 308–319.

[5] ———. 1990. "Why Personal Identity Is Animal Identity," *LOGOS* 11:71–81.

[6] ———. 1992. Review of *Identity, Consciousness and Value. Ethics* 102: 849–851.

[7] Locke, John. 1894. *An Essay Concerning Human Understanding*, ed. Fraser. Oxford University Press.

[8] Olson, Eric T. 1994. "Is Psychology Relevant to Personal Identity," *Australasian Journal of Philosophy.* 72: 173–186.

[9] ———. 1995. "Human People or Human Animals?" *Philosophical Studies* 80: 159–181.

[10] ———. 1997. "Was I Ever a Fetus?" *Philosophy and Phenomenological Research* LVII: 95–110.

[11] ———. 1997. *The Human Animal: Personal Identity without Psychology.* Oxford University Press.

[12] Parfit, Derek. 1984. *Reasons and Persons.* Oxford University Press.

[13] Quine, W. V. 1972. Review of Milton K. Munitz, ed. *Identity and Individuation, Journal of Philosophy* LXIX: 488–97.

[14] Shoemaker, Sydney. 1963. *Self-Knowledge and Self-Identity.* Cornell University Press.

[15] ———. 1984 *"Personal Identity: A Materialist's Account,"* in S. Shoemaker and R. Swinburne, *Personal Identity.* Basil Blackwell.

[16] ———. 1992. "Unger's Psychological Continuity Theory," *Philosophy and Phenomenological Research* LII: 139–143.

[17] ———. 1997. "Self and Substance," *Philosophical Perspectives* 11: 283–304.

[18] ———. 1999. "Self, Body and Coincidence," *Proceedings of the Aristotelian Society*, Supplementary Volume, LXXIII, forthcoming.

[19] Snowdon, Paul F. 1990. "Persons, Animals and Ourselves," in *The Person and the Human Mind*, ed. Christopher Gill. Oxford University Press.

[20] ———. 1991. "Personal Identity and Brain Transplants," in *Human Beings*, ed. David Cockburn. Cambridge University Press.

[21] ———. 1995. "Persons, Animals and Bodies," in *The Body and the Self*, eds. J. L. Bermudez, A. Marcel and N. Eilan. The MIT Press.

[22] ———. 1996. "Persons and Personal Identity," in *Essays for David Wiggins: Identity, Truth and Value*, eds. S. Lovibond and S. G. Williams. Basil Blackwell.

[23] Swinburne, Richard. 1984. "Personal Identity: The Dualist Theory," in S. Shoemaker and R. Swinburne, *Personal Identity.* Basil Blackwell.

[24] ———. 1992. "Discussion of Peter Unger's *Identity, Consciousness and Value*," *Philosophy and Phenomenological Research* LII: 149–152.

[25] Thomson, Judith Jarvis. 1987. "Ruminations on an Account of Personal Identity," in *On Being and Saying: Essays for Richard Cartwright*, ed. J. J. Thomson. The MIT Press.

[26] Unger, Peter. 1990. *Identity, Consciousness and Value*. Oxford University Press.

[27] ———. 1992. "Reply to Reviewers," *Philosophy and Phenomenological Research* LII: 159–176.

[28] ———. 1996. *Living High and Letting Die*. Oxford University Press.

[29] van Inwagen, Peter. 1980. "Philosophers and the Words 'Human Body'," in *Time and Cause*, ed. P. van Inwagen. Reidel.

[30] ———. 1990. *Material Beings*. Cornell University Press.

[31] ———. 1992. "Critical Study of Peter Unger's *Identity, Consciousness and Value*," Nous XXVII: 373–379.

[32] Williams, Bernard. 1970. "Are Persons Bodies?" in *The Philosophy of the Body*, ed. S. Spicker. Reprinted in Williams, *Problems of the Self*, Cambridge University Press, 1973.

PART IV

True Causes and Real Choices: Still without *All Power in the World*

9

THE UNIQUENESS
IN CAUSATION

There is a logical principle governing causation which, while it has consequences of considerable philosophic interest, never appears to be fully articulated or even recognized by any philosopher. I call it *the principle of the uniqueness of that which causes*. Expressed in terms of the verb "cause," and a notion of a *particular thing*, which delimits the relevant objects of the verb, the principle reads like this:

> If some entity causes, or some entities cause, a particular thing, then nothing else causes that latter thing and no other entities cause it.

This is an entirely general statement concerning the logic of causation, though of course it does not imply that anything ever is caused. In the antecedent, I talk of entities instead of things. This is to make clear that the principle governs persons and other conscious beings, insofar as they may be causes, as well as events, facts, physical objects and other entities naturally called things. It is quite obvious, I suppose, that our principle dictates as follows: If John's putting poison in Jim's food caused a certain particular thing, say, Jim's death, then Bill's shooting Jim did not cause that latter thing. I want it to be just as clear that our principle dictates this as well: If John's putting poison in Jim's food caused Jim's death, then John himself, who is a man and not that first fact or event, did not cause Jim's death. For convenience, however, we may also put our principle wholly in terms of expressions for things: If something or some things cause a particular thing, then nothing else causes the latter (and no other things cause it).

What are we to think of this principle, this *uniqueness condition* with which it presents us? I will argue that, properly understood, the evidence conspires to support this condition. Further, it is only by acknowledging this condition that we may get the best account of "cause," both verb and noun, while demarcating the sense most directly relevant to the topic of causation. Finally, I shall indicate some of the consequences of this principle.

1. On The Objects of Causation

Our principle concerns causation, and not any philosopher's invention however closely or interestingly related to it. This is due to our use of the verb "cause" in our statement of the principle. We are to test the principle by examining certain sentences which employ this verb. Avoiding some trivially irrelevant sentences with "cause" is trivially easy. Avoiding some other irrelevant sentences demands a bit more thought. This thought concerns the objects of causation. Our principle, we may say, only concerns those cases where the objects of causation are *particular things*, and where the object of the verb picks out a single particular thing.

Accordingly, the following sentence is never intended as an instance of our principle:

Drunken driving causes accidents.

For, the object word, "accidents," does not refer to any particular thing. Thus, our principle allows the following related sentence, denying uniqueness of what causes, to be consistent, as it obviously is:

Drunken driving causes accidents, and so do many other things.

The sentences relevant to testing have an object for the verb which refers to a single particular thing.

It is less obvious that the following sentences are also not directly relevant to the question of whether or not our principle is correct:

Bill's sneezing caused Betty to catch a cold. Bill caused Betty to catch a cold.

But they are not directly relevant. The point is that Betty's catching a cold may occur a number of times, or obtain on a number of occasions. Bill may cause her to catch a cold one time, someone else or something else may cause her to another time. Accordingly, our principle allows the following sentence to be actually consistent:

> Bill's sneezing caused Betty to catch a cold, and so did something else.
>
> Bill caused Betty to catch a cold, and so did someone else.

Without the explanation just given, to the effect that no particular thing is picked out by the object, many readers, I submit, would hear these sentences as inconsistent. This is because they would be *assuming* that a particular thing *was* picked out as caused, a particular case of Betty's catching a cold, and then our principle would govern their thinking which proceeded from that assumption. In that way, our principle receives some support, I think, even where the conditions are not proper for a direct logical test of it.

We obtain proper conditions when we begin with such sentences as these, where a particular object is picked out:

> Bill's sneezing caused Betty to catch a cold for the second time.
>
> Bill caused Betty to catch a cold for the second time.

For now, only one particular thing can answer to the object description: presumably, the event of Betty's catching a cold for the second time; possibly, the fact of her doing so, which may be the same thing as that event. In any case, we now encounter these directly relevant sentences:

> Bill's sneezing caused Betty to catch a cold for the second time, and so did something else.
>
> Bill caused Betty to catch a cold for the second time, and so did someone else.

These sentences not only appear to be inconsistent; they actually are. Thus, the sentences just above imply a uniqueness for their subject in relation to the object. And, it is the verb "caused" which is responsible for this implication. For with other verbs, otherwise identical sentences exhibit no inconsistency, nor even any appearance of one:

> Bill's sneezing helped Betty to catch a cold for the second time, and so did something else.

Bill observed Betty to catch a cold for the second time, and so did someone else.

This contrast confirms the idea that there is a uniqueness in causation, and that this uniqueness is not to be found just anywhere. For example, it does not obtain in the case of observation.

Even where an inconsistency is present, it may not appear to be. I think it clear, for example, that the sentence:

Men aren't men anymore

is an inconsistent one. But hardly anyone would hear it as inconsistent. The hearer's mind would proceed forthwith to an idea likely for a speaker to convey by means of the sentence, though not actually asserted by it, for example, that men aren't as virile as they used to be. The context would determine, more or less precisely, the consistent idea to which the mind would proceed.

Various causal sentences will likewise fail to appear inconsistent, even when they actually are so. One example of this is the sentence:

The flame caused the pan to get hotter at that time, and so did something else, the hot coals.[1]

I think that what this sentence actually expresses can be rendered as follows, so that the inconsistency emerges:

The flame caused an increase in the amount of heat in the pan at that time, and the hot coals also caused that increase.

The idea towards which the hearer's mind naturally proceeds, however, may be this rather different one:

The flame caused the pan to get hotter at that time, and the hot coals caused it to get still hotter (just afterwards).

This is of course consistent, and in no way violates any uniqueness condition. The flame causes one increase and the hot coals cause another. Those are two different things, and so they may be caused by things each quite distinct.

---

1. The apparently problematic status of this sort of sentence, and of the "mentalistic" sort of sentence soon to follow, was suggested to me by William Ruddick.

Another sort of example, where no comparative condition is explicitly involved, occurs in the realm of the mental:

> Bill caused Betty to be upset then, and so did someone else, John.

Again, I think that what the sentence actually expresses is inconsistent. But the mind will be apt to handle the sentence differently. For one, it may well move toward an idea involving comparatives:

> Bill caused Betty to be upset then, and someone else, John, caused her to be still more upset.

This latter sentence, concerning a different matter, is of course consistent. For another, the mind may move toward an idea involving different objects of the mental state or states:

> Bill caused Betty to be upset at him then, and someone else, John, caused Betty to be upset at *him*.

This too is quite consistent. But here, each person is said to cause something different. What our original sentence actually asserts, however, is neither of these, nor anything of the like. Its content is rendered, perhaps more clearly, in this following sentence:

> Bill caused Betty to be in a certain state then, that of being upset, and so did someone else, John.

This last sentence, which is indeed relevant, is quite clearly an inconsistent one.

While it is not to be found just anywhere, at the same time, this causal uniqueness is no narrow or special matter, confined to the verb "cause" and close cognates. First, general verbs of causality exhibit the same logical feature; we find it with "bring____about____" and "make ____(happen)____." Thus, the sentences we should expect them from do give us the revealing inconsistencies with these verbs:

> Bill's sneezing brought it about that Betty caught a cold for the second time, and so did something else.

> Bill made Betty catch a cold for the second time, and so did someone else.

Verbs with a causal element, but also with other more specific implications also conspire to suggest our uniqueness.

The verb "move" may be used intransitively, requiring no object but only a subject, as in the sentence "The stick moved." Here, the verb has no implication of causation. Alternatively, the verb may be used transitively, where an object of the verb is at least implied. This occurs in the sentence, "The man moved the stick." In all such cases, there is an implication of causality, the motion of what is moved is caused. In this case, the man presumably caused the stick to move; if he did not, then presumably he at least caused something which in turn caused the motion in question, or whatever. In any case, where the object of "move" picks out a single particular thing, a uniqueness condition applies, quite in parallel with the one with "cause." The same applies with many other transitive causal verbs: "create," "destroy," "build," "construct," "write," "compose," "paint," "open," "close," "fill," "empty," and so on, and so forth. To test directly, we must be sure the sentence picks out a single, particular thing as caused. For example, John may paint the fence, but also Bill may paint it another time. Here, John may be causing a particular coat of paint to go on the fence, or something of the like, and Bill is causing another to go on. Normally, when speaking of a fence being painted, we are not thinking of various coats, or various paintings, or whatever. Thus, we would normally hear the following as inconsistent:

John painted the fence, and so did someone else.

This appearance serves to confirm our uniqueness condition. At the same time, we now can see that such a sentence is not directly relevant for our logical test, and that we move toward such a test sentence with:

John painted the fence at that time, and so did someone else.

I am not saying that this latter sentence is logically adequate to our purpose. I am only suggesting that we have intuitions regarding a certain uniqueness in the verb "paint," and that this goes along with our intuition concerning the causal nature of the verb.

Let us suppose that John painted the front of the fence, and Bill the back; and that when they finished, the fence was painted. Did John paint the fence? I think not. John painted the front of the fence. Why do we have this feeling? Because John, we feel, caused the front of the fence to be painted, or to acquire a coat of paint, or whatever. But he did not cause the back to do so, and so he did not cause the fence to be painted. Rather, John and Bill caused the fence to acquire a coat of paint, or whatever; and so neither one, but the two of them, painted the fence.

Let us suppose that a monkey opens a door with a key. In casual talk, someone might say that the key opened the door. Someone else might say that the monkey did. If what they both say is really true, we should be able to conjoin them to form a truth:

The monkey opened the door then, and so did the key.

But this seems inconsistent, as does the logical consequence of it:

The monkey opened the door then, and so did something else.

As something inconsistent can't be taking place, what is actually going on? I think that the proper answer here is that keys don't really open doors; but that they are just used to open doors, by monkeys, people and so on, and perhaps are otherwise involved in the opening of various doors. In any case, however, the main point for us here is this: The inconsistency we feel in attributing the opening to each of two things at once goes along with our feeling that, in opening a door, something or someone causes some particular thing, and the thing caused involves or conerns the door. Perhaps, he or it causes the door to open, or to become open or whatever. Accordingly, as opening a door is causal, the uniqueness we feel present in cases of such openings confirms our idea about the uniqueness in causation.

I have been deliberately vague in my characterization of what is caused, calling it only a *particular thing*. My reason is that I am not quite sure as to the nature of these things, but wish to convey the idea of the relevant particularity. Many would urge that these particular things are events, particular events. If I insisted on particular events, an argument would be necessary. For, first, Roderick Chisholm has denied that events are particulars, claiming them always to be a certain sort of universal.[2] And, second, Zeno Vendler, while seeming to allow that events are particulars, argues that events are seldom if ever caused. He seems to think that what are caused are particular facts.[3] Our statement in terms of particular things is intended to be neutral amongst these various positions. But unless we have the particularity on which I am

2. Roderick Chisholm, "Events and Propositions," *Nous*, vol. 4 (1970), pp. 15–24. Also, see Donald Davidson's reply to Chisholm, "Events as Particulars," *Nous*, vol. 4 (1970), pp. 25–32.

3. Zeno Vendler, "Effects, Results and Consequences" in R. J. Butler (ed.), *Analytical Philosophy* (Oxford, 1962). Also, see replies by S. Bromberger and W. H. Dray, and Vendler's reactions, all in the volume just cited.

focusing, we will have no coherent idea of *causation* at all, but only some philosopher's invention. For present purposes, then, I may assume that our notion of causing a *particular thing* is adequately clear.

Often, however, historical discussions of causation have not even been this clear. In his *System of Logic*, John Stuart Mill offers the following definition of "the Law of Causation":

> The Law of Causation, the recognition of which is the main pillar of inductive science, is but the familiar truth, that invariability of succession is found by observation to obtain between every fact in nature and some other fact.[4]

While Mill speaks of a fact as the thing caused, the most likely interpretation of his meaning is that it is a universal fact, which may be instanced on numerous occasions. Indeed, in his interpretation of Mill's meaning, Bertrand Russell speaks of an event as caused, and it is an event which is a universal.

> An "event", in the statement of the law, is obviously intended to be something likely to recur, since otherwise the law becomes trivial. It follows that an "event" is not a particular, but some universal of which there may be many instances....What is meant by an "event" is something like striking a match, or dropping a penny into the slot of an automatic machine.[5]

Now, if one thinks, as Mill seems to do, in terms of the causing of such universals, it is all too easy to miss out on our uniqueness condition, which applies only to the causing of particular things. This would be so even if, as Mill himself does, one had thoughts which were extremely congenial to our condition. Indeed, in his most pertinent chapter, "Of the Plurality of Causes: and the Intermixture of Effects," Mill is most congenial to our way of thinking:

> ...We have regarded *a b c d e*, the aggregate of the phenomena existing at any moment, as consisting of dissimilar facts, *a b c d* and *e*, for each of which one, and only one, cause needs be sought; the difficulty being only that of singling out this one cause from the multitude of antecedent circumstances, A, B, C, D, and E. The cause indeed may not be simple; it may consist of an assemblage of conditions from which the given effect could result.

4. John Stuart Mill, *A System of Logic* Book III, Chapter V, Section 2.

5. Bertrand Russell, "On the Notion of Cause," *Proceedings of the Aristotelian Society*, vol. XIII (1912–13), reprinted in *Mysticism and Logic* (London, 1932), where the quoted passage is on p. 186.

> If such were the fact, it would be comparatively an easy task to investigate the laws of nature. But...it is not true that the same phenomena is always produced by the same cause; the effect *a* may sometimes arise from A, sometimes from B.[6]

Here, Mill begins with what appears to be a discussion of the causation of a particular fact or event: "the aggregate of phenomena *existing at any moment.*" And his remarks about an assemblage of conditions encourage us to spot important evidence for the uniqueness in causation. But by the next paragraph, Mill has reverted to thinking in terms of "universals," neglecting what might be discovered to obtain for a single, particular thing: "the *same* phenomena *always* produced by the *same* cause." Being relevantly particular, what may we gain from Mill at his best?

2. Causation by an Assemblage and Causal Over-Determination

We are clear enough, I take it, about the *objects* of "cause" in sentences relating directly to our principle. But it seems that we might yet advance clarity as regards the terms in the *subject's* position, that is, those terms purporting to denote whatever or whoever caused. In speaking of that which causes, our principle both speaks of some *entity* and also of some *entities.* The singular alternative is appropriate enough. But, in the statement of an alleged *uniqueness* condition, what is the latter, *plural* term doing?

Our principle must not rule out plurality. If it did, it would thereby wrongly rule out such consistent sentences as:

> The stone's striking the window and the window's being made of brittle glass caused the window to break.

We want to see, then, how there may be uniqueness in plurality. To do so, we take our cue from Mill, who has already instructed us in such matters: "the difficulty being only that of singling out this one cause from the multitude of antecedent circumstances....The cause indeed may not be simple; it may consist of an assemblage of conditions from which the given effect could result." In this light, let us consider the sentence, displayed just above, concerning the breaking of the window.

6. Mill, *op. cit.*, Book III, Chapter X, Section 1.

As we have remarked, our principle does not rule this sentence inconsistent. Indeed, the principle instructs us as to its consistent interpretation. The subject of the sentence denotes the unique cause of the window's breaking. What caused the window to break is *two* events, in Mill's terms, an *assemblage* of two events. As these events, or this assemblage of them, caused the breaking, nothing else did. In particular, *neither one of these events caused the window to break.* Accordingly, the stone's striking the window did *not* cause the window to break and, likewise, the window's being made of brittle glass did not cause it. Now, in some *other* case, we may say that a certain stone's striking a certain window caused a certain window to break. But then it follows that, in *that* case, the window's breaking was not caused by the stone's striking it *and* something else, say, the window's being made of brittle glass. It should be clear enough, now, how plurality and uniqueness may be relevantly compatible.

While whatever causes a particular thing may thus be a plurality, we have spotted a logical limit on what may cause it. There is no similar limit, however, on what a particular thing may cause; there is an asymmetry here. Any number of particular things may be caused by a single agent, event or fact; or by an assemblage of these. If an event, for example causes two particular things, then it causes each of them. If a stone's striking a window causes the window to break and John to hear a loud noise, then it causes the window to break, and it also causes John to hear the noise.

I think that things proceed in a relevantly similar manner for other verbs which have causal implications. For verbs that do not, like "precede," for example, matters proceed quite differently. We may best appreciate the difference by employing a Principle of Emphasis. Elsewhere, I have argued for this principle at considerable length.[7] Briefly, the idea is that by emphasizing key expressions, we do not alter what they mean or express, but we do help ourselves spot logical relations between the concepts they express. To spot the relevant difference between causation and precedence, then, we consider these following two sentences, where in each case our principle has been employed:

The stone's striking the window *caused* the window's breaking *and* the window's being made of brittle glass *caused* it.

The stone's striking the window *preceded* the window's breaking *and* the window's being made of brittle glass *preceded* it.

7. Peter Unger, *Ignorance* (Oxford, 1975), Chapter II, Sections 7, 8, and 9.

As emphasis properly brings forth, there is a strong appearance of contradiction with the first sentence, but none at all with the second. There is a uniqueness in causation, but no such uniqueness in precedence.

We may make our points another way, I suggest, by seeing how the word "also" works differently with "precede" and "caused." While the first of these allows an "also," the second results in contradiction or worse if the word is added:

> The stone's striking it *and also* the window's being made of brittle glass *preceded* the window's breaking.

> The stone's striking it *and also* the window's being made of brittle glass *caused* the window's breaking.

The reason for this, no doubt, is the relation of these sentences to:

> The stone's striking it *preceded* the window's breaking, *and so did* the window's being made of brittle glass.

> The stone's striking it *caused* the window's breaking, *and so did* the window's being made of brittle glass.

What is wanted to make the connection explicit, I take it, is an account of the element "so." In any case, as "precede" is wholly acausal, it manifests the symmetry which "cause" does not: Just as a given event may precede each one of any number of others, so that given event may be preceded by each one of any number of other events.

Linguistic intuition thus appears to be on the side of our principle. Acquaintance with the familiar philosophical topic of "causal over-determination," however, may lead many to suppose that our principle must be unsound. They would suppose that cases of causal over-determination don't conform to our principle. But when these cases of causation are properly described, there is no conflict, but only conformity to our principle of uniqueness. A couple of examples will indicate clearly enough how matters run here generally.

Regarding causal over-determination, the simplest sort of case is that where one event causes another, but should the causing event not have occurred, the latter would have occurred anyway, caused by some third event. For example, a certain stone's striking a certain window caused the window to break. But if John had not then thrown that stone, Bill, who was watching things, would have thrown a similar stone, a little bit faster, and the window would have thus been caused to break at the very same time. There is no problem here; for we may say that if the first stone's striking the window did not occur, and so did not cause its breaking, the second stone's striking the window *would have* occurred, and it *would have caused* the window's breaking. I am not suggesting that thoughts of this case would prompt many to question our condition, but it is good for us to have the case in hand before we come to a case which might.

A more difficult case, it might be supposed, is that where both stones were thrown simultaneously, both striking the window at precisely the same time. But, in fact, there is no difficulty here either. One thing we may say now is that the complex event of the two stones' striking the window caused the breaking. Or, we may say that the breaking was caused by (an assemblage of) *two simpler events*, the first stone's striking it *and* the second's. But, of course, this is not to say that one of these simpler events, or the other, caused anything. Whichever we choose, providing the situation is at all typical, we may go on to say this: If the first stone had not been thrown, the second stone's striking the window *would have caused* it's breaking, while if the second had not been thrown, the first's striking it would have. On the natural assumptions, these are the natural descriptions; on more complex assumptions, we would have other descriptions which conform to our uniqueness condition. Accordingly, whatever problems they may present, cases of causal-overdetermination, however complex, present no problems for our uniqueness condition.[8]

Regarding a plurality of causes, there remains to discuss a line of objection which is a bit more sophisticated than those worries so far encountered. A sophisticated philsopher may easily suppose that our condition necessitates an implausible divergence between the syntax of sentences with the verb "cause" and the semantics of these sentences. For it may be supposed that our condition implies an equivalance to exist between these two sentences:

John caused the window to break.

John caused the window to break by himself.

If there is an equivalence here, the expression "by himself" will make no semantic contribution to the sentence in which it occurs. It is implausible

---

8. Some recent discussions of these include J. L. Mackie, *The Cement of the Universe* (Oxford, 1974), pp. 43–47 and Louis E. Loeb, "Causal Theories and Casual Overdetermination," *The Journal of Philosophy*, vol. 71 (1974), pp. 526–531.

to suppose that such a syntactic element should make no difference semantically; so much the worse for our principle.

But our principle allows "by himself" to make its contribution. To see the difference it makes, we compare the above two sentences with:

John caused the window to break with someone's help.

Our original unqualified sentence is quite compatible with this last, but the sentence with "by himself" is not. If this third sentence holds, then John caused the window to break, not by himself of course, but with someone's help. Perhaps without the help, he would have caused it anyway; perhaps not; neither is implied by saying that he caused it with the help.

While it will now be granted that we have allowed for the contribution of "by himself," it may be thought that we face a problem on the other side. We cannot, it might be supposed, allow for a contribution of "together" to the semantics of:

John and someone else together caused the window to break.

We need to distinguish this sentence semantically from the unqualified:

John and someone else caused the window to break.

But, given our condition, how are we to do so?

The answer, I think, is to say that the opposite of "together" here will be gotten with "independently," or with an expression to similar effect, rather than with no qualification at all. Accordingly, both of the two sentences displayed just above differ logically from:

John and someone else independently caused the window to break.

The sentence with "together" is inconsistent with the last; the sentence with no qualification is consistent with it and, indeed, is entailed by each of these mutually exclusive qualified sentences.

This is a promising beginning, but what is the function of "together" and "independently" here, so that they solve our problem of semantic contribution. What are they really qualifying? I am far from sure of our answer here, but perhaps I may suggest something. When it's together, then the two people *did something together*—smashed the window with a log perhaps—and *by doing this thing* they caused the window to break. When it's independently, then *each did something in-dependently* of the other—perhaps John threw a stone while the other person threw another stone. There was no plan for them both to throw. Thus, by each doing his own thing, they caused the window to break.

Such suggestions work as well for various "objects" as for personal agents. For we speak of these objects as doing things. Thus, if the water caused Betty to catch a cold, it might do it by itself or, alternatively, it might do it with help from the cold air. Again, these two might cause John to catch a cold. They might cause it together or, alternatively, independently. In the first case, they might together lower his resis-tance, thereby causing him to catch the cold. In the second, the water may give him germs while the cold air, independently, prevents him from sleeping.

Where causes are facts or events, our suggestions may appear to find problems. But, then, what do facts do, and what events? Facts obtain; events occur; sometimes in conducive circumstances and sometimes not. If one event causes another *all by itself*, then perhaps it not only causes the latter but does so *without the aid* of conducive cir-cumstances. What about one event and another *together* causing a third to occur? Perhaps it is *by occurring together* that the first two cause the third. In contrast, they might cause it independently. If so, then, perhaps, what happens is this: They each occur independently—at different times, in different places, from different causes, or whatever. And by each thus doing something different, the two may indepen-dently cause the third event.

3. Toward a Systematic Account of "Cause"

The concept of causation is no philosopher's invention. To get a handle on it, we need to be sensitive to our language, which embodies it, especially to the word "cause," in terms of which the word "causa-tion" can be defined or understood. We speak of the *causation* of this by that when that is the *cause* of this. Not every sense of "cause," however, is closely relevant to such an understanding, as the following contrast makes clear:

John was the *cause* of the charity's being successful.

The charity was the *cause* which John favored.

In both sentences, the noun "cause" is employed in a very common meaning; but only the meaning in the first sentence is closely relevant to understanding causation. We want an account of the noun in its first meaning which will show how it is related to the verb "cause." I think that by adhering to our uniqueness condition we get the best, as well as the simplest, account. This will further support the principle I am advancing.

I propose that the basis of a good understanding of "cause," both verb and noun, is found in sentences concerning the causation of particular things:

> His smoking caused him to develop cancer.
>
> His smoking was the cause of his developing cancer.
>
> His smoking was a cause of his developing cancer.

On this basis, we may perhaps understand such a sentence as:

> Smoking causes cancer,

though exactly what form that extended understanding will take, I am unable to articulate. I do not think this inability need prevent us from thinking we have the proper basis however, nor need it detain us from trying to relate these three basic sentences.

The simplest accounting, I suggest, and the one furthered by our uniqueness condition, relies on identifying *the cause of* a particular thing with *that which caused*, or *is causing*, or *will cause* it. Thus, we may treat the first two of our sentences as logically equivalent. The uniqueness implied by the definite article matches that which our condition picks out for the verb. That this simplest accounting is correct is evidenced by the apparent inconsistency of each of these following four sentences:

> His smoking *caused* him to develop cancer, *and so did* something else.
>
> His smoking *was the cause of* his developing cancer, *and so was* something else.
>
> His smoking *caused* him to develop cancer, but (and, so) it *was not the cause of* it.
>
> His smoking *was the cause of* his developing cancer, but (and, so) it *did not cause* it.

We need only now explain the relation of our third sentence, where the *indefinite* article is employed, to the first two. What is *a* cause of an event; what are its *causes*? For *most* cases, I propose that a cause is *a part of the* cause, that it is a part of that which causes the event.

Accordingly, the *causes* of an event are the *parts of the cause* of it. In such a case, the cause will be some sort of complex or assemblage. The reason that I qualify my remarks, speaking only of *most* cases, is that the following appears to me consistent:

> His smoking was *a cause* of his developing cancer, *whether or not* it was *the cause*.

But if a cause is always a part of the cause, then it could *never* be the cause itself. Accordingly, we must explain "a cause" in terms a bit more complex. But they must be only a bit more complex. For we may accommodate the troubling case, and adequately paraphrase our third sentence, in terms of a simple disjunction of the two sorts of case:

> Either his smoking was the cause of his developing cancer or it was a part of the cause of it.

Other sentences follow suit. Accordingly, if *the causes of* that accident were drunken driving and the slippery road, then drunken driving was *a part of the cause*, and the slippery road was the only other part of it. If the window's being made of brittle glass was *an important cause* of its breaking, then its being made of such glass was *an important part of the cause*.

This account of causes concerns persons as well as events, and indeed anything which may be said to cause a particular thing. Thus, if John was a cause of the charity's being successful, then either he was the cause, in which case he caused it, or else he was a part of the cause, in which case he was a part of that which caused it. If the latter, then perhaps another part of the cause was the economy's booming. If these were the only parts of the cause, then the causes of the charity's being successful were the economy's booming and John. Neither of them caused it, but an aggregate, this time consisting of a person and an event, did cause the charity to be successful. We have hardly presented a complete account of "cause," even limiting ourselves to the relevant sense of the word. But we have, I suggest, made a good beginning in that direction. This further supports our idea of the uniqueness in causation.

Perhaps, this is a good place to remark briefly the relation of our condition to attempts to define causation in terms of (casually) sufficient and/or necessary conditions. While it has recently come under attack, many philosophers have favored the idea that the cause of something must be "sufficient" for its occurrence. It must be something which, at least in the prevailing circumstances, ensures the occurrence of the thing which is thus caused. Along these lines, there has been a tendency for the cause to become "larger and larger," with Mill it even swallows up any surrounding circumstances. Such a tendency serves to rule out there being anything else around which might play a part *in causing* the thing. This makes sense on our condition of *one* thing causing, of this being *the* cause, the *whole* cause, which therefore must leave out no part—no contemporaneous necessary condition.

Our uniqueness condition has no need of these conditions of which philosophers speak when seeking to analyze causation. Indeed, I find their words to lead to no conception which is either natural or clear to me. I wish only to help explain their tendency to speak in this particular technical manner. Insofar as our uniqueness condition is of help here, it is further confirmed by the behavior of these philosophers.

4. The Irrelevance of Ellipsis

Our principle concerns *anything* which might be supposed to cause a particular thing, not only facts, events and people, but physical objects, "universals," and so on. Our principle gives us a strict interpretation for many things we are wont casually to say, and bids us consider that such an interpretation is the correct one. For example, we are wont to assert indifferently:

> The slippery road caused the car to crash.
>
> The road's being slippery caused the car to crash.

In fact, however, the road's being slippery is a condition, fact or event, whereas the slippery road is a "physical object." The latter is a road which is, in fact, a slippery one. The road's being slippery is not any road, no matter how slippery that road may be. Accordingly, our principle bids us that at most one of the above assertions is true. I suggest that this is indeed correct, as is evidenced by the apparent inconsistency of:

> The slippery road *caused* the car's crashing *and* the road's being slippery *caused* it.

This contrasts with another sentence:

> The slippery road *and* the road's being slippery *caused* the car's crashing.

This latter sounds *odd*, I admit; but the point is that it does *not* sound *inconsistent*. Though it does not concern our principle, perhaps I should say that it seems more likely to me that the road's being slippery ·caused the car to crash, and indeed quite unlikely that the slippery road itself was the cause.

Let us consider another situation, one which prompts us to say rather indifferently:

> Those people caused John to feel depressed.
>
> Indifference caused John to feel depressed.
>
> Those people's being indifferent caused John to feel depressed.

Here, John's feeling is said to be caused by each of three different things: those people, who are certain particular entities; indifference, which is a "universal"; those people's being indifferent, which is a single, particular fact or event. Now, for all our principle says, indifference itself, the "universal," may be the cause, though I very much doubt it. More likely, I think, is that those people are the cause. To my lights, it is more likely still that John's feeling is caused by a certain event, perhaps those people's being indifferent. The point here, of course, does not really concern these relative likelihoods. It is just this: if any one of these is the cause, then none of the others can be.

(A way to allow various things each to cause of course remains open. We may then say, so far as our principle goes, at least, that those people caused John's depression, while their being indifferent caused John to feel depressed.[9] But I think this purely logical gambit presents little that is likely. More likely in the case is this, I think: Their being indifferent caused John to feel depressed, and it also caused John's depression, which he felt.)

In light of what has gone before, these remarks may seem so obvious as to be not worth making. But serious thinkers, in discussing causation and related issues, have said words to the opposite effect: They have spoken of expressions for the cause as being only elliptical, when these expressions were clearly ill-suited for picking out events or anything much like an event. For one, C. D. Broad writes:

> Of course I am well aware that we constantly use phrases, describing causal transactions, in which a continuant is named as the cause and no event in that continuant is mentioned. Thus we say: "The stone

---

9. I am here indebted to John Taurek.

broke the window," "The cat killed the mouse," and so on. But it is quite evident that all such phrases are elliptical.[10]

For another, Donald Davidson writes:

> ...If I poison someone's morning grapefruit with the intention of killing him, and I succeed, then I caused his death by putting poison in his food....
>
> The notion of cause appealed to here is ordinary event-causality, the relation, whatever it is, that holds between two events when one is cause of the other. For although we say the agent caused the death of the victim, that is, he killed him, this is an elliptical way of saying that some act of the agent—something he did, such as put posion in the grapefruit—caused the death of the victim.[11]

It is clear from his context that Davidson (unfortunately, I think) identifies what someone did with some event. In any event, he is claiming that an assertion like:

John *caused* Jim's death

is elliptical for something like:

John's doing something *caused* Jim's death.

But there is no reason to suppose the long sentence to be elliptical for the short. Is the description of the event elliptical for the simple name "John"? I doubt it.

What this talk of ellipsis does, however, is get us to examine such odd sounding sentences as:

John *and* John's putting poison in Jim's food *caused* Jim's death,

as well as our aforementioned:

The slippery road *and* the road's being slippery *caused* the car's crashing.

10. C. D. Broad, "Determinism, Indeterminism and Libertarianism" in his *Ethics and the History of Philosophy* (London, 1952); reprinted in Bernard Berofsky (ed.), *Free Will and Determinism* (New York, 1966), where the quoted passage is on p. 157.

11. Donald Davidson, "Agency" in *Agent, Action and Reason*, ed. by Robert Binkley, Richard Bronaugh, and Ausonio Marras (Toronto, 1971), p. 10.

Broad and Davidson would, I suppose, explain the admitted oddness in terms of redundancy, or something of the like. But I think that these sentences sound odd because the interpretations needed for their truth concern situations that are, if not downright impossible, which I suspect, at least most bizarre and unusual. I proceed, then, to articulate the interpretations for these sentences.

In the first odd sentence, a certain person, John, is part of the cause. Presumably, it is by doing something that he is. Possibly, it is by putting poison in Jim's food; more likely, it is by doing something else, say, by emptying Jim's antidote belt of all remedies. This is one way John figures in the cause; *he* is part of it. Another way he figures is this: Perhaps by putting poison in Jim's food, John is involved in a certain event, the event of John's putting posion in Jim's food. This *event*, and *not* John, is the *other* part of the cause of Jim's death.

In the second sentence, the slippery road itself was part of the cause of the car's crashing. Perhaps it was by *doing* something that it was. One thing the road did was curve around very sharply; perhaps it was by doing this that the road was a cause. Or, perhaps, it was not by doing anything, but by simply *being* a certain way, by being sharply curved at a certain point. Now, the road also figures in the cause in another, more indirect way. The road is involved in a certain event or fact, that of the road's being slippery, which is here asserted to be the only other cause of the car's crashing.

When one is thinking of an "object" or a person as causing, or as part of the cause, one will not be likely there and then to be thinking similarly of events involving those very entities. And, the converse is even more obviously the case. Thus, these interpretations, and the sentences interpreted, are clearly no part of everyday thinking or speech. This, I think, is all we need to note in order to explain the oddness of the noted sentences.

Of course, at some deeper level, these sentences, through their interpretations, may prove inconsistent. But to discover this will take argument; it lies beyond the evidence of the ear. However the arguments may run, they will not serve to revive any talk of ellipsis. What our causal sentences are asserting is clear enough for that line to be abandoned. If the sentences are in trouble, that cannot be helped by appealing to ellipsis.

Ellipsis is no more often in place with other causal verbs than it is with "cause" itself. We have already looked at the sentence:

The key opened the door.

This clearly is not elliptical for:

Someone opened the door with the key.

For, as we have seen, it may naturally be used on occasions where we say:

The monkey opened the door.

We might then think that it is elliptical for:

Someone or something opened the door with the key.

But where is the plausibility in this?

Let us suppose that after the monkey used this key to open the door, the monkey then pulled the key out of the door and let go of it. The key fell to ground, we may then suppose, at least as surely as we might suppose it true that the key really opened the door. Now, if something did X and it also did Y, then, I suppose, it is true to say that it did X and Y. Can we truly say here that the key opened the door and fell to the ground? I think not. If the monkey, after doing the rest, then fell to the ground, we could truly say that the monkey opened the door and fell to the ground. Why are we reluctant in the case of the key? Whatever more is going on, surely part of the reason is this: We don't really believe that the key opened the door.

5. The Intransitivity of the Causal Relation

Our principle governs the causation of facts or events, not only by other particular facts or events, but also by persons, objects, universals, assemblages of these, and whatever. But the case of one fact or event causing another has been of particular interest to many philosophers. This is largely because this case rather naturally submits to simple questions framed in the language of "classical logic." In this vein, our condition provides an unusual answer: Given the irreflexivity of this causation, which is all but impossible to deny, the causal relation is actually *intransitive*. What does this mean?

When it is asserted that an event A causes an event B, we may take it as being asserted that a dyadic (causal) relation holds between A and B, with A in the first place, that of the cause, and B in the second, that of that which is caused. This way of thinking is fully general. Accordingly, considerations of truth aside, it may be asserted that a given event, A, bears the relation to itself, that is to assert that A causes itself. In classical logic, there are three familiar "dimensions" for classifying dyadic relations: Those of reflexivity, symmetry and transitivity. In terms of these dimensions, what may we say about our causal relation?

It is quite clear, I suggest, that no event can cause itself; the causal relation is neither reflexive nor even non-reflexive; it is *irreflexive*. The stone's striking the window can't cause the stone to strike the window, nor can the window's breaking cause the window's breaking. A stone's striking a window on one occasion might cause it to strike that window on another, presumably later, occasion. But this is not an event causing itself; rather, it is an event which answers a certain description causing another which answers that same description. A finer description, implying uniqueness, will prevent such a confusion from arising.

The asymmetry of any dyadic relation will entail its irreflexivity, though the converse doesn't hold. This is entirely familiar. May we assert only the irreflexivity of the causal relation? Or, may we assert its asymmetry, from which that irreflexivity may then be presumed to follow? It is quite clear, I believe, that the causal relation is even *asymmetric*. If an event A causes an event B, then B cannot cause A. Of course, B might cause an event entirely similar to A, but then that event will be distinct from the event A itself. If the stone's striking the window caused the window to break, then the window's breaking did not cause the stone then to strike it.

It should be observed that this point about asymmetry is not any point about "backwards causation." Whether a later event can cause an earlier one is a different matter. Asymmetry alone cannot rule out the later breaking of the window from causing the earlier striking by the stone. Rather, asymmetry will say that if the breaking *does* cause the earlier striking, then the striking doesn't cause the breaking. Whatever may be the situation concerning causation and time, I can't see how one can properly deny the asymmetry of the causal relation.

We may also divorce from thoughts about time the question of the dimension of transitivity. But, in any event, here matters are more difficult. Some philosophers hold that the causal relation is transitive.[12] For them, if our stone's striking our window caused the latter to break, and the window's breaking caused John to feel annoyed, the stone's striking the window caused John to feel annoyed, although perhaps

12. A recent example of a philosopher who favors transitivity is David Lewis in his "Causation," *The Journal of Philosophy*, vol. 70 (1973), p. 563. (Unusually, on p. 565, Lewis seems to hold that causation is not reflexive, but is non-reflexive.)

indirectly. Other philosophers hold that such causing is not transitive, but not intransitive either, and so that it is a non-transitive relation.[13] For them, our stone's striking the window *may* cause John to feel annoyed and, again, it *may not*; which it does will, presumably, depend upon various circumstances of the particular case in question. I am familiar with no prominent philosopher who has held that the causal relation is intransitive, that in our situation, given the first two conditions, it *follows* that the stone's striking the window did *not* cause John to feel annoyed. But only such a philosopher would be right about the causal relation.

With our uniqueness condition in hand, the derivation of this unpopular consequence is neither long nor complex. We are to consider a situation where an event *A* causes an event *B*, and where *B* causes an event *C*. Might *A* cause *C*? As *B* causes *C*, nothing other than *B* itself will cause *C*. That is what our principle says. Thus, *A* will cause *C* *only if A* is identical to *B*, that is, only if *A* is really the very same event that *B* is. Might *A* be the same as *B*? We have said that *A causes B*. As causing is irreflexive, *A* does *not* cause *A*. Thus, *A* and *B* are distinct, and not the same. As the two are different, while *B* causes *C*, *A* does not. Therefore, the causal relation is *intransitive*.

Our derivation is straightforward enough. What is the truth? We consider test sentences:

> The stone's striking the window *caused* (the onset of) John's feeling of annoyance *and also* the window's breaking *caused* it.

> The stone's striking the window *preceded* (the onset of) John's feeling of annoyance *and also* the window's breaking *preceded* it.

If one makes no move to "explain away" the data, one will agree that, while there may be transivity in the relation of precedence, there is only intransitivity in the relation of causation.

Indeed, in this spirit we may do well to consider a problem posed by David Lewis.[14] What are we to make of such sentences as "Only driving errors cause auto accidents"? If we deny intransitivity, as Lewis does, we will have a problem. What about cases of excessive drinking

---

13. A recent example of a philosopher who favors non-transitivity is Michael Scriven in his "Causation as Explanation," *Nous*, vol. 9 (1975), p. 13. (Unlike Lewis, Scriven here holds causation to be irreflexive. But, almost equally unusual, he does hold causation to be non-symmetric.)

14. Lewis, *op. cit.*, p. 558. I am grateful to Lewis for pointing out to me how my account most simply handles this problem.

which cause driving errors—don't they *ever cause* auto accidents? Transitivists, and presumably most mere non-transitivists, will feel constrained to say "Yes." But, then, they will have to interpret the original "only" sentence in some such labored way as this: "Only causal histories that involve driving errors are ones that, in the place of that which is caused, contain auto accidents." Can this be what is said by the simple and apparently innocent: "Only driving errors cause auto accidents"? It would seem not. And our account says as much. For, on our account, those cases of excessive drinking, while they cause driving errors, *never do cause* auto accidents. Only driving errors *cause* auto accidents. Of course, we want a detailed account of this sentence, which we do not as yet have. But it seems that only intransitivity, and our uniqueness condition, will allow for a detailed account which is most plausible.

10

IMPOTENCE AND
CAUSAL DETERMINISM

When we are in a certain frame of mind, one which is not at all obviously muddled or confused, it is easy to think of everything that happens as caused by some earlier happening or happenings. Furthermore, we may then well think, events occurring at earlier times, by causing them, determine those at later times; by causing, the earlier leave no alternative but for the later to occur.

There are some other further suppositions, somewhat more radical, which are also quite natural, even if they do not occur quite so easily or frequently as those just previously expressed: As things are determined so that prior *events* are causing everything which happens, there is no chance for any *person himself* to cause anything. There is, then, no possibility for you yourself to make anything happen, prior events always and inevitably taking care of things completely. Accordingly, it is not within your power to act, or to *do* anything at all. You are totally, completely impotent.

These radical thoughts, focusing on acting, and on the power to act, merit our serious attention. They seem, however, never to have received the direct examination called for by their intuitive appeal. In the present paper, I shall try to remedy this situation. I shall argue, explicitly and in detail, that causal determinism is logically incompatible with the performance of any act at all, and even with the power to act, or to do anything. I shall argue, then, for the idea that causal determinism implies impotence, an impotence that is total and universal.

1. The Definition of Some Terms

By *impotence*, I will mean the *lack of power to act* or, in some use of the term, to *do* something. Someone may be impotent in certain areas, but not in others; thus, he will have no power to perform certain acts while perhaps able to do other things. Or, someone may be totally impotent, in which case he will not have it within his power to perform any act at all. It is this total impotence with which I will here be concerned.

By *causal determinism*, I will mean the thesis that every 'event', that is, everything that ever happens, is causally determined by some other event or events. By saying that a given event is causally determined by some others, I mean that the latter leave no alternative but for it to occur. But, I mean more too. For I mean that they do so *by causing* an event or events, perhaps causing the given event, perhaps only by causing some other or others which are suitably related to the given one. While various relations may thus be suitable, a condition on them all is this: the given event is caused by some other or others and, in that way, it is determined to occur. According to causal determinism, then, every event is caused by some other or others in such a way that its occurrence is inevitable.

In what follows, I shall argue that causal determination implies *total* impotence for *all* who ever might be. Thus, I argue that this thesis implies impotence which is *universal*. On the way toward this strong conclusion, I shall first argue for a closely related but somewhat weaker thesis. This weaker thesis is that causal determinism implies, perhaps not so much as that no one has any power to, and so never *can* do anything, but at least that no one ever *does* act. I will call my weaker thesis, *the thesis of radical incompatiblism*. However radical, this is, to repeat, the weaker of my two theses. My stronger thesis, that causal determinism implies that no one ever *can* act, I will call *the thesis of deterministic impotence*. Most of my efforts will be spent in arguing for the weaker thesis. The argument for deterministic impotence involves, I believe, only a relatively small extension of my argument for radical incompatiblism.

2. An Argument for Radical Incompatiblism

In this section, I will introduce the premises of my argument for the idea that causal determinism excludes there being any act which is ever actually performed. I will illustrate each premise by means of a brief example or two, but reserve any sustained discussion of a premise for a later section devoted to that purpose.

Our Argument for Radical Incompatiblism has four premises. The first premise states a rather immediate consequence of the thesis of causal determinism, as I define that view:

(1)   If causal determinism is true, then every particular event is caused (to occur) by some other event or events.

Suppose that a certain bottle is a certain shape, and then it is another shape. If causal determinism is true, then the event of that bottle's changing shape is caused by some other event or events, and thus by some event or events. Suppose that during a certain period a certain finger moves. That finger's moving is an event. According to causal determinism, the event of its moving is or was caused by some other event or events.

Our second premise specifies a requirement for anyone to *act*, or to *do* anything:

(2)   If someone acts, then that person causes at least one particular event (to occur).

Thus, if someone acts so that he moves a certain finger, then he causes something to take place. Perhaps he causes certain impulses to occur in his brain. If so, then he causes the event of those impulses occurring there. Or, perhaps he causes the finger to move. If so, then he causes, to occur, the event of the finger's moving. This second premise might stir a bit more controversy than our first, but it appears to be an eminently plausible proposition.

Our third premise concerns that which causes any given event:

(3)   If some event or some events cause a particular event (to occur), then nothing which is not some event or events causes it (to occur).

Suppose that *the onset of John's fatigue*, a certain event, causes his arms to flop limply into his lap, another event. It is common to say of such a case that *fatigue* caused his arms to do that. But fatigue itself is not any event or events, we may suppose, but rather, perhaps, a universal, or a (kind of) biological state. Granting all this, our third premise says that *fatigue itself* did *not* really cause this flopping of John's arms. Again, and more directly to the point, we may suppose that, before he became fatigued, *certain contractions of John's muscles*, some events, caused his arms to move briskly through the air. If it is true that John himself, the person, is not any event or events, then, our premise tells us, *he* did *not* cause his arms to move briskly then.

These three premises, if they be granted, all but establish our conclusion. But if radical incompatiblism is actually to be secured, we require one last proposition or premise. Our fourth and final premise, then, is this one, which concerns the nature of a person, at least in a certain rather minimal regard:

(4)   No person is any particular event or events.

According to this final premise, a person is one thing or entity, some event or events, something different. The premise implies that if a person is thinking about something, then it is not any event, nor any events, which then and there thinks. Perhaps this last premise will also stir some doubts. But I think that little can be said to contradict it which is plausible, and nothing which is true.

Reviewing our four premises, it will be agreed, I hope, that they together validly yield our desired conclusion:

(5)   If causal determinism is true, then no one ever acts.

For if this deterministic thesis is true, then, as all events are caused by events (1), none is caused by anything else (3). As no person is any event(s) (4), and so each is only something else, no one ever causes any event. Therefore (2), no one ever acts. In brief, and with a new order of presentation, this is our argument all over again. We may be confident that the relation of premises to conclusion is entirely logical.

Having validly derived this conclusion from them, we must return to examine our four premises. Can they really be true? I shall argue that a fair examination of each favors its truth, and that the fair examination of all favors the truth of our rather radical conclusion.

3. The First Premise: Causal Determinism and Universal Causation by Events

Our first premise is a quite immediate consequence of our definition of *causal determinism*. It says, simply, that if causal determinism is true, then every event is caused by some other or others. The thesis that every event is caused by some other event or events may be called *the thesis of universal causation (of events) by events.* This thesis is, apparently, different from the thesis of causal determinism. Our premise, allowing this, says that the thesis of causal determinism implies the thesis of universal causation by events.

This conditional premise, expressive of our definition, is, I suppose, quite trivially true. For our arguments to be of greatest interest, however, there must be some possibility of its antecendent holding, that is, of our deterministic thesis being true. In assessing this thesis, it is important not to assume that it claims things which it does not in fact claim. For example, various philosophers recently have been at pains to argue that, against certain traditional conceptions, it is no part of the idea of 'cause' that an event which causes another be 'sufficient for', or causally determine, that other.[1] Impressed with such arguments, one might suppose that our thesis is thrown in jeopardy. But causal determinism is quite compatible with this position as to the logic of 'cause'. For what our thesis declares is that those causing events which *do occur*, or at least enough of them, cause others in *such* a way, *whether or not* it is the only way, that they determine their 'effects' to occur.

In the final section of this essay, I will briefly discuss some logical challenges to our thesis, Most people will think, however, that the main threat is of an 'empirical' nature, coming from contemporary physical science. In this regard, let me say that trends in science can change, especially as concerns such large issues as this. There is a good enough chance of this occurring, I think we may agree, that we may be interested in the consequences of causal determinism.

4. The Second Premise: The Causation in Action

Our second premise, it will be remembered, is the proposition that if someone acts that person causes at least one event to occur; either he causes something to happen or he causes some things to happen. In stating this premise, I use the verb 'act' in a very general sense, having no particular relevence to the theater, so that our premise may have importance to philosophy. There is, I take it, a sense of 'do', whether or not it is the only sense of the word, that roughly corresponds to this sense of 'act'. In this sense of 'do', then, a man who is just growing

---

1. Two examples are G. E. M. Anscombe in *Causality and Determination*, Cambridge, 1971 and J. L. Mackie, *The Cement of the Universe*, Oxford, 1974, Ch. 2; there are other recent examples.

older is not on that account *doing* anything. Nor, I suggest, is someone who just lets something happen thereby doing anything: He must *be able to do* something about it, but that is a further matter.

Now, various philosophers hold that a person's causing something, or his bringing something about, is at least very nearly all of what action is all about.[2] So far as I can tell, however, nothing like this is even nearly true. I may, for example, cause you to have a heart attack, not in or by *doing* anything, but just by *being* in a certain place, say, a dark room where you are expecting no one to be. Mindful of such cases of a person causing, I should be the last to assert that such causing is even logically sufficient for one to act, much less the same thing as acting. Nevertheless, I do think it true that a person's causing something is *logically necessary* for him to act. Perhaps we may review various cases of action, to convince ourselves that this is so.

Most cases of acting or action, I suppose, involve movement. Typically, whatever else moves, there is movement on the part of the person who acts, of his body or some part thereof. If such movements are uncaused, they involve no action of anyone's. Likewise, if they are caused only by something other than a certain person, they involve no action of his. For movement to be involved in the action of the person, he must cause the movement to take place or else he must cause something else to occur, which in turn causes or contributes to the causation of the movement.

Movement is change, but not all change is movement. From a purely logical standpoint, a certain object may simply change color without there being any movement. How might such a change, supposing it to take place, involve action on the part of some person? The person will act, I submit, only if he causes that change of color, or else causes something which at least contributes to such causation.

Almost all action, and even doing, involves some change or other, and the causation by the agent of that change or of something which at least contributes to causing its occurence. In moving his finger, a man typically causes his finger to move. If it be possible that he not cause that, but he has acted, then he causes something else, perhaps the transmission of certain neural impulses, which caused the finger to move, or which at least contributed to causing the movement. But, perhaps, not every action need involve change, much less every case of doing something. For example, a person might hold his finger still, and in that way do something and even act. Here it seems there need be no change, and

2. For example, see Alan R. White's Introduction to his anthology, *The Philosophy of Action*, Oxford, 1968, p. 2: "To act is to bring about something, to cause it to happen; an action is the bringing about of something."

perhaps there indeed need not be any. But, what does this act involve which may be absent in the case where the finger simply does not move? In holding it still, the man causes the finger to be still, or he causes something else, say, the transmission of certain neural impulses, which in turn causes or contributes causally to that finger's then not moving.

Why do we regard someone's solving a problem, at least typically, as a case of his *doing* something? I take it that it is because we typically suppose the person to have caused the solution to occur to him, or at least to have caused something, say, the occurrence of certain related thoughts, which caused or contributed to causing its occurrence. If the ideas and solution simply do occur, then, for the man to *do* anything, he must cause something else, say, cause the solution to be recognized as such, or cause something which causes or contributes to causing such a recognition. If the man causes nothing at all here, then, even if the solution passes through his mind, he has not done anything. Concerning the solution, something will have happened involving this man, perhaps something from which an appropriate mind-reader would profit. But if the man himself causes nothing, then he fails to do anything.

The simple point I am making seems to me quite impossible to deny. But perhaps before taking leave of it I should discuss lines of thought in the literature which might prevent our having it in proper focus. In the first place, certain philosophers want to say that causing is, somehow, often or always out of place for people, though apparently related things are not. For example, G.H. von Wright emphatically says: "I am anxious to *separate* agency from causation. Causal relations exist between natural events, not between agents end events. When by *doing p* we *bring about q*, it is the *happening* of *p* which *causes q* to come."[3] It seems to me that at least quite generally, when someone *brings about* some state of affairs, he must *cause* it *to obtain*; he must *cause* its obtaining *to occur*. In our ordinary thoughts and speech, I submit, there is no separation, but only the universal application of our premise.

A second line of thought is that a person's causing something must be understood, and eventually defined, in terms of a person's acting or doing.[4] However this may be, I cannot see that our requirement does

3. G. H. von Wright, *Causality and Determinism*, New York, 1974, p. 49. A philosopher who seems to follow von Wright here, with unfortunate result, is Jaegwon Kim, in 'Noncausal Connections', *Nous* VIII (1974), 43–49.

4. Two philosophers who have this idea are Donald Davidson in his 'Agency' in *Agent, Action and Reason* (ed. by R. Binkley *et. al.*), Toronto, 1971, p. 10, and Zeno Vendler in his 'Effects, Results and Consequences', in his *Linguistics in Philosophy*, Ithaca, New York, 1967, pp. 164–165.

anything either to support or to contradict such a general notion. An analogy may be drawn with the proposition that if someone acts, he must believe something, Perhaps, it may be suggested, believing must eventually be understood, and even defined, in terms of action. Perhaps a belief is a certain factor in some sort of 'disposition' to act. But the just mentioned requirement of believing for acting may hold whether or not this analytical suggestion should prove correct. In any event, I think we may agree that these lines of thought are, at best, rather more speculative than the relatively simple requirement on acting which our argument employs.

I submit, then, that the condition that the agent cause something is logically necessary for someone's acting or even doing anything. Perhaps, it may be supposed, this condition has been secured only by understanding it in a way which renders it quite trivial. But a consideration of 'cause', forced upon us by our third premise, shows that this cannot be so.

5. The Third Premise: Why Universal Causation by Events Excludes Any Causation by Anything Else

It is with our third premise that we come to the heart of our Argument. This premise is a particular consequence of a very general principle governing causation. I think that this principle, though bound to provoke some controversy, is in fact correct. Thus, I view our Argument as a derivation from this principle (and from some less controversial ideas). It is a derivation of the intuitive thought, recognized in our Introduction, that causal determinism means no action for us. Accordingly, that intuitive thought will give support to the principle, while the support the principle receives from other quarters will pressure us toward accepting the intuitive incompatibility as genuine.

Here is that principle which, when I introduced it elsewhere, I named *the principle of the uniqueness of that which causes*:

> If some entity causes, or some entities cause a particular thing, then nothing else causes that latter thing, and no other entities cause it.[5]

Now, this principle, it will be noticed, is far more general than is needed for our Argument; that is, it is far more general than is our economically tailored third premise. It is not so much with what is caused that the principle goes beyond the premise. For the 'particular thing' of which the

---

5. In my paper, 'The Uniqueness in Causation', *American Philosophical Quarterly*, forthcoming.

principle speaks as caused may be taken by us to be always some particular *event*, given our very general use of the term 'event'. Or, if one likes, one may think of it as the particular occurrence of an event. In any case, it is in its lack of restriction on what causes that the principle is far more general then our third premise. First, in this regard, our principle says that if *any* entity or entities, not just some event or events, cause some particular thing (or event), then any other alleged causer is excluded. For example, if it is really true that *a stone* causes a window to break, then according to our principle, no person causes that window to break then, nor does any event or events, given, of course, that that stone is distinct from any of those latter entities. For our Argument, however, we don't have to worry about any stone's excluding someone from causing, but only about events doing that. Secondly, our principle says that if any entity or entities cause a particular thing, then *any other entity* is excluded from causing in the case. And, this means, of course, any other entity of *the same or any other category*, however we choose to delineate our categories. Thus, in particular, according to our principle if a certain event causes some other to occur, then *no other event* causes it. For another event is at least as surely an entity different from a given event as any person might be. As far as our Argument goes, however, we don't need to worry about certain events excluding others from causing. Rather, given the idea that a person is no event or events, which is explicit in our fourth premise, we need only to claim this: Should an event or events cause some other to occur, then *nothing which is not* some event or events will cause that particular event then to occur. Thus, it is in a doubly particular application that our general principle promotes the intuitive thought we encountered in our Introduction. As regards our third premise itself, then, our evidence for it may thus be divided in two. On the one hand, there is that evidence it recieves indirectly for being a consequence of the principle, which proposition is evidenced from various quarters. On the other, of course, is that evidence which more directly pertains to the premise itself.

As regards the indirect evidence, I have gone into it elsewhere in some detail, and so I will only briefly discuss it here, to give an idea of the variety and nature of the support. Consider, then, the following sentences:

(1a)   The influx of alcohol molecules into his bloodstream *caused* John to feel drowsy for the first time, *and so did* his leaning his head back.[6]

---

6. If one likes, one may consider instead the more explicity contrastive forms; in this case:

(2a)   The influx of alcohol molecules into his bloodstream *helped* John to feel drowsy for the first time, *and so did* his leaning his head back.

(3a)   The influx of alcohol molecules into his bloodstream *and* his leaning his head back *caused* John to feel drowsy for the first time.

(4a)   The influx of alcohol molecules into his bloodstream *and* his leaning his head back *helped* John to feel drowsy for the first time.

The first of these sentences is alone in appearing to express an inconsistency; the remaining three are apparently consistent. I suggest what is simplest, that this is in fact the case. With events in subject positions, 'cause' and similar verbs, e.g., 'makes' and 'brings about', demand uniqueness when the object refers to a particular thing, e.g., a particular event or occurrence. Other verbs, not only 'helps', but, e.g., 'contributes to', have a different logic. We note that whereas (4a) entails (2a), (3a) entails that *neither* of the subject events caused John to feel drowsy then. Where both help, each helps, but where both cause, each does not. 'Cause' and its fellows allow a *plurality* in their subject, but they require a *uniqueness* all the same.

We turn to confront those sentences most directly relevant to testing our third premise. Here, we have as subjects an event (or group of them) and a person:

(1b)   The influx of alcohol molecules into his bloodsteam *caused* John to feel drowsy for the second time *and so did* John (himself, by leaning his head back).

(2b)   The influx of alcohol molecules into his bloodstream *helped* John to feel drowsy for the second time, *and so did* John (himself, by leaning his head back).

(3b)   The influx of alcohol molecules into his bloodstream *and* John (himself) *caused* John to feel drowsy for the second time; (he did his part by leaning his head back).

The influx of alcohol molecules into his bloodstream *caused* John to feel drowsy for the first time *and* his leaning his head back *caused* him to feel drowsy for the first time.

I prefer the more chatty rendering; but there's nothing logically special there, due to the words 'and so did'. With both forms, to help bring out the contradiction, I employ emphasis, as discussed in my *Ignorance*, Oxford, 1975, Ch. 2, Sections 7 and 8.

(4b)   The influx of alcohol molecules into his bloodstream *and*
       John (himself) *helped* John to feel drowsy for the second
       time; (he did his part by leaning his head back).

Again, only the first sentence appears to express an inconsistensy.
The uniqueness in causation, then, transcends metaphysical categories. That, I suggest, is the most fundamental idea underlying the
intuitive thoughts of our Introduction.

Various philosophers have expressed an idea which might undermine
our argument if it were correct. This is the thought that a sentence where an
object or person is said to cause something must be elliptical, or the like, for
a sentence where an event is: some *event(s) of* the person's (or object's) doing
something, etc. caused the thing to occur.[7] But the evidence here encountered is not easily interpreted on such an idea. A more promising thought,
I suggest, is this. A sentence of the form '*C* caused *X*' is always equivalent to a longer sentence of the form 'By B-ing—, *C* caused *X*'. This would
hold for any value of '*C*', even an event. Thus, for example, by occurring
when it did, or even by occurring, the first event caused the second to occur.
As with most other things, so with causing: Our language gives no primacy
to events as against such entities as people and material objects.

Now, as already stressed, we have discussed various other implications of our uniqueness principle at considerable length elsewhere.
But we should, to avoid unfortunate misunderstandings, make two very
brief points in closing this present discussion of it. First, an event I
used for illustration, John's leaning his head back, if it is to occur,
requires that John actually lean his head back, and thus act. If causal
determinism is true, and our argument is correct, he won't. And so,
such an event won't ever actually occur.

Secondly, one might get the idea that while we may have to compete
with, and lose to, events in order to cause anything, we might always be
helpful to or contribute to the occurrence of various things, these latter
apparently being more 'cooperative' notions. But I suggest that these
verbs afford us no way out of the problems which we are encountering.
For if someone (or something) helps something to happen, he does so in
either of two ways. Either he does so in the manner, say, of a motionless
mountain which, not acting in any way, may help someone to feel
reverent. Or he does so in a more active manner. But, then, he must

---

7. For expressions of such a thought, see the passages by Davidson and by Vendler
cited in note 4. For some suggestions of a contrary nature, see my own passages in 'the
Uniqueness in Causation', Section 4.
    For another, continue to read the present essay.

help by *doing* something. And, that requires him to cause something to occur.

A fair assessment of it seems to favor our third premise, and also the idea that there is no relevant ambiguity or equivocation available with 'cause'. Accordingly, however weak our second premise might sometimes seem, it is strong enough to connect with our third. Our Argument for Radical Incompatiblism, then, seems to be drawing successfully to its close. Before we get there, or go beyond, however, it remains to review our fourth and final premise.

6. The Fourth Premise: The Difference between Events and People

Our fourth and final premise says that no person is any event or events. This premise is necessary to secure our conclusion. For if some events were people, then should those events cause others, people would cause the latter events. In that way, people would meet our requirement for action, and thus they might act even if causal determinism is true.

I think that most philosophers would grant us this last essential premise. But some might object even here. For example, an objection might come from one who made an attempt at viewing the world as a 'manifold of space-time'. While I am friendly toward new ways of trying to view the world, I cannot claim much understanding of what such a view entails. But I think not much understanding is needed to ward off any objection to our premise, from this or from any other view.

On such a view, the idea might be to think of a person, or a material object for that matter, as stretched out through time, so to speak, as having a temporal dimension. The same, I suppose might be true of an event. Accordingly, a view of the world as a space-time manifold, might promote in someone's mind the idea that people are events of a certain sort. But, then, along with whatever else it might encourage, the view would promote confusion. For a person, whether or not there are any such, must be capable of undergoing experience. No event or events, I submit, could ever experience anything.[8]

We may allow, it must be noted, that the advances of science, or something else for that matter, may properly get us to think that the world consists in nothing but four-dimensional events, granting that four-dimensional entites may be events. For we may insist that this

---

8. For a detailed discussion of these matters, see Michael A. Slote's *Metaphysics and Essence*, Oxford and New York, 1975, Ch. 2 and 3, most especially, Ch. 3, Section 1.

does not mean that we should think that people are events. If events are the only entities which exist, then there really are no people; for nothing will then exist which is capable of conscious experience. In no case, I submit, will our fourth premise be undermined.

Now, in the form in which they are expressed, certain of our premises may presuppose the existence of persons or of other entities which some philosophers may find questionable. But such a presupposition is not essential to the import of a premise. Without much ingenuity, any pemise may be rephrased so that there is no such requirement. We may do the same, of course, for our conclusion.

7. An Argument for Deterministic Impotence

We have derived our thesis of radical imcompatiblism from premises which even taken together, I submit, are quite acceptable ones. Thus, a proposition which is now quite acceptable for us is this: If causal determinism is true, then no one ever does anything. But I said at the outset that I wished to argue as well for a stronger proposition: If causal determinism is true, then no one ever *can* do anything. A person might do nothing, not because he can't, but, say, because he might just happen not to want to do anything. He may, then, have it within his power to do various things. But, if causal determinism is true, I shall argue, that will never be the reason.

The intuitive thoughts of our Introduction now come to mind. I suggest that we may naturally extend them: If causal determinism is true, then, because it is inevitable that events cause everything, we people have no power to do so. It is not that events happen to cause everything that occurs; while we 'stand back' though able to cause. It has already been *determined* that only events, and so not we people, will do all the causing that will be done in the world.

These thoughts are quite compelling. But how do they, or anything much like them, follow from causal determinism? Now, the events we usually have in mind, to be sure, are thought of as rather 'simple': the moving of a certain finger, or the breaking of a certain window. We view these as caused by other simple events: the contraction of certain muscles, or a certain stone's striking that window. But, in addition to such simple events, there are, in causal terms, certain more 'complex' events. Each of these more complex events is the event *of* one simple event *causing* another to occur.

Of course, these causal complexities do not stop here. If causal determinism is true, or even only universal causation by events, there is no stopping point. There are not only those events recently remarked, but also the events *of those* events being caused by others. And, then, the events *of these* most recently remarked ones being caused by others; and so on, infinitely.

Rather near the beginning of such a series, our thesis implies, such events as the following will occur. We will have, for example, the event of *a certain stone's striking a certain window causing the window to break (for the first time)*. As just suggested, this complex event may *itself* be caused, and it will be if causal determinism is true. Perhaps, the event of the window's being formed, or having been formed, of a brittle glass causes this complex event, that is, causes *the striking to cause the breaking*. Given causal determinism, it will thus determine the complex event; it will leave no alternative but for the striking to cause the breaking. This provides a good beginning, I suggest, for our Argument for Deterministic Impotence.

I think we may continue our Argument by saying this: If a given event has been determined to occur, then any event logically incompatible with its occurrence has been determined *not* to occur. We have already seen that the striking causing the breaking is incompatible with any event in which a person causes the breaking. Hence, due to prior events, it has been determind that, say, John's causing the window to break not occur, and so for any other person, and for any event he might conceivably cause.

Now, if a person ever acts, there must be the event of his acting. But what is required, logically, for the occurrence of any such event? It is required that there occur an event, or events, of that person causing some event or events. But it has been determined by prior causing events, we have agreed, that every such required event will not occur. Hence, it has been similary determined, for each event of a person acting, that it will not occur.

If prior events, by causing, determine that events of this last sort not occur, then they determine that no one acts. For each time, prior events leave no alternative but that, at that time, there is no person who does anything. Where prior events leave no alternative but that, at a certain time, no one does anything, then from the time(s) of those prior events to that certain time, no one *can* do anything. As causal determinism concerns any time, and allows us to go back without end, that thesis implies that no one *ever can* do anything. Causal determinism implies then, that there is no person who has any power to act, or to do anything. This is, of course, the thesis of deterministic impotence.

8. The Anatomy of These Arguments

Our arguments have now been set out; our conclusions have been derived. Certain features of our premises have been discussed. But some other interesting features have so far received scant attention. I will look to discuss some of these other features in this final section, trying to make a selection which will help us to understand what importance these arguments might have, and how they might relate to further questions for philosophic inquiry.

In the first place, it should be clear that in our first Argument, where we tried only to establish the incompatibility with action and doing, we made no use of the deterministic aspect of the thesis of causal determinism. We made use only of its causal aspect. In other words, a similar argument may be exhibited whose conclusion is that universal causation by events is incompatible with anyone doing anything. Indeed, if it is possible to have non-determining causes, as two cited philosophers, Anscombe and Mackie, have argued, then this thesis of causation just might be true, in the absence of any deterministic thesis holding true. If the causal thesis is correct, we may notice, then, whether or not there is determinism, there will never be any act performed by anyone. Whether or not anyone *could* act in such a circumstance is, of course, a further question.

In the second place, while I have focused on causation (of events) by events, the universal causation important to our arguments need not be put in precisely these terms. Rather, we might consider a causal thesis to the effect that whatever might conceivably be caused—events, occurrences, facts, or whatever—is in fact caused and, moreover, is not caused by a person. This point has some importance for us. For example, Zeno Vendler has argued that events never cause anything, but that facts or 'fact-like' entities do.[9] I do not find Vendler's arguments convincing. But let us suppose that he is right. What follows? It will follow that our causal thesis, as defined, is false. But, we may, it seems, rather trivially alter our definition of it, for example, as follows: In the case of every event that occurs, it is caused to occur by some fact or facts (to the effect that some event or events occur), and this causing is such that the (latter occurrence or) fact(s) determine the aforementioned event to occur. In line with this redefinition, we can construct arguments precisely parallel to those presented. Some other philosophers have more recently challenged our thesis on rather different grounds.[10] While I do not find their arguments convincing either, the supposition that one or more of them is right leads only to further redefinitions of

9. See Vendler, *op. cit.*, pp. 170–171.

10. For example, See Kim, *op. cit.*, p. 49 and Peter Achinstein, 'Causation, Transparency and Emphasis', *Canadian Journal of Philosophy* V (1975).

our thesis, and to further parallel arguments for our radical conclusions.[11] It is, thus, rather unimportant what is to be the precise form of our thesis of causal determinism or, for that matter, of the implied thesis of universal causation. For, so long as we distinguish the causing entities which they propose from people, and so long as we find no reason for similarly separating the things caused, we must conclude total, universal inaction and, with a deterministic aspect, as much impotence as well.

In the third place, while the more plausible universal causal theses, it seems to me, exclude people from ever being even part of the cause, our argument will work just as well for theses which allow people such a part. Thus, if it is suggested that a *complex* consisting of, say, a person and some events, may, under some thesis of universal causation, cause a certain event, we may reply as follows: First, we may say our notion of action requires that a *person* cause something, and not just some *complex*, which of course is *not* a person. And, second we may say that even if we revise our concept of action so as to allow causation by some such complexes to suffice, it is doubtful whether there will be any gain. For it is doubtful that the causes required for a concept much like our idea of action will *match up precisely* with those required by a correct thesis of universal causation. But, this precise matching is exactly what is required in order to escape effectively our conclusion of total, universal inaction.

In the fourth place, our argument for inaction contains an important lesson even if it is false that there is *universal* causation by events, or by anything much like them. The lesson is simply this: If there is a causal order of *things*, as opposed to *people*, then there must be a *gap* in that order *whenever we might act or do anything*. Our possibilities for action are only as great as the extent to which events, facts, situations or whatever are not caused by anything other than a person himself.

In the fifth place, it should be noted that even without our second premise, our arguments yield us some very strong conclusions. For we may derive straight off that causal determinism implies that no one ever causes anything to happen, and never can. This implies, what is much the same, that no one can ever bring about anything, or make anything happen.

11. Part of the failure of Kim's arguments, in my judgement, is his accepting the nonexistent separation posited by von Wright, between events causing and people bringing about. Achinstein's arguments are based on an idea of Fred I. Dretske, to the effect that emphasis alters the truth-value of various statements of philosophically interesting forms; see Dretske's 'Contrastive Statements', *The Philosophical Review* LXXXI (1972). I argue against this idea in *Ignorance, loc. cit.*

In the sixth place, I am mindful of the thought that as we do act, and indeed, do cause things to happen, this argument is a refutation of the thesis of causal determinism, and even of the implied thesis of universal causation. The same might be said almost equally, however, of any incompatiblist argument. As the history of the subject shows, this line has very limited power.

In the seventh place, perhaps most obviously, and, for us now, finally, the arguments of this essay say nothing whatsoever about any determinisitic thesis which is not causal in nature. Deterministic theses of this other sort may also be incompatible with any action. But, so far as these present arguments go, any such other thesis may be compatible with much action, indeed, even action which is freely performed and morally responsible. In this present brief essay, I hope only to have made some contribution, perhaps as definite as it is limited, to our thought about this area of difficult and vexing problems.[12]

12. I am grateful to several people for criticisms and suggestions, especially to my colleagues William Ruddick and John Taurek.

11

FREE WILL AND
SCIENTIPHICALISM

It's been agreed for decades that not only does Determinism pose a big problem for our choosing from available alternatives, but its denial seems to pose a bit of a problem, too. It's argued here that only Determinism, and not its denial, means no real choice for us.

But, what explains the appeal of the thought that, where things aren't fully determined, to that extent they're just a matter of chance? It's the dominance of metaphysical suppositions that, together, comprise Scientiphicalism: Wholly composed of such mindless physical parts as electrons, you are a being whose powers are all physical powers, physically deriving from the powers of your parts and their physical arrangements. Scientiphicalism conflicts with your having real choice.

Some fairly conservative alternatives to Scientiphicalism may allow for choice. Two are briefly discussed: On the further-fetched, you are a Cartesian mental being, a nonphysical being in powerful interaction with physical things. On the more conservative approach, you are wholly composed of physical parts, but some of your powers are radically emergent, including your power to choose.

Finally, it's argued that, if you choose, you must be, to some extent, exempt from natural laws.

1. Our Believed Choices among Actually Available Alternatives for Our Activity

Deep indeed is our commonsense belief that, often enough, we *choose what to do from among actually available alternatives* for our own activity. In particular, I deeply believe that, often enough, I choose what I'll think about from among actually available options for me. As sometimes happens, I choose to think about metaphysics, even while there are other alternatives available for my thoughtful activity, including an option to think about meat and potatoes. When I think about metaphysics *because I chose that alternative*, from among several available, there may be an especially clear instance of what's usefully called *full choice*.

As I'm using the term, "full choice" expresses our most central conception of choice: So, full choice must be *nonderivative* choice—which may be also called, more positively, *basic* choice. A committee may make choices, from among the alternatives available to it, but these will be only derivative choices and, so, not full choices. Derivative because the committee will make choices only when, in a more central and unqualified sense, some of its members, individual conscious beings, each make choices.

Again, some people may set things up so that a certain mindless machine, perhaps with built in radomizers, makes "choices" for them, or for other people. Even if the determinations made by the machine can be called choices, they will not be full choices. For, again, the selections will be derivative choices, dependent on the more basic choices of those who installed the machine, or, perhaps, on the choices of people using the device to go with the machine's determinations.

Only if an entity has the capacity for conscious experience will it have the capacity for full choice. And only if a conscious being can make *conscious choices*, wherein she's *aware of alternatives for her*, will she have the capacity for full choice. So, even if we may make some choices that are quite unconscious, driven wholly by unconscious beliefs and desires, that must be partly because we can make, as well, choices that aren't so unconscious.

If we didn't engage in full choice, at least from time to time, our lives would lack much of, even most of, the significance we commonly suppose our lives to have. In very central respects, they'd be no more significant than the lives of presumably choiceless happy clams. So, should gripping considerations pose a threat to our deep belief that we engage in full choice, they'd threaten our belief that our lives are, in such central respects, far more significant than those of choiceless happy clams. So, I think it fair to take our term "full choice" to express the essence of what many thinkers have meant by the philosophical term "free will."

Here, I try to uncover what are, in this present day and age, the most forceful apparent threats to our belief that we have full choice, or free will. No doubt with less success, I try to show that such threatening appearances don't really signal failure for the belief. Rather, they may signal problems only for metaphysical suppositions that, presently widespread, are questionable assumptions.

2. Free Will and Determinism, Full Choice and Inevitabilism: Not an Urgent Issue

In traditional discussions concerning whether we "have free will," the central issue is whether the truth of propositions to the effect that we sometimes engage in fully choosing what to do is quite consistent with, or whether it's really *incompatible* with, a thesis of Determinism, or Fatalism, or, as I like to put it, *Inevitabilism*.

According to what may be called *All-Too-Full Inevitabilism*, any event in which any of us is heavily involved, like your imagining a grey triangle an hour or so ago, was inevitable from times long before any of us first existed, even if perhaps not from a time before, say, an Almighty God made (the rest of) the universe.

Many will note that, in what's just been said, I've not mentioned laws of nature, much less said anything like: "Deterministic natural laws take the state of the world at a given specific time and yield, or determine, the state of the world at other specific times." Recently, it's been common to limit thought about Inevitabilism to such terms as those; but that's too limiting to do justice to the thesis. Better, I'll suggest, for us to think of the matter like this: In several recent centuries, *most of the reason to believe* Inevitabilism derived from reason to believe that the world was "governed by deterministic natural laws," in a sense indicated, pretty well, by the previous paragraph's quoted terms. (As I'll be suggesting, this reason was always far from conclusive and, indeed, never more than just pretty considerable.)

Toward gaining an appreciation of Inevitabilism, we may notice how we ordinarily think of the past and, by contrast, how we ordinarily think of the future: The past is absolutely settled and closed, in every real respect and regard; by contrast, the future is at least somewhat unsettled and open, in at least some real respects or regards. So, it is absolutely settled, a completely closed matter, whether yesterday one thing that happened was your imagining a grey triangle; either that happened yesterday or else it didn't happen, and *that's that*; there's simply nothing to be done about such a past matter. By contrast, it's at least somewhat unsettled and open whether tomorrow one thing that will happen is your imagining a grey triangle; presumably, it's *not* true that either it will happen or else it won't happen, and *that's that*. Rather, at least so far as we can tell, it's perfectly *possible for you to* imagine a grey triangle tomorrow and, equally, it's *possible for you not* to do that then.

Now, according to Inevitabilism, this ordinary thinking is all wrong: Just as it is with the past, so the *future* is absolutely settled and closed, in every real respect and regard. Just as it's absolutely settled what happened yesterday; *it's also absolutely settled what will happen to-morrow*; just as it's a closed matter whether one thing that happened yesterday was your imagining a grey triangle, absolutely fixed and completely settled, so also, according to Inevitabilism, it's completely fixed and settled whether one thing that will happen tomorrow will be your imagining a grey triangle. So, there's Inevitabilism for you, laws or no laws.

Anyhow, few contemporary readers will see much reason to believe Inevitabilism, or Determinism. For, nowadays, few will believe any "physical proposition" even remotely like a statement to the effect that, say, the distribution of matter at earlier times fully determines the distribution of matter at later times. In line with that, few will think that *anything* fully determines, or has it be inevitable, that there be a certain distribution of matter at later times, or that there be any wholly specific way that, in the future, is the only way for the world to be. And, in line with *that*, few will think that, for each future time, there *is* any wholly specific way that's the only way for the world to be.

Why do I think all that's so? Well, it's common knowledge that, nowadays, very few will hold with classical physics or, for that matter, with any science that has what's most plainly physical in our world be subject to complete antecedent determination. Rather, accepting "in-deterministic" physics with the same "objectivist" interpretation favored by most current physicists themselves, we agree that, even with what's plainly physical, there's plenty of room for random happenings, and plenty for purely probabilistic events, whether or not there's room for fully chosen activity.

Since few philosophers now believe a completely comprehensive thesis of Determinism, or Inevitabilism, few have a very urgent interest in a thesis of (Deterministic) Incompatibilism, according to which such a Deterministic view is inconsistent with our ever engaging in activity we fully choose for ourselves. (Of course, a fair number still have a *nonurgent* intellectual interest in this Incompatibilism, with able thinkers on each side.)

3. A Widely Disturbing Argument Presents a More Urgent Issue

More philosophers now take an urgent interest in another issue concerning full choice that, at least nowadays, may be the real heart of "the problem of free will." This more urgent issue may be presented by way of an argument strikingly forceful for reasoning so sketchy and bare:

> *First Premise*: If Determinism holds, then, as everything we do is inevitable from long before we existed, nothing we do is anything we choose *from available alternatives* for our activity.

> *Second Premise*: If Determinism *doesn't* hold, then, (while some things we do may be inevitable from long before our existence and, as such, it's never within our power to choose them for ourselves) it may be that some aren't inevitable—but, as regards any of these others, it will be a *matter of chance* whether we do them or not, and, as nothing of *that* sort is something we *choose* to do—nothing we do is anything we choose from available alternatives for our activity.

> *Third Premise*: Either Determinism holds or it doesn't.

Therefore,

> *Conclusion*: Nothing we do is anything we choose from available alternatives for our activity.

This argument is quite disturbing. Indeed, nowadays, able thinkers often take it to suggest that our concept of full choice is an incoherent idea, never true of any reality at all.

Such a severe judgment threatens to put us in the same boat with our choiceless happy clams. As I believe, that judgment's unduly pessimistic. But, then, what's wrong with our sketchy argument, so very wrong as to place it beyond repair? Well, there's little point in questioning the relation of the argument's premises to its conclusion; anything amiss with my presentation will just call for a reformulation. Nor is there a deeply serious objection to the argument's Third Premise, with the thought that either Determinism holds or it doesn't. So, for philosophical profit, we should consider just the argument's first two premises.

At least at this point, it's easier to get clear on the First Premise, about the implications of Determinism's holding, than on the Second, about the implications of Determinism's failing to hold. Mainly for that reason, I'll next discuss, briefly, the very appealing First Premise.

Then, I'll spend more of the essay exploring what's promoting much appeal with the Second.

4. Full Choice (Free Will) Is Incompatible with Inevitabilism (Determinism)

Not absolutely certain, I'm fairly sure that Inevitabilism, which I've argued is the heart of Determinism, is incompatible with full choice, or free will. What fosters this belief is a line of thinking so perfectly simple and, I think, so obviously correct, it should hardly be called a "philosophical argument."

Basically, it's just this: Let's suppose that, as regards anything that happens after a certain time long before I ever existed, at least from that time onward it is absolutely inevitable that the thing happen. Then, for each time throughout my existence—and forever after, there's really *just one* (perfectly specific) way for the world then to be. But, for any such time, I will have available alternatives, as regards what to do, only if there are *at least two different* ways for the world to be at that very moment or, perhaps, at the very next moment: one of these really different ways *for the world to be* will represent, or will provide, one actually available alternative *for me to do* something, and at least one other will provide *another* such alternative for me. So, throughout my existence whatever happens is so inevitable that I never have any actually available alternatives as regards what I do. So, nothing I ever do is anything I choose to do from actually available alternatives for my activity. Of course, there's nothing here that's special to me. So, if Determinism holds, none of us will have any full choice, or free will.

Of course, many philosophers will feel that this simple reasoning is badly objectionable. In response, they may resort to one or another philosophical story from the highly inventive work of David Lewis, much as I myself once did.[1] Or, they may make another objecting response. But, as I suspect, these are just so many only modestly plausible denials of what are our deepest beliefs about what must go on for us to choose from among actually available alternatives for our activity.

Of course, I can't support that suspicion with considerations all sensible readers will find conclusive. Realizing that, I won't say more

---

1. Lewis offers the basis for two sorts of response. On the one hand, there's his metaphysical system of many mutually isolated worlds, with counterparts of us in many of them. This can encourage one way of looking at matters of choice in terms of which nothing so metaphysical as what I'm trying to promote will ever seem to be both

about whether Determinism excludes full choice. Anyway, we may make more philosophic progress, as I've suggested, by exploring the appeal of our argument's Second Premise. That's what we'll next do.

5. Is Full Choice (Free Will) Incompatible with the *Denial* of Inevitabilism (Determinism)?

Even as it may help us focus on our essay's main matters, we now turn to discuss the great appeal, for many philosophers nowadays, of our argument's Second Premise. Precautionary wording to the side, its thrust is the thought that, if Determinism *doesn't* hold, then, some things we do, even as they aren't inevitable, will be a *matter of chance*—and nothing of *that* sort is something we *choose* to do. So, what this Premise says is that the denial of Inevitabilism (=Determinism) is incompatible with our ever doing what we choose, from available alternatives for our activity. And, this is to say that our doing what we so choose is *incompatible with* there being a certain *lack of inevitability*—with its *not* being true that, as regards anything that happens after a distantly past time, at least from that time onward it's absolutely inevitable that the thing happen.

Now, on the face of it, such an alleged incompatibility is wildly implausible. So, why have so many thinkers found our Second Premise, or statements much the same, to be so appealing?

When pondering this Premise, which has chance be inevitability's only alternative, we may bring to our thinking some powerfully constraining widespread metaphysical assumptions. To see how this may go on with even very able thinkers, we look at this passage from Peter van Inwagen:

> What happens if we reject determinism?...the quantum-mechanical world of current physics seems to be irreversibly indeterministic, ... Let

---

something truly real and any life-enhancing big deal. For a full treatment of this system, see his *On the Plurality of Worlds*, Blackwell, 1986.

On the other hand, his semantic ideas about the context-dependence of ever so many judgments can make it look like, in essays like this present paper, the author is just raising the standards for judgments about our choice to heights that are as unrealistic as they're divorced from our ordinary concerns for our lives. For this, see his "Scorekeeping in a Language Game," in his *Philosophical Papers*, Volume 1, Oxford University Press, 1983. In my *Philosophical Relativity*, Minnesota and Blackwell, 1984, I try to apply this semantic idea to the issue of this present paper, especially in "A Problem of Power and Freedom," which is section 2 of chapter III.

As I'm advancing in the present paper, both of these "Lewisian" ways of playing down what's required for us to choose from actually available alternatives must be ways of being misguided, as must be any other ways of playing that down.

us suppose for the sake of argument that human organisms display a considerable degree of indeterminism. Let us suppose in fact that each human organism is such that when the human person associated with that organism . . . is trying to decide whether to do A or to do B, there is a physically possible future in which the organism behaves in a way appropriate to a decision to do A and there is also a physically possible future . . . appropriate to a decision to do B. We shall see that this supposition leads to a mystery. We shall see that the indeterminism that seems to be required by free will seems also to destroy free will.

Let us look carefully at the consequences of supposing that human behavior is undetermined. Suppose that Jane is in an agony of indecision; if her deliberations go one way, she will in a moment speak the words' "John, I lied to you about Alice," and if her deliberations go the other way, she'll bite her lip and remain silent. We have supposed that there is a physically possible future in which each of these things happens. Given the whole state of the physical world at the present moment, and given the laws of nature, both of these things are possible; either might equally well happen.

Each contemplated action will, of course, have antecedents in Jane's cerebral cortex, for it is in that part of Jane (or of her body) that control over her vocal apparatus resides. Let us make a fanciful assumption about these antecedents, since it will make no real difference to our argument . . . Let us suppose that there is a certain current-pulse that is proceeding along one of the neural pathway's in Jane's brain and that it is about to come to a fork. And let us suppose that if it goes to the left, she will make her confession, and that if it goes to the right, she will remain silent. And let us suppose that it is undetermined which way the pulse will go when it comes to the fork . . .

. . . Does Jane have any choice about whether the pulse goes to the left or to the right? . . . If it goes to the left, that *just happens*. If it goes to the right, *that* just happens . . . it would seem that there is no way in which anyone could have any choice about the outcome of an indeterministic process. And, it seems to follow that if, when one is trying to decide what to do, it is truly undetermined what the outcome of one's deliberations will be, then one can have no choice about the outcome . . . [2]

Where I talk of what's a *matter of chance*, van Inwagen writes of what *just happens*; but the suggested thought's quite the same, as is the thought that what goes on with us will be *accidental*.

As will be worth attention later in our essay, what's quoted above is just as forceful where the behavior in question is purely mental activity, as with Jane's thinking more about lying. So, equally, it seems that, with

2. Peter van Inwagen, *Metaphysics*, Westview Press, 1993, from pages 191–93.

Determinism's not holding, Jane won't really choose even what she'll think about.

Anyway, before the passage quoted, in his text our author argued for the statement that free will is incompatible with determinism. And so, shortly after he has us thinking about ourselves in much the same terms we've just thought about his Jane, van Inwagen presents a disturbing dilemma for free will that, in all essentials, is quite the same as what's suggested by our own three-premise argument:

> But now a disquieting possibility suggests itself. Perhaps free will is . . . incompatible with determinism. But perhaps it is also incompatible with *in*determinism, . . . If free will is incompatible with both . . . , then, since either determinism or indeterminism has to be true, free will is impossible. And, of course, what is impossible does not exist.[3]

When we think about ourselves much as we've just thought about Jane, which we often feel compelled to do, then, I suggest, we're all but forced into such a disturbing dilemma. And, we're then all but forced, as well, into the disturbing dilemma suggested by our three-premise argument: Either what we do is quite inevitable, from times long before we existed, or else it's just a matter of chance what we do; so, in any case, we never do what we choose from available options for our activity.

But, *must* we think of ourselves in such terms as we've just thought about Jane? Or, are there alternatives available?

To give philosophically satisfying answers, we must take the trouble to think hard about what, exactly, are the metaphysical assumptions we're bringing to bear when we think of ourselves much as we've just been thinking about Jane. In subsequent sections, we'll do that.

For a usefully suggestive answer now, we may recall, from the history of modern philosophy, very different metaphysical visions. First, we can make such a radical departure from our customary metaphysical thinking as will have us entertaining Berkeley's Idealism. (With or without embracing Berkeley's theistic thoughts, this is, I think, a coherent view of reality, though I won't bother to argue that large point here.) With Berkeley, there is a world of many minds, and the various ideas that are the ideas of these minds. At all events, it certainly seems that the finite minds of this world, maybe you and me, can exercise our powers to choose: we can choose to think about metaphysics and, alternatively, we can choose to think about music. If we think about metaphysics, not music, that needn't be anything inevitable, and it also

---

3. *Metaphysics*, page 195.

needn't be a matter of chance; rather than either, we may do it because we chose to think about matters metaphysical.

To feel free from false dilemmas, we needn't go so far as to be Idealists. Recalling nobody less than the father of modern philosophy, we may entertain the Substantial Dualism of Descartes. (Both in its historical Theistic version and also in an evolutionary Nontheistic version, with this seminal metaphysician's Dualism there's another coherent conception.) Indeed, in the most relevant respects, Descartes' view of us—we're each a distinct temporally enduring nonphysical mental subject—is the same as Berkeley's. (Here, we put aside Descartes' unhappy remarks about your being a unit, with your mind and your body wonderfully intermingled.) For the old Dualist, as much as for the old Idealist, there seems plenty of room for full choice.

So, as it seems, our conception of full choice, or free will, isn't incoherent. Rather, it might only be that, in accepting the currently dominant metaphysic, we accept a conception of ourselves that's incompatible with our ever engaging in fully chosen activity.

6. Our Scientiphical Metaphysic and Our Currently Dominant Conception of Ourselves

By contrast with Substantial Dualism, any view now deemed intellectually respectable, among most prominent philosophers, will have us be just so many physical complexes, you being one especially interesting complex and me being another. *Give* or take a nuance or two, whatever categorical dispositions, or propensities, or "powers" you have will derive, in a fully physical fashion, from the physical propensities of whatever far simpler physical things serve to compose you and, of course, the physical relations among your simple physical constituents. All of them proceeding along just the lines of whatever are the basic physical laws, these derivations will be, in all essentials, quite the same as the fully physical derivations of the powers of your more complex physical constituents, say, your heart and your brain, from the propensities of the far simpler physical things that compose these organs, as with, say, their constituent protons, neutrons and electrons. Just so, all your powers will be just as fully derivative dispositions as are the "powers" of such absolutely choiceless physical complexes, and even such absolutely mindless entities, as geysers, planets, and cars. The differences concern only details: With you the details of the derivation are far more complex, of course; but, due to the complete comprehensiveness of physical law, all your own propensities are just as fully derivative as the powers of your car.

So it is that, when I think about myself in what seems an intellectually responsible enough way, my thoughts must comport with what
I've elsewhere called *the scientifical metaphysic*.[4] Noting that it's the
dominant worldview of the highly educated in cultures much affected
by the development of the natural sciences, I there gave a brief sketch
of this metaphysic. Yet more briefly, it's this: Distributed differently in
space at different times, there is physical stuff or *matter* in the world; as
it can exist whilst never experienced by any sentient being, this matter
is *mind-independent*. (My talk of the distribution of matter over time may
be, in several ways, rendered obsolete by advances of physical science.
But, for the main thoughts I mean to discuss, folks who know physics
assure me, this makes no difference.) Second, insofar as it's determined
by anything and isn't merely random, the spatial distribution of this
matter at a time is determined by the distribution of the matter at earlier
times—though it's allowed there may be a time before which there isn't
any matter—with the determination proceeding in line with our world's
basic natural laws, which are physical laws. Third, owing to the variety in
these material distributions, at certain times, like right now, much
matter composes complex physical structures or systems: salient among
these systematic physical complexes, and relatively rare, are those that
are alive. Fourth, among the more complex of even these living entities,
there are feeling and thinking physical beings.

Now, it may be useful to extend, or amplify, what's just above. To
remind us how very much the metaphysic thus secured is a particular
philosophical approach to science, rather than something science itself
actually delivers, I'll refer to the widespread worldview as the *Scientiphical Metaphysic*.

Fifth, on the Scientiphical Metaphysic all living human people are
highly complex physical entities, each with ever so many physical natural
parts and without any natural parts that aren't physical entities. Sixth,
like everyone to whom I'm now communicating, I myself am a living
human person, just as truly as I'm a being who thinks, and feels, and
consciously experiences; each of us is a highly complex physical entity,
wholly constituted by, or of, just so very many physical natural parts, with no
parts at all that are nonphysical. Seventh, absolutely every (concrete)
entity in our world is a wholly physical complex entity, wholly composed
of constituents that are themselves all wholly physical entities—for examples, a tree, a rock, a molecule, a human person—or, if not such

---

4. In "The Mystery of Physical and the Matter of Qualities," *Midwest Studies in
Philosophy*, XXII, 1999.

a wholly physical complex, it's an absolutely basic (nonmental) physical thing—for possible examples, a quark, or a superstring, or, perhaps, an infinitely vast insensate physical field. (On a Nonstandard Version of the Scientiphical Metaphysic, there aren't any absolutely basic entities; rather, there's an infinite sequence of "more and more basic physical constituents." As I suspect, a Nonstandard Scientiphical Metaphysic cannot be sustained. Whether or not that's so, it won't do anything toward having us be entities with important mental powers, including the power to fully choose.) Eighth, all our powers and propensities are physically derivative categorical dispositions, whether or not they're probabilistic, and all our behavior and activity, even our mental activity, similarly derives from the behavior of our physical parts (and of other nonmental physical things, physically simpler than us, that "serve to compose our environment".) Ninth, even as physically simpler things are governed by physical laws, insofar as their behavior isn't just random or a matter of pure chance, so we ourselves must be governed by the laws, insofar as our behavior isn't just random.

In the terms of our dominant Scientiphical Metaphysic, it's hard to think of myself as an entity that engages in activity he himself chooses from available alternatives for his action. I am beset with apparently insuperable problems. In this essay, I won't try to explore every problem, or apparent problem, our Scientiphicalism might mean, for my being able coherently to sustain our belief in full choice. Rather, I'll focus mainly on the seeming conflict between this belief of ours and the Scientiphical thought that we're purely physical complexes, all of whose powers are purely physical propensities, each with a Scientiphically respectable derivation. Near the end, I'll briefly address the Scientiphical idea that we're subject to, or governed by, (even just probabilistic) laws of nature.

Even with the suspected incompatibility that will be my main focus, I won't uncover a conflict as convincingly as, perhaps, was done with full choice and Inevitabilism. But, of course, that's to be expected. Rather than discussing a form of Incompatibilism discussed for centuries, I'm now trying to introduce for discussion new forms of Incompatibilism.

7. Simple Physical Entities and Their Basic Properties

If we're to make any good sense of our Scientiphical Metaphysic, then we had better be able to make good sense of what seem the metaphysically simplest forms, and the conceptually clearest forms, of this dominant worldview. So, we do well to focus on a form of the view where the

constitution of physical complexes has a basis in some physically basic
entities, or entity. What's more, we do well to focus on forms of the view
where, while there are many basic physical entities, each belongs to just
one of a very few basic physical kinds, with these basic kinds being mutually exclusive and exhaustive with respect to the basic entities.

To have matters be vivid, I'll employ ideas I first offered toward
answering this daunting question: How might we quite limited human
thinkers intelligibly differentiate between a world of spherical Newtonian Particles moving about in an absolutely empty void and a
world that's mainly a material plenum, or field, but with absolutely
empty spherical regions whose trajectories (of motion) precisely parallel
the paths of the Newtonian world's Particles? For a helpful answer,
I proposed that, in addition to two sorts of basic property for physical
objects long recognized, one well enough called *Spatiotemporals*, as with
shape and volume, and the other called *Propensities*, as with solidity, we
should recognize a third sort, well enough called *Qualities*.[5] More specifically, there will those Qualities well suited to be "spread though
space," the *Extensible Qualities*: these will be at least quite strongly analogous to absolutely specific phenomenal color qualities; so, we may well
label one *Red*, another *Blue*, and so on. While a Particle's Spatiotemporal
properties may be at least precisely mimicked by a counterpart void in
the Plenumate world, and while even a Particle's Propensities may be
quite well mimicked, not so with its Extensible Qualities. So, with Blue as
our supposed Quality, we may contrast our "problematically mirroring"
worlds thus: In the Particulate world, there will be many little Blue
spheres, each with a Gravitational Propensity to attract each of the
others, moving about in the vast empty space of the world, this mere
space evidently completely devoid of any such Quality even as it also
may lack real Propensity. In the Plenumate World, there will be Blue
instanced everywhere except where there are the many small spherical
voids; and, wherever there's the Blue plenum, there'll be, say, the plenum's "Propensity to pulsate in such-and-such a way"; and, with the
dynamical manifestation of this Propensity, there'll be, as an epiphenomenal upshot, the "movement of the voids".

Applying this framework for thinking of physical entities, we may
quickly move to contemplate vividly a world with electrons, and protons,
(and neutrons), pretty much as such particles were first conceived: So,
there'll be supposed many Small Blue Particles—very tiny physical

5. As with most everything else in this paragraph of the present text, I first offered
these ideas in "The Mystery of the Physical and the Matter of Qualities," cited in the just
previous note.

spheres serving as the world's electrons and many Large Red Particles—
not quite so tiny spheres serving as the world's protons. Each of the
Particles may have a weak propensity—I'll now leave off capitalizing
"propensity"—to attract each of the others, which will serve as the
world's gravitational feature: With a "forceful" propensity that's proportional to its Size—roughly, how much space is imbued by its instantiation of its absolutely specific Extensible Quality, each Particle
attracts every other to a degree that, in each case the same, is inversely
proportional to the distance between the centers of the Colorful objects.
This propensity, we're supposing, is a categorical disposition of each
Particle *with respect to*, even if not literally directed at, the Sizes of other
Particles—or, here the same, the Amount of Extensible Quality instanced in other Particles.

As well, each of the Small Blues may be disposed to repel strongly
each of the others, and also disposed to attract strongly each of the
Large Reds, even while the appropriate inverse holds for each of the
Large Reds. What's just been stipulated will serve as the world's electrical feature. This quite different propensity, we'll suppose, is a categorical disposition of each Particle *with respect to*, even if not literally
directed at, not the Sizes of other Particles, but, rather, the Qualities of
other Particles. So, a Large Red will repel another Large Red, not
because it is Large, but, rather, because it is Red. With these imagined
propensities, there's our supposed world's electrical feature. As will
be naturally supposed anyway, but as I'll now make explicit, each of
these Particles will be impenetrable by, or with respect to, all of these
other Particles. (For a nice supposition concerning neutrons, we may
suppose many Large Yellow Particles that have our world's gravitational
propensity, but don't instance any electrical propensity.) With a suitable
schedule of propensities supposed for our Particles, they'll be fit constituents for whatever more complex things may be counted among our
imagined world's fully physical entities.

8. Reciprocal Propensities and Physical Laws

What sort of further propensities might be on this supposed scheduled?
Except for such marginal exceptions as may happen with the likes of
"self-decaying entities," they will be *systematically directed propensities*,
"powers" inhering in each of just so many Particles, *for interaction with
other* (actual and, maybe, merely possible) Particles. For example, a certain Particle (of one basic sort) may manifest its propensity to have
another Particle (of another basic sort) spin faster. Then, just as there's

that power manifested on the part of the first thing, to increase spin on the part of the second, there must be, on the part of the second, the manifestation of a "receptive" disposition, to have its spin increase through just such interaction. Indeed, it's definitive of the physical that, with regard to any (basic) physical thing, the physical entity must have some such propensity for interaction with other (actual or possible basic) physical things, the (basic) physical things thus apt for mutual interaction then being each others *reciprocal disposition partners*. (Here, I'm influenced most by the compelling Neo-Lockean thoughts of C. B. Martin.[6]) What's just been offered implies that it's conceptually required of a (basic) physical entity that it evolve, or behave, in accordance with (basic) physical laws; it's required of it that it be "subject to," or "governed by," these laws.

It's no great exaggeration to say that *all a physical law amounts to is* that, as concerns such entities as are governed by the law, they *have certain propensities*. And, if we go on to make a provision for the singular case, what we've said might be no exaggeration at all: Where it's just one entity involved, as with Descartes' material plenum, to say there's a physical law governing the entity is to say that the thing has certain propensities: Governing the plenum there may be a law to the effect that, whenever the plenum becomes Purple a second later it will become Orange, and whenever it becomes Orange a second later it will become Purple. As I'm suggesting, this law amounts to *the plenum's having the propensity* to become Orange a second after it becomes Purple and *its having the propensity* to become Purple a second after it becomes Orange. So, the law "responsible for" the very regular cyclical change of the Color of our plenum isn't anything that governs the plenum from on high, or from anywhere else at all. Rather, as it amounts to the plenum's having these propensities, so the law inheres in the plenum. And, the gravitational law governing all the Particles in our previous world will inhere in that world's many Particles, which have the gravitational propensity for interaction.

In a world that's heterogeneous even at a particular moment, and not, say, everywhere just Purple and poised to become Orange, there will be, at any moment, a variety of basic entities (even if these might be

6. For a good example of Martin on these matters, see his contribution to D. M. Armstrong, C. B. Martin and U. T. Place, *Dispositions: A Debate*, Routledge, 1996 (Tim Crane, ed.), perhaps guided by the index entries for "reciprocal disposition partners." A nice new exposition of this idea, and its connection with other fertile Neo-Lockean conceptions, can be found in C. B. Martin and John Heil, "The Ontological Turn," *Midwest Studies in Philosophy*, XXIII, 1999.

just various substantial parts of a spatially vast physical field). In a world like our Scientiphicalism has us suppose the actual world to be, all the basic entities will be physical entities, all governed by basic physical laws. In any of this, there's nothing that's terribly mysterious, even if there might be, just possibly, something terribly restrictive.

Whatever the conception may involve, let's suppose that a notion of *objective probability* is applicable in properly metaphysical considerations. Then, even if it might fail in certain other regards, our Scientiphical Metaphysic can accommodate the thought that, rather than being deterministic, our world's basic physical laws may be *objectively probabilistic*: Then, the supposed fact that our world's basic physical laws are probabilistic will amount to the supposed fact that the world's basic physical entities have (at least some) probabilistic propensities: Instead of a Particle having the propensity simply to promote an increase in the speed of spin of another, certainly and always, the first may have the propensity to promote *with a certain degree of objective probability* an increase in the second's spin speed, with the second having a reciprocal receptive propensity, to have its spin increased with *just that degree* of probability.

Now, on the Scientiphical Metaphysic, all your powers will derive, in a fully physical way, from the propensities of your basic physical constituents, whether the derivations be deterministic or whether they be probabilistic. (If the basic propensities are all deterministic, so too will be all the derivative powers; if some are probabilistic, there'll be some probabilistic derivative powers.)

9. Objective Probabilities, Random Happenings and Full Choices

To make things manageable, we'll suppose that, whether the basic physical propensities be deterministic or whether probabilistic, the conditions favorable for their manifestation are such straightforwardly physical ones as the relative spatial positions of our Particles, their relative velocities, and other such manageable geometric-dynamical factors. And, your simplest constituents may be combined in ways spatially and dynamically very complex. Then, there'll be a complex derivation of all your powers. But, still, it may be an entirely physical derivation.

Now, let's return to consider our Scientiphical Jane. Composed of very many Particles, and nothing else metaphysically basic, all Jane's powers must derive, in such a straightforwardly physical fashion, from the basic propensities of her quite simple physical constituents. As it appears, none of these (derivative) physical dispositions can be a power of Jane's to choose anything, much less a power of hers to choose some thoughtful activity from among available alternatives for her. So, since it seems Jane can't ever really be making any choice or decision, it seems she can't ever really be in any state of indecision or deliberation. And, though we've been asked to do so, it seems very doubtful whether we can coherently suppose that there's a truth expressed with the sentence "Jane is in an agony of indecision; if her deliberations go one way, she will in a moment speak the words' 'John, I lied to you about Alice,' and if her deliberations go the other way, she'll bite her lip and remain silent."

By contrast, it's not so doubtful that a truth may be expressed with "there is a certain current-pulse that is proceeding along one of the neural pathway's in Jane's brain and that it is about to come to a fork. And . . . if it goes to the left, she will make her confession, and . . . if it goes to the right, she will remain silent. And . . . it is undetermined which way the pulse will go when it comes to the fork."

As we vividly suppose, a neural pathway is wholly composed of just so very many Blue and Red (and Yellow) Particles, impressively arranged, while a current-pulse consists of fairly few streaming Blue Particles. Now, when we imagine that our current-pulse comes to our neural fork, and it then goes to the left, what are we to suppose? Need we suppose "If it goes to the left, that *just happens?*"

Well if by it "just happens" we're to mean that its going left isn't a matter of full choice, *then we must* suppose that it just happens to go left; for, as we've agreed, there here *can't be* any full choice. But, as is quite natural, something quite different might well be meant with it "just happens."

If we're to mean that its going to the left *is a purely random happening*, beyond the reach of any probabilistic considerations, then we needn't suppose that it just happens to go left: Even as our electron-stream may have certain probabilistic propensities, so the fork it encounters may be a structure with certain derivative probabilistic propensities; and, even as some of the former may be (directed) with respect to the neural-fork, so some of the latter may be (directed) with respect to the current- pulse. Anyhow, in the circumstances prevailing at the supposed time, there may be an objective likelihood of .7 of the electron-stream's going to the left of the neural fork (and a .3 chance of its going to the right, and no chance of any other logical possibility's obtaining). So, then, if the current does go left, that will be the *objectively likely outcome*, not just a random happening.

Our current-pulse's going left may be an objectively likely outcome (or, in another case, an objectively unlikely even). But, though the pulse's going left needn't be "just a random occurrence," it seems that it won't be a matter of full choice. Nor, then, will there be full choice made should our Scientiphically Respectable Jane do what it is objectively likely that she do, namely, speak her mind—*or* if she does what it is *unlikely* that she do, and not speak her mind. As regards the question of her choosing some thoughtful activity from among available alternatives for her, our probabilistic Scientiphical Jane is in quite the same bad boat as her deterministic counterpart.

10. Can an "Infinitely Deep Sequence" of Physical Powers Help Jane Have Full Choice?

In considering physical things with probabilistic propensities, we departed from the terribly simple form of Scientiphicalism, and the most comfortably clear intuitive form, with which we began our exploration of the worldview. But, the involvement with some "Scientiphical complexity" did nothing toward having a Scientiphically Respectable Jane make any full choice. Will other departures from a most comfortably clear form of Scientiphicalism have our Jane making full choices?

Perhaps the most obvious move toward a less comfortable Scientiphicalism will have us abandon our Particulate vision and, instead, take up a Plenumate Scientiphicalism where there's just one vast perfectly nonmental and fully physical basic entity. An enormously heterogeneous physical field, the single basic individual might be infinitely extensive in all directions. Occupying all the world's infinite space, nowhere in this vast heterogeneous Field is there an absolutely physically empty region.

In such a *Fieldy* Scientiphical world, what goes on with a Respectable Jane will be determined, insofar as its determined by anything at all, by what goes on with the field, in which she "inheres." This will also be true of each of Jane's familiar parts, like her brain and heart; even as Jane's whole body will be (rather like) an exceptionally complex persistent pattern of pretty stable perturbations of the field, these parts will be (rather like) parts of such a complex pattern. Anyway, our belabored question about Jane's making a full choice, as to speaking her mind or remaining silent, fares no better than before: Now with her whole history so very dependent on just the evolvement in the Field, a very Scientiphically Respectable Jane won't ever, it seems, engage in full choice.

What may be the most radical attempt to depart from a comfortably clear form of Scientiphicalism, while still trying to uphold a Scientiphically Respectable view, comes with the suggestion that there's no basic entity at all, but, instead, there's an "infinitely deep hierarchy" of physical entities. On this suggestion, every physical entity will be *metaphysically superficial*, inasmuch as the powers of each derive, in a fully physical fashion, from the more basic powers of infinitely many others, all deeper in the hierarchy of physical entities and their propensities. Whether or not coherent, this conception is a familiar enough idea, rather common even in the daydreams of children.

If you're like many philosophers I know, then, at one time or another, you've engaged in an imaginative fantasy much like this: Within each of your atoms, there may be galaxies upon galaxies, many of them having planets inhabited by, amongst other things, little philosophers each constituted of, or by, quadrillions of atoms; and each of *these* atoms contains galaxies upon galaxies, and so on *ad infinitum*. Then, the powers of the planets in a given galaxy should physically derive from the powers of their atoms, which should derive from the powers of the atoms in the galaxies in those atoms, which should derive from the powers of the atoms in the included in those atoms, *ad infinitum*.

Is this fantasy a fully significant supposition? Or, have we conflated coherent thoughts about spatial inclusion with incoherent ideas as to powers? I suspect it's the latter. Trying to think of it as the *physical behavior* of a *physical entity*, we may try to think of the waving behavior of a certain little shirt, on a certain windy day, on a planet in a galaxy that's in one of the oxygen atoms now in your bloodstream—with *all of it* being "infinitely high up" in an infinitely deep hierarchy. How might this really be a thought as to the *physical* behavior of a *physical* thing?

That doesn't seem possible: On one side, we're barred from thinking of the waving of the shirt as a manifestation of nonderivative propensities of a physical field. On another, we're barred from having it be the upshot, in any sense, of the playing out of nonderivative powers of particles that constitute the shirt and its environs. Well, then, unless there's something very different going on at some *other* "level of resolution" for our world's physical powers, there's nothing more to any of this than an "infinite hierarchy of buck-passing" with nothing having any power at all, not even any "power to pass a buck"! Rather than an infinitely deep hierarchy of physical powers, what we've just been envisioning can amount, at most, to a world with an infinite nesting of pure "quality patterns," maybe marbled as nicely as can be, with spatial swirls infinitely larger and larger or, here the same, smaller and smaller. Far from any interaction among things each suitably set for doing that, what we have here is an absolutely "Humean" world, even if its Qualities be instanced in patterns that seem enormously regular and orderly. Indeed, with such an "infinitely deep hierarchy," it seems nothing has any real powers at all, neither physical nor even nonphysical.

Concerning this essay's main matters, the foregoing just might be, I suppose, a confused quest for overkill. Even so, it can't be much worse than a harmless digression: Maybe we can suppose a world with some such "infinitely deep hierarchy" of powers and, indeed, including so many powers of physical things. Among these physical things will be ever so many human organisms. So, we may imagine there'll be a Scientiphical Jane, with her current-pulse heading toward her fork. For being in an infinitely deep hierarchy of propensities, will this metaphysically more superficial Jane have full choice; will she fare *better* than her previously pondered counterparts? As seems certain, she will not.

11. Radically Emergent Beings with a Radically Emergent Power to Choose

Not much concerned with positive proposals, this paper's mainly aimed at presenting some Incompatibilist propositions, each concerning a conflict between a widely accepted Scientiphical supposition and, on the other side, our deep belief that we engage in full choice. Still, I'd like to provide some sketchy suggestions as to how, even in what's mostly a nonmental physical world, we might have full choice. First, a Cartesian suggestion; a considerable departure from our Scientiphical worldview, it's more conservative than any idealism. In the next section, there's a smaller departure.

On my Cartesian suggestion we're *radically emergent beings*: Each sustained by a different physical complex, each of us is an enduring nonphysical mental being, nowhere in space but surely in time, that has *radically emergent mental powers*, including a power of full choice. Though we have plenty of mental powers, we may be metaphysically simple beings, with no substantial parts whatever.

Toward vividly contemplating some such perfectly partless yet radically powerful beings, imagine a world where all the most basic physical entities are Small Blue Particles: When a quintillion such Particles are within a sphere of a certain small size, there will come into existence a metaphysically simple experiencer. The same point put differently: Each Small Blue has the propensity to sustain, when in a smallish sphere with nearly a quintillion others also sustaining it, a Cartesian self. When the point's put this way, there's not even a suggestion of objectionable magic: The emergence of a nonspatial mental being will be just *the manifestation of a propensity of our Particles for a certain sort of mutual interaction*.

Here's further specification for our emergent Cartesian selves: From the first moment of her existence onward, and for just so long as she exists, each nonphysical mental being will be in exceptionally close causal connection with the physical Blue Particle that, at the moment of the being's emergence, is nearest the center of the relevantly crowded small sphere. And, at least so long as she has a very close causal connection with any physical individual, each emergent Cartesian being will always be in closer causal connection with her "centrally initiating" Small Blue than with any other basic physical thing. As we may further suppose, our experiencer will be in somewhat less direct causal relations with many other Blue Particles that are interacting, pretty directly, with her Most Intimate Small Blue. That being so, certain of these interactions may constitute the workings of our being's sensory system, even as they may aptly affect the experiencing of the mental being. This models our conscious perception of our physical environment. And, making a few further such suppositions, we might have this: The relevant quintillion (or so) Small Blues constitute *the physical body of* the nonphysical being who's so closely tied, causally, to the body's original center.

About the world now imagined, two quite opposite further specifications seem salient: *First*, we may suppose that, once a mental being first exists, her continued existence is *not dependent on* what takes place with Blue Particles; even if there occurs the utter annihilation of them all, the experiencers always will exist. These supposed purely mental beings are *immortal*. So far as I can tell, they are *perfect paradigms* of what we should mean by "radically emergent entities."

Second, we may make this quite opposite specification: With the dissolution of the body of a Cartesian being, with the dispersal of her sphere's Small Blues, the being will cease to exist, completely and forever. Though such *mortal* mental beings won't be perfect paradigms of emergent entities, they'll qualify, well enough, as emergent beings.

Either way, as we've supposed, varying arrays of Small Blues will have various effects on the experiencing of an emergent experiencer; each emergent mental being will have, among her propensities, a passive power to have her course of experience influenced in certain ways. As it's so passive, this receptive power will be very different from a power fully to choose.

When our purely mental being has certain experiences, she may have certain thoughts occur to her. For instance, suppose she has a strong desire to have experience as of a cube. Then, typically, upon having such an experience, it will occur to her that she's having a quite satisfying experience. But, just as typically, this thought will be quite unbidden. Her propensity to have such unbidden thoughts is, again, far more passive than the power to choose.

How might our emergent being fully choose to *think about* metaphysics or, alternatively, choose to think about athletics? For starters, it must be possible for her to think about metaphysics *and also possible for her* to think about athletics. And, she must have in mind both possibilities for her activity. Further, she must be undecided, and unsettled, between them. Further still, she must have the *power to determine what will be her settled state* in this matter, whether it will be a state in which she (starts and so) is thinking about metaphysics or whether a state where she is thinking about athletics. Then, our emergent experiencer may exercise her power to choose what to think about. In doing that, she chooses to think about metaphysics, we'll suppose, and, for that reason, she starts thinking about that. As it surely seems, here's a perfectly possible case of a being making a full choice, between actually available courses for her activity. Quite unlike what goes on with our Scientiphically Respectable Janes, with a Radically Emergent Cartesian Jane there doesn't appear any impossibility in the idea of her having full choice. Rather, she can choose to have it that she'll be just a certain way, in which case she'll think about metaphysics, and she also can choose another way, where she won't.

12. Physical-and-Mental Complexes with a Radically Emergent Power to Choose

With less departure from Scientiphical Metaphysics, here's a second sketchy suggestion: Each of us may be a complex constituted of simpler physical entities, and each may have many Scientiphically Respectable derivative powers; but, unlike many more boring physical complexes, we'll *also* have *radically emergent mental powers*, powers with *no* Scientiphically Respectable derivation. Salient among these radical powers, there is our power to *choose what to do from among actually available alternatives* for ourselves, and, in particular, our power to *choose what to think about*.

On this view, it's a misleading simplification to say, with no amplification, that we're *physical* complexes. For, we may be mental beings just as much as we're complex physical entities. Among our very most central and peculiar powers, there'll be mental powers that have no Scientiphically Respectable derivation from any, or all, of our physical features. To avoid misleading, maybe we should say we're *physical-and-mental complex beings*: As with mere rocks, we have physical powers that don't (Respectably) derive from anything mental and, more peculiarly, we have mental powers that don't (Respectably) derive from anything physical.

About the suggestion that we're such radically powerful physical-and-mental complexes, this may be the main point: A complex being's many physical features may be *no obstacle to* her having, as well, many purely mental features, including a radically emergent mental power of full choice. With no such obstacle, it may be that, with each of a complex physical-and-mental being's basic physical parts, there is a propensity for serving, in apt physical conditions, to constitute a complex entity that has both Respectably derivative (physical) powers and also radically emergent (mental) powers.

By contrast with the world of Small Blues supposed in the previous section, in another world whose physical realm is exhausted by just such Particles, there may be, inhering in each of its Small Blues, a propensity toward serving to constitute physical-and-mental complexes. So, inhering in each of a quintillion well-arrayed Small Blues, there may be made manifest this propensity for interaction with each of the others: the propensity to be a constituent part of a mental-and-physical whole with the radically emergent mental power to choose. Now, once there is this whole with this power, it will have a power that's *not* a propensity for mutual interaction (nor any merely probabilistic propensity, certainly none concerning the whole's annihilation). Rather, it is a power to determine her own settled states and activities, from among available alternatives for the choosing whole, that she has in mind.

As we've observed, if a complex whole's powers should all Respectably derive from the powers of its physical parts, then, with few and trivial exceptions, the derivative powers will be propensities toward *interaction with other things*. In that case, it seems that there won't be any complex that chooses its own activity, from among alternatives for its own engagement. But, with the radically empowered wholes we're now considering, there are powers, far from trivial, that *aren't* directed at, or with respect to, anything else. Just so, its power to choose is, in the first instance, a power with respect to that very choosing entity, a power to settle *itself* in one way (for it to be settled) or else in another way, from among the various alternative ways *for it* to be. For instance, it may exercise this *self-directed* power by simply settling itself on—by simply deciding to be on—a course of thinking about metaphysics.[7]

---

7. A view much like that just sketched may be offered in the final chapter of Timothy O'Connor's fine new book, *Persons and Causes*, Oxford University Press, 2000.

13. Scientiphically Supposed Causal Closure of the Physical: How Much a Side-Issue?

As we've been observing, the central problems of full choice, or free will, concern our belief that we choose what to think about quite as much as they concern our belief that we choose how to behave bodily. So, questions concerning only the second of these deep beliefs can't be central problems of free will. Though that should be almost obvious by now, the observation still bears reflection.

For poignancy, let's imagine ourselves as Cartesian beings who may choose, fully and freely, to move our bodies in certain ways—to wiggle our Blue thumbs, for example. So, our imaginative thought runs, we're non-physical radically emergent mental entities that, at least from time to time, influence the course of physical reality. Now, this thought conflicts with a proposition that's accepted by almost all philosophers who, in recent decades, have written prominently on central questions of mind and body. Often going under the name "the causal closure of the physical," it's the proposition that, insofar as anything determines the course of (events in) physical reality, it's always only some sort of purely physical things that do so—some wholly physical events, perhaps. But, if we Cartesian beings succeed in wiggling our thumbs, perhaps because we choose to move our bodies in that way, then there'll be some *nonphysical* things—we Cartesian beings—determining some of the course of physical reality. So, then there'll be the failure of the (so-called) causal closure of the physical. And, perhaps less poignantly, there's this same consequence should we suppose ourselves to be physical-and-mental complex beings, with an emergent mental power to choose bodily movements.

For prominent current philosophers, is that thought far more disturbing than the thought that, with an emergent power to choose what to think, it may be only a certain mental being, and not any wholly physical thing, that determines some of the course of *mental* reality? I don't think so. Rather, philosophers endorsing the causal closure of the physical are just as committed to the thought that, insofar as anything determines the course of *our mental lives*, it's just what's physical that does so. A dualistic epiphenomenalist some may be, but, to my knowledge, few indeed will allow that anything nonphysical has any influence on any reality at all. So, it's misleading, at least, to say that the legions of Scientiphically-minded philosophers are especially concerned with the causal closure of the physical. Comprising Scientiphicalism as a whole, their metaphysical faith is rather more general.

Where central questions of full choice are our focus, we shouldn't narrowly train our sights on the causal closure of the physical, giving center stage to what's *something of a side-issue*.

But, of course, the question of causal closure *isn't entirely* a side-issue: Sometimes I've picked up a pen because I chose to lift the cylindrical physical object, even while my leaving it lie was an available alternative for me. Then, I engaged in full choice that's physically effective choice; the pen was lifted *because I chose to* lift it. Then, there's an effect on physical reality that's brought about through the effective exercise of a mental power of mine, not Respectably derived from features of physical reality.

According to the causal closure of the physical, and the encompassing Scientiphical Metaphysic, physical reality isn't ever affected by any such radically emergent mental power; rather, all that ever affects physical reality is something that's part of physical reality. So, those thoughts are in conflict with the idea that we engage in physically effective full choice. There's a very real Incompatibilism, our explorations are suggesting, between the causal closure of the physical and our deep belief that we do engage in physically effective full choice. Though not much less in Scientiphicalism's grip than my philosophical contemporaries, I find it harder to deny this belief than to deny causal closure. At any rate, here there's an intellectually uncomfortable Incompatibilism.

14. Is an Exemption from Natural Law Required for Full Choice?

Even if we should be metaphysically simple purely mental beings, a Cartesian idea hard actually to believe, that might still not be enough, I'll suggest, for us to have full choice: For, it may be possible for some such nonphysical simple mental beings to be *wholly subject to natural laws*. But, for a being to have full choice, she *must not* be wholly subject to these laws; there must be at least *some respects* in which, at least to *some degree*, she is *exempt from* the natural laws.

We've already argued that an entity's being subject to *physical laws* amounted to its having certain propensities. (Typically, these will be propensities for interaction with other entities.) In an extreme case, as with an infinitely vast material plenum, there may be just a single physical thing with propensities to go from certain states into certain other states. In one such simple case, a well-Qualified plenum may lawfully alternate between being all Orange for a second and being all Purple for a second. In a slightly more complex case, when Orange a plenum might have a .7 chance of next being Purple and a .3 chance of next being Green, and when Purple a .7 chance of next Green and a .3 chance of next Orange, and when Green a .7 chance of next Orange and a .3 chance of next Purple. Wholly subject to a certain physical law as to its Qualitative state, it may go through an always unpredictable sequence of Color states, perhaps infinitely lengthy; in all this, there are just the manifestation of the probabilistic propensities of this mindless material being.

It's equally imaginable that there should be purely mental Cartesian experiencers, each metaphysically simple and wholly nonphysical, but, all wholly subject to certain natural laws. One of the laws might be to this effect: When a being experiences phenomenal orange (and no other color), there's a .7 chance of her next experiencing phenomenal purple (and no other color) and a .3 chance of next experiencing (only) green; when experiencing phenomenal purple, a .7 chance of next experiencing green and a .3 chance of sensing orange; and, when experiencing green, a .7 chance of next orange and a .3 chance of purple. Subject to a certain mental natural law as to its experiential state, this mind may go through an always somewhat unpredictable sequence of experiences, perhaps infinitely lengthy; in all this, there's just the manifestation of propensities of bodiless mental beings.

There may be far more complex laws governing a simple mental being's phenomenal experience. As well, a metaphysically partless mind may have a complex endowment of dispositions as to its blatantly contentful thought processes: So, when thinking that yellow is more like orange than like purple, there may be a .3 chance she'll next think that blue is more like purple than like orange.

So far as choosing is concerned, however, a partless mental being that's so *wholly subject* to laws, whose *dispositions are all such perfectly* lawful propensities, seems utterly unsuited. To make full choices, even a Cartesian mind must be, at least to *some* degree, exempt from laws of nature. The laws must leave *some things open to her*; maybe it's left open to her to choose to increase the chance that she'll experience orange, or maybe to choose to decrease the chance she'll think that yellow is quite like orange; anyhow, there must be some powers she has that *aren't wholly* lawful propensities, or else she won't have a power of full choice.

15. Apparent Scientiphical Incompatibilisms and Future Philosophical Explorations

Central suppositions of Scientiphicalism, I've been suggesting, are incompatible with our having full choice, or free will. First, there's this:

We're purely physical complexes, with all our powers derived in a fully physical fashion from the rather simple powers of the mindless, choiceless parts that so wholly compose us. But, with only trivial exceptions, as with some physical objects' propensities to cease or decay, all a purely physical being's powers are just for mutual interaction. And so, none are appropriately self-directed powers, suited for being, or maybe just grounding, a power of full choice.

And, there are great problems with the Scientiphical thought that, except insofar as we may be involved in purely random happenings, we're wholly subject to natural laws: As we've just lately observed, any entity whatever—even any purely mental and utterly partless being— seems precluded from engaging in any full choice, if the being is wholly subject to natural laws.

I'll call each of these apparent conflicts a *Scientiphical Incompatibilism*. As it appears, each features a Scientiphical supposition that, if true, means we'll be hardly more significant than happy clams. Apparently, these new Incompatibilisms are important to consider.

As anticipated, I've not been able to make a very strong case for any Scientiphical Incompatibilism, not nearly as strong, anyway, as the case for thinking full choice incompatible with Inevitabilism, or Determinism. Why? Well, with this attempt at disclosing Scientiphical Incompatibilisms, we don't yet have much of an idea as to what it is about, say, one's having all her powers be propensities for mutual interaction, that should have full choice be ruled out for one should all one's powers be *just such* powers. And, on the other side of the conceptual coin, we don't yet have any good notion as to what it is about full choice that should have *it* ruled out for one should, say, all one's powers be propensities for mutual interaction. By contrast, we have a much better idea of what it is about Inevitabilism, and what it is about our having full choice, that may yield truth for the more traditional Incompatibilism.

For future philosophical exploration, then, these avenues all but present themselves: First, and on the one hand, some should explore the possibility that, though there's an *apparent* clash between Scientiphical statements and our belief in our full choice, there *isn't a real* incompatibility here. Those wanting to uphold the Scientiphical Metaphysic should explore this avenue most energetically.

Second, and on the other hand, some might explore how we might fill the void of understanding lately remarked, so that we might come to see what it is about our Scientiphical suppositions, and what it is about full choice, that means a conflict between the two.

Third, and finally for now, there should be attempts to develop metaphysical alternatives to the Scientiphical Metaphysic, worldviews that may be more conducive to our having full choice. Perhaps, we should begin this work by energetically exploring philosophical alternatives that mean only a pretty modest departure from Scientiphicalism, our currently dominant metaphysical conception.[8]

8. Over the course of a couple of years, I discussed most of this paper's ideas with many people, too many to remember to thank individually now. But, some I remember to have been particularly helpful are Gordon Belot, Ruth Chang, Keith DeRose, Kit Fine, Shelly Kagan, Barbara Montero and, especially, Dean Zimmerman. In my NYU graduate seminar in the Spring Semester of 2000, we discussed all the paper's present ideas, and some that didn't survive the scrutiny. The three Ph.D. students completing the course were each importantly helpful: Adam Pautz, Brad Skow and Elizabeth Vlahos. My thanks to all.

INDEX OF NAMES